GOOCH
My Autobiography

GOOCH

My Autobiography

Graham Gooch
and Frank Keating

CollinsWillow
An Imprint of HarperCollinsPublishers

To Hannah, Megan and Sally
Sorry for being away so often

First published in 1995
by CollinsWillow
an imprint of HarperCollins*Publishers*
London

© Graham Gooch and Frank Keating 1995

A CIP catalogue record for this book is
available from the British Library

ISBN 0 00 218474 5

Origination by Saxon

Printed by HarperCollins Manufacturing Glasgow

PICTURE ACKNOWLEDGEMENTS
The publishers would like to thank the following sources:
Allsport plate section pp 5 (top), 6 (top and bottom right),
12 (top left and right), 13 (top); **Tim Bradford** p 293;
Patrick Eagar pp 2 (bottom), 3 (top and bottom), 4, 5 (bottom),
6 (top left), 7 (centre and bottom), 9, 10, 11, 12 (bottom), 14;
Empics p 16 (top inset); **Alf Gooch** pp 1, 2 (top and centre);
Brenda Gooch p 15 (top); **Tom Jenkins** p 8; **Graham Morris** p 16
(middle inset and bottom); **David Munden** pp 6 (bottom left),
7 (inset), 15 (bottom); **Popperfoto** p 5

CONTENTS

ACKNOWLEDGEMENTS

Warm thanks go to Alf Gooch, first and longtime keeper of the log, Rose Gooch, Douglas Kemp, the late Laurie Hall, his widow Mrs Hall and their son Mike; Bill Morris, Doug Insole, Peter Edwards, Micky Stewart; and Essex and England colleagues down the years, especially John Lever, Keith Fletcher, Alan Lilley, John Emburey and Geoff Boycott. At CollinsWillow, Tom Whiting's efficiency kept the project on an even keel while designer Rachel Smyth maintained her cool; and copy editor John Bright-Holmes remains, as Mike Brearley once said of him, 'particularly helpful and helpfully particular'. Also thanks to Wendy Wimbush for assisting the story with her exact and enlightening stats, as well as to umpteen 'blunts and smudgers', members of cricket's writing and photographic press. And sincere gratitude to cricket lovers the world over for their support and encouragement throughout the past two eventful decades and more.

INTRODUCTION
by Frank Keating

When Graham Gooch, as ever meticulously, packed his trunk to play for England against Australia in his forty-second year in the winter of 1994/95, he also took on the voyage an unprecedented number of batting records, including more Test runs than any English batsman in the game's long history. Only one man, Peter May, has captained England more times; but in the job no England captain has scored more centuries than Gooch, who has led from the front by personal example. At the same time, no shy and seemingly uncontroversial man has been so regularly embroiled in controversy.

In the *Illustrated London News* during the early 1980s, Michael Watkins wrote a fond and pointed essay about Essex:

> 'There is a certain Essex quality which is imperishable. Stubbornness is that quality, downright cussedness that refuses to be brought into line. But there is no common purpose, no uniformity in this obstinacy; it is simply a series of unconnected statements of implacable self-confidence. One is aware of it in patrician Frinton and equally aware in proletarian Southend.'

Exactly. Stubbornness, cussedness, obstinacy, implacable self-confidence. Each description can be fairly applied to the cricketing splendour of Graham Gooch, especially as he persisted in occupying the crease for Essex and England into early middle age. Those four resolute and unfancy qualities represent the adult Gooch not only fiercely defending his wicket, but counter-attacking with thunderous defiance for two decades, especially when attacked by the West

7

Indies fast-bowling batteries, the most relentless bombardment the game has witnessed. Those words will also suffice to describe the unremitting and unapologetic self-defence of Gooch's own corner when pilloried as a 'rebel' for playing in 1982/83 in the apartheid state of South Africa.

It was a surprise when Graham Gooch asked if he could entrust to me the organizing of his lifetime's log. It was not my usual line of country, but in turn I surprised myself at relishing the task. I had known Graham down the years and admired him for his glistening deeds both around the fields of England and from his first days with the England XI in the sweltering, seething, and clamorous stadiums of the world. And I had much enjoyed his company; his steadfast straightforwardness, generosity of spirit, and the appealing dry humours that largely go unnoticed. He is the most companionable of men. Above all, he is an honourable man – and, more, he is honourable to the standards he sets himself. I admired the way in which, as a general, he did not treat his younger troops as callow boys; but he expected them to fulfil his own ideas of manhood ('If you fail to prepare, prepare to fail'). He likes to have men around him who are industriously in tone with this philosophy. But to him a team means more than its component parts.

With a few exceptions, sportsmen's biographies or autobiographies are usually disappointing. You might say that biography tells, but doesn't know; autobiography knows, but doesn't tell. For this reason Graham Gooch and I decided on what we hope is the best of both worlds – a split text – with third-person FK to establish time, place, and context, and then first-person GG to 'tell it exactly as it was'. For leading cricketers, every time they go to the crease and perform, in a sense they outline and then colour-in their own biographies. Study a batsman's series of long innings (and short ones, come to that) under pressure and you surely get more than a passing sense of his true inner character and what makes him tick as a man.

In the early 1970s, I dropped other distractions and became a full-time writer on sports. Cricket had been my boyhood passion and now I could indulge it. At around the same time, and five days before his twentieth birthday in the mid-summer of 1973, Graham Gooch was being given a lift in John Lever's clapped-out Vauxhall Victor to play his first game of county cricket, and enquire of the gods his destiny. Often, down the twenty-two summers and winters since, I would be witness to their answer as batsmen through the wicket-gate made their entrances and exits leaving, very much more often than not, the resilient and reassuring figure of Graham Gooch at the other end.

Not to mention resilience and reassurance at the business end as well. Particularly when it mattered most. Till England knew as well as Essex. Then all cricket, and beyond, hoorayed and golly-goshed at how, with a relentless and wondrous blossoming into his late thirties, Gooch was still able to hold his nerve and summon his spirit and zest to 'reassure' the public yet again as he continued to compose a series of innings truly epic in their valiance, commanding dedication, and skill; with any half-volley, it goes without saying, still being blasted over the ropes as they had been in his blacksmith's hammering strength of youth. Even into his 'dotage' Gooch can ransack any attack if the mood is on him; but his greatness came when all the industry at his last allowed him to discover the difference between 'scoring' a century and 'making' one; and once he realized that, well, for England he screwed his courage unflinchingly to the crease. And followers of the game gave thanks, never more gratefully than when he fashioned, against the West Indies, one of the finest captain's innings that has ever been played. For as G K Chesterton said, 'There is a great man who makes every man feel small. But the really great man is the one who makes every man feel great.'

After Gooch resigned as captain and, moist-eyed, passed the seals of office to his young squire Atherton, he continued in the ranks as best bat and eminence. At once, the Test match crowds (as did those around the shires where he played for his beloved Essex) overwhelmed Gooch's natural reticence – standing as one to applaud him in from batting, whatever his score; or when he fielded, out in the 'country' now and, mercifully at last, away from the close-in cannon's mouth. They stood to him and cheered and, between overs, slapped his back and offered their sandwiches or a six-pack swig, joshed 'Good old Goochie' to their neighbours and jostled in a flutter with their scorecards and autograph-books. A warm and heartfelt hurrah of honour for the grand 'old man' because they knew, and he knew, that he would soon be running out of summers, and there were other things to do – but most of all, before that happened, because they wanted the acclamation to make him realize with no doubt that they were gratefully aware that Gooch's noble cricket had, in itself, ennobled cricket.

1

'A QUIET BOY, ALWAYS HAS BEEN'

FK

Rose Gooch gave birth to her second child and only son not long before midnight on 23 July 1953. Rose's baby, Graham Alan, noisily weighed in at a hefty enough 8lb 13oz. As was the custom then, confinement and delivery took place at the Gooch's home at 14 James Lane, Leyton, in the borough of Waltham Forest and the county of Essex. Leyton also happily answers to east London and if the prevailing sou'westerlies are breezing across Hackney Marshes, it is possible to hear the sound of Bow Bells – the peal which traditionally is the first sound a definitively genuine Cockney ever, as they really do say, 'cops in his shell-like' – with far more resonance and regularity than a few miles up-river in the heart of the city.

When the new baby was born, Rose was forty, her husband Alf thirty-nine, and their daughter Brenda already six. The couple of rooms which the family rented in the little terraced house at James Lane were now too restricting, and the local council were soon able to move them to a nearby flat of their own at 1 Mills Court, Leytonstone. At the bottom of Mills Court was a children's playground, fenced in and safe from traffic, and it was here that Rose's new toddler first 'played ball'.

Some forty years later, on 3 October 1994, Alf celebrated his eightieth birthday and, with a proud glint in his soft-boiled eyes, recalled Mills Court and the first time he rolled a ball to his baby son. 'From the very first, you know, he had an innate balance, a feel and an eye for it. And once he'd got the ball, he'd always cussedly want to keep it.'

The year Alf met Rose at a dance at Leyton Town Hall was 1939.

'He was a strapping six-footer!' Rose remembered. 'He looked so handsome in his Army clothes; not quite "dashing", mind you, because he was no great dancer at first. And what was most obvious was that he didn't have no money.' They both laugh fit to burst.

Both Alf and Rose lived through Hitler's 'Blitz' which ravaged London and laid much of it to waste. Rose was from an indomitable Leyton family of East End publicans, Alf the son of a Merchant Navy sailor from Plaistow, hard on West Ham country. The docks, the factories, the very streets and houses around their homes became the epicentre of the civilian horrors which London suffered between 1940 and 1945. Days and nights were punctuated by the fearful wail of air-raid sirens.

'Oh no, it was no good staying in all the time, or living down the bomb shelters,' says Rose, half a century on and matter-of-fact. 'You had to get out, had to have fun, else we'd have all been totally miserable, wouldn't we? Of course, we went on dancing, Alf and I went dancing all the time; or the pictures, everything – plus diving under tables, or ducking into doorways when the siren went, or waiting for the "all-clear" before moving across the streets and on to somewhere else. It was no good staying home and letting it all get you down, was it?'

After basic training in 'ack-ack' (anti-aircraft guns) Alf was due to be posted to Egypt – he had been a keen goalkeeper and occasional striker with Witney Town and Oxford City when working there pre-war – but, the day before embarkation, an old soccer injury flared up in his knee and he was attached instead to the searchlight batteries which strobed the night skies to track the serried, droning approach from the North Sea across the estuary marshes of the Heinkels and Dorniers and Junkers, their bomb-bays laden with dreaded cargo. Later, in Germany's final desperate throw, the liquid-fuelled V2 rockets came noiselessly. The very last V2 was aimed at London on 2 March 1945, and it exploded, without the slightest warning, on the Walthamstow–Leyton boundary-line, demolishing a dozen houses, killing eight people and injuring 111, on the corner of Grove Road and College Road, E17. This was, as the crow flies, less distance than a decently middled six by the man who was born eight years later in the rented flat at 14 James Lane.

From the western corner of James Lane, it would need a

red-blooded hook shot of the adult Graham to clear Leyton High Road and the railway station and land on the playing field which, until 1933, was the headquarters of Essex County Cricket Club. The doyen of cricket writers, E W Swanton, described the Leyton ground of those days as 'that grim yet not wholly unattractive enclosure which had brought all great cricketers, in their time, to the East Londoners' very doorstep'.

Leyton's budding cricketer was lucky with his schools. At five, young Gooch went to Cann Hall mixed-junior at Leytonstone, where cricket was on the syllabus. Two teachers who covered all subjects, Douglas Kemp and Laurie Hall, were also sports enthusiasts. At cricket, Kemp would umpire and Hall do the scoring. Kemp, now eighty-three, still lives nearby in South Woodford, and remembers, 'Graham was a quiet boy, never pushy. I took the scholarship classes so he was never in my "stream"; he was never academic, he just did as much as he had to. But at sport he stood out. At cricket Graham was always head and shoulders above every other boy. It was already noticeable how keen he was – yet even from this distance I remember him as a very fair player who never boasted about his precocious prowess. He was a grand lad on the playing field, and never once forgot that cricket and football were team games, not unlike another, older, lad I took when I was involved earlier in district schools' sides – Bobby Moore from the Tom Head school nearby.'

Graham's other Cann Hall schoolmaster, Laurie Hall, retired to Devon in 1975 where he became scorer for Sidmouth CC and the lollipop traffic man outside All Saints School. Ten years later, at the instigation of Hall's son, Michael, Graham sent a ruby wedding anniversary card to his old schoolmaster and his wife, signed by all the England team playing in the 1985 Test match at Trent Bridge – a kindly touch picked up by the following week's *Sidmouth Herald*, which sent a reporter to interview Hall. He recalled, 'At Cann Hall, Graham already had outstanding ability. He used to open both batting and bowling and, in truth, simply *was* the team. In one school match, the side was all out for 14. Graham scored 12, one of the other boys made one, and there was one extra.'

Graham's secondary school, Norlington in Leyton, all boys, unusually had artificial cricket nets in the school playground. The child's horizons had at once been broadened by sport. After the carpenter Alf (who became a head-of-department at the Hackney firm of John J Dunster & Sons, which made 'shiny-wood' cabinets for radio and television sets) had knocked off on Saturday lunchtimes, he would regularly take his son on bubble blowing gen-uflections, accompanied by Uncle George, to the Upton Park shrine of West Ham United. At Cann Hall junior school young Graham had, if anything, preferred soccer. He ended his time there as captain of the school teams both in summer and winter, and what might have early inclined him towards the warmer-weather game was an innings of 40 for the school when he was only nine years old.

Thus it was that, when the boy was eleven, he had his name in the public prints for the first time, in the Waltham Forest Schools' Cricket Association Handbook (price 6d.): 'The Under-13 XI showed considerable promise. Best batsmen were D O'Neill, who scored 59 runs, and G Gooch and E Dunkley, who each scored 43.' On the strength of this, Alf took his son to the Ilford indoor cricket school, which was run by Bill Morris, a white Jamaican who played 48 matches for Essex between 1946 and 1950 (78 innings at 17.93 (highest score 68), 43 wickets at 46.16). Bill Morris, everyone says, was a very good coach. A sharp, blond, and matey Ilford teenager, four years older than the shyly untalkative Graham, hung around Morris's school most hours of the day and night. His name was John Lever. He remembers: 'With his short hair-cut, his long parka and his thick-soled shoes, Graham was very much what we used to call a "mod" in those days. Yet he had an old-fashioned approach to play-ing cricket. All he wanted to do was whack the ball as hard as he could. I bowled at him myself under the watchful eye of Bill and I will never forget the look on the coach's face when I pitched the ball on leg stump and Graham flipped it in the direction of square-leg with all the time in the world.'

Bill Morris, now seventy-seven and retired in Kilmarnock, still remembers 'this big-boned twelve-year-old clocking John Lever all over the place'. He went on: 'Graham just had a natural aptitude for batting – and for looking to belt the ball at every opportunity. He always had a lot of "right hand" in his shots, but one of the secrets of coaching is often to leave well alone, don't blind with science and technical verbiage, just help steer and encourage into a natural level of standard and aspiration. When not at the wicket, Graham was a very shy and reserved boy and not at all communicative. But he was a well-mannered young lad who just loved his cricket; as a bowler even as a kid he had the action to swing the ball; he was also a pretty good wicketkeeper, but I think he got too tall for that and decided to concentrate everything on his batting; the reticence would vanish and he'd come animatedly alive when he was batting.'

Says Alf Gooch: 'Bill's indoor school obviously did Graham the world of good in many ways. He was a quiet boy, always has been. It was the devil's own job to get anything out of him at all, and that's never changed either. He'd just come in, ask for his spam-and-chips, wouldn't bother telling us anything even if he'd scored a hatful of goals at school or a pile of runs like most other boys would. He was never cocky or pushy. He was a very straightforward boy. I never once had to bawl him out, never had a ruckus with him at all. In fact, he was very slow to come forward, I had to tell him more than a few times to be a bit more assertive. Except, obviously, when he had a bat in his hands and the ball was whizzing down. He was no great scholar. Not interested really. His reports were all variations of "could do better". But he was always a very honest lad, like he grew up to be ... as honest as the day is long.'

By the time Graham was born his father was a stalwart wicket-keeper with East Ham Corinthians CC and, long before the family could afford, proudly, its first little second-hand Austin Cambridge, it would be up early at weekends for 'the cricket', ready for journeys hither and yon around south Essex by public transport – Alf with the cricket bag in one hand, Rose with the sandwiches and young Brenda, and the baby swinging between them in his carry-cot. All of this was strongly, if unconsciously, nurturing the boy's life-lasting fidelity to his county and its cricket.

GG

I took to a ball from the very start. Some kids do, some don't. Mills Court was three blocks of council flats, each only four storeys high, and down at the back by the bicycle sheds was a tarmac and grass playground area where all the kids would play with a scuffed old tennis ball, football mostly at first. If it was only me, even when I was only a toddler, Mum would be watching me happily messing around with a ball for hours.

When I was about ten we moved to 34 Montague Road, a small terraced house, but it meant that I had a room of my own at last because, in the two-bedroomed flat, Auntie Doll had come to live with us when my grandma died, so I had been sleeping in a bed in the corner of Dad and Mum's room. Auntie Doll has lived with my parents ever since, and has been almost a second mother to me.

From day one, the wall at the back of the new house took a real pounding as I banged a ball against it like there was no tomorrow. Cricket in summer, soccer in winter. I was a right-footer but made myself pretty useful with my left. Hour upon hour against the wall. I still reckon that unceasing practice was the way to sharpen reactions and make ball-sense second nature, so in my case, not to mention Don Bradman, it really served a purpose. All the while I would commentate to myself, like I'd heard on the radio or television: West Ham scoring memorable goals at football if it was winter, Essex v Kent or England v West Indies in the summers. Same when Dad and I used to play that 'Owzat!' game with two little roller-dice, one marked one-to-six for runs, the other 'run out', 'bowled' and so on; and everything logged neatly in our scorebook, of course. We had just a tiny black-and-white television then, but I well remember the excitement of the West Indies cricket tour of 1963. Gary Sobers was the great star and, along with millions of other kids of my generation, my first cricketing hero. Frank Worrell was the captain. I don't suppose I've really thought about it for years, but I can still name that whole wonderful side – Conrad Hunte and Easton McMorris opened, then Kanhai, Butcher, Sobers, Solomon ... and wasn't there a white fellow, David Allan, who was wicketkeeper before Deryck Murray? And, of course, the great bowling attack was Wes Hall and Charlie Griffith with the new ball and Lance Gibbs's spin to follow. Not to mention Sobers as well!

England had the likes of Micky Stewart, John Edrich, Colin Cowdrey, Ken Barrington, Brian Close, Fred Trueman and Fred Titmus. The captain was Ted Dexter. It would have been 1964 when Dad took me down to Lord's for the Gillette Cup final. We sat on the grass behind the boundary rope at the Nursery End; you were allowed to do that then. We were on the grass on the corner in front of the Mound Stand. All I remember, apart from the general excitement of the day, was Ted Dexter batting for Sussex. And in 1968,

Dad took me to The Oval to see the Australians. We sat on the third-man 'curve' between the gasometers and the Pavilion, and saw Basil D'Oliveira make his big hundred, 158.

Most of my first recollections were of cricketing. The weekly family outing was simply 'the cricket'. Dad was assistant fixtures secretary and wicketkeeper of the East Ham Corinthians. He played some Saturdays and every single Sunday, usually an all-day game. Sundays were up-early days, Mum making the sandwiches, the jelly, the salad, the lot. Then down the A12 in the Austin Cambridge to Fairlop and the Old Blues ground, cricket gear in the boot, myself and my sister Brenda in the back with the picnic hamper. Dad was always a brilliant woodworker and he made this hamper-box which strapped in all the plates, cups, knives and forks.

It was a good ground; in the old days Essex used it for their pre-season training sessions. I can still see Mum now, sitting in her old deckchair with her knitting, or then going in to help make the players' teas. Quite happy, too, although she had never apparently been in the least bit sporting as a girl.

I didn't so much watch the cricket, I was up and down the boundary all day bashing a ball around with the other kids or, sometimes, in the nets. So that's how I learned, and got my first informal 'coaching' from Dad when he wasn't out on the field. He used to bat around no. 8 – he was pretty big and hefty with sloping shoulders and we used to rib him about being the same shape as Colin Cowdrey.

Whenever I think of those days at the Old Blues ground I remember Dad's pockets. Yes, his pockets. He was a roll-your-own cigarette smoker – he's given up now – and would carry around his tin of Old Holborn and one of those little Rizla rollers. Then he had his keys, and all his loose change and, I dare say, a few boiled sweets. And he'd put the lot in his pockets – and go out and play. As a wicketkeeper, too. Same when he was batting. All those things rattling about in his pockets – when he ran you could hear him coming for miles. Didn't it hurt him when he dived? Funny, lots of his fellow players did the same, but not with tins of baccy and Rizla rollers too. Perhaps it was to do with the war, or being in the Army, or making sure all your possessions were safe. Just as well Dad had packed up his goalkeeping by then!

At the end of every season Dad would bring the club's kit home and spend the winter repairing all the bats, sanding them or rehandling them. And then re-polishing the balls to have them looking like new for the next spring.

In the winters, although Leyton Orient was obviously our nearest local league club, Dad's Plaistow roots made him a Hammer through and through. Mum's brother, Uncle George, lived at Leyton and the three of us would go regularly to watch West Ham at Upton Park. Dad's woodwork came in handy again when he made me a sort of attaché case, a box which closed and a handle to carry it. Once inside the ground you opened it up and there were four legs inside, and you'd screw them into the four corners and, hey presto, little me had my own orange-box to stand on and watch the match. Like every soccer fan we had our favourite regular Saturday routine. We'd always park in the same side street – I still park my car there when I go and see the Hammers now – and we always stood, as you go in, on the right corner, just above the corner-flag and halfway up the terracing. Then, suddenly, for some reason that Dad never told me, we swopped sides and ends and made our regular patch above the corner-flag at the North Bank end.

We went to West Ham regularly in the early and middle 1960s. When I was about seven or eight, Bobby Moore was just coming through, and Geoff Hurst, and then the young Martin Peters. I learned the meaning of the word 'presence' by watching Bobby Moore. If Pelé was the finest attacking footballer there has been, he said the finest defender who ever marked him was Bobby.

I could still name you two or three of the teams I watched in those days. Even on the mistiest or most drizzlingly grey day they were marvellously entertaining, playing fantastic attacking football. Everything was colour and warmth and fervour: the fans in the famous, now long gone 'chicken run' singing and swaying in unison, and me on Dad's special box-with-legs with my claret-and-blue scarf and pom-pom hat and rattle.

We won the FA Cup in 1963. See if I can recite the team over thirty years later ... Standen (also a cricketer) in goal; Bond and Burkett; Bovington, Brown, Moore; Brabrook, Boyce, Byrne, Hurst, Sissons. Then they won the Cup-Winners Cup in Europe the next year, and in 1966, of course, Moore lifted the World Cup for England at Wembley, and the scorers were Hurst and Peters.

For that World Cup final, Dad had to book his week off from work months before so we were at a holiday camp – we went to a holiday camp most years. The one at Littlestone, near Romney, was my favourite. But in 1966, we were at Freshwater, on the Isle of Wight. On the afternoon of the final about a hundred people crowded into the hall, in the middle of which was one small black-and-white television set, which looked particularly ropey, with one of those little wire indoor-aerials on top of it.

Anyway, the match kicks off, and the picture keeps going fuzzy and the sound starts buzzing: then it 'comes back' and is okay for a minute or two, before the picture goes again. Everyone moans.

So one bloke picks up the indoor-aerial and moves it around to try and settle the picture. He walks this way and that, and then right behind the set – and at once and miraculously the picture and sound becomes perfect. 'Hold it there! Hold it there!' everybody shouts.

Only one problem. The poor bloke is three yards immediately behind the set. He just stands there in this position, grinning weakly and just holding the aerial, exactly so, for the whole of the match, including two periods of extra-time and Bobby getting the Cup from the Queen. And he never saw a bit of it. He might have looked an idiot – and felt even more of one – but the memory of it makes me smile to this day. In all my life, that was probably the most generous and sustained example of out-and-out sportsmanship I have ever witnessed.

So that was how I saw Bobby Moore lift the Cup for England when I was just thirteen. We used to say that Bobby was going up those 39 steps to get the Cup at Wembley 'so many times that he'll soon get "medal fatigue"'. Moore was my one top-ace sporting hero; he was 'local' West Ham, like my Dad. Later, when I was an Essex cricketer, I used to meet him at functions and still feel a bit in awe. He never really changed, did he, in appearance or gentlemanly manner? When, in 1985, he agreed to play in a football celebrity match at Southend for my 1985 benefit – alongside me in midfield for 'my' team – I honestly had to pinch myself and say, 'Is this the best dream of all come true, me receiving passes from Bobby Moore, and then him urging quietly "outside you, Graham!" or "push it through!"?' He played the whole first-half and later shook my hand and said he'd really enjoyed it.

I sometimes wonder whether the example Bobby set as captain of West Ham and England might have unconsciously become lodged in my head and come to the fore when I became captain of Essex and England. I never had Bobby's elegant perfection and genius at reading a situation, but if nothing else, we were both hard-working perfectionists on the practice pitch and, as players at our different sports, the records show we both revelled in the big occasions. Moore was fastidiously neat and tidy, just as I am. Even from the early days he had written into his contract an allowance that, at away games, he could have a hotel room to himself because he couldn't stand some of the slovenly ragamuffins whom he'd have to share with, littering their clothes all over the floor. I'm the same. My colleagues rib me, not only for having the neatest room on the circuit but the tidiest cricket 'coffin' as well.

Moore went to Barking Primary, then to the Tom Hood school in Leyton, my childhood patch. He met his wife, Tina, at the Ilford Palais, just as I did Brenda. Trevor Brooking, the Hammers' next England great after Moore, Hurst and Peters, told me that Bobby was in essence an extremely shy man and not one for meaningless chit-chat or small-talk at parties. On the practice pitch he was dedicated and determined, Trevor said, spending hours alone, ironing out little points of technique, just as I do. Moore would work unstintingly, say, at perfecting a curved pass with the outside of his right foot because he knew his left was comparatively the weaker; and he'd put in hours on his famous 'drag-back' tackle; nor did Trevor ever see him waste even a five-yard ball in training. 'If you waste a ball in training, the odds are you'll waste it in a match.' And his captaincy was a matter of leading from the front, by example. Once, in a tense Cup semi-final replay in front of 40,000 against Stoke City, the West Ham goalkeeper, Bobby Ferguson, was injured and carried off. The regular stand-in goalie was Clyde Best, the big Bermudan. Moore held out the goalkeeper's jersey for Clyde to put on. He refused. 'No way, not tonight. I'm too nervous,' said Best. Without a word, Moore put the jersey on himself – and saved a penalty from Peter Dobing.

I knew he was ill. I knew it was cancer. But everyone was always saying 'the worst is over, he'll be okay'. When Bobby died on 21 February 1993, aged only 51, we were touring India and were in

Bangalore for a one-dayer. It was the middle of the night. I was asleep. From London, the *Daily Mirror's* Chris Lander, who knew I was a West Ham man, telephoned me with the news. Sure, I was very upset. Moore was a central figure in my boyhood. The Hero. Well, I used to go down to West Ham every 'home' Saturday, didn't I? Without fail.

In those days, too, I was probably, as Frank Keating suggests, more soccer-mad than cricket-mad. Dad and Uncle George would never set off for the match till I'd got home from playing for the school on the Saturday morning. At junior school – Cann Hall mixed-infants, Leytonstone – if you got in the team we had our own strip, green-and-gold stripes. I was so proud of it. And my best Christmas present ever was a pair of brown football boots with a great big toecap and nail-in studs. Think of the delicate little 'slippers' footballers wear now!

At Cann Hall I was captain of both football and cricket. I was lucky that two of the teachers particularly loved their sport. Both Mr Hall and Mr Kemp lived to see me as England captain. Along with Dad, their early enthusiasm was an important factor. Mr Hall retired to Sidmouth in Devon in 1975 and, when Essex played the minor county at nearby Exmouth in the 1991 NatWest trophy, I arranged tickets for him and his wife. He was frail and ill and in a wheelchair so I was not able, as I had planned, to take him into the Essex dressing-room to meet the players, but Dad and Mr Hall had a good chinwag about old Leyton times through the day, and so did I. Sadly, it was Mr Hall's last outing, for he died later that summer.

Whether I was too keen on sport to bother, or whether I just wasn't clever enough, I always knew I wouldn't be going on to the grammar school. So I went to the Secondary Modern, now called Norlington Junior High School. It was a couple of miles from home, about half an hour's walk. But it wasn't the school I wanted to go to; that was called George Mitchell and was even further away. Perhaps the reason was that it had a really good local reputation as a soccer school. Also it was a mixed school, whereas Norlington was boys only. However, looking back, I don't regret going to Norlington at all, but if I had gone to a mixed school I believe I might have been much more comfortable in boy-girl relationships once I'd become a teenager. At fifteen or sixteen I used to be very uneasy in mixed company. It wasn't until I got a scooter when I was seventeen that I felt confident enough to ask anyone out on a date, and by that time, of course, I was doing my apprenticeship. Even then, though, these were not real one-to-one dates with a particular girl, just a few of us boys sometimes and a couple of girls going along to the pictures, or a pile of us would go to the dancehall and stand around.

Sport was always my main thing. I was always very shy anyway, quiet and reserved. People used to remark how I never said anything. Even though sport continued to go really well for me, I never pushed myself forward. In district games, a teacher would ask 'What number do you bat?', and instead of saying 'Well, I open the batting, sir', which was true, I'd mumble that I'd bat at no. 6 or 7 – so of course I'd get put in at no. 9 or no. 10. Maybe I was frightened of being pushy and then making a fool of myself. Dad always used to tell me to assert myself more, but I never could.

Mum never worried about things like that. Her great worry was getting me to eat properly. Till I was past twenty, every day she'd say, 'What do you want for tea?' And every day I'd say, 'Just spam-and-chips as usual, Mum.' Or sausage and chips. Or – the height of my culinary daring – corned beef and chips. Actually it was all my mother's fault, because she made the most brilliantly tasty chips in the whole of London and East Anglia. She still does.

As well as football and cricket at school, I was in the badminton and cross-country teams. In the classroom, I never actually disliked the school work. I quite enjoyed history and geography, although I preferred metalwork to my Dad's woodwork. I was quite good with my hands. All my school reports were variations of 'Could do better' or 'Just a little more effort and concentration, please'. One said, 'Neat enough to make a good office-boy'. But I kept my head down and was mostly out of trouble. Discipline was strict and nobody minded using the cane or the slipper. It was a good school. My best friend, whom I still see occasionally, was Graham Hammond. He was a Leyton Orient supporter. He joined British Telecom, and now has his own business in telecommunications. We used to hang around together, pretending to be cool and streetwise. But we were never in any trouble. And I was too big and gawky to be bullied. Drinking beer never appealed to me. I tried a cigarette once, but never again.

I got a few CSE grades, but no GCEs, so Dad and I made the decision together that I leave at sixteen and take an apprenticeship. Even though my cricket was going well by then, and I'd set my heart on becoming a professional, I agreed with Dad that, in top sport, 'there's many a slip' and a trade behind me would be a solid insurance for the future. So, with metalwork being one of my good subjects, I signed a four-year apprenticeship as a toolmaker, first with the Association of Toolmakers in Ilford beginning with a year at Redbridge Technical College (who gave me Wednesday afternoons off for football or cricket!) and then, after they were taken over, with a firm called Goldring, nearer home at Leytonstone.

All this time, however, I had been getting more and more into my cricket, not only for schools' teams and district sides from a wider and wider area, but also for adult clubs. I played a few matches for Dad's East Ham Corinthians. Then Walthamstow, one of the leading club sides in the area, asked me if I'd like to join them. But I was already going to Bill Morris's cricket school and he said, 'Oh no, you don't, come and play for Ilford'.

Dad first took me to Bill Morris in the mid-sixties. Dad reckoned that his own coaching and advice had run its course, and that I should be aiming for a better standard of cricket – 'the more satisfaction you get, the more the enjoyment', he said. Bill was a super coach, very imaginative, but strict and at times quite fiery. On one of the first occasions I went for group coaching in the Easter holidays when I was twelve, I was messing about at the end of a net and not paying attention and he bawled me out in front of everyone else. I burst into tears.

After a few sessions with the group, Dad began taking me up for private lessons with Bill, which cost £1 for a half-hour session. Bill obviously thought I had something he could work on; raw as it was, I had a good hand-eye co-ordination, and Bill began putting some technical gloss on my batting. I could hit the ball all right and, from the beginning, he drummed into me the need for patience and gave me ideas about shot selection and how to plan an innings. He tightened me up, but never tried to cramp any inborn flair. Like all great coaches, Bill was brilliant at identifying weaknesses, which he set about eliminating, and strengths, which he encouraged. Simply, he turned me from a greenhorn schoolboy into a cricketer who might even go further. I was still very shy and reserved – but with a bat in my hands and a ball coming from 22 yards I felt utterly confident, even belligerent. I liked to give the ball a real whack. Perhaps I was compensating for my shyness by taking out my pent-up aggressions on a cricket ball?

I spent hours at the cricket school. It is nice to start adult cricket somewhere truly romantic, isn't it? – and my first game for Ilford 3rd XI was at the Becton Gas Works ground, down the A13 near West Ham's Upton Park. Bill must have been about fifty then, but he was still a good batsman and played for the Ilford Second XI, and soon I was promoted and would open with him: the middle-aged old pro and the callow schoolkid. Once, at Ilford, we put on 160-something for the first wicket against Winchmore Hill. At that time, Bill had the idea of turning me into a wicketkeeper. He said the Essex captain, Brian Taylor – known affectionately by all as 'Tonker' – was coming towards the end of his career and Essex would soon be needing a bright kid who could bat a bit to take over his gloves. But I liked bowling too. In fact, in my teens, I was really a Jack of all trades and master of none. I used to score quite a few runs here and there but never a huge weight of consistent runs like some all-conquering schoolboy prodigies; and when I wasn't keeping wicket I took wickets pretty regularly as, say, second- or third-change bowler.

This 'bits 'n' pieces' versatility set me off on my first big adventure, a tour to East Africa with the London Schools' Cricket Association, to Zambia, Tanzania, Kenya and Uganda. Lots of cricket as well as all the sights – safaris, the copper mines, the Victoria Falls. The Isle of Wight was the furthest I'd ever been before. We left on 23 July 1969, my sixteenth birthday. We didn't stay in hotels but were billeted with families who were involved with the local cricket clubs, two boys to each home.

From the first stay, in Lusaka, Zambia, I was put down to share with the oldest boy on the tour, who was just seventeen – a south Londoner from Peckham Manor school by the name of John Emburey. The future England and Middlesex off-spin bowler became my most enduring friend in cricket. You wouldn't have recognized him then, though. He was tall and as thin as a stick insect.

When we arrived for the game in Kenya, our English host drives John and me to his house. He is married to a German, a very severe and abrupt woman. Or so she seemed to us. In fairness, she was probably fed up at having two gormless kids foisted on her.

As John was a south-east Londoner and me north-east and both from working-class families, we were terribly conservative, not to say fussy eaters. I was still the bane of my mum's life, refusing to eat anything but spam or bangers or corned beef, with of course chips. John was the same. So, on the first night in Lusaka with the German lady, she plonks our supper plates down on the table. It was presumably a German dish, a sort of sauerkraut hash, and had probably taken hours to prepare. We looked at it, horrified, and then we looked at each other. There was no remote way we were going even to look at the food again, let alone eat it.

We left the lot ... did not touch a morsel. Our hostess was not best pleased and began ranting in clipped German. We were scared stiff of her. We went to bed. Next evening, she was waiting for us. She said she was 'having people in to play bridge and you will have to stay in your bedroom, not dare to come out, do you understand, and I will bring your food to your room'.

So she brought in what looked to us like an even more revolting concoction. We stayed in our room but could not bring ourselves to eat any of it. Next day we complained to the teacher who was our tour manager: 'Sir, we are not very happy at all, we haven't eaten for two days and there is no way we are going back to that frightening German lady.'

So that evening he came back with us and tried to get it sorted out. In the end, after a big confab, we apologized and she apologized. And then she dished up another of her awful looking German meals, but it was so soon after the peace treaty that John and I knew we would have to eat it. We really suffered. We nearly threw up. But we ate the lot. Our first experience, if you like, of cricket tourists as ambassadors.

It was a marvellous, eye-opening tour for me. I got a few runs down the middle order, and took one or two wickets. I was also reserve wicketkeeper. Out in the bush one night, near Ndola, our host took us and all his servants outside, pointed up to this huge full moon in the night sky and told us that an American spaceman, Neil Armstrong, had just landed up there and was actually walking on the moon. His servants laughed. He explained it to them again, slowly.

They walked away thinking their boss was totally barmy.

Three years later, I went on a second junior tour of an altogether higher cricketing standard. The England Young Cricketers tour to the West Indies in 1972 was managed by Lancashire's old England Test player, Jack Ikin; and our captain was John Barclay, who was at Eton and later went on to captain Sussex. His initials were JRT, the 'T' being for 'Troutbeck', so he was known as 'Trout'. I was just nineteen –we flew out to Montego Bay two days after my birthday – and among others on the trip who went on to play county cricket were Geoff Miller, Graham Clinton, Bernard Reidy, and Andy Stovold. The latter, who did brilliant service for Gloucestershire for years, was my particular buddy on that tour. His full surname was Willis-Stovold, and his Dad's name was Lancelot. I was his reserve wicketkeeper. The day before we left Heathrow, we had played two practice matches at Lord's, against the Combined Services (when I was no. 9 and didn't get a bat, but clean bowled a certain Lieutenant-Commander R C Moylan-Jones, RN, for 16). And on the eve of departure we played MCC and I was put in at no. 3 and Andy and I had a good partnership. When we got to Jamaica, Dad sent me out a cutting from the *Daily Telegraph*, the match report by the old radio commentator, Rex Alston. It said, 'the two players who caught the eye in a decent partnership of style and purpose were the two wicket-keepers Willis-Stovold (22) and Gooch (47) who both batted with commonsense and proper aggression'.

Dad had bought a little cine-camera for me to take on the trip, and I went high up into the 'bleachers' when we played at Sabina Park in Jamaica and filmed a startlingly athletic run-up by a local fast bowler called Michael Holding. I got a half-century against Trinidad Youth, and 48 against Barbados Youth at Kensington Oval, before I was clean bowled by a smiling young man of beanpole proportions named Joel Garner. At the Bourda Test ground, against Guyana Youth, the openers Graham Clinton and Bill Snowden, the Cambridge University captain, were taken by surprise and ransacked for next to nothing by a tall kid who was an extremely quick and accurate in-slant bowler, by the name of Colin Croft.

On the plane home, we were given the *Trinidad Guardian* for us to read. In it, our manager, Jack Ikin, who had been very kind and encouraging to me, had given an interview to sum up the tour. He never mentioned the West Indian fast bowlers we had encountered, but said that, of the home sides, 'the googly exponent Imtiaz Ali impressed me, as did the all-rounder Gregory Gomez and, from my England tourists, the captain Barclay had particularly excelled with his line and length and leadership; but the three who look to me to be genuine Test team prospects for the future are Geoff Miller, Bernard Reidy, and Graham Gooch.'

The following spring, Dad bought me *Wisden*, with my first proper mention in it – 'Gooch, Reidy and McLaren showed a proper appreciation of the needs of the one-day game … and McLaren and Gooch in particular delighted their manager by hitting the ball back over the bowler's head and over extra-cover.'

For me to make the tour, Dad had to ask the managing director of my toolmaking firm, Goldring, if I could be allowed some time off. By now, I had only a year left of my apprenticeship, but I had read that dog-eared cutting from the *Trinidad Guardian* again and again. And the mention in *Wisden*.

Did I really have a chance of making a reasonable fist of first-class cricket?

2

EAST SAXONS FLAYED AND OTHER CONQUESTS

FK

Gooch the youngster had knuckled down to his four-year appren-ticeship with what was already characteristic diligence. 'It was really quite interesting work. You had to be more meticulous than you might imagine; I was quite good at it, certainly I enjoyed it.'

Meanwhile, the local newspaper, the *Ilford Recorder*, was keep-ing the Essex county club fully informed of the young toolmaker's remarkable progress on the cricket field.

'MAIDEN TON BY GOOCH PUTS ILFORD IN FINAL ... A superb unbeat-en maiden century by 16-year-old Gooch – who slammed no fewer than 5 sixes and 12 fours in his 120 – helped Ilford Colts to their third successive Bailey Cup final against Shoeburyness last week ...'

'GOOCH FLAYS EAST SAXONS ... Boy ends rout with two glorious sixes over square-leg'

'GOOCH RUN BLAST CONTINUES'

'GOOCH RAGING 90 IN 100 MINUTES SINKS MET POLICE'

'TON-UP IN BOUNDARIES! ... Hutton were totally demoralised by a savagely ferocious 136 by Ilford youngster Gooch on Saturday – his 7 sixes and 16 fours contributing 106 of his runs in boundaries.'

And there was one other particularly evocative report from the *Ilford Recorder* in July 1972. 'ILFORD V WESTCLIFF-ON-SEA: GOOCH C CUTLER B BAILEY, 87'. The bowler was the forty-eight-year-old Trevor Bailey, of former England and Essex eminence. Whether any of the boy's 11 fours and 3 sixes came off deliveries by Bailey (three for 36) was not mentioned, but doubtless Bailey himself would have purred at seeing what an uninhibited talent Bill Morris had unearthed for his old county. Bailey served Essex for two decades as all-rounder and captain (1961–66) and latterly as secretary, not to mention England too as an all-rounder.

Essex had blooded the fifteen-year-old Gooch in one 2nd XI game against Northamptonshire 2nd XI at Northampton in 1969. Graham kept wicket and, at no. 11, did not bat. In 1971, on his holidays, the trainee toolmaker had three 2nd XI innings (average 15). The following summer, while laying local cricket sides to waste at weekends, he kept his head down over his lathe; but in 1973 he showed real signs of blossoming. Essex 2nd XI surprised even themselves by winning the county's first-ever trophy, and in 11 innings for them Gooch averaged 24, took 34 wickets, and *Wisden* commented that he 'showed fine all-round ability'.

That season, he played for the 1st XI in a handful of Sunday League knockabouts; also in the Gillette Cup pipe-opener against the still Minor County, Durham (did not bat), and in the losing second-round tie against Gloucestershire at Chelmsford on 1 August, when he was out, lbw b Brown, 3. A fortnight before, at Westcliff, he had made his debutant's curtsey in the first-class game, as a nineteen-year-old, and in a low-scoring game on a broken wicket he went in at no. 5 and made 18.

A week later, in the Sunday League, at Northampton, he hit a beefy 27 in a stand of 66 with Brian Hardie, and took two wickets (Steele and Sharp). He was beginning to contribute. But not yet to many conversations. He was still painfully shy. The captain, Brian 'Tonker' Taylor, bluffly tried to jolly the boy out of his shell, till he gave up, sighing, 'Well, at least it shows he's well brought up'. One time, the captain-elect and England batsman, Keith Fletcher, looked at Gooch trying to be invisible in the corner of the dressing-room and enquired of the others, 'Does it speak?'

Graham would have to let his bat speak his volumes. His unease in company at that time was exacerbated by being asked, on his apprentice's pittance (he was still playing as an amateur), to chip into the beer kitty after matches; not only could he ill afford the pound or so, but he could not twig the matey taproom custom when all he wanted to drink was a lemonade. And young Gooch's introversion was compounded, of course, by the fact that, working through his apprenticeship, he had played, comparatively, so little cricket at the club as not to have been able to ease himself gently into its social life or the general camaraderie of county cricket. Suddenly in 1973, from nowhere, he was in the thick of it. Small wonder he was mute.

Essex had some character all right, and some characters. Also, down the century, one or two very fine players. But not as a consistently winning combination? When Graham Gooch pootled up on his metallic mauve scooter, pads and holdall strapped on his back, bat tied to the running board, Essex 1st XI had not achieved a single trophy in ninety-seven years.

Keith Fletcher still smiles at the memory. 'If Graham hadn't joined the Essex dressing-room, and, say, he'd gone to Surrey at The Oval or to Middlesex at Lord's or another county, he might have turned out to be introverted and morose all the time. When he was a kid, us senior players would rib him to bring him out of himself. In the end he became one of the funniest blokes of our lot, with the driest humour and the most observant impersonations of anyone. Yes, he was quiet all right at first. But it was also a quiet determination to succeed. He'd know exactly who to talk to in order to sort out his game. He was a bit of a wicketkeeper at first, but I knew that wouldn't last long and that his batting was always going to take precedence. He had full-bloodied shots and had time to play them, which is the crucial thing. But away from the wicket, he looked awkward and sort of dozy. A very "retiring" boy. But we brought him out of himself. Because he was doing his apprenticeship, he wasn't around the club as much as others early on, so at first he was more uneasy than most. He had this little Vespa, and short-back-and-sides and crepe soles, like a "Mod", which was the fashion at the time. He didn't look like a young professional sportsman who'd be going right to the top – till he went out with a bat in his hand, that is. Then you knew he was a natural sportsman all right.'

John Lever concurs: 'With those sloping shoulders, ungainly posture, flat feet and knock-knees, nobody would have thought of Graham then as a likely looking prospect – until a ball was flying about and suddenly he would be better co-ordinated than any of us. He really worked at his fitness from the first. And his whole game. He was as determined as he was stubborn about it. He was going to improve himself and that was that. When he realised his wicket-keeping might upset his batting, he went for his bowling in a big way so he would be doubly valuable to the one-day side. He learned to swing it both ways, and once, early on when I got injured, he took seven wickets against Worcester. The ball was swinging all over, and when he came off I joked, "Great stuff, Goochie, but if I'd been playing they'd have been my wickets really." "Look in the paper tomorrow if you want to see whose wickets they are," he said. You couldn't fault him really, not for fitness, skill, or single-mindedness.'

GG

I'll always remember it. No first-class cricketer forgets his debut in the 'big time', the red-letter day when he walks out as a county player. After all, he has presumably spent a good few teenage years working towards it, and day-dreaming about what might happen. For sure, my first-class debut remains unforgettable, but mainly because I nearly didn't make it.

John Lever was four years older than me and already capped by Essex, but as I lived at Leytonstone and because we were both club members of Ilford CC, he was detailed to give me a lift to Westcliff for my first Championship match, against Northants. Now JK, being established in the team and already as nicely cavalier and carefree, says, 'No worries, we're in good time if we get to the ground dead-on an hour before play starts'. Of course, there was none of our present-day team-talk and warming-up jazz in those days. I can still see it now, JK's old silver Vauxhall Victor standing outside his house. So I load up and off we go – the A12 and then the A127 dual carriageway for Southend. Of course I was nervous, wondering whether we'd field or bat, about their bowlers and the weather, everything. But JK is just driving along without a care in the world.

Then BANG! The engine explodes. Victor is vanquished. Smoke everywhere. No more power. We stutter and shudder to a halt halfway across the inside-lane grass bank.

We are a few hundred yards from the Rayleigh Weir roundabout (it's an underpass now) and still a good five or six miles from Westcliff which, of course, is Southend really, the posh bit. But the day-out holiday traffic is whizzing past on its way, oblivious to a broken-down, steaming wreck, on the verge. And the clock is ticking on. So I get very hot under the collar. But not as hot as under the bonnet of the Lever Vauxhall Victor. There's another great billow of smoke as JK opens it with a rag. One of the spark-plugs had blown from the engine and it must have hit the underside of the bonnet like a bullet. The hole was there. It sheered off, just like that. This Victor had played its last game – possibly for ever, certainly for today.

But what about me? It must have been around five-to-ten now, for an eleven o'clock start. If I didn't show up soon, in the dressing-room, obviously they'd give my place to someone else. Is Keith Pont playing today, or Robert Cooke? Who's twelfth man?

Across the dual carriageway, a few hundred yards on the other side, was a petrol station. We dodge the traffic and get across. We ask to use the phone. But who knows the number of the Westcliff cricket ground? There are two grounds in Southend, both alongside each other. Are we playing at Southchurch Park or Chalkwell? Anyway, mercifully, we finally get through. Stuart Turner answers the phone. Good, faithful, Stuart, always reliable. We explain where we are. He is none too happy but he says, okay, he'll come and pick us up in his car. Not as easy as it sounds, because we're on the other side of the dual carriageway with our bags and kit – by this time I'd progressed from my little 'grip', which I used to strap on my Vespa with those elastic hook straps, to a proper pro's big cricket bag. We go back across to JK's now very dead car, still gently steaming in its last rites. We unload, and wait on the grass verge. The clock is ticking on.

Suddenly a friend pulls up. It's Ivan the taxi-driver, an Essex member who sometimes helps sell scorecards. 'Jump in,' he says. JK looks at me. What did I think? He's the boss. And it's my debut. And I'm already in a terrible fret. 'But what about Stuart?' I ask. JK knows what to do. It's now past 10.15 and he allows me to reason with him that if Stuart cannot find us, it would be better if two turn up than three go missing. Especially if one of the two who make it is on his first-class debut. So we load up into Ivan's taxi.

We arrive at the ground and change. I'm still in a state: Turner is still out looking for us, and we are not where we said we'd be. When Stuart finally gets back he's none too pleased. I don't blame him. Then, at once, Northants begin batting, and Stuart and JK have to go out and open the bowling. Stuart was probably still fuming at me, because he dismisses Peter Willey in no time. And JK ends up with two for 20 in his nine overs. Northants are all out for 161. We bat. I go in no. 5. Mushtaq Mohammed is bowling his leg-breaks, 'Doc' Dye taking wickets at the other end. Straight-off I hit four fours off

Mushtaq, but not really dramatic ones because they were all full-tosses. Then Bob Cottam comes back, and gets me lbw for 18. The debut I nearly didn't make. We win by seven wickets.

Funny, I'd been driven to my first 2nd XI game – Northants again, at Northampton – in a Rolls-Royce Silver Cloud by the captain, Johnny Welch. He picked me up at the George in Wanstead and I sailed up the M1 like royalty. A bit different to my first 1st XI game in JK's silver-sprayed old Vauxhall Victor; but I'd already had an old banger of my own since I was eighteen, a 1963 Ford Prefect, the model immediately after the famous 'jellymould' type with the big mudguards. It cost £60 and Dad lent me the money – I was only earning £10 a week in 1971 as an apprentice – and we patched up the bodywork and resprayed it battleship grey, more sober than the metallic mauve of my Vespa!

Essex had long given up the idea of me being a wicketkeeper. They had realized I'd grown too big for it. And that season with the 2nd XI I had occasionally bowled swingers. In fact I took 34 wickets. Even so everybody's eyes at the club must have popped out when they read that I'd taken seven for 70 against Middlesex 2nds at Chingford. Middlesex had a Rhodesian all-rounder in their side, Sam Black, a good cricketer. And the Chingford ground is only a small one, and that helped because, when this fellow Black comes in he starts tonking the ball all over. He hit them into adjoining gardens, and into the roads, and over the trees. In the end, he lost six balls – and suddenly the two umpires and the club officials look at each other and realize there were no more usable balls available. So they were reduced to looking into everyone's bags in the pavilion. What they came up with was this grotty old ball which must have survived a thousand very long and sustained net practices. It was gouged and scarred and as soft as a sponge.

Middlesex were winning easily on account of Black's amazing assault. And I'd been bowling when the last decent ball vanished over the chimney-tops. So I kept bowling. I might have been shy in those days but I was no mug when it came to recognizing a good thing. I'd gone nought-for-plenty – and now I ran in and bowled with this last-gasp ball, and it swung every which way, but mostly it just shot along the deck. No batsman could play it! So that old ball helped us to win the 2nd XI Championship.

Of course, I didn't play many 2nd XI games because I had my four-year apprenticeship to do. Anyway, with Essex, when I began, the 2nd XI was really a glorified club side made up of a few promising kids and some old hands, because sometimes there were only a dozen professionals on the staff and they'd all be in the 1st XI. So when I started mixing with the county team I didn't know anybody even reasonably well, except John Lever and Keith Pont. Luckily John was a really confident character, but in the first full season I played, 1974, he had a shocker of a season. He could not have taken more than 25 wickets. But he stuck at it, knuckled down to learn his trade and develop his skills, so that he was a fine bowler by the time he played his first Test, for Tony Greig's side in India in 1976/77, when they bowled the Indians out for 122 in Delhi, JK taking seven for 46.

Lever was a one-off, not just as a 'character' in the Essex mould of Ray East and Robin Hobbs and, a bit later, of Pont, but as a bowler too. The great things with JK were his stamina and his love of bowling. There are certain bowlers who may be very good, but they give the impression they don't like bowling – okay, a fired-up four-over burst, but then that's it for an hour or two. Lever was different. When he had the ball, you couldn't get it off him. Fletcher just had to say, 'One more, JK?' and he'd be told, 'No, I'm okay for two or three more, at least'. He just wasn't happy unless he could reel off ten or twelve overs on the trot. And even then, when he was taken off, he'd march away moaning at the injustice of it all. But what a treasure for a captain. Many years later, Angus Fraser was out of exactly the same mould when I was captain of England: 'One more, Gus?' 'What are you talking about, I'm just settling into my rhythm.' Ian Botham was another, strong as an ox, ninety-minute spells no problem to him either. Ian and JK were two of a kind, especially on tours in the heat – marathon spells, close-of-play, socialize to the hilt, then get up next day and vie about which of them was going to bowl unchanged till lunchtime. They made a marvellous pair together. No wonder they were regular room-mates abroad. Like for like. Wonderful team men, but disciplined bowlers, too.

JK would have been a much better batsman, but he never bothered with it, never practised, even though he had a good technique. He usually had his own bat and gloves, but never any pads. He'd just borrow off other players, even in a Test match. Although he wasn't our no. 11 – that was always David Acfield – his batting was always good for a laugh, like once against Sussex at Hove in my first season in 1974. Sussex had this Indian off-break bowler then, called U C Joshi. He'd got a few wickets against us, and John was watching the play in front of the pavilion, waiting to go in to bat. He says, 'How can anybody live with themselves if they get out to this chap? There's no remote way he's going to get me. If this Joshi was to get me out with that sort of innocuous rubbish he's tossing up, I'll, I'll …' and he considers what outrageous thing he would do. 'Tell you what, I just won't come back to this pavilion ever again.'

In time, Joshi duly gets another wicket and JK gets up and goes forth to bat. At once they are all going up with a shout … Lever, caught at the wicket, Joshi, for 1.

Back in the pavilion we are all in fits of laughter, and even more so when we realise JK is not returning to us from the middle, but walking in the opposite direction. At Hove, at the furthest left-hand corner across the field away from the players' pavilion, is a grassy hillock where they put a lot of deckchairs. That's where Lever goes. He's clean bowled. He looks at his stumps, turns and walks over into the far distance, climbs on to the hill, and sits down all by himself in a deckchair and takes off his pads. And he sits there in that solitary corner, until we're all out and go in to field, when he deigns to come across and join us, and open the bowling. Typical, glorious JK.

If it hadn't been for Joshi, who was a good little spinner, I might never have got to know Ken McEwan. He was a South African and Tony Greig had recommended him to his own county, Sussex. But they had Joshi as well as Geoffrey Greenidge from Barbados as the two overseas players permitted in those days. So Ken came to Essex, played himself in during his first season in 1974 – which was also mine – and the rest is history. He was a tremendous batsman, charm and power and timing, all the strokes, and he could pace an innings any way you needed it. Also, more than just in his brilliant cricket, McEwan was a fundamentally vital cog in that 1970s team of ours which went on to take everyone and everything by storm in the 1980s. But my first, proper, cricketing introduction to him, left him far from pleased. In that first season when, basically, I began as 'sub' for Keith Fletcher when he was on Test-match duty, I made a faltering start with a 'pair' in my first match against Gloucester at Bristol. At least I knew I had begun at rock bottom and things could only improve from here.

Then I got a few runs against Sussex in the next match. When I had my next chance I hit 94 against Lancashire at Old Trafford, which was satisfying especially as they had a good attack – Lever and Shuttleworth and Lee, and the spinners Simmons and Hughes. That was the innings that showed me I might have what it takes. But still I had not shared any sort of partnership with McEwan; he got a duck in that Old Trafford match, for instance. The opportunity came a few weeks later at Taunton. Brian Close, in his forties, had come down from Yorkshire to take over a young Somerset side and teach them all about cricket. In their innings he had scored a good 75. When we went in, we lost both openers but then McEwan really began to play. He was smashing them all over, going like a train. We'd put on about 30 and were both thinking 'there's more to come here, this could be our first big partnership'.

So, of course, somehow I stupidly orchestrate a ridiculous run out. Totally my fault, and we finish up staring at each other at the same end. I'm 30-odd, Ken's in the 90s. 'Sorry, Kenny,' and off I walk back to the pavilion.

'Nay, nay, nay, lad,' shouts Close, 'it's not you to go, it's McEwan who's out.' Now if I'd been more experienced I'd have just kept on walking and that might have been the end of it. But when Close kept ordering me back, 'Nay, lad, it's not you who's to go, it's him, it's McEwan who goes', like an idiot I turned and stood there. Close is causing this huge row because he knows, quite simply, that Ken is clocking them all over and has not only got 90, but is looking good for a very brisk double-hundred as well. 'Nay, nay, it's not the lad out,' and so he brings the umpires into it and now he's got them, Arthur Fagg and Alan Whitehead, into some serious reconsideration. So a bit more insisting, 'It's McEwan who must go', from Close, and then Fagg is pointing at Ken and giving him the finger of doom. So off goes Ken, not best pleased to put it mildly, and I stay in, none too happy either. And when I then get out for 37 (c & b Moseley), Close is really chuckling to himself like an old hen, isn't he?

That match marked the first time I laid eyes on Vivian Richards and Ian Botham. They were both, if not exactly scrawny, then 'slimline' and hadn't turned into the great strapping fellows of their prime. Viv got a duck, lbw, playing back to Robin Hobbs's googly. Ian was still bowling little medium-paced 'dobbers', but he could already swing it, coming in all jaunty off about fifteen paces and with a good sideways-on action. Within two or three years, of course, he'd put on weight and three or four yards of pace and was running in fully intent on some fireball-quick mischief – and English cricket was never quite the same.

During that first season it was rewarding to play on the same field as legendary players I'd first heard of in my boyhood, on the radio or on television. Brian Close was one. Then Yorkshire played at Leyton that year, at the festival and on the ground very near where I was born, and I fielded to Geoff Boycott while he made 68 out of 131 all out. It was fascinating to be able to watch a master at work in such circumstances, when everything around him was disintegrating. Keith Boyce took the first six wickets for us in that innings and to every other Yorkshire batsman except the imperturbable Boycott he looked unplayable.

In that 1974 summer I only had 25 first-class innings and never came across any of the world's genuine quick bowlers; but that gap in my education was soon filled in the opening county match in April 1975. We played Hampshire at Bournemouth and they sent me in at no. 4 after I'd drooled away the day before in the field in awe at the batsman who became, there and then, my all-time cricket hero, Barry Richards, as he laid us to waste without breaking sweat. When I go in, I am still in a sort of daze of admiration for him. And this bowler at once menacingly propels himself seemingly off the sightscreen, slithers in like lightning, and before I've even picked my bat out of the blockhole the ball is smacking into the wicketkeeper's gloves thirty-five yards behind me. 'Jeez,' I thought to myself, 'first Barry Richards, now Andy Roberts; boy, you have suddenly joined a very different and totally new ballgame.'

Roberts was the first of the 'lightning quicks' to come in and shake up the batting orders of county cricket; not only the top-order bats-men but the tail-enders even more. Come to think of it, Ian Botham had already made his name by standing up to Roberts and hitting him – matching fire with fire – to win a Benson & Hedges Cup tie for Somerset against Hampshire in 1974. That was Ian's announcement of himself to the wider world and he deserved the plaudits he got. Not many men in those days took on Andy Roberts and won.

A couple of years later, we went down to Portsmouth. A pretty dodgy pitch, but this time Andy doesn't seem too interested. He bowls half a dozen overs, then slopes down to fine-leg. If we had but known it, it's mid-summer and he's in his final season for Hampshire because in the autumn the Kerry Packer 'revolution' was about to burst on us. So he retires to the outfield, but still the two medium-pacers, Rice and Taylor, bowl us out for 113. Hampshire go in and, although they are five or six down in no time, the mid-order and tail dig in. Taylor gets a good century and the captain and wicketkeeper, Robert Stephenson, also gets a few. So we go in again, and by the end of the second day we are still 76 behind – McEwan out, Fletcher out, Gooch out – with only five wickets left to avoid an innings defeat. Ken had made 40-odd, and Roberts had got him, sure, but generally the West Indian still didn't seem very interested.

Before going out next morning, however, and with a forecast of some rotten weather moving in up the Channel, one of the guys heard the canny old captain, Stephenson, telling Roberts that if he rolled over our tail, he could forget Hampshire's next match, away to Worcester, and have the week off.

So Roberts steams in, even faster than the rain that was moving in over Dorset. He has Keith Pont lbw at once. Don't forget, in the whole low-scoring match, this finest fast bowler in the world had only taken one of the wickets to fall up to this point. Ray East goes in to join Stuart Turner, who never gives anything away. Roberts is bowling for his week off from the Worcester match, so he is bowling very quick indeed. Essex, in a match that has gone badly wrong from the start, are playing for the dignity of a draw, and so have one eye on the weather coming in from the south-west.

Turner and East nudge and nurdle and hit some runs. They have put on 30-odd, which was superb for, even from the pavilion, Roberts was looking an extremely nasty proposition.

Then he bowls this wicked delivery which snakes back into East, and which he somehow fends off as he jumps, and the ball comes off his body and loops up in a gentle parabola before it starts falling. In the close cordon, at third slip, Hampshire had a promising young-ster called David Rock who reacts quickly, takes a forward dive, full length, scoops up the ball brilliantly, rolls over in celebration and holds it up. A big catch. But the batsman, Ray, is standing there, nonchalantly rubbing his shoulder and looking all-innocent at the umpire, the bluff Australian Bill Alley. Alley gives East 'Not out'.

Nobody on the field can believe it, least of all the bowler. Roberts goes back to his mark smouldering with rage. Ray snicks a single and gets up to Alley's end, then takes his glove off, wrings his hand and examines it. 'What's wrong with your hand, mate?' enquires the Aussie umpire. 'The ball hit me right on the knuckle,' says Ray. 'On the knuckle,' says Alley, 'you bastard, you signalled that it hit your shoulder.'

'No,' says Ray, 'I didn't walk because the catch didn't "carry", it was a "bump-ball".' Says Alley, 'It was not. It was a brilliant catch and a fair one.'

And, of course, listening to all this, his eyes popping out with fury and amazement, is Andy Roberts. Retribution will be imminent.

So play resumes and Ray is worried, thinking to himself, 'Raymond, lad, you might just have pushed your luck a bit too far here in enraging the world's most dangerous bowler ... who's looking for a week off.'

Turner gets a single. East to face Roberts, who is rushing in most vengefully ... and as the West Indian coils himself into his delivery stride, Ray takes two sideways strides from the stumps, allows the whizzing ball to knock the lot out, and walks off.

There was no way he was going to be targeted by Mr Andy Roberts for the rest of his career, thank you very much.

So we lost by an innings, courtesy of Mr Roberts, who finished the morning with five for 20-odd and, presumably, had his week off. However, innings defeats, if not exactly the norm when I first joined the club, had occurred most seasons two or three times. The club had been flat broke and if having only twelve or thirteen professionals might have made for complacency and a lack of competition for places, it also engendered a very contented companionship and team spirit. Although I never played a season under his leadership, it was obvious that Brian Taylor's regime laid the foundations of Essex's later success. His 'sergeant-major' approach was obviously much loved and he never let things get too much out of hand. He even got the joke at Derby once when he put Keith Pont, in only his second game, at third-man at both ends – so Pont borrowed a push-bike from a spectator and rode it round the boundary between overs.

Between innings Tonker would come back to the pavilion and announce curtly, 'Same batting order, but better batting.' He really rated Robin Hobbs. He would even play Robin in Sunday League games, in which he'd bat at no. 9 or no. 10 and wouldn't get a bowl with his leg-spinners. 'First on my list, first on my list,' snapped Tonker. 'Hobbs plays for his fielding.' He was right there. Robin, a lovely man and good cricketer, was a brilliant fielder. Robin and Ray East could even extend their off-the-cuff double-act on to the field. In my first season, at Leyton Robin made a brilliant stop at cover-point, diving to hold the ball like a goalie going for the bottom corner, and then doing a flamboyant gymnast's tumble-roll to celebrate the fact. Then he got up and just lobbed the ball to extra-cover to pass on to the bowler. Ray was at extra-cover. He caught the lob, dived on to the floor and did exactly the same gymnast's roll.

I was nine when Keith Fletcher first played for the county and he was my No.1 Essex hero. In my first season, Keith did not make too strong an impression on me as, of course, I was mostly in the team as his substitute when he was away at the Tests. But after that his home Test appearances were more spasmodic, and then began his great run as captain. Keith had begun his career at Essex in 1962 at the age of eighteen when Trevor Bailey was captain and trying to keep the club afloat on shoestring budgets. But even then, Keith tells me it got up his nose that the team seldom presumed to win – when they went to the likes of Surrey or Lancashire or Yorkshire there was not even the remotest contemplation of victory even if they played above themselves. 'We were often looked on as cannon fodder,' he told me, 'and those big teams were mighty pleased to see us; for one thing we were a matey crowd, but most important we could be relied on to boost every opponents' averages.' Fletch was particularly influenced by the Yorkshire side of the 1960s because although, he said, they were difficult characters – the Closes, the Truemans, the Boycotts, the Illingworths, all bickering and getting in their own two pen-n'orth – they were great players and they would obviously all pull together on the field where it mattered. He used to say that what influenced him profoundly was that, whenever Yorkshire got into a situation where they could drive home the advantage, they did just that. When they got you down, they kept you down and trod on you.

In a way, Keith Fletcher served his captaincy apprenticeship by playing against – and of course *with* in the Tests – captains like Close and Illingworth. It helps, of course, to have a decent team under you, and he was fortunate, when he inherited Essex's captaincy from Taylor, that the likes of Lever, Hardie, East, and Turner were a nucleus approaching maturity, which coincided, of course, with the arrival of Kenny McEwan – a piece of tremendous fortune.

Fletcher was more astute than any other captain at filing away in his mind opposing batsmen's habits or weaknesses. Once, at Chelmsford, I was bowling away-swingers against Northants. I got a wicket and in comes David Steele, with his glinting spectacles, grey hair, and sailor's high-seas gait. Fletch sidles up to me. 'To get himself going, this cock likes to push his leg out and play through midwicket. First ball, give him a little in-swinger and I'll go leg-slip.' So I do, and get it dead right. Steele pushes out his leg, his bat follows the ball, and he's caught Fletcher at leg-slip. Steele could not believe it. They had to get a wheelbarrow to lift him off.

That first team I got into was also boosted by Keith Boyce in his last couple of years before retiring. I've never seen such a natural athlete. Keith used to have a house near me, so I travelled quite a bit in his old Ford Anglia. He was a free spirit; he lived life, as they say, to the full. If we were batting, he'd be going in at, say, no. 7. So he'd pad up with the openers, then stretch out on that bench just outside the pavilion with orders not to be woken till the sixth wicket fell and he was in. And when his batting came off, well, he was a superb hitter. But before the injuries caught up with him, it was his bowling and lithe fielding that were sheer joy.

When Boyce played for the West Indies against England in 1973/74, they say he saved his most hostile stuff for the entrance of Fletch, his new county captain. At Trinidad, he bowled six searing bouncers at him in one over, at the end of which Fletch walked down to the umpire and said, 'Hey, what about "intimidation" then? That was six balls, six bouncers!' Said the umpire, scornfully, '*Bouncers*, man? Those were six *long-hops*.'

Because Fletcher looked a touch diffident as he shuffled out to bat, and was generally an undemonstrative country man, I think the powers-that-be were uncertain about him. His 'face didn't fit'. But he was a genuinely top-class batsman. In my early years, in fact, we relied on him too heavily. He was our best player by far, and if he failed the rest of us had a tendency to fold up like a deck of cards. To bat at the other end to him in those formative years of mine was a crucial bonus in my cricketing education. What do university blokes call one-to-one lessons with their professors – tutorials? Those part-nerships with Fletch were my tutorials. He was an especially brilliant player of spin bowling. I know the general rule is to play forward to spinners, but Keith played back to them a lot – certainly he'd never commit himself to the big 'fast forward' too early like some batsmen. I learned a lot from Keith about playing spin. When you're defend-ing, for instance, 'don't hit the ball, let the ball hit the bat', and use 'soft hands' just to stun the ball gently and drop it down. If you go for it with 'stiff' hands, a slice or a nick can fly anywhere.

Keith also understood spinners as a captain. He realized they gave him further options to keep the game alive and not let it drift. In that respect he was always fortunate, of course, in having Lever's stamina and willingness to call on, for even when JK looked close to flagging after reeling off a dozen overs, Fletch might quietly signal the wick-etkeeper, Neil Smith or David East, to stand up to the stumps, and that would make JK livid so he'd put in a couple more overs at full pace.

Smith and East were both popular. It is important that wicket-keepers remain the 'life and soul' during long days out in the field. David's nickname (because he could be a bit of a chuntering old woman occasionally) was 'Ethel' and he bridled at it, especially when addressed as such by junior members in the 2nd XI, which natur-ally made the name even more popular with us. David equalled the world wicketkeeping record of eight catches in an innings held by the Australian Wally Grout. That was in a fantastic match at Taunton against Somerset when Ian Botham was captain. Because one day had been lost to rain, Fletch persuaded Ian the pitch was cracking up and talked him into the idea that we could not possibly hope to get 290-odd in 90 overs. We got them with about twenty overs to spare and I got 170, mostly because Ian kept bouncing me and I kept 'tap-ping' him on to the roof of that old 'cider' club pavilion down at square-leg near the church.

But what I remember most about that game, was the performance of Keith Pont's kid brother, Ian, in his debut match for Essex. Ian was a very raw fast bowler, extremely lively and, if he got it in the right place, capable of knocking anyone over; but if he got it wrong the ball could go anywhere. Rather like a youthful Devon Malcolm.

We lose the toss and Fletcher gives young Pont the new ball. He roars in, and at once gets Peter Roebuck to nick it and give David East the first of his record pile of catches. Funny, I say in the slips to Kenny McEwan, we might be in luck here because Viv Richards is not coming in at his usual no. 3. The great man, we hope, might have been out all night with his captain and be snoozing it off in the dressing-room – Ian Botham's motto then was 'never come back the same day you go out'. So in comes Nigel Felton at no. 3. Pont immediately tears in and gets the other opener, Nigel Popplewell, caught behind. So, two down for not many, and Pont on a high. So in comes the Emperor at no. 4. And sure enough, he does look a touch sleepy, a little lackadaisical. He still has his rolling strut in his walk to the crease, of course, he wouldn't be Viv without that.

But what's this? The kid Pont is standing halfway down the pitch, all aggressive and threatening, and actually trying to out-glare the famous fellow. In the slips, Kenny and I are thinking, 'Hang on, Ponty, hang on, that is not the way to do it, just keep it all tame and low key. Can't you say, nicely, "Good morning, Mr Richards, sir".'

So Viv takes guard. The lip-curling Pont offers the batsman one more glare, and then goes back thirty yards to begin his run-up. Viv scratches his mark with his bat, adjusts his cap, and turns round to us in the slips as if to ask, with a quizzical frown, in that distinctive Antiguan drawl, 'Who is this Ponty, ma-an?' Kenny and I pretend not to hear.

The debutant Ponty charges in. Viv always likes to get forward, doesn't he? If you bowled short at him, he was a great puller, and if it was really short he could still rock back and hammer it square for four. Anyway, this time he begins to push forward, and Pont digs in this vicious ball, short, but not bumper-short. It really flies. Viv adjusts, goes to rock back and pull it, but it's a bit too quick and surprises him. He snaps his head back, the fizzing ball just nicks the peak of his cap and knocks it off, and as Viv spins round he overbalances and falls over in the crease. A touch inglorious for a monarch in his immaculate, newly-pressed flannels.

Viv gets up, dusts himself down – and there's Pont, having followed through like a train, seriously eyeballing the discomfited
superstar in his crease. Kenny and I in the slips grimace quietly to
ourselves, 'No, Ponty, no, you haven't worked out this first-class
cricket properly at all, have you, son?' And I just whisper 'Greg
Thomas' to remind Kenny of the time, in a Test match in the West
Indies, that the greenhorn Glamorgan pace bowler similarly tried to
ruffle Viv by showing him the ball after a bouncer and saying, 'It's
round, it's red, and it's about this big'. Next ball, another attempt at
a venomous bouncer, Viv smashes clean over the grandstands and
out of the ground before laconically telling Thomas, 'You know
what it looks like, so you go and fetch it!'

So what's going to happen now? Pont snorts back to his mark. Viv
recovers his composure, settles in at his guard, and you can hear him
muttering to himself, pumping himself up, 'C'mon Ponty, ma-an,
c'mon'. Pont explodes into his delivery stride. It's another good ball.
Quick again, on a length, it both rises and seams away towards us at
slip. Viv rocks back – and all these years later I can still hear those
two noises, BANG!-BANG!, like successive gun shots. Viv hits the
ball, the ball cannons into the advertising boards square on the offside. It went like a tracer. I have never seen a ball hit so hard nor leave
the bat so fast.

Pont, undeterred, has a little stare, a little sneer, and goes back to
his mark. Vivian's geared up and wide-awake now, and he's knocking his bat down vertically a few times, ostensibly to push the rub-
ber-grip down but a characteristic habit of his when the adrenalin's
really flowing. Kenny and I look at each other and wonder where the
next one's going – Yeovil or Shepton Mallet? – and whether the
maestro will complete his big double-hundred by tea time or not. At
mid-on, Fletch, obviously thinking the same, surreptitiously signals
the field to spread out a bit.

Third ball. Pont turns and thunders in. Because the first delivery
was a really good bumper, and the second a fuller length which is
smashed for four, Viv understandably expects the third to be another bouncer, so just as the bowler unwinds into the delivery Viv puts
his weight on his back foot in readiness.

Give Pont credit. He disguises a slower ball, almost out of the
back of his hand. Viv spots it, but too late, and as he readjusts to

come forward and crack it back over the bowler's head, he's not quite 'there' and he nicks it – and it just carries to the forward diving David East behind the sticks.

I V A Richards c East b Pont 4.

Richards turns and walks back to the pavilion. Having now bagged three wickets on his debut, Pont, thoroughly elated, follows through to embrace the wicketkeeper, which he does, and then turns to look at the departing batsman, and asks us, 'Who was that young black lad, anyway?'

Chronologically, I have jumped the gun a bit with that tale of first-match innocence, but I was so much of a wide-eyed fledgling myself that, when I scored my first century in county cricket, I even apologized for it. It was at Chelmsford at the end of that 1974 season, my fifteenth match or thereabouts. Leicester's captain, Ray Illingworth, set us over 240 to win in around three-and-a-half hours. Soon we were 150 for six. Neil Smith and then Robin Hobbs stuck around with me. I remember hitting John Steele for 16 runs in an over, and then celebrating my first county century by driving the great Australian quick bowler, Graham McKenzie, over long-on for six. As he followed through I found myself saying to him, 'Sorry, Mr McKenzie'. We won by two wickets.

3

WHAT EVERY YOUNG CRICKETER DREAMS ABOUT

FK

Gooch's realization of 'a totally new ballgame' on receipt of that first delivery from Andy Roberts came in spite of the fact that, with 46 and 53, he had top-scored in both innings against the hostile West Indian at Bournemouth in that match which opened the 1975 county championship season. It was Gooch's first full summer on cricket's round-Britain whizz.

That first-match aggregate of 99 was lauded by Henry Blofeld in the *Sunday Express* the following weekend:

'I saw Gooch's 46 and 53 against Roberts, and he batted with remarkable skill and assurance. Gooch told me, "Roberts is the quickest I've ever faced. I decided to go back and across to get into line and give myself more time." At twenty-one, Gooch is very high on my list of England players of the future. He scored his maiden first-class hundred at the end of last summer against Leicestershire, captained by Ray Illingworth, who told me: "The boy has the ability to go all the way. He is a big lad, hits it hard and, crucially, has time to play. That one against us was an extremely good hundred."'

In fact, Gooch's account for the new season had already opened. Four days earlier, on 26 April, he had top-scored with 59 in Essex's winning Benson & Hedges first-round tie against Middlesex at Lord's. It was his first 'grown-up' game at cricket's headquarters, the ground to which Gooch would become so fondly attached over the next two decades. He had first played there, of course, on the eve of the Young Cricketer's tour of the Caribbean three years earlier.

On the last day of May, Gooch scored his second first-class century, on a picnicking Saturday at Essex's comparatively pastoral 'out' ground at Castle Park, Colchester. The *Sunday Times* sent their eminent soccer writer, Brian Glanville, to enjoy a day in the sun:

> 'Gooch's attractive 100 included on-driving, off-driving, a pull for six, a notable hook for four, an occasional deft late cut. For one so large he is a remarkably light mover, and he is adventurous rather than impetuous.'

The England touring team (captained by Mike Denness and including Keith Fletcher) had returned from its 1974/75 winter in Australia seriously demoralised, not to say shell-shocked, by the opening attack of one of cricket's legendary pairs of fast bowlers, Dennis Lillee and Jeff Thomson. The England stalwart, Geoffrey Boycott, had declined to tour under Denness, and when Dennis Amiss and John Edrich had hands broken, England sent for the veteran Colin Cowdrey in the month of his forty-second birthday, but even his staunch bulk, and all the experience logged in making his sixth tour of Australia, could do little to divert the rout.

Now, at once, the Australians were back in England, staying on for a shortened tour after a thrilling World Cup in mid-summer, during which they had played some equally stirring cricket. So Fleet Street, as it does, set about enjoying one of its periodic fits of sneering despair about the spineless wimps of the English cricket team and demanding new blood, new attitudes, and new faces.

After Gooch had followed his century at Colchester (against, among others, the England bowler Derek Underwood) with, in early June, 85 against Lancashire (Lee and Shuttleworth), and 90 against Nottinghamshire (Rice, and Latchman's seven for 65), the *Daily Express* excitedly and definitively decided on the new saviour of English cricket, and the sports editor dispatched its chief back-page colour man, James Lawton, to watch Gooch make 82 in as many minutes against the students of Cambridge at Fenner's in Essex's next match. The bandwagon had begun to roll as insistently as Lawton's prose:

'The boy with the build of a blacksmith has the classic fresh complexion and the image of a youthful contemporary of W G Grace. He bats with immense power and optimism. But for England? The key phrase is the chorus, 'He must not be rushed.' Did the Aussies rush the nineteen-year-old Neil Harvey? Did the West Indies hustle the teenage Garfield Sobers? Or Pakistan the seventeen-year-old Javed Miandad? No, the latter just strode from the pages of Rudyard Kipling. Gooch must be allowed the same sort of natural momentum – and MUST BE PICKED FOR ENGLAND, preferably before middle-age.'

The pack followed Lawton. And the selectors, as so often, followed the pack. Gooch was picked in the beginning of July to play for MCC at Lord's against the Australians in the tour's pipe-opener, less than a fortnight after their dramatic, losing World Cup final against the West Indies. The MCC captain was the middle-aged Cowdrey who, the week before at Canterbury, had scored for olde tyme's sake a memorable and undefeated 151 to win Kent's match against the tourists; as well as Gooch, the MCC team included other young Englishmen of promise, such as Bob Woolmer of Kent, David Bairstow the Yorkshire wicketkeeper, and Philip Slocombe of Somerset.

MCC batted and the Australian fast bowlers, Lillee and Thomson, pawed the turf and opened up with all the venom they had displayed on England's woebegone tour in the winter. In his first eleven deliveries, Lillee took the first three MCC wickets – Lumb 2, Johnson 2, Cowdrey 0; the latter was to get a dreaded 'pair', the third of his long career. At 11 for three, Gooch walked in to join the Lancashire opening batsman, David Lloyd. And the man-child just nervelessly stood up and, as they said of the legendary American golfer Bobby Jones, 'gave it one'.

Gooch hit 75 in a stand of 109 with Lloyd. The large crowd clucked contentedly as Lillee and Thomson and then, particularly, the left-arm swinger Gilmour, were sent on their way with lusty dismissiveness. In the committee-room the selectors – Alec Bedser, Sir Len Hutton, Ken Barrington, and the former umpire Charlie Elliott – beamed and called for the wine waiter. Up above the Warner Stand, in the press-box, purple Quink was called for:

'Gooch, unconcerned, simply outfaced Lillee and hit him through the offside in a refreshingly natural way; likewise when, without fuss, he pulled Thomson and Gilmour for sixes.' (Michael Melford, *Daily Telegraph*)

'A fine upstanding attacking innings when, at 11 for three, almost everyone else would have been in the trenches.' (Clive Taylor, *Sun*)

'Gooch with his high natural talent and temperament played, beyond argument, the most impressive innings by a young English batsman against quality bowling for years – the selectors must give him the no. 4 spot in the Test matches.' (Alex Bannister, *Daily Mail*)

To think it was just a year to the week that Gooch had tremulously made his wretched 'pair' at Bristol in his first county match of 1974. Now twelve months later, Alf Gooch, working at Dunster & Son in Hackney, had heard a radio bulletin from Lord's at midday, asked his boss for an owed half-day, talked himself into Q-stand ('I think you'll find that's my son batting out there'), basked in the obvious relish in the crowd at the new batting arrival, and saw Graham's last 20-odd runs before Gilmour bowled him. And on the following Sunday, Alf cut out and proudly stuck in the family scrapbook an article in the *Sunday Express* by the old hero Denis Compton: 'Young Gooch's power and confidence is what we have waited years for. He impressed me so much at Lord's that he must play in the whole Test series, even if he fails in the first.'

Fleet Street, the selectors, and the cricket public had created another new saviour for English cricket, but they were asking an awesome lot. Gooch had not even played a full season at county level. In 1974 he had scored 637 first-class runs, up to the MCC match he had made another 647; add his 15 in 1973 and, well, a career aggregate of less than 1,300 runs was an awful few to be taking with him into first Test at Edgbaston in 1975, especially against the rampaging Australians. Certainly, at twenty-one Gooch was the youngest batsman chosen for England since Colin Cowdrey in 1954. In his gleaming new county cap, he tuned up with 41 and 35 for Essex against Derbyshire at Ilkeston, where he gave the last of his interviews before the match, to Chris Lander of the *Daily Mirror*:

'Preparing for his first Test match at Edgbaston tomorrow, the happy-go-lucky Cockney boy said yesterday, "To play in your first Test match against Australia is what every young cricketer dreams about. No, I'm not frightened of fast bowling. Batsmen must live with it if they're going to succeed." Gooch praised his father, Alfred, "a club cricketer who taught me the value of playing with a straight bat".'

Then he drove to Birmingham.

GG

I cannot recall too much about my first Test match. There was a practice session at Edgbaston the afternoon before and I drove down in my battered little red Sunbeam Imp. I was the selectors' only 'experimental wild card'; and the rest of the Mike Denness side was John Edrich, Dennis Amiss, Keith Fletcher, Tony Greig, Alan Knott, Derek Underwood, Chris Old, John Snow, and Geoff Arnold. Not surprisingly, I felt terribly uneasy: two-thirds of them had been playing Test cricket when I was still at school, let alone doing my tool-making apprenticeship. Keith Fletcher then was still far more a local hero than a close friend, because I had played mainly as his replacement. And it was he who had first asked about me, 'Does it speak?'

To be frank, I felt conspicuously out of place in the nets and in that Edgbaston dressing-room, like a frightened kid on his first day at big school. Nobody took me under their wing, or not that I was aware of. Still, in fairness, I had joined the big-man's league, and everything was up to me: I had to get on with it.

The team stayed at the Raven Hotel, Droitwich, which was a good twenty or thirty miles away from the ground. I had to make my own way there in my Imp. We had a team dinner, at which the talk was desultory: in-jokes, tomorrow's weather, the pitch, and Lillee and Thomson. It did not seem too positive, but who was I to say? Becoming suddenly an England Test cricketer had, if anything, increased my shyness.

At least, after the dinner, I thought we'd all get in the bar for half-an-hour's drink which would put me more at ease. I went and phoned Mum and Dad and then went into the bar. There was not a soul around. They had either gone early to bed at 8.30 or, more likely, out to a pub somewhere. Either way, they had not bothered to include me. I wasn't to know that two or three of them (Alan Knott and Derek Underwood, for instance, and of course Mike Denness himself) would in years to come be really good friends, but I certainly couldn't imagine it that night as I took one more look into the completely empty bar at the Raven before going to bed, apprehensive for the next day.

At breakfast in the hotel dining-room, at least Sir Len Hutton stopped to have a word with me. He seemed a kindly man, but a dry one. 'Good luck,' he said. 'Er, tell me, young man, have you ever played against the Australians before?' I thought he was making fun of me. 'Yes, sir,' I said. 'You're one of the selectors who picked me after I scored 75 against them for MCC at Lord's last week.'

Denness won the toss and put the Aussies in. It had not been a straightforward decision; there was much discussion between the fast bowlers and the leading batsmen. It was thought the overcast conditions would help the swing bowlers (and when it is overcast and humid at Edgbaston, as I was to discover down through the years, the pitch somehow looks greener than it actually is once the sun has broken through). John Snow had not toured and was back for England, but nevertheless it was still a daring decision to put the opposition in. After the bad England defeats in the winter, Denness's job was obviously on the line and he had only been appointed for this one Test. When the Australian openers, McCosker and Turner, batted through to lunch, nobody actually said as much but you could sense the Edgbaston members and people around the pavilion thinking that we put the Aussies in to postpone the moment Lillee and Thomson were let loose.

I was nervous, desperate not to make a mistake. I fielded at mid-off and fine-leg, down by the main scoreboard and opposite the pavilion end. (I was reminded of this eighteen years later, the very next time I fielded there are Edgbaston, which was after I'd handed over the England captaincy to Mike Atherton and I could come out of the heart of the action and take a little breather on the boundary. In 1993 I had a laugh with Mike, saying 'Hang on, pal, I haven't been down there for nearly twenty years'.)

After Australia's opening stand of 80, England did not do badly at all. At one time, Australia were 186 for five, but then Edwards and Marsh added 79 and Thomson made 49, so they finished up, midway through Friday, the second day, at 359 all out; reasonably okay, but only a working score.

Edrich and Amiss went in, but after just one over a thunderstorm burst. And how. It absolutely hosed down. In those days, the wicket remained uncovered during the hours of play. The downpour was short, but extremely sharp, and the pitch was saturated. It meant that the umpires had to add on the extra hour. So when play recommenced on this soaked wicket, it was fairly obvious what was going to happen.

Edrich battled on, but Lillee got Amiss for four and then Max Walker, in perfect conditions for him, dismissed Fletcher for six and Denness for three. I went in at 46 for three – and came back, three balls later, at 46 for four.

I was caught down the leg-side by the wicketkeeper Rodney Marsh who was standing back to Walker. No excuses, but I always think that's an unfortunate way to get out, an inswinger that starts middle-and-off and then whips down to miss the leg stump, and as you push out just to cover it you get an inside edge. Non-ball, non-shot, really. But if it scuttles down to the fine-leg boundary for four, the commentators say, 'Oh, what a lovely leg glance'.

On this occasion, however, the ball ended up in Marsh's gloves and that was that – wretchedly disappointing. Not even time for me to be sledged! England, eventually all out for 101, followed on and after further rain I came in at 20 for three in our second innings. This time round I survived seven balls. The penultimate one, from Thomson, was a juicy low full-toss outside off-stump. Instead of helping myself to a nice calming boundary through the covers, I stared at it nervously and far too cautiously and missed it. The next ball was a genuine beauty – on that damp flier you simply had to get it in the right place – and it pitched middle, left me like a very fast, rising leg-break, and I got a nick: c Marsh b Thomson 0. A pair. I was a glaring failure.

Fletcher was at the other end, and as I walked past him back to the pavilion he signalled to me, 'Bad luck, that was unplayable enough to have got anyone out as readily on 150 as on nought'.

That was the Saturday evening. Greig was out immediately after me, then Fletch for a brave 50 and England, having followed on 250-odd behind were 90 for five at the close. Sunday was a rest day, so I drove myself home for some of Mum's chips, and all the way back again. I was disconsolate. The other players pretty much ignored me. Were they smirking behind my back? I was far too 'out of it' to be enjoying my first taste of Test cricket.

There were still two days' play left, but on the Monday morning in the car-park at the Raven, I was surprised to see that wise long-time pro, John Edrich, loading up his car with all his gear. 'This game won't last till tonight, let alone tomorrow,' he said.

Now I was not so naive as to think that England's last five wickets could bat out two more days, but this gave me an insight into the mind of the experienced professional. Loading up, ready for a quick getaway from the ground, was not so much defeatist as pragmatic. Prepared for the worst. And, if we did happen to lose on this Monday, I had another twenty-odd mile drive from Edgbaston to pick up my stuff at the hotel, and then get back on to the road again. Which is exactly what happened. It rained some more, but England had still lost by an innings and 85 runs before three o'clock that afternoon.

What also sticks clearly in my mind to this day was Rodney Marsh, a truly competitive cricketer, batting Australia back into the game on the second day. The ball went out of shape and about five minutes were lost while the umpire had to 'rough up' a new one to the same condition. First delivery after the hold-up, Marsh got out. He was livid about the delay, he was purple. He marches back to the pavilion, fuming, then SMASH! We could hear it out in the middle, the sound of the dressing-room's glass door being shattered into little pieces. I don't know whether Marsh must have put his bat through it, or simply slammed it behind him too hard, but the result was the same.

After England's disaster at Edgbaston, Tony Greig took over the captaincy from Denness for the second Test at Lord's, which ended in a draw. Greig led from the front and got a good 96, and in the second innings Edrich, a gritty, world-class batsman, made a really big hundred (175). I made six in the first innings (c Marsh b Lillee) and 31 in the second (yorked by the off-spinner Mallett), but did not bat at all well. So I feared the selectors' worst; for one thing, although nothing was actually said, I got the distinct impression that the new captain did not rate me as a player; for another, David Steele, a month before his thirty-fourth birthday, had come into the batting line-up for his first Test and had played brilliantly.

My fears were confirmed. Although I was very disappointed on learning that I had been dropped, I was not exactly suicidal. I was picked to score some good runs and I hadn't come up with any; end of story. People still say to me all these years later that I was obviously brought in too early, but I disagree. When is too soon? When is too late? I agree with Keith Fletcher on this. Whether it seems too soon, or too late, the point is that, whenever the opportunity comes, the crucial thing is to grab it with both hands. I didn't, so I had to go away and work for another opportunity to come up. Look at David Steele in that match at Lord's. Never had a chance before – but up it comes at last and he grabs it, making 50 in the first innings and a good 45 in the second.

The crowd really took to Steele. He went in at no. 3 with England in the mire and Lillee with his tail up. I don't think the Australians or the crowd could quite believe what was happening. Most of them hadn't even seen Steele before, his prematurely white hair in direct contrast to the blue of his gleaming new England cap, Elastoplast round his bat, his 'Groucho Marx' walk, and the wonky tilt of his cap-peak framing those peering, glinting spectacles. One newspaper dubbed that entrance, 'THE BANK CLERK GOES TO WAR'.

Not only that, but he arrived at the crease a bit late. In all his matches at Lord's for Northants, he would have used the visitors' dressing-room, which is exactly the other side from the 'home' team's. It is disorientating when you first come down that identically-built set of stairs which twist round 'left' instead of 'right'. So one of the openers gets out immediately and down the stairs goes Steele, but he turns down one flight too many, and ends up peering into the tiled members' loo below the Long Room.

So back up he climbs, finally gets out to the crease, says a matey 'Mornin' all' to the Australians, who are too amazed to answer back, before Lillee comes in to bowl to him off his long run ... and Steele hooks him off his front foot as if it's Sunday morning in the park.

Although he was obviously tensed up for his first Test, he was decent to me in that match. Right up to the mid-1980s, Steele was one of the best liked and richest of characters during my time on the county circuit. Naturally, everyone called him 'Stainless'. I remember how, when at the non-striker's end, he used to turn and peer with myopic intensity at the bowler running in. Brian Edmeades once refused to bowl if Steele persisted staring, and demanded that the umpire tell him to stop.

At Chelmsford, opposite the river end, there is that lovely big clump of chestnut trees. Kenny McEwan once hit a stupendous big hundred against Derbyshire, when Steele had moved from Northants to captain Derby. Two or three times Ken hit Steele's bowling into the middle of the trees. 'McEwan,' admonished Steele in his Staffordshire accent, 'don't you ruddy South Africans know that you're not meant to knock down horse chestnuts till it's conker-time in October.'

McEwan hit 180 that day. He was out when Peter Kirsten came on with his little off-spinners. And Ken hit this absolute steepler. It went up miles! Guess which poor boundary fielder was waiting underneath it as it at last began to drop? David Steele, of course, staring up to the heavens, glasses glinting in the sun. And he held it, a super catch. Thereafter, wherever Derbyshire played and a huge soaring hit was made, for or against them, Steele would always grade them as to comparative height – 'a two-thirds-McEwan' or a 'half-McEwan', the ultimate being, of course, a gushingly acclaiming, 'By Jove, that's a hell of a skier, that's a genuine full-McEwan, that is'.

I once struck an off-spinner from Geoff 'Dusty' Miller on to the slate roof of the Chesterfield pavilion. When the ball came back, Steele was due to bowl the next over. 'Sorry, Youth, I can't,' Steele said to Dusty, whom he always addressed as 'Youth', as he threw back the ball to him. 'There's too much tile in it.'

Once Miller, who only made two or three hundreds in his career and should have had more, had reached 98 not out in a match. He was batting with Steele, who had made more than a few himself. There was a mix-up in the middle of the pitch, neither really to blame. Steele could have 'crossed' to sacrifice his wicket and let Dusty get his century. But the older man suddenly dived back into his crease, and Dusty had to go. No apologies.

At tea, the still furious Miller was waiting for Steele at the dressing-room door. 'You selfish bastard, Stainless. You knew I was on 98 and a century means much more to me than you, and you dive back in instead of sacrificing yourself. I bet you didn't even think about me.'

'Actually, I did' said Steele, 'and I agree it was a difficult one. My first thought was indeed of the "noble gesture". Then I thought, oh, bugger it, I know the Youth's on 98 but, then again, it's a super flat wicket, a lovely day, easy bowling, and, oh, bugger it, so I jumped back in.'

Now it was my turn to jump back into county cricket, but not with a splash. For this new and newly discarded Test player could scarcely scratch another run. After the Lord's Test, in my next 11 innings for Essex to the end of that 1975 summer, I made just 150 runs, with three more ducks and four knocks in single figures. The terrible trot was only relieved, ironically, with 68 against the Australians at Chelmsford.

Perhaps the 'pair' of Edgbaston had dented my confidence, but I determined to keep learning, and try to graft a relentless consistency on to my game, for only when the latter goes without saying can a batsman grumble about not regaining his Test place. I was already aware of that, as well as the fact that it was all very well having glorious and occasional 'spurts' like I'd had in that June when I was really firing, and had hit 220 runs in three innings during Essex's Ilford week, with 170 of them coming in boundaries. I knew I had to knuckle down and learn how to make every innings tell.

At the end of the summer, a friend of Dad's who had been on holiday on the south coast brought him a clipping from the *Southampton Evening Echo*. It was the sports column written by my hero, Barry Richards. It read:

'Young players must be learning all the time. Young Gooch has wonderful potential, but he has obviously found that once you are in a Test side you have to set your own standards and that the judgement of others is much fiercer. Getting to the top, when everybody is on your side, is not the hardest part. Staying there is the real challenge. But Gooch will make it, as long as he is not now left back "in the wilds" for too long.'

That really cheered me, and it trebled my determination.

Still, I had (just) passed 1,000 runs in a season for the first time. And away from the county circuit I fell in love with and got engaged to Brenda Daniels. She was a book-keeper and secretary, the daughter of a motor mechanic from Chadwell Heath, close to my neck of the woods. We'd first met when I was a shy nineteen and she was a wonderfully spirited eighteen, at a dance at the Ilford Palais. I was there with a bunch of guys from Redbridge Tech. She had come with another fellow, but in spite of my seemingly permanent 'two left dancing feet', she obviously thought I had 'something', so we took it from there. So much so that, three years later, in the winter of 1975/76, we took ourselves off to South Africa where I had been offered a modest job as well as a lot of good cricket, in the Cape Town sun. No end of English cricketers wintered down there in those days, coaching and playing club cricket. Besides, I was a Test player – if only twice.

What we did not know was that it marked the beginning of my long and fond – some might say, notorious – relationship with South Africa.

4

A NEW GOLDEN AGE?

FK

Gooch, even in South Africa, could not escape from his debut ducks. On 1 November Paul Fry, in the *Cape Herald*, wrote:

> 'Forget Gooch – without further ado, my advice to the Western Province selectors, and it is a view shared by just about all local cricketers I have spoken to, is: Forget Gooch. Nothing personal, but we have enough local batsmen without calling on a fellow who has come out to sell sports goods for a few months and to "assist" Green Point's Hylton Ackerman as a player-coach.'

An unsigned and cruelly pointed note in the Cape's *Sunday Times* also asked: 'How much can a two-Test, two-duck batsman with an average of 9.25 teach our cricketers?'

In fact, down the century no end of Test batsmen, who were later to be installed in the game's all-time pantheon, began their international careers with the dreaded nought. Test history's most prolific scorer, Allan Border, made a duck in his first international. So did England's doughtiest of Test 'fighters' Ken Barrington. More to the particular point, recall off-hand some future England captains who walked back with a painful 'blob' against their name in their first Test innings – Bob Wyatt, Len Hutton, Tony Lewis, Mike Brearley, and Mike Atherton.

Gooch, however, needed to wind down in the Cape sun more than he might have imagined. The young cricketer's reaction to his traumatic debutant Test matches was still plain to all. He played for the

Sea Point club, Green Point, which provided the young couple with a pleasant flat. Brenda worked in an office, and Graham at Logan's sports store in the city centre, serving at the counter and selling anything and everything, from trainers to ping-pong balls. Apartheid was still at its most defiantly entrenched – although the Green Point club at that time was the first in the area to include non-white players – and Graham could not fail to notice it (and to bridle) when Afrikaans speakers came into the shop and demanded to be served by an assistant in their own tongue, not a shy young 'rooinekk', speaking estuary-Essex.

This first visit to South Africa introduced him to the pleasures of a glass of wine. On the whole he preferred the Cape reds. With the sun and the spectacular beaches all around, for the young couple it served as a paid-for pre-nuptual honeymoon. The real thing was to take place the following October, 1976, when they married at St Chad's church in Chadwell Heath, where they had bought their first home, a somewhat run down, three-bedroomed terrace house. The best man was Keith – his sister Brenda's husband – who was a printer. They booked a guest-house in Blackpool for their honeymoon; it was a long way from Cape Town and the sun, and it rained for two days. They had no idea that Blackpool was so kiss-me-quick tacky. They cancelled their booking, had a night in a better hotel in the Lake District, and returned, chastened, to Essex. In the next decade they were to move house five times – always 'upwardly mobile', first to the Gidea Park area, then the more salubrious (and nicely named) Hutton.

In July of 1976, Gooch hit 136 against Worcester at Westcliff – his highest score so far – and 106 of which came in boundaries. A fortnight later, the selectors told Gooch to hasten to Headingley as a standby for the fourth Test against the West Indies, so he knew he was not totally forgotten. In the event, he was not needed, but before re-joining Essex, he watched attentively the first morning's play from the dressing-room balcony.

It was the story of the summer encapsulated. Tony Greig had said the visitors would 'grovel', but the boot was on his own foot. At Leeds, the West Indian openers, Greenidge and Fredericks, savagely took England apart – 50 runs in eight overs, 100 in 18 – and they came in to lunch at an astonishing first-morning's 147 for no wicket in 27 overs. Coming up the steps after being submitted to such a flogging, the captain Greig acknowledged Gooch with a nod. 'Phew, that was some batting,' muttered Gooch, adding the matey Cockney throwaway, 'every one a coconut.' It was not the time for what Greig pointedly interpreted as a cheeky young sprog's superciliousness.

With England's 1976/77 winter tour in mind (it took in the historic Centenary Test at Melbourne), two of the selectors, Bedser and Barrington, insisted on Gooch's playing in the three one-dayers at the end of the West Indies tour, but he dismayed himself with 32, 5 and 3; and by the time his next opportunity for England came along, all of two summers later, Greig had abandoned the helm of England for World Series cricket with the Australian magnate Kerry Packer.

So the next time Gooch walked out for England, on 16 June 1978, at Lord's against Pakistan, it was in a new position as opening batsman, and under a very different type of captain, Mike Brearley, former Cambridge scholar in Classics and Philosophy. In addition, Packer had unknowingly, but luckily, enforced upon England the precocious likes of Gower, Botham and Edmonds. Did we but know it, another 'golden age' of English cricket was beginning on that sun-blessed mid-summer's day at Lord's in 1978 when Gooch joined Gower and Botham and his new colleagues in the nets.

Barrington welcomed Gooch back into the cadre, cheering the young man at once and settling his apprehensions by telling how he (Barrington) had played his own first two Test matches in 1955, and failed with scores of 0, 34 and 18, after which, like Gooch, he had been banished back to the county slog for three more learning and grafting years. 'And when the brought me back,' beamed Barrington, 'well, I did reasonably all right, didn't I?'

In these three years of 'exile', Gooch had moved to opener, launched himself into a determined fitness routine and worked, with a heavier bat, assiduously at every aspect – including his fielding – although John Woodcock, cricketing eminence of *The Times*, was none too sure about the latter:

'Gooch's reappearance will have England suffering in the field. That is a pity. But not everyone can be a Randall. Unless he finds a place at slip, Gooch may be rather too large and heavy to be much more than a buffer at mid-on or mid-off. For Essex last season, Gooch's regular place in the order was at no. 5. He is benefitting now from going in first. Fletcher, his county captain, thought it might make him concentrate better, and it seems to have done so.'

Gooch and his captain went forth to bat, Brearley in his prototype, homemade helmet, Gooch in white sunhat. (He would not don the helmet till the following winter.) Brearley was soon gone, then Clive Radley as well. At 19 for two, Gower joined Gooch, and as Michael Melford grinned in the *Daily Telegraph* next morning:

'The sight of two bold young England batsmen at last unruffled by the loss of early wickets, or by the occasion, and showing every desire to let fly at anything resembling a half-volley was truly and greatly heartening.'

Gooch and Gower put on 101 in a beguiling hour-and-a-half. The author Geoffrey Moorhouse, at Lord's writing his classic book *The Best Loved Game*, also prophetically glimpsed the future that day – it was to be pointedly rounded off in the evening with a century of spectacular belligerence by the no. 7 batsman, Botham. Wrote Moorhouse:

'The distinctive things about [Gower's] batting are its neatness, its air of total calm, its economy of effort and its fluent movement from quick back-lift to untrammelled follow-through ... The reassuring figure of Gooch works stolidly at the other end. He is built like a guardsman, and that expressionless face with its black moustache surely saw service in England's old imperial wars, defending Rorke's Drift and marching up the Khyber Pass ... He is a hitter of the ball who puts all his beef behind both cut and drive. When Sikander [Bakht] lets him have a bouncer, Gooch shifts his head a fraction but otherwise does not budge, and I don't suppose he'd do more than grunt if the ball hit him square between the eyes. In these two batsmen, in Leicester and his worthy cousin Essex, England are served by rapier and broadsword out there.'

They each fell together at 120, 'a flaw that appeared in the batting of both (and it is that what made each innings beautiful, where it might have been merely faultless)', added Moorehouse. However Botham's 108 off 104 balls then took England to 364, and Pakistan were twice out for less than 150, Botham taking eight wickets for 34 in their second innings. England won the rubber 2–0, and then beat New Zealand 3–0.

Now Brearley would lead, as Field-Marshal, his two successive winter tours to Australia. With him in both 1978/79 and 1979/80, as assistant manager, went the new mentor, Ken Barrington, whom they called the 'Colonel'. Kenny would guide with affection the bonny, bold belligerence of Botham, the rapier of Gower, and the trusty broadsword of Gooch.

GG

I came home from Brenda's and my first Cape Town adventure full of the joys and raring to go. Nineteen-seventy-six was a productive summer for me at Essex, and I easily scored my 1,000 runs. Then, twelve months later, my batting was going nowhere. I scored little more than 800 first-class runs during 1977, with only one century. I put on weight and felt lethargic, and there was little consistency or discipline about my cricket.

I was still a very natural batsman, but I was playing almost the same way as when I was sixteen or seventeen – just going out to biff it around with the philosophy, 'If it's my day, then you bowlers better watch out; if it's not my day then, okay, there's always another innings tomorrow.' Definitely not the way to approach serious cricket. I remained a talented strokemaker, if everything happened to click, but the rough edges were becoming ever more apparent. So half the time I just lost my wicket and, if I'd bothered to think about it, I was getting myself out through increasingly sloppy mistakes and errors of judgement. Possibly, too, county bowlers had worked out how to attack my weaknesses. On the one hand, I used to play too much through the leg-side; on the other, I was too regularly being caught around the cover or mid-off areas. In 1977, I think I came near to being dropped – certainly I was demoted in the Essex order behind some of the younger players, like Mike McEvoy, and that shook me.

So after Brenda and I were married in October, I took a long, hard look at myself and decided to take a grip. It began with a conscious realization, for a start, that everything successful in nearly all top sport stems first from fitness. So I began running. I was still playing weekend football for the Old Fairlopians, whose ground was three or four miles from Chadwell Heath. So I either ran there to play and Brenda would pick me up afterwards, or the other way around. Then I might run first thing in the morning, or in the evening. This was the start of what the press years later would call 'Gooch's obsessive fitness regimes ...'

When I started touring again with England, I wrote to John Lyall, the manager of West Ham United, and asked if there was any chance of my coming down to train with the team. He wrote back, 'Yes, we'd love to see you', so that became a regular winter fixture as well.

For two winters I was an 'expediter', working in the Buckhurst Hill offices of Such & Searle Shipping, a company owned by Ron Cundale, a friend of Doug Insole, who was, and remains, an Essex stalwart, scoring over 20,000 runs between 1947 and 1963, and captaining the side throughout the 1950s. (Ron Cundale was another devotee of Essex cricket, and in 1985 was chairman of my benefit committee.) My job was to expedite ships' orders. If a cargo boat or a tanker was coming into port, the expediter would have to make sure that anything they needed by way of stores, provisions, even engineering equipment, would be ready to go aboard during the ship's stay in dock. And if it wasn't, the expediter had to chase it up. It was just for the winter months, and the money, of course, was more than useful.

On which subject, that bad summer of 1977 was the one big time I fell out with Keith Fletcher. It was about my salary. Essex originally had a wages structure of a certain level basic rate and annual increments for long service, but once anyone was a capped Test player he automatically went on the top money at once. So as soon as I played a Test I went straight to the same salary as any of the senior players who had played for ten years or so. I didn't find that a problem, of course, but perhaps Essex did. So after the 1977 'realignment' of wages, it turned out that uncapped or junior capped players had a money increase which brought them almost in line with me. For any ratio of £1,000 in their rise, it seemed my increase was only about

£200. It was not my fault they had decided on this realignment, but I was the one missing out because of it.

I got it into my head that Fletch was to blame, and I confess I acted a bit childish and immature over it. But I still fell out with him for a while. And Keith was more than a bit fed up with my behaviour. I told John Lever and he said, 'Well, go to the committee and complain'. So I went down to London, to see the club's vice-chairman, Tiny Waterman, in his plush offices in Birdcage Walk near St James's Park. He was a lovely chap. He sat me down and listened to my moans. He just heard me out, basically. Nothing came of it, I didn't get anywhere. But it really did me good to air my grievance and get it off my chest. Not that I won that one, but I have always been stubborn for my rights. Sometimes to the point of foolishness.

When I got back that day, I told Lever all about it. John said, 'There is one very simple way to win your point and get a much more decent lump in your bank account each month.' 'How?' I asked. 'Make a concentrated and determined effort to get yourself back in the England side,' he said. JK was right.

My first contract with Essex in 1974 was for £1,075. A year later, my match fee for my first two Tests was £200 each. For my third Test match, three years later in 1978, the sum was £1,000 (with infinitely better kitty bonuses for winning, and more besides). That represented a basic fivefold increase in just three years. Revolutionary. Only two things were responsible for that, and one followed the other directly: the Packer World Series Cricket and Cornhill Insurance. As simple as that.

Mr Packer never approached me, I was still a nobody then. But his signings made it easier for me to get back into the England team.

Suddenly, after Mr Packer, the establishment had to court, and be courted by, the sponsors. When Ken McEwan joined Essex in 1974, they said that because he was an overseas player his perk could be to drive the club van. What an honour! It was a Commer van, a sort of prehistoric transit-van which doubled up as the transportation for all the kit and clobber for away matches. It even had Essex CCC painted on the side. I became friends with Ken, and I often travelled in it with him. There was always an old kitchen chair in the back, and if anyone needed a lift they had to sit on that in the back, swaying around from side to side. I'll never forget going up to Manchester, the night before my first-ever big Championship innings, that 94 against Lancashire. On the way, someone threw a brick through the windscreen – we never found out if it was something to do with having 'Essex CCC' on the side – and we had to find a garage to repair it. It was almost dawn before we reached our hotel. Imagine an overseas player these days, a new Kenny McEwan, being thankful for the perk of an old two-seater van from his club, with a grotty kitchen chair in the back for any third passenger!

Once Mr Packer had come on the scene, I wrote around in 1978 to a few local garages in the area asking if they'd like to sponsor me to drive one of their cars. Jim Hair, of Wickford Park service station, said he would be delighted, and I stayed with him and his Toyotas for sixteen years.

Meanwhile, in that winter of 1977/78, while I was working in the shipping office, the penny was beginning to drop about my cricket. Fitness first, and I could already 'feel' my new determination paying off there. The money row with Fletcher, and Lever's blunt advice, also geared up my resolve. Then during the pre-season, Fletch told me he'd had a brainwave. Mike Denness, my first-time England captain and now an experienced veteran, had left Kent and joined us as an opening bat for 1977, going in first with either Hardie or the University player, Matthew Fosh. It had worked only reasonably well. At the end of the previous summer I had been dropped down to no. 6, so Fletcher now said, 'You're going to swap with Brian (Hardie). He drops down, which might suit him better, and you go up and open with Mike, which will make you concentrate more and tighten up your game.'

The decision, especially as it came at the same time as my conscious resolution to get a grip on my whole batting attitude, helped me enormously. That one decision of Fletch's, I am convinced, was the making of me as a cricketer, the crucial turning-point. As opener I just had to tighten my technique and cut out anything sloppy or too chancy; I would not be having to 'dash' for a last quick few runs after Mike, Brian, Kenny and Keith had done all the important work, but I'd be facing the new ball and in many, or most, cases facing the opposition's best bowlers. I was being offered, literally, the number one responsibility.

Fletcher is a genius. Overnight, I found I had a new role, a new goal. I must not fail this one – this was sink or swim. I knew I had an inborn and powerful shot-making ability; now I would have to graft on technique, discipline, and patience. It would take time and hard work, sure, but with Keith's decision to try me as an opener came, simply, the start of my success as a proper and serious cricketer.

Around that time, too, I began using a heavier bat – around 2lb 14oz as opposed to the standard 2lb 8oz – with a number of rubbers on the handle to make it more comfortable to grip. The weightier 'pick-up' suited my style of play; the 'almost' thick edges would now carry for four. It wasn't till a couple of years later in Australia that, with Ken Barrington's guidance and suggestion, I began experimenting with the high 'bat raised' stance, and what convinced me to stick with that permanently was seeing, on return from the tour, some videos which Brenda's Auntie Grace had made off the television which showed how crouched my style was and how my head kept 'falling over' towards the slips. I watched the tapes again and again and each time I was staggered.

But I am jumping the gun again. For first base, as a new opener, I walked in to open the batting with Mike Denness in the very first match, in April, of the 1978 season, against the University of Cambridge, and scored 40. Less than two months later, when Barry Wood was injured after the first Test against Pakistan, I was called up by England to open, with Mike Brearley, at Lord's in the second. I got 54, had my first of innumerable century partnerships with David Gower and, to all intents, never looked back.

The following winter, 1978/79, Brearley's side to Australia was sent as direct competition to Packer's World Series. I did not exactly set either the Swan River or Sydney Harbour on fire, but I played in all six Tests, although I might have been pushed to hold my place but for injuries to a couple of other batsmen. I then had quite a good summer at home in 1979, with the World Cup, Tests against India and everything topped, gloriously, by Essex's first two trophies in our history – the Championship and the Benson & Hedges Cup, when I hit a century in the final.

England then had another short tour to Australia, a sort of 'kiss-and-make-up' healing of the Packer rift. Before the first Test at Perth, Brearley came to my room at the Hilton and told me I was dropped because they were going to play three spinners. I was terribly disappointed, and Ken Barrington really had to talk me through it that night. (That was the match when Dennis Lillee caused a commotion when he tried to use an aluminium bat.) I won back my place for the last two Tests of the three with a century against Queensland. Then in the Melbourne Test, the final one, in February 1980, I ran myself out – for 99! It was the last ball before tea. Lennie Pascoe bowled it. I was well aware what my score was, but, yes, that time I must admit to the nervous nineties. I pushed it towards mid-on. I obviously thought it was travelling faster than it was. I called and set off. Kim Hughes came round and fielded it, and I know I'm struggling. I was out by about six inches. I glumly led them all into tea. Back in, I just said to Brearley, 'Spot the deliberate mistake'. Ian Chappell, the Australian captain, looked at me as though I had a screw loose. 'What, don't you like scoring centuries, or something?'

As I grew older and wiser down the years any actual nervousness in the nineties was not a factor at all. Even if I'm on 89, I haven't given a century a thought or consideration. But once I'm on, or passed, 90, I say to myself, 'Steady, boy, don't cock it up now, don't do anything silly or hasty, just let it come, let it come'. That 'let it come' is the operative phrase, because there can be two fatal things that happen and I've seen it many times with both club or Test batsman. Some go into their shell, so paranoid that they cannot even hit a ball that's begging to be hit; the others go to the opposite extreme and try and 'make' the hundred. Especially when they are between 96 and 99, they set themselves up to play the shot which will do the trick, play it to the wrong ball and as a result they're walking back to the pavilion, cursing. The knack is to continue playing each ball on its merits – and the right one will come in the end. Easier said than done, though.

Ninety-nine is only one run short of the magical figure with which records are logged, so really it should be no big deal, for you've obviously batted well. Still, I wasn't looking at it so realistically that night in Melbourne. Many years later my Essex chum, Mark Waugh, was bowled by Tufnell one short of his hundred when playing for Australia against us at Lord's. Afterwards one MCC member had sorrowfully approached Mark with a betting-slip. He had wagered £100 at 1,000–1 that the first four Australian batsmen would get centuries. Mark Taylor had made 111, Michael Slater 152, and

David Boon 164, so Waugh's failure to get just one more single had cost this fellow £100,000.

Ian Chappell's sarcasm in Melbourne had brought up a relevant point, however. I had now played twenty matches for my country and 99 was my top score. A century was eluding me. Though there is, honestly, no end to the learning process, I had at least begun to get the hang of opening the batting; but, altogether, in 225 first-class innings, I had only scored ten centuries. For an international batsman, that was still pretty mediocre.

In less than five months, June 1980, the coveted three figures were at last hoisted, and against the West Indies, too – Andy Roberts, Michael Holding, Joel Garner, and Colin Croft; the first of the fearsome quartets that the captain, Clive Lloyd, could let slip. It was a tremendous challenge every time I faced them (and arguably it was even more daunting later with the likes of Malcolm Marshall and Curtly Ambrose). No calamity this time in front of a jam-packed house at Lord's. It had taken me almost half-an-hour to get from 95 to 99. I just kept saying to myself, 'Wait. Wait for it.' At last I prodded a riser from Colin Croft down on the leg-side and Chris Tavaré urgently called and we scuttled through for a single. Clive Lloyd was first to come in and shake my hand which somehow made me even more proud of myself. And Mum and Dad were there somewhere. It was a long way from that block of flats at Mills Court, Leytonstone, where Mum used to watch me whack that scuffed old tennis ball against the wall. And also from the day when Dad first brought me to Lord's on the bus and we saw Ted Dexter in the Gillette Cup Final.

A couple of months before, in the spring of 1980, *Wisden* had rather sniffily criticized the new stance I had worked out with Ken Barrington: 'Gooch would surely benefit from a more relaxed stance. His stiff, awkward position with bat unnaturally held aloft must surely prove a severe strain when he plays a long innings in a hot country.' But there was no mention of my 'unnaturalness' in the Almanack's following edition when it described this first happy Test century of mine – 'Gooch played with an authority and power seldom seen from an Englishman in the last fifteen years or so.' I finished with 123. It was a dull day and there was rain about and a few stoppages. It took me two-and-a-half hours before Michael Holding had me lbw just before tea. Tavaré, as became usual for him in a Test, just dropped anchor. His share of our 145 partnership was only 26! I hit 17 fours and one six, a gift-wrapped full-toss from Viv Richards which I deposited on the Grandstand balcony. In the *Sunday Times* that weekend, Robin Marlar wrote, 'Gooch became a star on Thursday. He is now as near to a reincarnation of Walter Hammond as we have seen.' Generous words from a man whom the boys on the circuit knew as Robin 'Snarler' for the 'crispness' of his criticisms.

We had lost the first Test at Trent Bridge by two wickets, and this second match at Lord's was ultimately wrecked by the weather, which also affected the next three which all ended in draws. I made 83 at The Oval and 55 at Headingley and, with an aggregate of 394, was the series' top scorer on both sides. In the first year of the 1980s, this first experience of the West Indies attack was to hold me in good stead for the next decade and beyond.

That first Test century cemented my enduring love-affair with Lord's, the first heavily emotional rumblings of which could be heard in my heartbeats eleven months before in front of another capacity crowd at 'headquarters'. I could have retired happily there and then after Essex won the 1979 Benson & Hedges final. I was overflowing with exhaustion, utter relief and true pride at seeing old Essex players and lifelong supporters openly weeping with joy as they greeted the county's first trophy of any sort in our 103-year history. I made 121 in 140 balls and shared crucial partnerships with Kenny McEwan and Keith Fletcher, who both played gloriously that day. I remember thanking my lucky stars that here I was, carrying a century of Essex expectancy on my shoulders, but still learning all about professional cricket from those two fine players.

Only a few weeks later, for we had been miles ahead of the pack all summer, Essex clinched their first-ever County Championship to set in train a run of five more Championships in the following thirteen seasons, plus the NatWest trophy and two Sunday League championships. Only the legendary formidable sides of Yorkshire and Surrey in the middle of the century could better that sequence – and those two, of course, had no one-day competitions to divert them. Also, we could have won the Championship in 1989 but for being deducted 25 points for an unfit pitch, and we were twice pipped for Sunday League titles on minute mathematical calculations. If those had come down on our side the teams that Taylor and

Fletcher built for Essex would have been hailed as the very best in County Championship history.

I was also learning by observing my England captain during those years. The first thing to say about Mike Brearley is that he is simply a very nice man. Part of his brilliance as a captain was the fact that he could relate to all people: players who didn't have the public school or university upbringing, and those at the other end of the scale, like myself, who had come from a working-class family and secondary modern school. He could relate to everybody. That, to me, was the secret of his success: his man-management and handling of people. However, one of the things that gnawed away at him was that he desperately wanted success with the bat, and to be accepted as a quality Test batsman. He was a more than reasonable performer, but never a dominating batsman.

Mike could certainly get the best out of his players. No one more so than Ian Botham, on whom he had a very positive effect. Ian was just embarking on his Test career then, and just beginning his tour-de-force as the giant all-rounder. But Ian respected Mike and was even, in some ways, in awe of him. I believe the age difference helped because anyone could see what a well-travelled, scholarly and knowledgeable person Mike was. He also had a brilliant cricket brain and the ability to sum up a situation in a trice and act on it. The difference in Botham's performance when Brearley returned as captain in 1981 was too great to be coincidence. He liberated Ian again, restored his confidence and allowed free rein to his talents. Brearley, some say, overbowled him in his great years, but if I had been captain at the time, I would also have thrown the ball to a great bowler who thrived on hard work, loved to bowl, and who had the talent to dismiss any batsman in the world with an unplayable delivery.

In the dressing-room, if Ian began horsing around at inappropriate times, Mike could put him down crushingly and Ian would immediately be as good as gold like an admonished schoolboy. No malice either given or taken, though. And on the field, if Mike wanted even more of an effort from Ian he would chivvy him up with the ripest of insults. In fact, Mike was more 'schoolmasterly' strict than I'd been used too with Fletcher, particularly on not pushing dressing-room buffoonery too far, and also on punctuality; and he liked to call 'school assembly' sort of team meetings, where everyone was expected to chip in with their bit. Fletch was much more tolerant of larking, and always used to say, 'No problem, everyone knows exactly how far he can go'. He was delighted when Tony Lewis defined the Essex spirit to him once – 'You plan your cricket like a war, but play it like a party game.' Keith would far prefer quiet little chats with individuals when the need arose to the communal 'think-tank' get-togethers which Mike liked to call.

When he did get us together, however, Brearley could be really tough. In 1979, in Sydney, we had a disastrous first day, bowled all out for 152 and only 50 runs ahead at the close with nine wickets still to get. We had batted very badly and then bowled and fielded worse. As we were hobbling off at the close, Mike Hendrick, one of the most senior players, was distraught and said, seethingly, to nobody in particular, 'We all need a right bollocking – and we need it right now.' 'He's dead right there,' said Brearley, and he let us file into the dressing-room, quietly closed the door, and tore into us, collectively and one-by-one. Such livid anger from such a civilised man trebled its impact – and we went out and played it tremendously tight next day. Then Derek Randall played a stimulating marathon innings for the cause and we won the match. A couple of years later, when we played Sri Lanka's inaugural Test in Colombo, we were performing miserably at the end of a drawn-out losing six-Test tour of India. This time it was Bob Willis who read the riot act. When we went out next day, John Emburey skittled them (six for 33) and Chris Tavaré knocked off most of the runs.

Brearley sometimes had a very short fuse but, like Fletch, never held grudges. Brearley would blow up, let fly (even over something that seemed pedantic), and then it was at once back to normal and it was never brought up again. He had a quick spat at me once or twice about my fielding. He nicknamed me 'Zap', as in Zapata the Mexican, not only because of my droopy moustache and floppy white sunhat but also, pointedly, he put two and two together and thought I was dozy in the field. I said I most definitely wasn't dropping off, I was concentrating like mad, it was just that I might have looked it to him. 'Well, please try not to look it then,' he said, 'everybody has got to be *seen* to be trying to motivate everyone else.' Fair point.

It was good to be in the same room when Brearley and Botham were rubbing sparks off each other, but Brearley's always were, in the end, the brightest. It was also fascinating to observe the relationship between the captain and the other 'great' in his team, Geoffrey Boycott. The cultivated, academic and rounded man, Brearley, who knew that really, deep down, cricket was only slightly important in 'real' life and not the be-all-and-end-all; and the dedicated, single-minded, often tunnel-visioned Yorkshire batsman and perfectionist who had worked and grafted to raise his high standards ever higher. The truth, it seemed to me, is that there was a fond – if sometimes, warily fond – mutual appreciation of their totally different qualities.

Geoffrey was obviously and by far the better player; but what seemed to me to grate on Geoffrey was that Mike never once asked him, the 'master', for the tiniest piece of advice about batting technique (when it could have been rewarding for Brearley had he done so). But that is long gone now. Nevertheless, Geoffrey will still tell you all these years later that Brearley, everything considered, was the best captain of any he played under; and Boycott's captains included the likes of Ted Dexter, Mike Smith, Colin Cowdrey, and his two fellow Tykes, Brian Close and Ray Illingworth.

One certain clash of will, in which Brearley famously prevailed, occurred just before the Sydney Test on the second of those late-1970s tours. It was a wet wicket and batting was going to be uncomfortable, certainly against Lillee and Dymock and Pascoe. At the team dinner, Geoffrey appears wearing this sort of surgical-scarf wrapped round his neck, and announces that, sorry, he's ricked his neck playing golf and cannot play next day. 'Aye-oop,' chorus all the lads, mocking, 'you're kidding, it's a damp and dodgy pitch and you're funking it, aren't you?' And all of us, to a man, took up our white cloth napkins from the dinner table and wound them round our own necks, sending him up rotten.

But Brearley did not get the joke. He suddenly went 'spare' with Boycott: 'You're in! You're in! You're playing, and that's all there is to it!'

He bawled him out similarly in the dressing-room next morning when Boycott was still whingeing on about his neck. Mike wasn't going to let his best batsman get away with it. Nor did he. Boycott went out to bat – and he didn't have a lot of trouble moving and jolting his neck when Lillee & Co started peppering him with bumpers.

That night, the team lark with the table napkins was just taking the mick and taunting Boycott over his efforts to pull out. We knew he was the best. Boycott was an extremely courageous batsman, always, and he had a wonderful technique against the fastest and most hostile of bowling. I count myself privileged to have been able for those three or four years to admire his stupendous defensive technique at close quarters and his all-round 'building' of an innings. We suited each other's game, and he unquestionably is the favourite Test match opening partner I ever had. And, when you tot them up, I had more than a few opening partners for England.

Opening Partnerships of 100 or more runs

225	M A Atherton	India	Old Trafford	1990
204[+]	M A Atherton	India	Lord's	1990
203[+]	M A Atherton	Australia	Adelaide	1990/91
176[+]	M A Atherton	India	Oval	1990
170	M A Atherton	New Zealand	Edgbaston	1990
168	M A Atherton	Pakistan	Headingley	1992
155	C J Tavare	India	Madras	1981/82
146	B C Rose *	West Indies	Oval	1980
144[+]	G Boycott	West Indies	St John's	1980/81
132	G Boycott	India	Delhi	1981/82
127	W N Slack	West Indies	St John's	1985/86
125	B C Broad	West Indies	Trent Bridge	1988
123	A J Stewart	Pakistan	Lord's	1992
116	G Boycott	Australia	Melbourne	1979/80
112	W Larkins	West Indies	Port-of-Spain	1989/90
112	H Morris	West Indies	Oval	1991
111	G Boycott	West Indies	Trent Bridge	1978
108	M A Atherton	West Indies	Trent Bridge	1991

[+] denotes 2nd innings
* 155 runs in all were added for the 1st wicket, but Boycott retired hurt (3*) when the total was 9.

Having partners of different styles, rhythm, and 'pace' is vital. When Boycott and Brearley opened in the 1979 World Cup Final against West Indies, they batted very well to give us a platform for the presumed final assault. They put on 129 for the first wicket – but by that time the rest of us were going to have to score at nearly eight an over! So we were runners-up. Nevertheless, I still love World Cups. I might not have gained a winners' medal in that 1979 World

Cup, but I did ensure one personal 'trophy'. In the semi-final at Old Trafford against New Zealand I clattered Brian McKechnie for a straight six to the Stretford end. It exploded into and through the sightscreen like a shell, and left a perfectly formed hole. They never mended it. For the next ten years, whenever I went back to Manchester, I would check to see if the hole was still there.

Chris Tavaré played a few very good innings for England, but the times when I was out first and he came in at no. 3, Boycott would get frustrated because Chris, being Chris (in Test matches anyway, in county cricket he could score really quickly when he needed to), and Geoffrey being Geoffrey, the scoreboard workers could almost go on an extended coffee-break. Boycott once asked the captain officially if someone else with a touch more dash could come in first-wicket down and although the idea was thrown out, he did have a valid point, because it is always vital to keep the runs ticking on somehow. Once, at Bangalore in 1981, Chris and Geoffrey were in for hours; only one wicket had fallen but everything was so totally becalmed and desultory that John Emburey could stand it no longer, and asked permission to go back to the hotel to write some letters home. Or fill-in his tax-return. Anything for a bit of adrenalin. It was a comment rather like Ian Botham's about another limpet deadbat, John Steele of Leicestershire. Ian told me that 'if Steele was batting in my garden, I'd have to get up and close all the curtains'.

Mean to lesser mortals, but equally, I suppose, as nicely cheeky as Beefy is, was, and ever will be. But now, suddenly, this life and soul of the party was actually going to have to organize himself. Brearley stepped down from the captaincy – permanently, as he thought, and for sure we did – and Botham was his and the selectors' first choice as heir and captain. This was going to be an interesting; never a dull moment in prospect. What Mike had left Ian with, however (Brearley was no idiot, he must have noticed the crazy fixture-planning), was a daunting baptism – head-to-head reciprocal tours, by and of the mighty West Indies. When we turned up for the Caribbean trip, we were quite happy and content that he was captain. But we also wondered what we were letting ourselves in for.

5

'SIMPLY WHAT IT'S ALL ABOUT, BRIAN'

FK

Gooch finished the last workout of his winter with the West Ham footballers and then reported to Lord's to meet his fellow tourists. This 1980/81 England tour would, of course, be his second official cricketing trip to the Caribbean. He was twenty-seven years of age.

At Lord's, the bespoke blazers, bats, and general cricket kit and equipment were being doled out by a square-shouldered familiar-faced barrel of a middle-aged man who chivvied around and humped the touring clobber into a semblance of order. It was Ken Barrington, on his fourth successive tour as England's assistant manager. Few could say with greater conviction that they had 'seen it all'. He was in his early fifties now but up to 1968 he had been a famed and stalwart England batsman, posting the majority of his twenty Test centuries on foreign fields. That year he had retired from cricket at the age of thirty-eight, after suffering a heart attack following an innings at Melbourne.

One of the myriad reasons why Barrington was universally loved by his 'boys' in successive England teams was that, as an outstanding coach and general all-round father-confessor, he never once was heard to come the old soldier (even though his nickname was 'the colonel') and berate his modern-day charges with 'This is how we used to do it in my day...' Except, that is, on two subjects: cricket tourists' food ('What are you complaining about, boy, I averaged 70 once on the '62 tour to India on a total diet of fried eggs and oranges; even Indian cooks can't muck about with fried eggs or oranges, can they?'); and cricket tourists' travel arrangements – 'Club Class in a jet plane? A handful of hours to cross the Atlantic? You're in luxury, boy,' he'd beam. 'On my first tour to the Windies with May's lot in '59, couldn't leave the cabin for a week, empty banana boat called the Camito, tossed about we were, like a cork in tempests and hurricanes. Seasick? Cabin was awash with it. Talk about tempest fugit, eh?'

Already, after only two tours abroad, there was some ambivalence in Gooch's mind about touring. If the cricket was good, he relished it and felt not only charged and motivated but highly fortunate to be indulging in his passion at the very peak of his competitiveness and his commitment. But the hotel-hopping and airport-lounging was already a chore. There were few compensations: he was no barfly, no over-social animal, certainly no disco dancer. If he was not playing or practising or training, time hung heavy. Golf was an occasional diversion. Fortunately, as in the previous two winters, John Emburey was on this tour again as England's leading off-break bowler. But their cockney appetites were still wary of exotic foreign food. Basically, Gooch was a home bird. At least this time, at mid-tour during the Barbados Test, Brenda would be coming out with some of the other players' wives for a fortnight.

Tours now, if more manic, were far shorter than in Barrington's day, of course. A tour of Australia up to the early 1960s, for instance, was topped and tailed with a month's sea voyage each way. The team would leave home in September and return in April. How would Gooch have coped with that? In fact, when Barrington went to Australia with Dexter's side in 1962/63 he was a pioneer of cricket tour flying. Daringly, the team had travelled from London to Aden by flying-boat, and then picked up the liner Canberra, on its maiden voyage to Fremantle, via Ceylon.

That was the time Ken Barrington had asked if he could fly at his own expense and meet the team in Colombo. His father-in-law, who kept a pub in Reading, was ill, and Ken wanted to delay as long as possible to help his wife, Ann, behind the bar. The feudal squires at Lord's would not even consider it. The first letter Ken opened in Colombo told him Ann's dad was dead.

Clive Lloyd's West Indians – Vivian Richards the emperor, the four fast bowlers the glinting jewels – were probably, to date, the most relentlessly powerful international cricket side in history. To all intents, they were unbeatable. In his first-class opener, under the sweltering wooded mountains and the samaan tree-parasols at Port of Spain, against Trinidad, Gooch hit 117, posting 173 for the first wicket with Boycott. The really serious battery began at once in the first Test match which followed when, in reply to West Indies' 426 for 9 declared, Gooch made 41 (b Roberts) of England's 178 all out.

Three hours for 41. Courage for the cause. He had pasted on to his helmet that morning the timeless George-and-Dragon emblem of the England touring teams. Three into 41, that's just over 13, but this is not Chelmsford, nor Colchester. The throng either dances, or bays for blood ... Roberts, Holding, Garner, Croft, turn and turnabout for lethal freshness. Before every over Gooch would re-set his guard, after every over he would tug off his helmet and bathe his face and neck in an already sweat-sopped white handkerchief ... dispassion-ate, defiant, hangdog, brave. Whenever not facing the bowling, with the already familiar and singular touch (like, in another sport, Pancho Gonzales searching with his forefinger, and finally finding that one droplet of sweat to wipe from his eyebrow before serving) he would grimacingly 'teeth' off his velcro-strip at the wrist of his gloves and hold them at his left hip to dry. Roberts, Holding, Garner, Croft, forward or back, back or forward ... a yorker dug out ... leave that alone ... 'wait on' ... 'come one' ... back foot many more times than front ... leave that one too ... dodge this lethal blur ... and that one. Can you get whiplash injuries at batting? Forward and back, ducking, dodging ... 'wait on' ... watchful, poring over it, watchful, ever watchful, for the cause. As sportsmen say, 'at the end of the day, this is what it's all about, Brian'. All the learning, all the skills, all the daydreams and night-dreams, all the practice-makes-perfect coming together as one. Three hours for 41. For the cause.

In the second innings Gooch made 5 (lbw b Holding) as Boycott, this time with 70 of an all-out 169, raised the tattered flag of defi-ance. England crumpled to a dreadful innings defeat.

Barrington was almost the most distraught. On this sun-baked field twenty-one years before, in the corresponding Test he had scored a defiantly doughty century (121), during which he had been felled (no helmets then) by a bumper from Wes Hall when he was 93. The writer Alan Ross was there for the Observer: 'The seam of the ball might be indelibly imprinted on his skull. Barrington went down, looked as if he might stay down, doggedly got to his feet. He had batted a notable recovery for England, from 57 for three to 227 for four. At the close, the centurion could lie back and take his ease, legs crossed as honourably as any Crusader's.' England had won that match.

Next stop, Guyana. Bob Willis, much liked vital cog and vice-captain, flew home for a knee operation and England sent for Robin Jackman, the Surrey sparrow, who had wintered and coached in South Africa for years. So Guyana's President, Forbes Burnham, banished the England team on account of Jackman's 'connections with South Africa's apartheid'. After some humbling, political dallying, the next Test in Barbados at last got under way. The West Indies batted and Jackman, in his first Test, bowled with chunky heroism before Botham cut off the West Indies tail. They were all out for 265.

Barrington was overjoyed. All England had to do now was survive the new ball and work painstakingly to build up a first-innings lead over the next couple of days. 'Boycs and Goochie have just got to go steadily through them swing-doors, walk calmly up to the reception desk and book themselves in for bed and breakfast,' was how he explained the tactic. Alas, Michael Holding opened to Boycott with one of history's most lethal, enthralling overs. Five balls which had you fearing for 'Sir' Geoffrey's life, before the sixth tore his off stump from the ground.

So much for B & B. Barrington put his big, hairy, consoling arm on Boycott's shoulder, then did the same about every ten minutes as his boys were blitzed out for 122, Gooch top-scoring with 26. When Barrington was not consoling, he sat slumped in the corner of the pavilion balcony, chain-smoking grimly, fretfully.

That evening, at the Holiday Inn, Barrington and Boycott asked the BBC TV reporter, Michael Blakey, to replay Holding's over to them, which he did, re-running it time and again until they had seen enough, as they said, 'to work on'. No replays in his day, remarked Barrington. He had to rely on superstition, and only change the routine when it did not work. He always put his left pad on first, always carried the half-crown in his blazer pocket that Peter May had tossed with in Barrington's first Test in 1955, and in the back pocket of his flannels, whenever he batted in a Test, the good-luck telegram that

Ann would unfailingly send him. The day he made his highest Test score, 256 at Old Trafford, Ann changed the usual wording, this time putting '*Vincit qui patitur*. I love you. Ann'. Gubby Allen translated for him: 'He who perseveres, conquers'.

At least the wives had arrived. Ken and Ann went out for a quiet seashore supper. By 10.30 pm they were back at the hotel preparing for bed. Ann had bought a sun-hat that afternoon, and Ken sat fooling around with it as Ann went into the bathroom. Seconds later she heard a muffled grunt. She knew. She raced next door to shout for the team physiotherapist, Bernie Thomas. Even though he used a ventilation tube while his wife, Joan, pumped at Ken's chest, there was no response.

GG

I answered the soft tap on the bedroom door at about 7.30. Instinctively, I knew something was up. Ian Botham and the tour manager, Alan Smith, were there. They said he was dead. Then they went grimly on down the hotel corridor, telling the others. I went back to Brenda. Ken had meant a lot to her as well. He was the only 'official' who made the wives feel welcome when they came out; others would, sniffily, just tolerate them. Now we both just sat there and cried our eyes out.

There were tears, too, when the team gathered on the pier outside the Holiday Inn. We lined up and stood in silence for a minute. Then we did the same at the ground, with the West Indian team and the whole crowd, before the day's play began. I just could not stop crying. Ken was such a good man. His influence on me was massive. An uncle, a friend, a wise counsellor. He was humorous, always looked on the bright side, and had that marvellous funny way with words when he got them a bit wrong, and we'd rib him about it, and we'd laugh. 'Well, you know what I bloomin' well mean, don't you,' he'd say. And now we'd never again see that smile or hear that laugh. I vowed to myself that when we batted – pretty obviously it would be to try yet again to save the game – I would offer up my will and determination into the innings as a dedication to Kenny's memory and in thanks for all he had done for me, both in cricket and life. All the little things he had tried to help and instil into me as a player I would channel into this innings. It just might help, as a mark of respect and gratitude, to make less sorrowful this most soul-destroying day of my life. But first we had to attempt to get the tragedy, as best we could, out of our minds and go on to the field and try to contain the West Indies batsmen. Concentrating on the task in hand might even help.

Unfortunately, I had split the webbing on a finger on my right hand the morning before when taking part in slip-catching practice. I couldn't field because of the danger of another knock which might have widened the split and prevented me batting a second time. All I could do was sit in the corner of the dressing-room balcony at the Kensington Oval and watch. It gave me plenty of time to think of what Ken had meant to me in particular, to the team in general, and to everybody associated with England's cricket.

He was more than an assistant manager in charge of the cricket side, a man who bowled in the nets until everybody was finished, then took part in giving fielding practice. He had to arrange the practice venue, as well as the transport to get us there. He organized the laundry and generally looked after us on and off the field. He was always ready to listen to anybody's problems. His room door was never closed. On the tour to Australia the previous winter, after I had been left out of the side for the first Test in Perth, Ken spent a lot of time building up my confidence, instilling in me the need to bat for a long time, and never to waste the chance to cash in when the ball was running my way. 'Book in for bed-and-breakfast,' he always said to his players.

'Remember,' he told me, 'it is criminal to throw away a chance of a big score when the opportunity is there. One big score may easily be followed by a run of little ones and you'll be glad of that big score to fall back on.' Those were sound words. I determined to remember them when I batted in the second innings.

I felt a good score was in me, and that I could take on the West Indies fast bowlers once I had managed to survive the new ball, when anything can happen. This Test was only our fourth first-class game in seven long weeks. Despite the constant interruptions to our programme by rain and the Guyana affair, the lack of good practice facilities, which was disgraceful, and the shortage of visits to the crease in first-class matches, I felt in fairly good form. Not as good as the previous summer when I scored my first Test century against them at Lord's in entirely different circumstances, but good enough to have a try.

Not that anyone from the beginning expected England to win on a wicket which appeared to have been specially prepared for the West Indies pace attack. It wasn't doctored in the way pitches have sometimes been changed overnight in mysterious circumstances, but there is no doubt in my mind that the wicket was prepared to suit them and not us, in much the same way as some county sides at home prepare wickets to suit their own bowlers rather than the opposition. It's part and parcel of the game and happens all over the world except, for the most part, in England where we seem to go to extraordinary lengths to prepare a fair Test wicket, whatever the Australians may have said in the past.

I wasn't hopeful of winning because I thought the task was beyond us. To beat the West Indies we needed to have made a score in the region of 500 in our first innings to be able to apply any pressure. Even if two or three batsmen came off together, they bowl their overs so slowly with their four-man pace attack that it would take us almost two-and-a-half days to score that many runs. Then we would have the task of bowling the West Indies out twice in the remaining half of the match. We would be lucky to manage that. We were very down on luck. Especially that day in Barbados.

As we feared, Viv Richards made a big century (182 not out) and Lloyd declared 522 ahead. We would have to survive five full sessions. My finger injury seemed okay, and I went out to settle a score with destiny. At once, after just 11 balls, we were 2 for two – Geoffrey Boycott was caught off a Holding flier, then Mike Gatting was bowled first ball by a shooter. It was perilous stuff. David Gower and I dug in. I thought of Kenny all through. 'Make it count. If you get to 40, make it to 60; if you get to 60, make it to 80. Make it count, don't give it away.'

David and I put on 120. He was out for 54. Only one other player got double figures in the innings – Peter Willey, who made 17. We were all out for 224. I made 116 of them and was eighth out. At home, Dad kept the cuttings. The *Daily Telegraph* had said, 'In the harrowing circumstances of a death in the family, Gooch's innings was one of true valiant courage.' *The Times* said, 'In profound sorrow, Gooch discovered heroism.' All I know is that my second Test

century is one I will always treasure. It was all for Kenny. I hope he
was proud of me that day.

He himself had made a Test century here at Barbados on his first
tour in 1959/60. And it must have been around the early 1960s that
I first laid eyes on him, when Dad took me down to Surrey to see a
benefit match one Sunday. I could only have been seven or eight at
the time. I got Kenny's autograph. When, later, I used to ask him
about his great days, he used to laugh and say, 'No, I was just the
dogsbody, they used to send me in as cannon-fodder, to blunt the
attack and sweep the stage for the Mays and Dexters and Cowdreys'.
But he had a heck of a record: 6,808 Test runs and averaging 58.67.
Very few batsmen in history have that high an average. Of course,
Geoffrey batted with him often for England. He says Kenny would
get very tense before going out. Wally Grout, the Australian wicketkeeper, said when Barrington came in to bat, he was so determined
'you could almost see the Union Jack trailing behind him'. Of course,
Kenny's father was a soldier.

With his record, I fancy not too many bowlers had Kenny in
'two-man's land'. That's the phrase he used to Mike Hendrick once
in Australia. He was facing Mike in the nets, and Mike bowled him
a real 'jaffa' – another of Kenny's favourite words, meaning 'great
ball' – and he shouted down the pitch, 'Nice jaffa, Hendo, it really
had me in two-man's land'.

One day in a hotel there was a smorgasbord laid on for lunch. He
said with relish he was going to try 'some more of that smogglegas'.
Kenny said when he played his first Test in Trinidad – he got a century in that match as well – there had been a major riot, only quelled
'when they sent in hundreds of plain-clothes protectives'.

John Emburey was witness to a brilliant hat-trick of Kenny and
his words. Kenny was commiserating with John about bowlers having to face a diet of short-pitched fast bowling. He said, 'It's a good
job you have helmets these days, John, else there'd be one or two fer-
tilities; with the ball coming at you like a high-philosophy bullet, you
tailenders are expected to be like those Japanese kalahari pilots.'

We had one of the last great team jokes with Kenny at Trinidad,
before the tour disintegrated with the Robin Jackman dispute. One
of Kenny's jobs was not only to organize practice, but also the transport. Usually it was a coach but in Trinidad it was taxis – 'Bozo Bros

Taxis' – big chrome-and-winged American gas-guzzlers which had all seen better days. About four or five were ordered each day for a specific time, and we'd be waiting in our whites outside the lobby. But you know the laid-back West Indian philosophy about time-keeping: great wide smile and 'Nine o'clock, ten o'clock? Same difference, ma-an, no problem, ma-an'. Anyway, Bozo Bros taxis were never there on time, and Kenny used to tear his hair out (he once said to me that, as a boy, he had a great bushy head of black hair, 'just like those fuzzbies the guards wear outside Buckingham Palace'), and be permanently on the telephone to them from the lobby.

The evening before the first Test – all Bozo's best having been booked by Ken for first thing in the morning to take us to the ground – there we all were in the team dining-room, talking about this and that and the morrow, and Kenny is probably already having had a couple of sighing whinges about Bozo's. Graham Dilley surreptitiously slips out of the room, picks up a phone in the lobby, rings through to the dining-room, puts on his best West Indian accent, and asks for Mr Barrington. Paul Downton answers it. 'A call for you, Colonel, Bozo's Taxis.' Ken gets up and takes the call. The conversation goes something like this:

'Hello, sir, hello, Mr Barrington, sir. Just a check call, sir. Did you order five taxis for nine in the morning, or nine taxis for five in the morning, sir?'

'Ruddy 'eck,' says Kenny, and then confirms that the former order is the right one. He comes back to his seat and announces, 'Oh, Gawd, can you believe it?', and he picks up the previous conversation at the table. A couple of minutes go by and the phone goes again. Bozo Bros for Ken. 'Right, what is it this time?'

'Mr Barrington, sir, Bozo's Taxis again, sir. I have just been checking my order book for the morning, sir, and we seem to have overbooked. You see, there is a cricket Test match beginning tomorrow and very many people are coming in for it from the airport. So I can only let you have two taxis at nine o'clock, and they will make three journeys each. I hope this will be convenient, sir?'

By this time, all the team's in the picture and we're becoming convulsed in giggles, especially as now Kenny, every so often, is putting his hand over the mouthpiece and relying to us, in despair, the full gist of the taxi man's conversation. So Kenny ends this particular call with 'Okay, if we have to we'll do it in shifts, it's not too far to the ground, I suppose, but you'll really have to get your drivers here dead on time, all right? Okay, thanks, I know you'll do your best, won't you?'

He comes back to the table, on we go, and Dilley comes back with a suitably straight face – and David Gower and Geoff Miller decide it's their turn to have a go.

The phone rings again. 'Flipping 'eck,' says Kenny, 'what now?' 'Mr Barrington, sir, this Mr Sylvester Bozo, one of the four joint managing directors. I have some very bad news, Mr Barrington, sir. I have to report that the two taxis booked in your name for tomorrow morning, sir, have just been involved in an accident.'

'What, two ruddy accidents at exactly the same time?' says the incredulous Kenny.

'No, sir, just one accident, but I'm afraid it was the two taxis which collided with each other. They are both write-offs, sir. I will try and come up with an answer to our mutual problems, sir, and ring you right back.'

Kenny put the phone down. 'Ruddy 'eck, what a palaver...' He was now in such a state, talking about not paying Bozo's, even for the work they'd done so far, and cancelling the exclusive contract they'd tendered for prior to our arrival, that he still hadn't noticed that all of his team were now either under the table in suppressed mirth or had decided, at exactly the same time, to take out their handkerchiefs for some extended nose-blowing.

The phone again. 'Mr Barrington, sir, Bozo's here. I have some wonderful news for you. I have just hired a 30-seater bus for your journey tomorrow morning ...'

Kenny puts his hand over the mouthpiece and beamingly relays with utter relief the great news to us. 'Boys, we're in business, old Bozo's come up trumps at last and got us a bus ...' Then his face falls as he picks up the remainder of Mr Bozo's sentence.

'What d'you mean, one slight snag?' says Kenny groaning.

'Only a slight one, Mr Barrington, sir, but I am unsure how to resolve it. You see, the bus has unfortunately mislaid its steering-wheel.'

Shouts Kenny down the line in utter exasperation: 'If I knew where your ruddy office was, Bozo, I'd be right round there mislaying your personal ruddy steering-wheel and all,' and he slams the phone down in fury.

Gower and Miller saunter back in. Bairstow has already slipped out. We are now all paralytic with bottled-up laughter. Kenny is still so fuming as not to notice. 'Ruddy 'eck, no steering-wheel, can you ruddy believe it?' He just keeps shaking his head and repeating it, like that Herbert Lom character in the Pink Panther films.

The phone rings. 'If it's a Bozo, tell 'em I'm not here,' says Kenny, head in hands. 'I never want to speak to a Bozo or anything to do with them ever again.' Downton takes the call. 'Oh, great,' says Paul, 'yes, I'll tell him, he'll be delighted, thanks.' Paul relays the message to a suddenly delighted and overwhelmed Kenny. 'It's all right, they've found a steering-wheel, they've fitted it, and they're going to give it a quick road-test to check it's all perfectly safe and tickety-boo. It will be here at the Hilton dead on ten-to-nine, and, most important, because of all the inconvenience tonight, as well as the bus they are sending round the pride of their fleet, a Studebaker Convertible, to take "the esteemed Mr Barrington" to the ground.'

Ken is consumed with joy. His great smile lights up the room. He looks ready to call for the tallest and coldest pina-colada in the Hilton. 'Well, good old Bozo, told you they'd ruddy turn up trumps if you pester them enough, didn't I, boys?'

The phone rings again. 'If that's Mr Bozo,' says Kenny, 'I'll speak, and thank him for all the trouble he's gone to.' He takes the phone. The happy warm glint in his eye fades to cold greyness ... 'What do you mean? Both write-offs? Gawd help me. I just don't believe you. What do you mean, "the bus has just crashed into the Studebaker"!'

'Hey, hang on a tick,' he says, as, slowly, the penny begins to drop. He surveys the room and, for the first time, sees half the team rolling on the floor. Then he looks at the telephone in his hand, and puts it to his ear again. He'd rumbled it at last. 'Hang on a minute, this Bozo's got a ruddy Yorkshire accent ...' He looks round the room again, "Ere! What's going on? Where's that ruddy Bairstow?'

Dear, much loved Kenny. Thinking all these years later about that story and his 'ruddy Bozo Bros Taxis', and seeing him again, in my mind's eye, waiting with us outside the Hilton for those taxis to arrive, looking at his watch all the time, and getting in a state, I can understand what Boycott meant about Kenny getting all tensed up before he batted. And after all – although, typically, he'd never remind you of the fact – Ken had to bat against the likes of Hall and Griffith (who, he always felt, 'chucked' his paciest deliveries) and there were no helmets then, nor proper thigh-pads or chest guards.

Of course helmets or chest guards were superfluous in that over which Michael Holding had bowled to Boycott. People say it was the most lethal over ever bowled. I don't know about that, but what made Holding stand out was that he was a superb athlete. He could leap straight to his task. Most fast bowlers need two or three balls, some an over or two, to warm up. Not Michael Holding. He could just turn on the ignition and move straight into overdrive. Straight into top gear, you know, 0 to 60 in 3.2s. And because of his 'liquid' athleticism, you couldn't really hear him running up. That was why they used to call him 'Whispering Death'. Those first five balls Geoff faced from Holding were, as near as damn it, unplayable. They were extremely fast, and very bouncy, fliers, but not bumpers that you could duck. He had to play at them all. Short, and coming up at your throat. In fact, Geoffrey dealt magnificently with two or three. He gloved one, I think. Clive Lloyd said afterwards he'd never seen Holding, or any man, bowl faster. So five shortish, very nasty risers, the huge crowd sensing Holding's really on song and humming – and with the sixth, and Geoff obviously expecting another to leap up at his Adam's apple, he didn't quite get into line, Holding pitched it up – and it picked out the off-stump and sent it flying. Geoff just stood there in utter disbelief, as if he'd seen a ghost, then he shook his head and walked away. It was the classical 'killer' ball, but the greatness was not the one single and terminal delivery, but the six together in context, the five snorters and then, like the bullfighters say, the *coup de grâce*. Classic fast bowling.

In those days Holding moved it around too. He was very quick, the 'Rolls-Royce'. By this time Andy Roberts was not as lethally fast as when I first faced him at Bournemouth, but he was very wise and cunning. He was still given the new ball first. He had a dangerous away-swinger, and was superb at varying his pace, even with his bouncers, which was a real art. After those two would come Joel Garner, the beanpole. Garner was naggingly accurate and with his height, 6ft 8in, he had a terribly awkward bounce, similar to Curtley

Ambrose years later. Both also had tremendous yorkers. But the 'wild card' of that first (to us) notorious quartet was Colin Croft. He had great stamina and strength, and was very nastily fast because he'd be aiming from a different angle; his action had his left foot coming down wide of the popping crease, so that the ball was spearing in at you all the time. They were four quality bowlers all right.

By the end of that series, Roberts got injured and Malcolm Marshall came in. He was only young then, but when he matured, he was the real genuine quality article, the fast bowler supreme. Of all the West Indian quicks he gave me the most trouble. Those who bang it in always suited my style of batting better – and Marshall had a dangerous skiddy bouncer – but he pitched it up that little bit more and moved it around, and I've always had more trouble against that type of delivery.

It wasn't all pace, pace, pace, however. In the one-dayers the West Indies could not just keep switching their pace quartet, and in those days it was usually Viv Richards and Larry Gomes who shared the spare overs with their accurate but gentle dobbers.

So what with the Jackman affair, the only match we played in Guyana was the one-dayer in Berbice, to which we were flown to a clearing in the mountainous green-forested South American jungle in old khaki-coloured troop helicopters. At the team meeting beforehand, the captain, Botham, comes up with his master plan. 'Right, lads, when Mickey Mouse and Pluto come on we've got to cash in, tap them all over Guyana for plenty.' Mickey and Pluto? 'Yes, Mickey Mouse Gomes and Pluto Richards.'

The match begins. Roberts and Holding open the bowling, four or five overs each. Geoffrey and I keep them out. Then Clive Lloyd comes up with his own master-stroke. What is it? He puts on Mickey Mouse and Pluto. Pluto immediately clean bowls Boycott, and then Mickey, one after the other, gets Gatting, Gower, and Roland Butcher. They each bowl their full overs – Pluto 10–0–26–1, Mickey 10–2–30–3.

It was rotten luck for Ian Botham that his captaincy coincided with two successive series against the West Indies. Mike Brearley never captained once against them, and the one chink in Botham's record is his comparatively mediocre performance against West Indies. But overall he was as talented a cricketer as I've ever seen. He had boundless ability at batting, bowling, and fielding – some of his slip catches were miraculous. As a bowler his stamina and willingness was legendary and he'd try this and try that and then try something else outrageous, and he'd either go for runs or get wickets; batsmen never knew what was coming next. He once said he got no satisfaction from bowling a maiden, even in a Test match. Why? 'They're boring,' he said.

He was a free-spirit, all right, and his competitive confidence, which governed all aspects of his cricket and his life, was possibly what made him the giant he was in those seven or eight years of his Test match prime. It was a bit sad in the end at Durham, seeing him bowl those diddly-doddlers and getting carted all over the ground – I wonder if he remembered Mickey Mouse or Pluto? – because in his pomp he could run in, at top speed, and beat the best in the world. Sometimes he overdid the bouncer, but that was also part of his bombastic competitiveness.

In many ways Ian was a good captain. Tactically he was sound, and was always willing to experiment. As a general team man and inspiration in the dressing-room, captain or not, he was faultless. And he looked to lead from the front, that's for sure. I'm not the type to follow a match through the day once I'm out – I might catch a bit here and there – but whenever Botham batted I'd be out there watching. He always made something happen.

One time when he didn't lead from the front was in that Barbados Test. Botham was in and Holding was revved up and steaming and, padded up on the pavilion balcony and waiting to bat, were the tailenders, Emburey, Jackman, and Dilley. Holding whips down another, which again gives Ian a shave of the hairs of his nostrils, and he whiplashes his head back. He throws down his bat, holds open his arms and, with a shrugging gesture towards the pavilion, makes as if to say, 'How can anyone play this stuff? It's not only impossible, it's lethal'. And the three tailenders quaking on the pavilion 'scaffold' look at each other and think, 'Well, if he can't play it, what chance have us three got?'

It was during that Barbados Test that I had a couple of little runins with him. There is an old sailing boat there which runs up and down the coast for hire for cocktail parties – you know, Caribbean sunsets, romance, rum punches. It is called, rather obviously, the

Jolly Roger. The England team is always invited for one evening cruise on every tour and it can be very pleasant. On this occasion, after a long day in the field, I was lying down on the front part of the ship, enjoying the warm, balmy evening, and I suppose I closed my eyes, dozily. Next thing I know Ian has sneaked up to me, rolled me over ... and there I am falling twenty feet into the water.

I think he tends to be a bit paranoid about people who like to live their life to the full during the daytime, and then enjoy a sound night's kip to prepare for the next day. The other Barbados run-in with Ian was about my early morning runs. A year or two before I decided that fitness was one of the key ingredients, even the very basis of sport. A morning jog on wintry Essex pavements, through the frosty fog and worrying if no. 48's rottweiler is still chained to its kennel, is one thing. Quite a different sensation is to get up early at the hotel to a glorious Caribbean dawn. Come down in the lift, run down the hotel pier and you're on the lovely wide beach. Run for half an hour or so, have a swim and shower, then breakfast. Bliss. When Brenda was there for her stay she ran with me. For a jogger, it was heaven: early enough to miss the sultry, tropical heat, everything fresh and cool and sparkling. Which all conspired, and inspired, the captain of the England cricket side to call an extraordinary team meeting.

Ian gets up, looks at me, and announces: 'I'm banning forthwith all early morning jogging.' I say, 'You can't be serious?' He says, 'I'm dead serious.' He goes on, 'It's making you tired in the evenings, I've noticed a few times lately that you're nodding off after supper. It's this early morning jogging that's the cause of it so, as simple as that. Your skipper is banning all jogging. End of story.'

I am almost speechless. 'Hang on a minute ...' and I know I should have said that the only reason he was aware I went for early morning runs on the beach was because he saw me at it while he was on his way back from a party. But I just looked at him and said, 'Ian, people in glass houses shouldn't throw stones', and then I said I wasn't going to take this ban from him. I had mighty respect for him as a man, as a cricketer, and because he was my captain, but I wasn't going for a moment to suggest he change the way he chooses to live his life, so he shouldn't try to change how I lived mine.

In the end it all blew over. We each growled a bit, then everyone's happy and laughing about it. Don't get me wrong. I'm not complaining about Ian having a few drinks and being the life and soul of the party. I've no gripes about that. But giving me that ticking off for running so much in the mornings that I was too tired to socialize in the evenings, well, it was just laughable.

A serious point thrown up by that little incident, however, is that, as captain, Ian's lifestyle did not sit easily with setting an example to his players. How can you instruct someone, like he tried with me and my running, when deep down inside you know it's probably yourself who deserves a reprimand.

When you are just a player, okay, live life how you want, as long as you turn in the performance on the field. But when you are captain, you have to be able to detach yourself a bit, take a step back, not be aloof, of course, but not be 110 per cent 'one of the lads'. Being the latter, for a captain, is almost impossible when, next morning, you might have to crack the whip. In fact, in Guyana, after Bob Willis had left for his knee operation, Ian asked if I would be his vice-captain, but I suspect Lord's vetoed the suggestion and Geoff Miller was appointed.

If Ken Barrington's death was its most wretched low point, the tour itself was dismal generally. Three months in the sun and away from an English winter might sound delightful, but I was already beginning to feel that it could be overrated. Still, I ended with a big century, 153, in the final Test in Jamaica – which made it a trio of Test hundreds against the West Indies in just nine months – so I came home content with my form and that I had established myself in the team. How wrong can one be?

At the beginning of the summer of 1981, Botham lasted only two more Tests as captain, before resigning at Lord's saying, 'I'm not going to give them the pleasure of sacking me'. The selectors brought back Mike Brearley and, with Bob Willis fit again, Mike pumped up Ian and, well, the rest is history. Ian's century at Old Trafford was, simply, a brilliantly controlled Test innings; but his more famous one at Headingley (which we won after following-on) was an unbelievable last-desperate-fling that just went on and on. Then, at Edgbaston, Australia were cruising home only for Ian to charge in and take the last five wickets for one run. It seemed like the *Boys' Own Paper* story come to life.

I played in the series, but was a complete failure, averaging a paltry 13 in five Tests, and was deservedly dropped for the sixth. I promptly hit four hundreds in Essex's next four matches which, coupled with Keith Fletcher being named England's new captain, got me on to the tour of India for the winter.

When I was put out of my misery after the fifth Test the selectors also dropped David Gower (who had averaged 'only' 25 in the series, but nearly twice as much as me). David and I met up again at Colchester for Essex's match against Leicestershire. When the two counties had met earlier in the season, I made 164 and 87, and David 67 and a sublime and typical 156. This time David made 0 and 22, while I continued my late flurry of form with 75 and 105, 80 of them in boundaries. Both of us were still wondering if we'd be on the England tour to India, but the reason I remember that game still is a heated mid-pitch altercation I had Leicestershire's bowler Les Taylor. I hit him back over his head for a couple of straight sixes and Les so 'lost his rag' that, for the next ball, he charged up and 'ran through' his crease and let fly a bouncer at my head. It was my turn to take umbrage and we squared up to each other and had some very harsh 'eyeballing' before the umpire Ken Palmer stepped between us before it came to fisticuffs. (Les went on to play for England, albeit for one Test only, and I became quite good friends with him.)

In the next match of the Colchester Festival, against Glamorgan, I dropped a further reminder to the selectors by getting 113 in 90 minutes, but the reason that game was memorable came in Glamorgan's second innings when, on a viciously broken wicket, the Pakistani Test player Javed Miandad played just about the greatest innings I have had the pleasure to witness, when he scored 200 out of 311 all out.

For the sixth Test at The Oval Paul Parker and Ned Larkins were brought in to replace David and me, but neither of them distinguished themselves, so David and I found ourselves selected for India with Fletch as our captain. Unfortunately, it was another miserable tour, one of the dullest series in history. We lost the first Test, and then Sunil Gavaskar's Indians slowed everything down to a snail's pace, and we followed, playing them at their own weary game. I started the tour insecurely, made a decent hundred in Hyderabad, and then began to play much more fluently. In the fifth

Test in Madras, I cannot remember exactly why, but I got intensely annoyed while waiting to go out to bat. We had just fielded for over two days while they pottered along to 481 for four declared; maybe I was realizing that Test cricket wasn't all it was cracked up to be? Anyway, I went out to bat fuming, lashed Kapil Dev for three successive fours and got a hundred in 139 balls.

In this match I opened with a new partner. The previous week, not long after breaking Sir Gary Sobers' world record Test aggregate of 8,032 runs in the Delhi Test, Boycott had gone home. The official reason was 'mental and physical tiredness'. However, he had been particularly cantankerous and went to play golf when he was meant to be back at the hotel ill in bed, and although none of us was best pleased with that, quite a few were privately wishing they could have gone back to England with him. When Chris Tavaré and I went out to open the innings in Madras, Fletch told Tav just 'to bat as long as you can'. Tav took him at his word, and batted five-and-a-half hours for 35. In county cricket Tav could lay into an attack with gusto and some fine strokes. By contrasts, in Tests, he just dropped anchor. Tav was very quiet. Once on that tour, I shared a room with him, and he scarcely uttered a word. We nicknamed him 'Rowdy'.

After the heroics of the summer before, Botham was mobbed everywhere. But it was an anti-climax to follow the summer of 1981 with such a turgid series. Ian still ended up at the top of the Test batting averages (with 55 to my 54) and, of course, he bowled his boots off. Even before the war of attrition set in, of all the Tests the banker draw was always going to be at Bangalore. On the eve of the match, at the team meeting at the West End Hotel, Fletcher said that, on this flattest of pitches, our bowlers must concentrate on their length and line. 'Right,' he says, 'let's go through their batting line-up and discuss any little flaws we might have noticed. First, this Gavaskar, thousands of Test runs, not a bad little player, eh?' Bob Willis says the titchy genius can only be regularly vulnerable early on if we pack the slip cordon and pitch it up, and never drop it short.

'Hang on,' says Botham, 'not when I'm bowling. Gavaskar played some games for Somerset last year and I know his weaknesses if anyone does; he's only five-foot and a bit, and has just taken to wearing a helmet. I know he doesn't like it up at him. I'm going to bounce him out, you see. Get him hopping.

'Right, who's next?' 'Srikkanth,' says Fletch, 'the twirly little dasher. He can be off and away and on 50 before you realize he's even on the scoreboard.'

Says Both: 'Leave him to me, he might hook but it's a panicker's hook. Give me two men back for the hook, Fletch, and I'll bounce him out. Straight down long-leg's throat, no problem.'

'Hang on, Beefy,' we all say, 'this is Bangalore, the flattest pitch in the world, it looks like it's white, rolled-out marble.'

'It won't seem like it to that Dilip Vengsarkar,' says Botham, 'he's shit-scared, he is, and the great thing is he knows I know it too. I can see it in his eyes. So I'll bounce it all of him tomorrow – and I'll do the same to that film-star type who follows him, Patil. Just one spot-on frightener to ruffle his hair and he's looking for the pavilion he is.'

'Vishwanath next,' says Fletcher. 'Now here's a little cove who really can bat.' Before any of us can utter, Botham says dismissively, 'A midget like his brother-in-law Gavaskar; two back deep, bump him, thanks very much. Next?' As he pulled the side of his forefinger vengefully and horizontally across his throat, the great English legend just had a two-word retort at mention of Kirti Azad: 'He's dead.' And so he goes on through the tail ...

When India go in to bat we put the Botham Plan A into operation. Alas, Plan A proves a two-day foot-slog. Srikkanth goes off like an express train and makes 65; Gavaskar sets out his stall for 172, Vengsarkar scores 43, India make 420-odd and Kirti Azad 'lives' happily for 24. In the sweltering heat, Botham bowled unchanged all morning and half the evening, banging it in. He ended with 2 for 137. But at least it illustrated once again Botham's blazing and bountiful strengths at his peak – competitiveness and hostility, stamina and stomach for the fight, and, carried on from the night before, utterly unquenchable self-belief.

Apart from bouncers, there was another matter on Ian's mind at Bangalore. Quite a few of us in the team were concerned about it as well for Botham's 'adviser', the veteran Fleet Street journalist Reg Hayter, and his solicitor Alan Herd, were flying in from London to see him. There was some serious, secret, parleying to be done.

6

'COUNT ME OUT, COUNT ME IN'

FK

Gooch knew perfectly well why Botham's two advisers had flown all the way to Bangalore. While we dozy, unenquiring journalists were assuming that it had to do with a few Indian deals – and the BBC holding their client's hand as he accepted, live across the satellite skies, their 'Sports Personality of the Year' trophy – Gooch, and about half of the team were aware that Hayter and Herd had come to dissuade Botham from being part of a clandestine cricket tour by English players to South Africa. By staying 'legit', Botham could earn far more in endorsements as a national totem than South Africa could ever afford. So most of the players involved in the subterfuge – telephone messages and cables were cloaked in chess code ('castles and knights meet in bishop's room tonight') – fully expected that the trip, which would follow on immediately from the Indian tour, would be cancelled by the South Africans, especially when Gower also pulled out. Gooch's dilemma and his depression continued; as well as, he admits, his dithering. He could not possibly confide in his best confidant, Fletcher, now his England as well as his county captain. Brenda and her friend, John Emburey's wife Suzie, had stayed on after the Delhi Christmas and would see out the rest of the tour, which was to end with Sri Lanka's inaugural Test match in Colombo. Brenda was dead set against the South African adventure. She 'sensed' the establishment reaction and worried for Graham's career and reputation. The Embureys, on the other hand, were for it. At Kanpur, during the sixth and final Test against India, Gooch made up his mind and telexed the South Africans that he was pulling out of all negotiations.

In Colombo, however, he telexed again: 'Count me in'.

Back at Gatwick Airport, Gooch and I said our cheerios. For all the cricket tedium of the tour, he had been a particular friend among a good bunch of fellows. I would be seeing him again very shortly, however, for I had promised to take him to his first rugby international at Twickenham the following Saturday. We made the arrangements for meeting. 'See you then,' he said. Poor Graham, he could not confide in anyone, not even in Alf and Rose who, faithful as ever, had turned up to meet their son and daughter-in-law. Graham's solicitor was also there. 'Something fishy's going on here,' thought Alf. Graham said he had to go and meet a man at the airport hotel but, could they wait? He wouldn't be long.

Just long enough to ask for £20,000 more than the offered £40,000 to join the South Africa tour. He also stipulated that he have a binding contract of three further winter seasons in South African cricket guaranteed in the event of a ban by Lord's. 'No problem, sir.' He wished he'd asked for more. All signed and sealed, done and dusted, then Alf drove the family home, and Graham, ever the assiduous correspondent, settled down to write some letters by way of explanation and expiation, including a touching one to me, apologizing for the subterfuge 'even during all our matey debates and differences on apartheid when we were in India', cancelling our rugby date 'with sadness', and ending, 'by the time you read this I will already be in South Africa'.

I knew that. The whole world did. For all hell broke loose.

The story was the banner-headlined front-pager throughout Fleet Street and far beyond. Every broadcasting newsroom followed suit:

REBEL 12 ROCK ENGLAND (*Daily Telegraph*)

BLOOD MONEY BAN FOR LIFE (*Daily Mirror*)

Point, counterpoint. The House of Commons whipped itself into a froth. The Prime Minister, Mrs Thatcher, was said to be 'furious' and then 'disappointed' (both reports seem doubtful, for she was almost certainly celebrating a nice bit of blatant 'market forces Thatcherism', but officially she had to be seen paying lip-service to the Gleneagles Agreement). The Labour Party spokesman railed at 'Englishmen selling themselves for blood-covered krugerrands'.

Point, counterpoint. And when Gooch was made captain of the side, his name became synonymous with the tour. 'Why shouldn't

Gooch play where he wants to? If it's against the law, why pick on our sports stars? But it isn't against the law,' reasoned the *Sunday Express*. 'Gooch is a political pawn, and a very greedy one,' answered the *Sunday Mirror*. And on and on. In the Commons, the up-and-coming Labour MP, Neil Kinnock, scathingly spoke of 'dirty money earned by ... '– and he coined the phrase which was to stick – 'this Dirty Dozen'; at which the Conservative George Gardiner begged to differ: 'By giving encouragement to those who have fought against apartheid, Graham Gooch and his team deserve, not blacklisting, but a medal for helping to create a more just and humane world'.

In *The Times*, John Woodcock wrote of the 'hysterical reactions' of people who should know better, and continued: 'You would think that Gooch and Emburey, though doing nothing that as citizens of a free country they are not perfectly entitled to do, have disqualified themselves for good and all from playing for England again. For myself I sincerely hope ... that they will be in Australia later this year, warmly welcomed as members of the England side.'

Alan Lee, who was then working for the *Mail on Sunday*, wrote: 'I fancy most of them have worked out their options and decided either that they have little time left in Test cricket or that the long and arduous official tours are no longer attractive. Graham Gooch, the most exciting specialist batsman in the country, and potentially England's senior opener for years to come, is the most poignant name on what will inevitably become a new blacklist. Gooch detests apartheid. His one previous trip to South Africa, six years ago, left a profound impression and he has for the past year wrestled with his moral conscience in the knowledge that, one day, the rumours would end and South Africa would really produce the cash for the tour.'

In the *Guardian*, I wrote that I had little doubt the 'rebels' would be banned by Lord's – and, everything considered, deserved to be. Nor was it difficult to guess that it would be a three-year banishment. The truth was, deep down, that Lord's (generically, good dyed-in-the-woad English cricket) would love to have done what Gooch and his men had, and gone out to resume playing cricket with the South Africans, traditionally their oldest friends after the Australians. But another side of Lord's was, understandably too, in fear of losing its perceived leadership of world cricket. (Rather like

Mrs Thatcher and the Commonwealth's 'Gleneagles'; although she stridently told the House of Commons and the Labour leader Michael Foot that, 'if we demanded sportsmen not visit South Africa, we would no longer be a free country ourselves', few doubted she was really cheering Gooch and his men for being there). Lord's knew they had to be pragmatic as well as dogmatic. Hence the three-year ban – for you only had to look at the upcoming tours to and by the England team. The only seriously threatening fuss about Gooch's 'rebels' would be kicked up by India, Pakistan, and the West Indies. The following tours had already long been planned:

1982:	India and Pakistan to England.
1983:	World Cup in England.
1983/84:	England to Pakistan.
1984:	West Indies to England.
1984/85:	England to India.

And of course, the end of the ban in 1985 happened to coincide with a visit by the Australians, surprise, surprise.

Later, of course, the South Africans organized many tours similar to this pioneering expedition. The sponsors, we learned much later, were funded by massive tax incentives from the government; this tour was sponsored by South African Breweries after Holiday Inns had pulled out when Botham and Gower said 'No'. There were even 'rebel' tours by West Indians and Sri Lankans.

Gooch's tour began in Pretoria. In a way everything ended there too: all his depressions in India, and the arguments with Brenda, discussions with the Embureys, and despair at not being able to confide in Fletcher; the 'insecurities' of professional sport, and the fact that, in less than two years already, England had dropped him twice; third time, terminally unlucky? He had already played with many men who had been capped a few times for England, did well enough, but not quite well enough to keep their place or their earning capacity. Might he even have to cash-in on his diligent toolmaking apprenticeship? For a start, both Graham and Brenda wanted a family. And South African Breweries were certainly going to help pay for it. And so, at the end of the first week in March in Pretoria, he went forth with Geoffrey Boycott to open the batting. Boycott was out for 13,

Gooch for 33. Then the 'South African Breweries' XI collapsed. 'Did you feel any undue pressure?' a reporter asked him. 'No, not on the cricket side.' 'What about anything else?' 'I'm not answering about anything else,' said Graham.

But he was going to have to answer it for the rest of his career, possibly for the rest of his life.

GG

Throughout England's tour of India in 1981/82, I suffered four months of personal torment. Should I or shouldn't I go to South Africa? It didn't help that the cricket in India was so mind-bogglingly tedious – India, having taken a 1–0 lead in the first, Bombay, Test then sat on it for the whole six-match series. Indeed that had a lot to do with my final decision to go, for it made me realize that touring and Test cricket was not all it was cracked up to be. Apart from Brenda, who was dead against the expedition from the beginning, I was on my own. One day I found myself agreeing with her, the next day I'd reasoned and wrestled my mind back to the fact that to go on the tour would be for the best. Come what may John Emburey was going. I had no-one else to turn to. Not my Dad – he'd be against anything that even suggested any tangle with the cricket establishment – nor my Essex mentor, Doug Insole who was part of the cricket establishment, as was the present England captain, Keith Fletcher.

But having made the decision, I will still stick by it. To the grave. That's me, take it or leave it. There is no going back. I felt that I was perfectly within my rights to go, and I still do. What's done is done. I made a decision in good faith, for what I considered at the time to be in the best interests of myself and my family. So how can I have any regrets if I did what I thought was right? I was under no contract to anybody. Living in a free country meant, surely, that I could be free to hire my talents anywhere I wanted. Just like any businessman. The deal and the money were very good, I admit. Of course it was. But what's wrong with that? For a month's work it was six times as much as I'd get in five years or more as a county pro. So who else would turn that down as a totally legal and legitimate bonus on your income? If taking it meant I 'was wracked by the insecurities of a working-class man', then okay, I was 'wracked by insecurity'. But that's daft. If a company salesman gets a windfall bonus by cashing in on his special talent and skills does he turn it down or is he labelled as a 'dirty money-grabber'? Of course not.

So why, people ask, when eight years later Mike Gatting went on his (aborted) 'rebel' tour, didn't the same things apply? Why wasn't I on that one? Because a) circumstances and aspirations change; b) I wasn't 'invited' to go – and successfully sued a tabloid newspaper which said I had signed up; c) I wasn't going to put my family through all the aggravation again; and d) on the theoretical assumption that I had been asked, it was not propitious for any number of reasons for me to go on that second tour.

But in 1982 it had been. So I made my decision. And I stick by it.

I walked out to bat with Geoffrey Boycott in Pretoria precisely a year to the week after he himself had, out of the blue, first sprung on me and five others the fact that a cricketing trip to South Africa was being hatched. The twelve-month saga which was to alter my career, my life and, both for better and worse, many people's perception of me, began in Guyana, ironically at the very same time that the Jackman 'affair' was to reach its humiliating conclusion with England's expulsion. Some in the team learned then that they were top of the 'shopping list' should ever an unsanctioned tour to South Africa by England players take off.

Boycott invited the 'famous five' to meet in his room at the Pegasus Hotel in Georgetown. There was nothing else to do anyway in that boringly awful week. Bob Willis had flown home injured, of course, or else he would have been there too, so Ian Botham, David Gower, John Emburey, Graham Dilley and myself listened to Boycott's outline proposition that a tour was secretly being organized to take place in October, at the end of the upcoming 1981 English cricket season; failing that, exactly a year hence, after the Indian tour, at the turn of February/March. Either way, it appeared that the chosen dates would not conflict with any England or county commitments.

We knew that Boycott's connections in South Africa were strong; he had regularly wintered there down the years, and had even tuned-up in the sun for this West Indies tour with a few pre-Christmas weeks in Johannesburg. On that occasion he had met a sharp young English-born record producer who was keen to expand his entre-preneurial ambitions beyond the music business. His name was

Peter Cooke, and he told Boycott he had outlined (Baldrick-like) a daring and cunning plan.

Geoffrey had doubtless heard such stuff before. For a number of years there had been no end of talk and whispers about South Africa hosting unofficial cricket trips involving large sums of money. But nothing had happened. This time it did. Cooke and one of the sponsors, Holiday Inns, came to London and, among the others who had shown to be theoretically willing, met Brenda and me and said the project was still 'on', for a month at the end of England's tour to India. They kept stressing the need for secrecy and subterfuge – which immediately got Brenda's hackles up, and on the way home she let rip. 'Don't touch it,' she insisted. Brenda is absolutely straight, she's right down the line and conservative, with an in-built wariness of anything that smells of intrigue. Perhaps I should have taken her first instincts on board, there and then.

For my part, while I was teetering about moving on to the next stage, another part of me was already debating in my mind that, if I did go on the tour I was breaking no law, nor any contract. England picked and paid you by the match, and my Essex agreement ran only from April to September each year. In between, I was contracted to no one. My stubborn streak, my 'sticking up for my rights' was coming to the fore. Another point: if I'd been, say, a bright young businessman very successfully going out to sell cat-food or whatever to the South Africans I could readily qualify for the 'Queen's Award for Industry'. They don't have to employ subterfuge. Why were bright young cricketers singled out?

What with the original rumpus in Guyana over Jackman, and the general rumours about South Africa at the end of the summer, the TCCB sent every contracted county player a letter warning of the possible repercussions in taking part in unofficial winter tours to South Africa. I reckoned that was sheer cheek: since when has the TCCB ever been worried about what county players do in their winters? When, for instance, quite a few were on the dole? One or two of our Essex players read the letter when it was handed out in the dressing-room, scoffed, scrunched it up and tossed it in the bin.

With the tour to India imminent, Boycott and Geoff Cook – who had just come into Test cricket late in his career after playing a number of winters in South Africa – were both asked publicly to renounce apartheid before the Indian Government would let them in. Why only cricketers? Why not every single person who flies into Bombay? The world was going crazy. In the name of both diplomacy and the quiet life, they both did so, in order that the tour could go ahead. (Did the TCCB ask Sunil Gavaskar or Bishan Bedi to renounce India's caste system before letting them come to England with the Indian team? Or Clive Lloyd renounce Comrade Forbes Burnham?) Even so, the two Geoffs refused adamantly to 'promise' the Indians that they would never again visit South Africa. When we arrived in India, by the by, I bought Brenda a diamond ring, 'mined and cut by De Beers of South Africa'. So it's all right apparently for the Indian government to trade with South Africa.

Once the tour began and the tedious Test trek set in, and when phonecalls were received, the subterfuge increased – 'Spassky might be ringing tonight during the pawns' game in the bishop's room' or whatever. Once at Kanpur I had to take a crackly, barely audible call from South Africa in the packed and jostling lobby of the Meghdoot Hotel. If anyone had bothered to stop and listen to my convoluted chess analogies they'd have thought I was out of my mind.

In fact, it was that call at Kanpur which announced that Holiday Inns had pulled the plug on their sponsorship. It did not surprise us too much, for by now, of course, Botham and Gower had pulled out. On their decision, Dilley said 'Thanks, but no thanks'. Gatting had already done the same after that first London meeting, because he thought it might affect not only his annual Middlesex contract, but also his new sports-shop business.

So we were left with Boycott, committed obviously; Emburey and Willis, both still counting themselves in; and me, very fast getting cold feet. However many aspects of the whole scenario I was going over and over in my mind – moral, financial, political, cricketing, security-insecurity, family and friends – I realized too, with the list of non-starters lengthening, that back at home there would be perceptions of 'saints and sinners', heroes and villains. Who wants to be seen as a villain? I telexed South Africa to say they had to consider me 'extremely doubtful'.

I was mortified I could not confide in Keith Fletcher; nor even with John Lever, who was on the India tour with me. Nor was I remotely proud of myself, in Delhi, when the tour manager, Raman Subba

Row, an extremely pleasant man whom I respected, asked outright at a team meeting if anyone had heard rumours about a projected tour to South Africa. Nobody uttered a word, but I knew that, in this instance, my silence was nothing less than a downright lie.

Then, as we approached the tour's last fortnight, at Colombo, and with my mind made up not to go, I innocently asked Subba Row if my return ticket home could be re-routed via Cape Town because Brenda and I had been thinking that a quick holiday with our old friends in Green Point might give us the break we needed. Raman was a bit taken aback. What, South Africa? I reassured him, on my honour, that it was for a genuine holiday. What Raman must have thought of me a few weeks later still does not bear thinking about: as soon as we got to London, I wrote to him to insist that the request, at the time, had been totally genuine; but he must have thought the worst of me.

Because, in Colombo, I changed my mind again. Brenda was still dead against me going, but John Emburey was more keen about the whole project the nearer 'D-Day' approached. After a final-final consideration of pros and cons, I telexed South Africa saying that, on arrival in London, I would be asking for more money as well as a firm guarantee that the team would not be labelled 'England'. They telexed back by return: 'No problems'.

We also learned in Colombo that Chris Old, Mike Hendrick, Alan Knott, Peter Willey, and Wayne Larkins – all recent England players who were not touring in India – had all been signed up back home. Then Emburey and I recruited Derek Underwood and John Lever, who both felt their England days were numbered. In making this point John said that 'an end of Test career' bonus for him, a thirty-three-year-old fast bowler who had never played regularly for England anyway, made complete sense. But for me – he thought I was an idiot to go. That gave me pause for thought. But I knew I was too far in now, past the point of no return.

At the Gatwick Hotel, we were given all the details. They agreed without hesitation to my demand for more money and a cricketing contract for the following winters. That was Wednesday. We were due to fly out to Johannesburg on the Sunday. Then, dramatically, this was brought forward to Friday when, it seemed, Lord's had begun to smell a rat. I discovered later that Donald Carr had telephoned Willis and Emburey on the Thursday to ask what they knew. In the end, of course, Bob, so enthusiastic all through the planning and 'plotting', withdrew at the last minute. He was an important loss as player, and the probable captain, and for the credibility of the expedition. In the event, whatever (or whoever) had made him change his mind, it turned out well for Bob.

There was only time to do some laundry, write some letters, including the one to Subba Row, and tell Mum and Dad what was happening and what I might have let them in for. Dad at first could not quite take in the full implications. By the time we were in Johannesburg he knew all right, as his phone began to ring incessantly and Fleet Street's vitriol began to splatter around him. When I came home a month later, his continuing upset was very painful for me to bear. He thought I had impugned the family name and its respectability, as well as my own good name and standing in cricket, just for the sake of a jolly good and easy payday.

On arrival, mellowed by the wining and dining aboard, we had one night at Johannesburg's Balalaika Hotel (before transferring to the Rosebank). I telephoned Brenda at home. She told me the news had broken – and how! – and that the reaction in Britain was obviously going to get even worse. 'Traitors' and 'mercenaries' were among the mildest of descriptions. She was obviously feeling wretched and miserably hemmed in. And she was the one who, throughout, had warned me off the adventure. Was she being proved right at a stroke? I felt desperate for her, and wondered too how Mum and Dad were coping. I was overwrought enough to find myself saying to Brenda, 'you have got to be either with me or against me', like it was an ultimatum. It was not a happy phonecall. Brenda could come out and join me in a week's time. Till then, with far more flak to fly, she would be bearing the brunt. Till the Fleet Street mob arrived in South Africa.

It did not take them long.

All these years later I can hold a hand on my heart and say, 'What happened, happened, and I have no regrets'. I took the decision, lived with it, and served my three-year ban (which was as painful as it seemed punitively an over-reaction when it came) without a murmur of complaint. What might have happened, and had I stuck to my change of mind in Kanpur and not gone to South Africa, is anybody's guess. During that three-year ban, I might have 'played' myself out of the England team. Who knows? Or even been made captain three or four years earlier, got sacked, and strolled away from the Test scene altogether in my thirties. Again, who knows?

But two matters have always bothered me. Important ones. Once Willis had pulled out at the eleventh hour, the obvious captain was Boycott, but the players looked at me and said, 'Why doesn't Goochie do it?' Without any real thought, in fact I was quite flattered, I said 'Okay, if that's what you want'. I had found myself captaining Essex a couple of times and thought, 'Well thanks, boys, it will be a good experience'. The upshot, of course, was that I was seen back home as the ring-leader of the tour, even that I had hatched and plotted it. It was now 'my team'. Overnight 'Dirty Dozen' became 'Gooch's Dirty Dozen', 'Gooch's Rebel Gang', whatever. I have had to carry it for years. A decade later, few cricket fans, let alone anyone outside the game, could readily name, off the tops of their head, even half a dozen of us – let's rephrase that as 'six'! – who played in South Africa in 1982. Except for 'Gooch, the Pirate Captain'.

Later, one summer after the storm had blown over, I noticed a father gesture towards me to his son, a nine or ten-year old, with his autograph-book. 'That's Graham Gooch,' said the father. The boy looked at the name and turned to his father, saying, 'Dad, isn't he the man you call "the traitor"?' I didn't want to add to the father's embarrassment, so I smiled, if palely.

My other sorrow about the tour concerns Keith Fletcher. The twelve players contracted were in South Africa but with an obviously busy schedule of matches – we still had to work out the itinerary and fixtures – we needed a couple of others at least, especially a batsman. We thought of Geoff Cook, but he declined. So did Derek Randall and Paul Parker, who were playing in Australia. Well, there was only one thing for it now, I said, I'll ring Fletcher. He was at work in his gumboots in his beloved country garden, neglected through the winter. I knew it was asking a lot even to consider the offer, as incumbent captain of England. But he did us the honour of saying he'd think about it for twenty-four hours. He rang back next day to say, 'No, sorry, but the captaincy of England means too much to me for whatever money is on the table'. In next to no time, of course, Keith learned that he was sacked by the new chairman of selectors,

Peter May, and that Bob Willis was his successor. In the circumstances of the past year, it seemed to us a highly ironic appointment.

You can buy the London newspapers in Johannesburg, but a day late. We were not best happy with most of the lurid knee-jerk coverage; but we thought back to Bangalore, and all the meetings Ian Botham had attended to help work out the deals and the details when we read in his 'exclusive star column' in the *Sun* a couple of days after our arrival that, however huge his offer of money to join us had been – 'one thought kept flashing across my mind: I could never have looked my mate Viv Richards in the eye again'. At the time, of course, he had cited 'financial considerations' as his reason for pulling out of the tour.

But eight readers' letters to none in the *Daily Telegraph* all in favour of us and our rights, cheered our spirits. And I cut out and kept in my wallet, and on my bedside table, an article from *The Times* by Lord Chalfont, who wrote:

'It is not reasonable, or indeed tolerable, that citizens of this country should be deprived by harassment, blackmail or threat, of their freedom to pursue their sporting activities either for pleasure or for gain, wherever they wish to do so. There is no law in this country, as there is in some others, which forbids travel abroad. United Kingdom citizens are therefore free to go to South Africa whenever they wish, on business or for pleasure.

'The Government may, in its wisdom, forbid certain categories of commerce or trade for reasons of state; sporting bodies may justifiably decline to allow representative teams to travel under their auspices. No-one has the right to tell an individual law-abiding British citizen where he may play his games, earn his living or enjoy his leisure.'

In our room at Cape Town's De Waal Holiday Inn, we nervously switched on the BBC's World Service to listen to the evening news after the Lord's meeting back in London. The first headline item (winging round the world) was as if a thunderbolt or meteor had exploded from the radio. Three years. Three! It was a stunner. Brenda and I just sat on the bed, each staring silently at the nearest wall. A three-year ban from Test cricket. For all of us. We guessed there would be some sanction, one Test match, or a Test series, or even a twelve-month penalty. But thirty-six months! It was a hell of a long sentence, especially when you are convinced of the innocence of your 'crime'. No law broken, no contract abused, no chance to state your case in 'open' court; while here we are, with every group in South Africa – black, white, coloured, Indian – learning from and enjoying our cricket and our bridge-building in international sporting relations. For we were the first cricket team of any distinction to visit South Africa in fifteen years. Does apartheid make for a rotten regime, totally unfair, revolting, and distasteful? Of course it does – and so thinks, from my experience of them, almost to a man, every South African cricketer I have ever played against, as well as the crowds that have watched us of whatever race.

Why doesn't the Roman Catholic Church, say, ban Italian footballers for three years for playing matches in Ulster? If I go and watch West Ham am I, just by being there, condoning soccer hooligans? Anyway, with this ban on us, where now stood the great motto of Lord's – 'All teams to be selected on merit'?

As Brenda and I sat there in silence, my mind was racing, wrestling with all these various wild, haywire thoughts. I was both seething and feeling sorry for myself. So all Brenda's warnings had come true. She had been right all along. She could now have taunted me, 'I told you so'. But she didn't, not once. She was obviously as upset for me as I was for myself. The three-year ban was for all of us, even Geoff Humpage, the Warwickshire wicket-keeper batsman who, in the end, became our notorious 'thirteenth man', but then at once looked as if he might be surplus to requirements once we had also signed Bob Woolmer, now living in South Africa, and Arnie Sidebottom, the Yorkshireman who had been playing for the Orange Free State.

The rest of the side was just as shocked – some reacting with fury, others more philosophical. As captain, and knowing we had three more weeks of cricket – against some top-class international players keen and very hungry to show, in their own backyard, what they could do against these so-called 'stars' from the 'outside world' – I had to give the impression that legal action when we returned home certainly would get the ban rescinded, so that now we should concentrate on the job in hand. (All the legal implications and possibilities were examined closely and minutely by our lawyers when we got home, but after Packer, Lord's had worked hard at getting their 'restraints-of-trade' defence watertight. We took no action.)

In the end, the cricket was not bad at all. In the circumstances, we did not give it away, considering our hassles and turmoil and the fact that more than half our side had come straight from an English winter. I scored our most runs – over 500 in all, with a mid-fifties average. I was pleased with myself, deep down, for coping and for being steady and, so to speak, staunch under very heavy fire, which came from all angles, not least from Clive Rice and Vintcent van der Bijl, the principal South African bowlers.

Then it was home to face the music. I said it was best to go as a team. We braced ourselves for a rowdy demonstration at Heathrow – but there was none, only the usual battery of microphones and cameras. On the plane, I had told everybody to face up squarely and honestly, for we had done nothing wrong in our view, and to confine any discussion to matters of the cricket. I took the main questions, obviously, as the perceived new 'Bluebeard, the pirates' captain', and I put on my best and, in the last month, suddenly well practised monosyllabic tone and deadbat face, simply answering the cricket queries – 'Yes, thank you, we enjoyed the trip, it was just another tour for us, and they deserved to win, but there was some reasonably decent cricket that we played' – steering clear of any topic with wider implications. Reporters and broadcasters soon get bored with that (as I knew even then), so they flutter their eyes to heaven despairingly, and wander off knowing there's nothing there which won't end up on the cutting-room floor at *News at Ten*. Until, that is, we saw Boycott, and his girlfriend Ann, scuttling through the cameras towards the exit. Ann was holding a newspaper in front of her face, and Geoffrey his coat to cover his, like crooks coming out of court and into a Black Maria. At a stroke, every TV news bulletin had its top feature and dramatic pictures – the most famous one of us all coming home like a criminal, admitting his 'guilt'. I was livid, furious. Brilliant bat Boycott, expert cricketer; but sometimes totally infuriating.

The first crucial need for me was to patch it all up with Dad and Mum. My father was still, as he put it, 'ashamed' of me: family name tarnished for ever, and my 'loyalty' to Essex and English cricket in tatters. All the media coverage had got to him and had made his son seem an imposter of ill-repute to the one he had known and brought up. Not only did it make me wretchedly upset, I even thought for some time that the breach, and Dad's opinion of me, might never be properly repaired. But over the next few weeks and months – ever so slowly – as I took pains to explain to him all my reasoning and motives for the trip, and my now even heightened sense of responsibility because of it, he gradually came round to seeing that the immediate, knee-jerk, versions of the story relayed to England, might have been tremendously one-sided. Our grudge was mercifully, and completely, mended in time, and Dad and Mum continued to be my very best supporters, travelling all over to watch me play, just as they had done since I was a junior at Ilford 3rds.

What helped enormously with Dad's coming round was that, during our dramatic month in South Africa, Brenda had also done the same and reversed her worries and warnings of the whole previous year. She saw that, for better or worse, having made my decision and stuck to it honestly and vigorously, I had come out of it a stronger and more self-assured person than when I went in. Stubbornness can win you brownie points! Brenda also now realized that, for all the ferocious and, even, frightening flak she had taken the brunt of at home – as well as the ban which had so upset her – it nevertheless meant that she could now spend her next three winters in Cape Town with me and Western Province.

Essex, of course, were none too happy with me or John Lever. Doug Insole, very grave, came round to our house. He thought I had been irresponsible, not only to Essex and my valued relationship with him, but particularly to myself. JK and I went to see the club chairman, 'Tiny' Waterman, to put our point of view which also differed from his. But Essex's warm, close, loving sense of 'family' prevailed (just as it did in the end with Dad), and although, amicably enough, we 'agreed to disagree', there was none of the rancour we heard was emanating from two or three other counties who turned so vindictively against some of the tourists.

So my 'normal' cricket resumed. Not one Essex player railed against JK or me, nor showed any grudge or jealousy, although I must say that Keith Pont, a character and my one-time representative schoolboys' XI captain, was coaching in Cape Town during the tour and, when we played at Newlands, he came to the ground and unveiled a big banner which read 'I'M AVAILABLE!'. At that particular time, too, we might have grabbed at him as our 'thirteenth man'. Sadly, Keith never sustained his glittering schoolboy promise.

Nor did Keith Fletcher ever show the slightest resentment to me or JK. It is the mark of the man. He knew there would, and should, be a punishment from officialdom for us. But he realized, too, that we had gone into it with our eyes open. Just as he had done to consider it all before rejecting our offer. Poor, good Fletch, the two-time loser, rejecting a small fortune in the cause of England, and then England kicking him in the teeth. When the new chairman of selectors, Peter May, told him on the telephone that he'd got the boot, Keith just got in his car and drove blankly around the countryside for hour upon hour in his dismay and despair. The next match we played was a Benson & Hedges qualifier against Hampshire at Chelmsford. Keith was silent, pale, seemingly on auto-pilot. The dressing-room was as quiet as a graveyard in our embarrassment, and our feeling and fondness for him. One of our resident court-jesters pathetically felt it his duty to break the ice by jocularly saying, 'Fletch, you should have taken Goochie's £45,000!' Has a lead balloon ever more heavily crashed to earth? Total silence.

The match began. At one stage we were 14 for six, including Fletch, till Turner and East pulled it round valiantly to save Keith's face and to show him that, for just this one day and one passing passage, we all totally understood why he had momentarily lost his grip.

I suppose my own lack of runs early that summer of 1982 might have had something to do with reaction setting in from South Africa. I took a time to get going. By the standards we had begun to set ourselves, it was a mediocre season, but with Fletch, JK and me now on permanent, uninterrupted county duty until 1985, we all built up an unbelievable head of steam for 1983 and 1984, gloriously winning and then at once retaining the Championship and, in the respective summers, being runners-up to Middlesex in the Benson & Hedges final (which we should have 'walked'), and handsomely winning the Sunday League. In truth, Essex's rampage had only just begun.

Three last, final thoughts on South Africa and that still unfair tag, 'Gooch's Dirty Dozen'. That first 'banned' summer back, on 10 June 1982, I scored 9 (c Wright b Newman) against Derbyshire at Chesterfield. Someone else made exactly 9 that day – Allan Lamb –

at Lord's in his debut Test match innings for England against India. Allan, with the broadest of white South African accents, was born and brought up at Langebaanweg, which is less than an hour's drive away from Cape Town's De Waal Hotel, where Brenda and I had listened, stunned, to the announcement of the ban. No offence to Allan but, as *Wisden* noted at the time, it made the whole situation 'ironic, if not absurd'.

Twelve summers later, accompanied by the general rejoicing which greeted South Africa back to play in England for the first time in twenty-nine years, on the eve of the historic 'homecoming' Test match in 1994, their coach Mike Procter said at Lord's, 'The occasional tours to our country, which began with Graham Gooch's side in 1982, were a true godsend. Some, variously, called them "rebels" or "mercenaries". I never saw them as rebels: to me they were brave men, supportive of multi-racial cricket in South Africa and they were right to make a stand against the hypocrisy that hangs round the whole question of sporting links with each other. Those tours were the best thing that could have happened to all South African cricket at that time.' The applause for that speech was led by black members of President Mandela's new multi-racial government.

The final 'South African Breweries' English XI' innings of that tour began on 27 March 1982, at Durban, when, once again, I walked out to open the innings with Geoffrey Boycott. It was our last opening partnership. We put on 67. I had valued – and will always treasure – opening with Geoffrey. I did not know then that it was, in fact, the end of a beginning, and another step forward.

7

LET THE BAT DO THE TALKING

FK

Gooch knew that if it was financial security he was after, the South African tour would certainly provide it, and sooner rather than later. A consideration in terms of any 'insecurity' was his knowledge that a Test-match career was always at the whim and gift of the selectors; and they had dropped him the summer before. He was aware, too, that his batting style, at that time, was not conducive to consistency. But had he been an England regular – and in retrospect it is hard to imagine him not being so – the three-year ban cost him three overseas tours with England at between £10,000–£12,000 a time, and fifteen home Test matches at £1,500 each. That was over £50,000, but taxed. He was in profit, but not by a fortune.

Graham's oldest cricketing friend, John Emburey, says that Gooch is so famously stubborn that, even if he admitted it 'deep down' in his soul (which he doubts, anyway), Graham would never announce that it might have been a wrong move to go on the tour. 'Nevertheless, the South African experience changed him,' says John. 'Obviously it was not pleasant having all the "anti" reaction directly associated with his name, as in "Gooch's rebels", but a more important factor was his captaining the team on the cricket field. Suddenly Graham was not only the spokesman off it, but in charge of a bunch of tremendously experienced cricketers who had been household names when he himself was only a boy – men like Alan Knott, Dennis Amiss, Derek Underwood, and Geoff Boycott. The responsibility of having to shoulder both burdens changed Graham's outlook a lot, and as well as coming out of it far tougher, he also became more introspectively detached, more insular.'

111

Emburey and Gooch, of course, had first me on their way to East Africa with the London Schools side over a dozen years before. Recalls John:

'The enduring first memory I have is of the confidence of this young kid from Essex. He had a cocksure manner, a certainty about himself. He might have been putting it on, as they say some intrinsically shy boys do, but certainly to me he seemed very knowing and out-going. What he said, the rest of us followed. He was already aware that physical fitness was going to help him get to the top, and once there keep him at the top. On that first day, at once Graham got down and put in seventy press-ups on the trot to prove it. I was finished if I did four straight off. (Even in our forties dotage now, at Lord's I might drive my car round from the Pavilion to the Nursery end for nets; Graham will jog there and back.)'

'Graham as a kid was a different animal to the Graham of the early and mid-1980s. I think he turned in on himself a bit and became more withdrawn, reticent and quieter than I remembered him as a boy. Whether that was just a natural growing-up development as he became more of a well-known public figure, or whether it was a direct result of his reaction to that South African tour, I honestly couldn't say. Possibly so; possibly not.

'I think he just decided that the best idea was to let his bat do the talking. And the way he batted meant there was a heck of a dominant figure in there somewhere. During our ban, we had two winters in Cape Town with Western Province. Before we went, I always used to bowl pretty well at him. I was confident as a bowler about asking him all the questions. But since then he's taken us at Middlesex to the cleaners at Lord's no end of times. Me in particular. In Cape Town I bowled an awful lot to him in the nets. He loves his nets. So he obviously worked out a way of playing me. Ever since, when Middlesex v Essex comes around, he'll jump on me from the word go, never let me settle into a groove or rhythm. No look-see, no let up, he'll just go for me. He loves to dominate at the crease, and he's always particularly liked off-spinners (slow left-armers have a better chance against him: Tufnell has always bowled well against Graham). For me, it has become increasingly daunting to bowl at him. He can sometimes seem to hit fours and sixes at will, and you know he can 'work' or milk any balls for singles or twos any place on the field he wants. No, when I'm bowling and he's batting, we take it very seriously. There's no repartee between us. He doesn't talk to me, and I don't talk to him. But he's a tremendous man, and a tremendous cricketer.

Essex's disappointing season of 1982 – seventh in the Championship, sixth in the Sunday League – was in stark relief to their anticipation of it, with the permanent presence of the England-banned Gooch and Lever. Gooch played glumly at first, and after a first-ball duck against Derbyshire, Fletcher and the opposition captain, the former international opener Barry Wood, had together to jockey him out of it. Although, with typical stubbornness, Gooch would not admit it, there was no doubt that the ban was still sorely troubling him. His next winter back in South Africa, but now without hassle, proved to be a rest as well as a cure. With the Embureys living almost next door, Graham and Brenda enjoyed an idyllic time. In midweek, he joined a school coaching programme, forerunner of Ali Bacher's township schemes, organized by Mobil. For Western Province he opened the batting with either Adrian Kuiper or, more often, Lawrie Seeff. In nine provincial games, Gooch hit 600 runs and, returning the following southern summer, he bettered that with another 600 runs in seven games, including a Western Province opening record of 293 with Seeff.

In 1983, Emburey did have one smile at his friend's expense. With Gooch in imperious one-day form (a bombarding 176 from 117 deliveries against Glamorgan, for instance), Essex still contrived dotty collapses after having the contests sewn-up in both the NatWest quarter-final (against Kent) and in the final itself of the Benson & Hedges Cup at Lord's where Middlesex pinched the game at the last (Emburey 11–3–17–0) after Essex, chasing a puny 190, stood at 79 for no wicket and 127 for two (Gooch 46, Hardie 49) and 151 for four, yet still managed to lose by four runs. In the same calamitous week, Essex were way behind in the Championship but, undaunted, they gathered themselves for a voluptuous final sprint and clinched it at the very last, against Yorkshire at Chelmsford (Gooch 111, Lever 11 wickets in the match including his 100th of the season).

Gooch made an ultra-patient 110 in over five hours to save the match against Leicestershire in August – a birthday present for the arrival of their first-born Hannah (he had taken three hours off from fielding the day before to be present at the birth), but Gooch was still given to occasional serious fret and brooding that his consistency was letting him down in the first-class game, so that when Essex had played Somerset at Taunton in midsummer, the West country opening-bat and (already) perceptive writer, Peter Roebuck noted in his diary on 6 June:

'This evening Gooch scored 34 lugubrious runs in 33 overs. He must be finding it difficult to excite himself playing in ordinary county games with no prospect of Test selection. It's no wonder that sometimes these brilliant cricketers find the daily routine of cricket dull and seek their excitement beyond its boundaries. They must sometimes feel like concert pianists only able to play pop tunes in bars, unable to stretch their finest abilities.'

Yet to his friends, even when a television was on in the dressing-room showing the Test matches and all the surrounding hype and crowds and colour and fame, Gooch kept insisting he felt no pangs of regret, no sense of missing it. (In fact, later some evenings he would admit to worry that all 'pangs' were absent in his breast.) Nor did he feel, he said, the remotest jealousy for those who had taken his place for England: he wished them a hundred every time, and one believed him totally.

The following spring, 1984, in what was to be a resplendently successful defence of their championship trophy, Gooch and Essex springing straight from the traps with the highest score of his career to date, 220 in 315 minutes, with 146 in boundaries, against Hampshire at Southampton ('Well, obvious wasn't it?' he would recall with a knowing chuckle exactly ten years later. 'No Malcolm Marshall; he'd already joined the West Indies tour that summer.') When the West Indies came to Essex in midsummer, the still-banned Gooch was warmly satisfied to make a point in his 101 out of the county's 267 against Garner and Walsh (Marshall did not play). In two months of the tour, it was the first century by any English player against the West Indies, who had arrived at Chelmsford hot from cruelly annihilating England in the first Test at Edgbaston by an innings and 180 runs. It was the opening scene-setter to the home side's horrific and humiliating 5–0 'blackwash' in the rubber. But the tabloids, contrary to the last, were demanding Gooch's return, pronto. So, less stridently, was the cricket establishment. For the Australians were coming in 1985. And Gooch's ban would have ended by then.

Gooch wintered in Essex that year. The county had, in the old feudal term, 'granted' their loyal professional a benefit for 1985. You are not meant to organize benefits yourself, a committee of friends does the honours for you. But you get out of a benefit what you put into it, which is hard work and a ceaseless slog round the pubs, clubs, quiz nights, supper evenings and garden fetes of your constituency. Gooch dived into the task with a will. Everyone said he was brilliant at it. In all, his benefit made him £154,000 tax-free, dramatically almost double that of Fletcher's Essex best the year before, and beating comfortably Boycott's all-time benefit record of £148,000. The one-time toolmaker was well on the way to security now. To prove the point, with Brenda and baby Hannah, they moved into their new handsome stockbroker-belt house in the district of Hutton. By the spring of 1985 his untiring work had given the benefit almost a momentum of its own – generously helped by another glamorously successful summer by his Essex confreres whom he helped to win the NatWest trophy and the Sunday League title; and they were runners-up in the Benson & Hedges Cup.

So it was to rejoicing and forgiveness all round that he buckled on his pads for England again for the first time since Sri Lanka's inaugural Test match in 1982 when he had telexed Johannesburg, 'Sorry, on second thoughts, count me in'. In England's three international one-dayers, which kicked off the six-match Ashes series against Allan Border's Australians, Gooch allowed nobody – including the many who had judged his sentence fair and moral – the slightest flicker of doubt that his banishment, nevertheless, had cost English batting dear. In those three matches, with honest vengeance in him, he hit 57, 115, and 117. He was acclaimed to the echo. He was back. It meant a tremendous amount to him, and to Alf, who had been made redundant, and to Rose, who were both there.

Botham, Gower, Gatting, Lamb, and Gooch. Thus the *dramatis personae* and programme notes. In that heady summer of 1985, they frolicked. The remainder of the performance starts here. Gooch, now thirty-two, was the oldest of these five mighty different, and differently mighty, engaging friends and, yes, musketeers. They still had a long route to travel together. Long and winding.

Meanwhile, Gooch was, as is his way, just relieved and quietly content at last to have slipped off the front pages of the newspapers and, he hoped, remain a member of the team on the back pages.

GG

I finished the 1985 summer on a real high. In my last six first-class innings I scored over 700 runs, including that treasured first Test century (196) against Australia at The Oval in the sixth Test when we regained the Ashes. It had taken me 40 innings and ten years since my traumatic Test debut, but it was worth waiting for. In the middle was that horrific, self-inflicted run out on 99 in Melbourne. At The Oval I was 94 not out at tea. As I sat there waiting to go back on to the field with David, I thought of Ken Barrington – 'Don't give it away now, don't give it away'. It was a feeling to savour when Craig McDermott at once bowled me a full-toss which I tapped through mid-on to the boundary. It was thrilling to have that partnership with David. We put on 351 runs together and flayed the Australians all round the ground. When he's going so glitteringly well, it scarcely seems like a Test match.

Essex won the NatWest final at Lord's the following Saturday in dramatic fashion, by one run. Derek Pringle and, especially, Keith Fletcher keeping their nerve in the last over against Derek Randall's genius improvization. And the very next day, at Trent Bridge, we as good as clinched the Sunday League title again against Notts. Brian Hardie and I had another field day – at Lord's we had put on 202 for the first wicket, the highest partnership for any wicket of any Lord's final in history (Brian's original strokeplay asserting itself quite wonderfully), and the next day we hit a record Sunday League opening stand of 239. And Richard Hadlee was playing in both matches!

Then Lester Bird, the deputy prime minister of Antigua, began to criticize me and England's forthcoming winter tour of the West Indies. At the end of my Test ban I had done a few radio interviews in which I'd said 'I've no regrets about what I did, I've served my time, end of story,' and, of course, all or part of it was transmitted to the West Indies. And the letters start flying around.

In the middle of the summer, Charles Palmer, then Chairman of the TCCB, came up to see me at the Mottram Hall Hotel in Manchester and said, 'There's a slight problem, Graham. One of the West Indian governments wants you to clarify your statement that you have no regrets about going to South Africa'.

'Yes,' I say, 'dead right. I don't have any regrets, none at all.'

Palmer implied that those sorts of comments were going to cause big problems, so would I make a, er, 'clarification statement'. Sure, I said, whatever that means; if it would help, sure I would. But I would not be retracting anything I'd said, because it was the truth. To cut a long story short, memos and phonecalls and letters went back and forth. Even Sir Sonny Ramphal of the Commonwealth Secretariat becomes involved. Suggested wordings and statements were flying about, my solicitor got involved, the lot. All hassle. At the end of the season, when we were playing Middlesex at Lord's, I had to ask Fletcher if I could bat down the order if we won the toss, because the authorities wanted me in for a meeting. Everything was getting very uptight.

But I tried to be helpful and in the end we came up with the following statement:

'Let me say that I strongly oppose apartheid. My visit to South Africa was certainly not motivated by any intention to support apartheid and naturally nothing I have said has been intended to be contemptuous of anti-apartheid opinion in the West Indies, or anywhere else in the world.'

In the end it was more cringingly apologetic than I'd have liked but, okay, Lord's thought it would do the trick and I wanted to do the right thing by them so that the tour could begin with no problems.

But Lester Bird was still not happy. His answering statement said, 'We would categorically say that Mr Gooch will not be welcome in Antigua. The attempted apology falls short of what is required, I think, for Caribbean people to accept that he should come and visit this country.' That's when I should have said to Lord's, 'Okay, forget it, count me out of the tour, I've done my best to help you, but if Lester Bird is still not satisfied, let him stuff it'. Next, Bird sends an open letter to *The Times*, which they print, and it seems to say that I am now, suddenly, acceptable. Then on it drags – the tour wasn't starting till the New Year – and when the newly appointed TCCB chairman Raman Subba Row (whom I felt I had let down at the end of the Indian tour) personally persuaded me to go, I agreed, although it was still against my better judgement. Anyway, he assured me that a 'truce' had been called in the 'Lord's-Lester' slanging match.

The tour proved to be an unmitigated disaster from the very beginning, both from the view of the cricket and the double-crossing. There were placards and demonstrations against me, but okay, I could live with those although it was a touch 'rum' to see them while sitting in the coach from the airport in the next seat to Allan Lamb! But when Lester Bird comes out with a press statement saying he had made me 'apologize' for going to South Africa and that I regretted going ...

'Mr Gooch's statement contains three elements which I had suggested were necessary to ensure his welcome to the Caribbean. He has stated that he would not return to South Africa, that he does not support apartheid and he has regretted the circumstances which took him there in the first place.'

'Hang on a minute', I say to the tour manager Tony Brown, 'I'm not having that, I don't regret what I did'. I told Tony that I'd been as helpful as I could before we arrived, and they'd told me that was the end of the matter and there would be no more carping, and now here was Lester Bird breaking the agreement and saying things that were not true. I said I wanted to put the following statement out in our British press refuting what Bird said:

'On 29th August, *The Times* contained comments attributed to Mr Lester Bird, Deputy Prime Minister and Foreign Minister of Antigua, misrepresenting my views. Although through the High Commissioner for Antigua in London Mr Bird has confirmed that he welcomes my statement and that there is no objection to my visiting Antigua as part of an English cricket team, he is quoted as saying: "Mr Gooch ... has stated that he will not return to South Africa ... and he has regretted the circumstances which took him there in the first place".

I have never made any such staement and the purpose of this further statement is to set the record straight.

I am a professional cricketer and a British citizen. As such I must and will reserve the right to visit South Africa, or any other country I choose to play cricket ... As to the 1982 visit, I wish to make it quite clear that I have no regrets about the visit. In the light of the circumstances as they existed at that time, I made the decision which I believed to be the right one and which I stand by.

I am obviously aware that my decision was not popular in all quarters; I received and have accepted and served a three-year ban from Test cricket. As far as I'm concerned, that incident is now past history.

Finally I would like to emphasize that neither my 1982 visit to South Africa nor my views expressed in this or other statements are made with any political motivation of any kind. I strongly oppose apartheid and nothing I have said or done has been intended as in any way contemptuous of anti-apartheid opinion, whether in the West Indies or elsewhere in the world.'

The TCCB, however, refused permission to have it released as they claimed it would stir things up even more. 'So you're going to let him get away with slandering me?' I put it to them. 'That doesn't bother you? All right,' I said, 'the last Test is in Bird's Antigua, I'll skip it and fly home.'

'You can't do that,' they said.

So the upshot was that they refused me a right of reply to Bird, and then said I had to go on to Antigua. I had spoken to Peter May in Barbados, and Subba Row in Jamaica. The latter was very sympathetic, but said they had to deny me the right to 'clarify' what Lester Bird was saying about me, otherwise it would all blow up again. Sorry, I say, I'm not very happy at all, and I think I'm being let down badly by the TCCB who are quite content to allow my integrity to be besmirched by some petty politician. So, as the Antigua Test gets nearer, the TCCB secretary Donald Carr flies out from London and we have a long meeting. In the end David Gower, as captain, asked if I would stay for the last Test and go to Antigua for him and the team. So I said, 'Okay, I'll come', but I left our authorities in no doubt that I felt very let down in being used as a pawn in a political game. Say one thing one day, another the next, who cares? If that's diplomacy, you can keep it. It rankled with me for a long time that those who should be backing me preferred to bow to a politician's rantings. To cap it all, I got the feeling that the interlude had Lord's marking me down as 'not officer material'.

So my two tours with England at each end of the three-year ban were disastrous. I seriously thought of giving up touring there and then, although I realized that that would not be looked on at all favourably. The following winter, in fact, I did turn down the tour to Australia, when the twins, Megan and Sally, were born. Then, in 1987/88, I said I'd happily play in the World Cup in India and Pakistan, but not go on Down Under for another tour later in the winter. Don't get me wrong, I love the cricket, it's the wear and tear of touring and the hotel life that's the problem. Perhaps I would have been happier if I had taken to drink, or the Walkman, or cowboy books. Seriously, though, a whole winter away is a long time for a man with a young family.

On that 'Lester Bird' tour the pitches – especially practice pitches – were so ropey as to be dangerous. David Gower took a lot of stick for announcing 'optional nets' but, to be honest, often it wasn't worth practising.

The tour started off badly and got worse. There was a one-day international before each of the Tests. In the first, at Kingston, Patrick Patterson, who is very fast, was in his West Indian cap for the first time. In his first two overs he got Tim Robinson and Gower for ducks. Then Gatting and I got us into the 40s, when Gatt went to hook Malcolm Marshall. He missed and the ball smashed into his nose. He had to go back to London for surgery. It was a grim day all round: Alan Lamb, Peter Willey and myself each got 30-odd, but we were well hammered.

For the Test which immediately followed, the pitch looked just as lethal. When Marshall and Garner began it didn't seem too bad, but then they let Patterson off the leash and up the slope. He got Robinson at once. Gower and I clung on somehow. Because he was always such a languidly classical bat, it is often ignored that, all through his career whenever it was called for, David was full of guts and immensely courageous when the fast bowling was at its most dangerous. It was an understated courage, and he would laugh it off later in the evening with a typical quip; but I knew, from the other end, how many times I was witness to his fearlessness and genuine 'bottle'.

That day in Jamaica, David stuck it out till Holding came on and got him lbw, and then Patterson immediately had David Smith caught at the wicket. At that point, for the first and, I think, only time, I began saying to myself 'Graham, it might be doing yourself a favour if you got out, this boy Patterson is really firing and it could get very nasty indeed. If you don't watch it, you could be hit very badly.' It was the only time I thought I might be hurt at the crease. Now I found that I was crouching very low, knees really bent, even before Patterson was into his delivery stride. Not a good feeling at all. Lamb, like Gower, is full of guts, and we stuck out the period to lunch. But immediately after, that wizard little demon Marshall conjured up something totally unplayable and Garner caught me in the gully. I'd got 51, Allan made 49, but we were all out for 159. Not a bright start to a series.

One of the disconcerting things about facing the Windies' ultra-quicks on their own lightning-fast tracks is that no fielder is in front of the bat, so it's as if you're the only one in the spotlight – you are too, for that matter – because all that's in vision is the umpire, the non-striker and the bowler steaming in. You know the ring of five slips, two gullies, and two leg-slips or whatever, is behind you in a cordon, but you never actually look at them. You just hear them.

This has never worried me. If anything it gingers you up and makes you concentrate more, although they think it might unsettle you, dislodge your game and your 'groove'. It might work with some batsmen, new young ones perhaps, but it has never got my back up. David Boon, that fine Australian batsman, told me the best one yet. David is a short, squat, stocky fellow, a bit like Gavaskar. He once did a little jump in the crease to play down a ball from Curtly. And as he throws the ball back from slip Desmond Haynes encourages the bowler, 'Well done, Curtly, he's in the elevator, but he's still only on the seventh floor – let's take him up to the twelfth!'

Merv Hughes is thought to have 'invented' sledging. But Merv is a cuddly baby compared to his predecessors like Hogg, Lillee, Thomson and, especially, Pascoe. Nick them through the slips and they sneer 'Shit shot!' or 'Arse wipe!' or 'You couldn't even middle it with a surfboard!' Nor has this ever bothered me either. Pascoe was originally of Yugoslavian descent, and looked like a wild man down from the hills. One time, the light was getting murky and the Aussies wanted to keep England out there batting, so the captain Ian Chappell tells Pascoe to pitch it up – 'No bouncers, Lennie, else the umpires will have us off'. At once Pascoe bowls two snorting screamers right up the batsman's nose. 'Off we go,' say the umpires, with Chappell berating Pascoe for being a total idiot. Says Lennie, 'Sorry, skipper, a leopard can't change his stripes!'

The one Australian who always 'got my ruddy goat', as Kenny Barrington used to say, was Geoff Lawson. I can't exactly say why, but I had a run-in with him in the Nehru Cup in India around this time. It was at Hyderabad, very hot and steamy. Lawson thought I'd nicked a ball from him and started bleating about me not walking. I said that talk from an Aussie of 'not walking' was the richest thing I'd heard in years. So Lawson blows his top, and then, of all people, Allan Border sticks his oar in and supports Lawson, so I have a go at him too. Very heated for some moments. Anyway, on we go, and Ned Larkins and I put on 180-odd for the first wicket, Ned playing a truly thunderous innings. Afterwards, Allan came up and apologised profusely and said the heat of the moment had got at him. We naturally remain the best of friends.

That West Indies tour of 1985/86 was ruined for me by the political antics of Lester Bird; but it was definitely a no-contest as a Test series. We suffered another 'blackwash' on some rottenly uneven wickets, losing twice by ten wickets, once by an innings, once by seven wickets, and in the final Test by a massive 240 runs. I managed only four half-centuries in the series, but that still had me second in the Test averages, at 27, behind the 37 of captain David Gower, who batted with real guts all through. In my ten innings, Marshall had me four times, and Holding and Garner twice each. My only consolation was the 129 I made in the second one-day international in Trinidad. Even so, we all returned from that tour a chastened bunch – myself in particular for reasons not to do with cricket.

I don't think I've ever been more pleased to get home.

8

CAPTAINS AND UMPIRES

FK

Gooch had hit his seventh Test match century, 183 at Lord's in 1986, against New Zealand and Richard Hadlee at the peak of his craft, but generally, even as Essex won their fourth Championship, his season was mediocre and he finished 59th in the first-class averages, his lowest for twelve years. He even wondered if, at thirty-three, his reflexes might be beginning to wind down.

Within twelve months Gooch felt certain of it.

He skipped Mike Gatting's triumphant England tour of 1986/87 for the Ashes in Australia and played the modern father to the new twins Megan and Sally – sleepless nights, nappy duties, pram-pushing, supermarket shopping-lists and all. But he enjoyed his winter. He trained with West Ham three days a week, humped topsoil around his new garden and put in quality time with his new batmaker and sports equipment firm, Stuart Surridge & Co. He hoped he might work towards a permanent and prestigious job with them when he retired, as he thought he inevitably would, in two or three years.

As Essex's conscientious new captain, he began the 1987 season with zest, determined to claim back his opener's sentry-post for England – in which Chris Broad and Bill Athey had wintered well in Australia. Gooch tossed his gauntlet down flamboyantly in Essex's first Championship match at Bristol. He almost contemptuously ran the Gloucestershire bowling ragged, hitting 171 off 206 balls. Athey and Broad were worried men. Not, however, for long, because what followed that blazing announcement was a sequence of 0, 0; 0, 0; 27, 2 in the Championship, and two more noughts in Essex's first two

Benson & Hedges Cup matches. Six ducks in nine innings, and his batting confidence was in shreds.

He scratched a few innings together, but to all intents never recovered it. His captaincy, on which he had embarked with such fervour, fell into the same decline as his batting. He found the organization and the delegation debilitating. Obviously and understandably he blamed the captaincy on his woebegone batting decline. And then vice versa. Increasingly, in his depression, he allowed things to drift until his eminence grise, Fletcher, who was still playing for the side, was as good as directing operations in all but name and tossing-up. Matthew Engel reported a match for the *Guardian* in which he noticed Graham moving, say, fine-leg finer with a wave, and then at once, with a more surreptitious gesture, old Keith waving him squarer. Engel christened Essex's new captain 'Flooch'. By season's end Gooch had given the leadership back to Fletcher officially.

Then happened at once – by fluke or divine providence – a quite amazing resuscitation, both actual and spiritual. At the end of August, Lord's was staging its celebrations for the 200th anniversary of the MCC: the ancient club's XI against the Rest of the World. At the eleventh hour a leg injury forced the New Zealand batsman, Martin Crowe, to cry off. The nearest man to hand, just up the A12, was Graham Gooch. The day before, Gooch had asked Fletcher and Doug Insole whether, having given up the captaincy this time, it would preclude his having another go in the future. They had both said, 'No problem'. It was a burden from his shoulders.

Next day: packed house, glorious high summer, Gooch's most preferred setting in the world. MCC batted, Greenidge and Broad opened. The Rest of the World fielded a formidable attack – Imran Khan, Courtney Walsh, Kapil Dev, Roger Harper, and the Pakistani mesmerist Abdul Qadir. Broad soon succumbed. Gooch came in at first-wicket down. He pottered uneasily, prodded and fretted and overdid the 'gardening'. His friends worried for him.

Then, out of the blue, he leaned into a straightish off-drive from a delivery from the bounding Kapil Dev. It scorched the grass, took off on that tiny green slope in front of the pavilion and exploded with a single fierce retort into the freshly white-painted picket-fence. It startled the members at their pre-prandials.

That one defiantly booming stroke did the trick. Gooch was on his way; the season's moth was now the butterfly speckled in bright colours. For the next four hours, Gooch's innings established the match, and the auspicious occasion itself (these phoney junket-wars can so often turn turgid) as one of grandeur for the memory. For the next four days (rain wrecked the fifth) there was a resplendence around St John's Wood as the likes of Imran, Rice, Gavaskar, Border, Hadlee, Marshall, Greenidge, Kapil, Gatting and Gower strutted on their stage.

And Gooch's century had led the parade. After that first boundary, he hit 17 more and, on the way, conducted a masterclass in how to play the wiles of the leg-breaker Qadir. When he was on 117, and having a merrie Englander's stand of 103 with Gatting, Gooch went down the wicket and straight-drove, hard, the West Indian off-spinner Roger Harper. In a spectacular and unforgettable split-second passage, the tall bowler, in a single pantherish and prehensile movement bent, fielded the drive, and threw down Gooch's stumps as the batsman sensed danger too late and tried unavailingly to divert the ball with a dive.

Run out. Gooch stood up, dusted himself down and, all smiles, shook his head in admiration and offered a nod of acclaim to Harper. As he walked back to the pavilion, the applause of the throng for such a feat of fielding changed to a different resonance, to one of gratitude for an innings which had so gloriously set the tone for the whole revels, and every person remained standing till Gooch had vanished from the famous field into the pavilion.

The Bicentenary party at Lord's – Gooch made a belligerent, celebrating 70 in 118 balls in the second innings, outshining Greenidge in a second-wicket stand of 135 – ensured his place in Mike Gatting's World Cup side for the 1987/88 tournament in India and Pakistan. In the semi-final, Gooch scored an extravagant and highly original century, sweeping the Indian left-arm spinners to distraction, but Allan Border's revitalized Australians won the final.

After the World Cup, Gooch stayed with England for the short and notorious three-Test tour of Pakistan, when Gatting had the altercation with the umpire Shakoor Rana, but he chose not to take part in England's trip to Australia, for the second Bicentenary Test, or to New Zealand.

GG

In my opinion, the England team was totally out of order to become embroiled in disputes about the umpires on the 1987/88 tour of Pakistan. The siege mentality settled on us early and the result was just about the most remarkable day I have known in cricket, when we all stood around at Faisalabad, waiting to play. In the first Test at Lahore, we felt the Pakistanis had enjoyed some luck with umpiring decisions in our first innings, and it reached boiling point when, at the start of the second innings and facing a deficit of 217 runs, Chris Broad was given out caught at the wicket off Iqbal Qasim. I was at the other end and there was certainly a noise of some sort as the ball beat the bat. Chris stood there and said, 'I didn't hit it, I'm not going,' and he started to exchange heated words with the close fielders. 'I am not going,' he said, 'you can like it or lump it, I'm staying.' It wasn't just fleeting. He stood there for ages. In the end, I came down the wicket and told him he just had to go. He still refused. Eventually I persuaded him to see sense.

Perhaps I should have stayed down my end, leaning on the bat handle and then we might have been able to go home early! Broad's Test career might have ended there and then if he had refused to budge, but our tour management gave him only a stern reprimand. I attended that disciplinary meeting and spoke against disciplining Chris, which in retrospect was the wrong approach. I just sprang to his defence in the heat of the moment, but, looking back, it was daft of me to take the side of a player over an umpire. We should have fined him – not only for the gravity of the offence but also to alert the rest of us that dissent is simply not allowed, whatever the provocation. I soon came round to that way of thinking when I became England captain, although I don't blame Gatting for feeling, that day, that Broad had been subjected to enough censure. Thus the pot was still simmering when we got to Faisalabad for the second Test.

Those pictures of Gatting and Shakoor Rana shouting at each other were very disturbing if you had cricket's best interests at heart. It looked disastrous on television and, although we mentioned the incident when we got back to the dressing-room, we had no inkling that it had looked so bad or that events would move so swiftly. Shakoor Rana was wound up about his honour being questioned, a matter of pride which they are very hot on in Pakistan, and soon we had a major incident on our hands, with the umpires refusing to begin the game again until the England captain apologized. We all supported Gatt at our meeting and many players felt we shouldn't take the field under any circumstances. In the end I just had to say to the young players, 'Do you realize what it means if you do that? You'll be breaking your tour contract and you could well never play for England again.' Some of them hadn't thought it through, and I said we should go out and play, after issuing a statement that we deplored what had happened and that we fully supported our captain. Gatting was under immense pressure and I felt desperately sorry for him. But when the ridiculous 'barmaid' affair was slung at him during the first Test at Trent Bridge the following summer, it was pretty obvious he was being sacked for Faisalabad in retrospect. Gatt has been a thoroughly excellent sportsman and has never once caused any other umpire a moment's bother, but the whole affair just mushroomed at Faisalabad and he eventually lost control.

Then, immediately after Faisalabad, Lord's gave us a 'tour bonus' of an extra £1,000 each. Nobody could believe it. At first, when I heard '£1,000' mentioned, I thought they meant a fine. I reckon they could sense serious rumblings of mutiny. Back in London later, Doug Insole told me that, at Lord's, when they mentioned '£1,000' to him he muttered a stern 'quite right, too' – and it was ages before he realized they'd been talking about a bonus, not a fine.

Imagine a Faisalabad happening at Lord's! 'Not going to finish the game?' They would have come down like a ton of bricks, ordering us to get out there immediately or our Test careers were over, and to worry about any statements later. That has to be right: you can't play cricket without umpires, no matter if they seem incompetent, and it is the captain's job to stamp out dissent. On that tour of Pakistan I was worried about the way the cricket was heading. We couldn't say it was their fault, because our captain had been seen jabbing his finger at an umpire, and in the process undermining his authority. There are good umpires and bad everywhere in cricket. Some Pakistani umpires are good, some English umpires are not and vice versa. But if a cricketer is not prepared to take the rough with the smooth it would be anarchy and cricket would be dead in no time. Without umpires there would be no game.

Whenever any question of umpiring comes up I always try to tell myself – and especially if I think I might have been 'sawn off at the knees', as we professionals put it, that very day with a poor decision – is that they all love cricket. They wouldn't be doing the job if they didn't love cricket in the first place. When I first came into the game in the 1970s, there were lots of umpires who had played the game in the 1950s: Arthur Jepson, Jack Crapp, Sam Cook, Dusty Rhodes. Lovely characters. As captain, you have a form to mark at the end of each match on the umpires' performance' and it goes back to Lord's. I nearly always just ticked the 'Good to Satisfactory' box. One really bad decision doesn't affect this – anyone can make a howler – but if, say, there were three real blunders from one umpire in a game, then I would mark him 'down' a bit. Once, the story goes, our captain 'Tonker' Taylor had marked down the old Aussie umpire and character, Cec Pepper, 'for over-excessive and noisy farting'.

Basically, the way to bracket umpires is in three types – a bowling-umpire, a batting-umpire, or a captain's umpire. The last one does make a bit of sense, seeing that the captain is marking him up after the game, but I suppose it's a hark-back to the old days of the amateur captains when they could be very strict, even tyrannical, with 'working-class' umpires. And sure, sometimes when you are given 'not out' in a very close lbw decision, you can say to yourself 'yep, a good "captain's decision" that'. A famous bowler's-umpire was someone like Eddie Phillipson, the former Lancashire opening bowler, who would give lots of lbw's, no fear nor favour nor favourites. If it hit the pad, up would go the finger. Once David Acfield had Eddie at his end, so naturally David was being a bit appeal-happy. Up goes another lbw shout. Not out. But Eddie mutters to Acfield in that Lancashire accent of his, 'Just turn it one more inch, Ackers, and we'll get the bugger in a minute, you'll see.'

A famous benefit-of-doubt umpire is Dickie Bird. Very hard for a bowler to get a narrow decision out of Dickie, ask any bowler the world over. Dear old Dickie: I can't remember whether it was Somerset v Northants at Taunton or at Northampton: however, Allan Lamb comes out to field and, after a couple of overs, he 'realizes' he's got his mobile phone in his pocket, so he hands it to Dickie and asks if he'd mind putting it in his bigger pocket for the duration. Dickie refuses at first and starts a song-and-dance, complaining about modern players and new-fangled 'devices' and what the

Bognor Holiday camp,
en I was about six and
eady a mustard-keen
ammer'.

Isle of Wight, 1966.
I developed from pitch-and-
putt and in 1982 achieved a
hole-in-one in Calcutta.

Dawlish Warren Chalets,
1964, and a decent enough
straight-drive back over
Mum's head.

st Ham Corinthians in 1965, when I was 12. I'm the sheepish-looking one in my Essex Schools
, and Dad is seated, second from the right. The umpire, Al Spooner, was a founder member of the
b and died in 1994, aged 96.

In my London Schools blazer before the East Africa tour of 1969, alongside Malcolm Howlett, a really promising all-round sportsman who was to die tragically of cancer only three years later.

England Under-19 tour to West Indies at Bridgetown, Barbados with yours truly in the back row, centre. Others to make their name in county cricket included, in the front row, John Barclay (third from left), Graham Clinton (third from right), Andy Stove (far right), and in the back row Geoff Miller (third from right).

Counter-attacking against Roger Knight of Surrey in the B & H final, 1979. Still a most memorable century for it helped Essex to its first trophy in 103 years.

Opposite left: A glaring failure. Marsh celebrates my second duck in my first Test in 1975. Little consolation that it was a snarler of a delivery from Thomson.

Spot the deliberate mistake. Hughes runs me out from mid-on for 99 at Melbourne in 1980. 'What, don't you like scoring centuries or something?' jibed Ian Chappell.

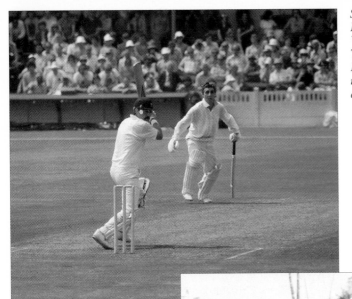

Shoring up the innings with Mike Brearley in the 1979 World Cup semi-final at Old Trafford against New Zealand. Mike was the finest of captains who brought the best out of everyone.

Much loved friend and counsellor Ken Barrington in discussion with my co-author, Frank Keating, and Mike Gatting just days before he died on the England tour to the West Indies in 1981.

Another one 'for Kenny' ... opening out when Clive Lloyd (at slip) brought on a spinner during my treasured century, dedicated to Barrington, at Bridgetown in 1981.

John Lever would bowl his boots off for Essex and England – and still be fit for more larks. Here in Sri Lanka in 1982 we both made our final decision to make the SAB tour to South Africa.

With Geoffrey Boycott in the SAB XI's first 'Test' against South Africa at Johannesburg in 1982. My only regret remains agreeing to be captain of what became known as 'Gooch's rebels'.

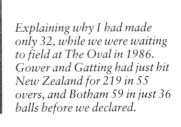

Explaining why I had made only 32, while we were waiting to field at The Oval in 1986. Gower and Gatting had just hit New Zealand for 219 in 55 overs, and Botham 59 in just 36 balls before we declared.

Third Test, Edgbaston, 1989. Not Alderman this time, but Lawson, as I 'fall' across my crease and am again lbw. During that summer, Alderman and Lawson each dismissed me four times.

It felt just as excruciatingly painful as it looks, physio Laurie Brown examines the injury at Trinidad in 1990 which might have cost us not only that first Test but the series.

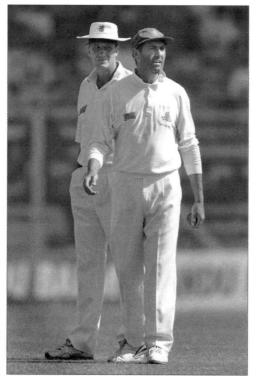

Above: I enjoy playing tennis, and felt privilege when Brenda and I were invited into the Royal Box at Wimbledon in 1992. Not that it seemed so from this photograph.

Left: My best and most enduring friendship in cricket. John Emburey and I first stood togethe at slip over 24 years ago for the London School touring team.

England v India, First Test, Lord's, 1990. The scoreboard tells the tale – but the Indian wicketkeeper More could tell you another. Nine-and-a-half hours before I was out, he had dropped a sitter when I was on 36.

My two best supporters. Dad was my first coach, and Mum still makes the tastiest chips in Essex.

Captaincy can be a fretful job when the team is up against it.

world's coming to; but in the end he agrees and puts it down at the bottom of his ample great pocket. A couple of overs later, just as the bowler is beginning his run-up from Dickie's end, in the pavilion Ian Botham is dialling a number ... The phone rings shrilly in Dickie's pocket. Total consternation and blind panic from the umpire who is now dancing about like a cat on hot bricks, thinking he's got a hornets' nest in his pocket; utter panic and shellshock. The whole field is collapsed in laughter.

Jack van Geloven, a pleasant, if rather strict northerner who used to play for Leicester, later became an umpire. At Tunbridge Wells once, against Kent, last ball before lunch, Ray East is caught at midwicket, the fielder diving forward and just scooping it up. Ray thinks it's a bump-ball so he just stands there. Van Geloven has a little think and then, up comes his finger, 'Out'. On the way in for lunch, Ray walks in with Jack, saying, 'Okay, I'm off, Jack, but I could swear it was a bump-ball.' 'Get away, lad, that was a fair catch, you're out.' All through lunch, as we're all sitting there, Ray is still rucking on that he wasn't out and it was a bump-ball. Jack sits there having his tuck and thinking quietly, 'I dunno, what's the world coming to? East was out and that's all there is to it.'

So the bell goes. Out go the umpires, out go Kent. East is in the dressing-room, putting on a different coloured helmet, different gloves and bat. And out he goes again. Van Geloven had no idea, of course. Ray is at Jack's end, and just as the bowler is about to deliver the first ball after lunch, East turns his new helmet to Van Geloven, looks him straight in the eye, and says, 'You did say that was a bump-ball, didn't you, Jack?' Van Geloven leapt out of his skin and nearly collapsed on the spot.

People like Van Geloven, the veterans who have seen it all, and done it all as players, are like old and firm friends, sort of uncles in charge on the beach. Remember old Arthur Jepson of Nottinghamshire? Dusty Miller comes in to bat once. 'Mornin', Arthur.' 'Mornin', Dusty lad, did you use the motorway this morning ...?' or ''ee, lad, I've a gippy tummy after that breakfast she gave me', that sort of general friendly chat. So this time, when Arthur says, 'You'll have no trouble on this pitch, Dusty lad, the others don't seem to realize it, but all you've got to do is get right forward every time and this bowling's a heap of crap.' Right, thinks Miller, nice nod and wink there from old Jeppo, thanks very much. So next over, Dusty is facing, and Arthur is at the bowler's end. First ball, he plays the most extravagant forward-defensive of all time, right down the track with his long left leg. Just like Arthur had said. It hits him in the middle of the pad. Big appeal. Finger up. 'That's plumb, lad, sorry!' said Jepson as he sent him on his way.

Once I was given out at Leicester, lbw, down the legside when the ball just clipped my trouser flaps which had come loose from my pad-straps. A ridiculous decision. It annoyed me. But it all evens up. More than a few times I've been certain I've been run-out and I'm given in. Well, the batsman probably knows best there, he's closest, but if they say 'not out' you stay.

In 1985, Ian Botham had a little run-in with Alan Whitehead. Alan, as the whole circuit knows, is a very strict umpire. So he no-balls Ian, who is a very rare no-baller, and the batsman is caught on the boundary. But 'no-ball'. Botham says something and it all gets a bit heated. And later, Lord's fine Ian. But this never took into account his exemplary record as a fair and honest player. He likes umpires, as much as they like him.

In 1990 against India at Old Trafford, the ball nicked my shoulder but John Holder still gave me out. Okay, I probably deserved that, because when the Indians appealed I stood back and gestured that it had clipped my shoulder and I hadn't hit it. Possibly John Holder had said to himself in that split-second, 'Right, sod him. He's trying to tell me my job, so he's going.' So up went his finger and I had to go. Fair enough. For that gesture, I deserved to as well. His decision was 'out'. Why should I try to alter it with a bit of dramatics? I still don't think it was actually out. But he gave me out; so, in cricket, I was out, end of story. Apart from that tiny 'gesture' – and occasionally looking over-intently at my bat at an lbw or caught-behind as I walk away, as any club cricketer might do every weekend, I have not shown any 'dissent' in my life. I know that umpires are not going to get it right every time; that would be humanly impossible.

Nevertheless, I reckon that umpires' natural human fallibility cost me a bit after word went round that I was prone to lbw decisions – that I played 'in front of my pad' – and why not? That's the sort of thing the umpires chat about with each other in the pub after a dull day – 'Goochie's lbw's, oh, the lad's so prone, ain't he?' In other words, once wicket-to-wicket late-swing bowlers began tucking me up and getting me lbw, the buzz was never far away from our umpires' rooms that I was a sucker for the leg-before. 'Ooh, yes, old Goochie's playing across the line is something terrible these days, we just have to give him out, don't we, boys?'

In other words, your reputation catches up with you with umpires. Just as Mike Gatting's drama with Shakoor Rana caught up with him. He was out on a pretext which seemed pathetic at the time ('We totally believe you, Gatt – but you're fired!'), but it had mighty repercussions.

9

'NOT A NATURAL LEADER'

FK

Gooch, with relief, had handed the captaincy of Essex back into Keith Fletcher's safe-keeping and at once put the travails of 1987 behind him in the first match of the new 'four-day' Championship against Kent at Chelmsford beginning on 21 April 1988. On a bitter two-sweater April day he hit a best-ever 275 in 399 balls, sharing a fourth-wicket stand with Derek Pringle of 259 and, in so doing, passed Percy Perrin's record aggregate total for the county. As he had not held a bat in the middle since India pre-Christmas, he found an aching wrist beginning to trouble him when he was well into the 200s, so there was a moment's relief when, with a lazy shot, he allowed himself to be bowled by Kent's slow left-armer Richard Davis. At once, though, he could have kicked himself. As he walked back in, he was not remotely elated; he was furious. Would he ever get the chance again to get to a triple-hundred? Very many batsmen could set out their stalls for 300; but very few reach the magic figure, because the context of the match gives them no chance. And here, he had fallen just 25 runs short when 300 was there for the taking.

Still, the innings kick-started a truly vintage summer. In all, he was to hit 2,324 first-class runs at an average of 65, with six centuries and fifteen half-centuries; he only failed to make a half-century in five out of 25 matches. Essex, by the by, won this first four-dayer against Kent by eight wickets. They were chasing a target of 169 in 25 overs and won with four overs to spare, thanks to a partnership between Gooch (70) and the county's overseas signing, one Allan Border (55). Gooch was to savour many such rewarding partnerships with the Australian captain during his brief sojourns at Essex.

With Fletcher back, officially, as club captain, Gooch was now increasingly happy to resume 'doing the honours' – and certainly when Fletcher announced his imminent retirement from the game at the season's end. This time, Gooch took to the leadership keenly, even with relish, and there was no further suggestion at Essex that his batting was affected by the job. Quite the contrary. A good thing, too, because before the end of the summer he was to captain England.

In the first Test at Trent Bridge against the relentless business-as-usual West Indians, England at least halted bravely a losing streak of ten successive defeats against the Caribbean champions, thanks to a stupendous last day rearguard led by Gooch himself to save the game and win a draw of some nobility. He batted with remorseless grit, in partnerships with Gatting and Gower, for seven hours to make 146, his eighth Test century and his fourth against the West Indies.

It was during this match that a sequence of events was set in motion which topsy-turveyed England's cricket and its captaincy. The Trent Bridge Test was saved on the Tuesday. Two days later, the Fleet Street tabloid, the *Sun*, filled its front page with just five words 'GATTING MADE LOVE TO ME' and two separate single-column pictures of Gatting and a Midlands barmaid who worked in a pub near the team's hotel, the Rothley Court. On Friday morning the popular Gatting was summoned to Lord's and unceremoniously and ludicrously sacked as captain for, as selectors' chairman Peter May said, 'inviting female company to his room for a drink in the late evening'. In an accompanying speech of illogical gobbledygook, May said he believed totally Gatting's denial of any impropriety, but he was fired anyway. As Gooch had predicted, the Shakoor Rana incident was now being called to account.

But, for the moment, the whole calamity was probably summed up most aptly by the headline in the faraway *Melbourne Age* – 'GATTING CAUGHT RUMOUR, BOWLED HYPOCRISY'. In the *Sunday Times* in London, the former captain Mike Brearley wrote, 'Perhaps the TCCB does not believe Gatting's denial of the more lurid versions of the story; but in that case it not only condemns a man on suspicion, it also covers up its reasons'. And the *Guardian's* Matthew Engel wrote:

'Cricket has never functioned this way. Firstly, it is impracticable. It may be possible to control footballers totally the night before they play a dozen games a year. Cricketers often play international cricket more than one hundred days a year, never mind all the county and ordinary touring matches. It is absurd to make such strict rules and everyone knows it (we'll see how long the manager's curfew lasts). Nor is it right. Everyone knows how the game's greatest geniuses – Sobers, Miller and Compton to name only the most obvious – have made their own pre-match rules. Cricket is both a team game and an expression of individuality; a cricketer is entitled to be judged on his cricket. If he fails, he should get dropped; it's as simple as that.'

Emburey took Gatting's place for the next two Tests, Christopher Cowdrey the following one and, when he was injured, Gooch was offered the last of the West Indies series. He realized the selectors thought him a despairing 'bottom of the barrel' choice, but he enjoyed it, especially rallying the by now shattered England side to display some spunk and gumption for the first time since the opening Test at Trent Bridge; and although they lost at The Oval, they were very much in the contest until the final day. Gooch also captained England in the one-off match against Sri Lanka and then, after much idiotic indecision, the tour to India was correctly cancelled following a week of potty perversity by the Indian government, which had welcomed Gooch the winter before to grace their World Cup, and would do so the following year for their one-off and only begotten Nehru Cup.

Before the tour to India was called off, the selectors had prevaricated over appointing Gooch. This upset some – both the prevarication and the fact that it was Gooch. The old-boy network could not fathom the man from Essex. The three big guns of cricket's printed establishment boomed out. John Woodcock snorted in *The Times*:

'A good batsman, uneasy with the mysteries of captaincy, Gooch is being treated at the moment with the deference that might have attended a W G Grace in his heyday. It seems to me that our administrators have gone mad. Either that or I have.'

In the *Cricketer*, E W Swanton concurred:

'Among those who have seen most of Gooch as a captain I have found no-one who regards him as at all a natural leader, either in terms of personality or tactics.'

Only in his celebrated annual notes, written at the same time for the 1989 edition of *Wisden*, did the editor, Graeme Wright, display a fresh and warm confidence in Gooch as leader. And prescience?

'Gooch has an ability,' he wrote, 'to distance himself sufficiently from his team-mates to gain their respect as a leader. He will not be one of the lads. I do not share the concern that his batting will suffer from his being captain. Essex consider he is capable of doing the job and they are a county who plan carefully and have a commitment to success.'

Very soon we would see who was nearest the mark.

GG

In 1988, I had decided not to tour India and agreed with Robin Jackman (by now the Western Province coach) to spend the winter over there. That was England's embarrassing 'summer of the four captains'. When Mike Gatting was sacked at Nottingham, I wondered just how more ridiculous things could get. The answer was a lot more, for it began a long trail that eventually led to my being the undisputed captain of England, which, you never know, might never have happened if, first, I had stubbornly stuck to my agreement with Robin and Western Province (or if they had held me to it), and second, if Gatting's Nottingham 'birthday party' had not been picked up by the tabloid rags.

At Trent Bridge, in the first Test, we played our best cricket of the series. We had already beaten the West Indies 3–0 in the one-day internationals, and the draw at Nottingham ended a run of ten successive Test defeats against them. I did well, scoring 73 in the first innings and 146 in the second, and we made a total of 546 runs for the loss of only 13 wickets. But the West Indies scored 348 for nine in their only innings and there simply wasn't enough time for a result. So Gatt was dropped and the captaincy for the next two Tests – at Lord's and Old Trafford – was given to John Emburey. But then a problem arose. The fourth Test was at Headingley, where England have often gone into the Test without a recognized slow bowler. So obviously it made no sense to pick John as captain if he wasn't even certain to be in the team. I already knew that I was also in the selectors' minds. I wasn't actually asked if I would be prepared to captain the side, but an informal sounding-out process was put into action after the Old Trafford Test early in July by Doug Insole.

I had to tell Doug that it might prove awkward. Giving me the captaincy now would mean that they also had me in mind to lead the side on the tour of India that winter, when I had already contracted to play for Western Province. So the upshot was that the selectors brought in Chris Cowdrey who, at that time, was not even in the England team. Chris is a popular player, but he was not quite up to Test class either as a batsman or as a bowler. There's no question, though, that he was a very good captain – he had done a fine job leading Kent – so when he came in at Headingley I told him he had my full support. The trouble was, we now had a captain who had played only a few Tests abroad, as well as two key batsmen, Tim Curtis and Robin Smith, who were playing their first Test; and this against the best Test side in the world! Not surprisingly, they were much too good for us and we lost by ten wickets. But Chris didn't do anything wrong. He was made captain for the fifth Test at The Oval but, early that week, suffered an injured foot when playing for Kent. So he missed that Test, and was dropped after it. I felt sorry for him. He was pretty upset and said so. I don't blame him.

On the Tuesday before the Test I was playing at Hampstead Cricket Club in a six-a-side benefit match for a friend of mine between some of the Middlesex and Essex players. Apparently Micky Stewart, the England manager, had been trying to catch up with me all day. Eventually I was called to the public pay-phone on the wall under the stairs at the Hampstead clubhouse. The phone is next to the bar, but over the din of noisy drinkers I could hear Micky say: 'Hang on, Graham, the chairman of selectors wants a word with you.' Obviously, they were at Lord's and Micky had Peter May with him. A few moments later Peter May came on the phone and said: 'Christopher is injured. We'd like you to take the team out at The Oval. Would you accept?' 'Yes, with pleasure.' I obviously presumed it was a one-match appointment, since Chris was injured. So it didn't look as if it would affect my contract with Western Province. Then things began to change. We had Robert Bailey playing at The Oval, and he did pretty well in his first Test. Robin Smith made his first Test fifty and Neil Foster bowled brilliantly to take the first five wickets in the West Indies' first innings, when we dismissed them for 183. We left them to make 225 in the final innings, and though they got them with only two wickets down, it was England's best performance since the first Test at Nottingham. And I really enjoyed being captain. In fact, at The Oval, England had the summer's fifth captain, because on the Monday I injured my hand when dropping a catch in the slips off a no-ball from Phil DeFreitas and ended up in hospital. Derek Pringle therefore took over for the rest of the match. My finger had split open like a sausage when you put it in the frying pan. So I didn't take any further part. It was the ring finger on my left hand, not the most important one, and I might have been able to play if I'd had to. But there wasn't much point in risking it. Anyway a fortnight after The Oval came the Lord's match against Sri Lanka. I was retained as captain and so I had a say in selection.

That was the first and last time I had any close dealings with Peter May, who resigned as chairman of selectors that November. I never got to know him very well; nor, I think, did most of the other players. We felt he was a little remote, but that, I imagine, was caused by his shyness. We easily beat Sri Lanka so, suddenly, it was clearly possible that, in spite of my talk on the subject with Doug Insole, I might be asked to skipper the side on the tour of India. Sure enough, before the end of the Test at Lord's against Sri Lanka, May asked me if I was prepared to go to India as captain. Naturally, I said 'Yes'. There was no indication at that time that the Indian authorities would raise any objection to the selection of any players in the party who had links with South Africa. I had, admittedly, renewed my links by agreeing to play for Western Province that same winter. But players like Emburey, who also had South African 'connections', had played in the World Cup in India and Pakistan a year earlier without any objection from India. I don't think Lord's had done anything irresponsible or cocked a snook at the Indian authorities by selecting me and others who had played in South Africa. So I asked Western Province to release me from the contract which I had signed during the summer. I owed them that much out of a sense of decency. They were good about it and agreed to allow the contract to lapse. By then, however, the problems over the tour had blown up. There was a lot of coming and going between the Foreign Office, Lord's, and the Indian Government. It was suggested they called it off because I had been made captain. There were half a dozen of us with South African connections, but my name was as usual at the top of the list and the Indians were reported to have said that it was an affront to them to make me captain. To me that was rubbish. The previous year we had been accepted and granted visas to play in the World Cup. What had changed since? By now I didn't feel angry or even sad. I'd learned you just have to accept that politicians make decisions to suit themselves. The following year India happily accepted me to play in the Nehru Cup, a prestigious event for them, yet I hadn't made any statements or promises about South Africa to suit the politicians.

People often ask me why I was prepared to take on the England captaincy in 1988 when, only the previous season, I had resigned as skipper of Essex. The first answer is easy: there is really no similarity between the two jobs. I didn't give up the Essex job because I didn't like it, but because it was affecting my form as a batsman, and I felt I needed then to devote all my attention to that side of my game.

Increasingly, through the early 1980s, Keith Fletcher had been preparing me to take over as captain. A 'seamless' handover was what Essex prided themselves on, and when I happily took charge for the 1986 season – everyone still forgets we won the County Championship that year – I was, uniquely in the competition since the war, only the sixth Essex captain in forty years.*

If 1986 was a brilliant season for me, the truth about 1987 was that my batting form fell off disastrously, and I found myself blaming the most obvious factor – the captaincy.

The trouble in 1987 was that I was expected to be captain, manager and opening batsman all in one. It couldn't be done, and so I had a disastrous year with the bat. Not only did I have to look after the boys on the field, making sure they knew our tactics and game plans; I also had to make sure that everyone was fit and ready before I could

---

* The others were T N Pearce, 1946–49; T N Pearce and D J Insole, 1950; D J Insole, 1951–60; T E Bailey, 1961–66; B Taylor, 1967–73; K W R Fletcher, 1974–85.

even think of myself. I never seemed to have enough time to prepare myself or plan the way I was going to bat. Often, it seemed I hardly had time to put my pads on before I was out there to face the first ball. In 1989 we managed things differently – I would not have taken the job on again otherwise. Keith Fletcher had become second-team captain, but he spent a lot of time with the first team, even though he wasn't officially designated manager. The effect was to take off my shoulders a lot of the little tasks I had been saddled with in 1987 – such as organizing practice-nets and the like – rather as Micky Stewart does with the England team. So I started 1989 with the prospect of skippering both England and Essex. Unfortunately it didn't work out like that.

I assumed that the appointment of Ted Dexter as chairman of selectors, with Micky Stewart as his right-hand man, would make little difference to my personal position. I felt that having one supremo, with Micky as his aide, was, if anything, a change for the better. The quality of the selectors is much more important than how many there are. But I still felt that the TCCB had only gone half-way. They were rightly paying Ted to compensate him for having to give up his media work. But if they are going to pay big money I do not understand why they failed to go the whole hog and publicly adver- tise the post as a full-time, salaried job. Otherwise there was bound to be a feeling that the position was going to be offered only to a member of the cricket establishment or someone with access to it.

Dexter's first task, of course, was to appoint a captain to take on the Aussies in 1989, and the way that was undertaken was – from my point of view – disappointing to say the least. Three names were mentioned – David Gower, Mike Gatting and myself. Dexter inter- viewed David and Mike, but he never even talked to me. Eventually it came out that Gatt had been the first choice; but that only became public knowledge when it was later revealed that the TCCB had applied their power of veto. The only time anyone spoke to me was when Dexter rang me at home to tell me David was going to get the job. That was fair enough. David is a great guy and a great player; but I had led England in the last two matches played. David gave me a ring to commiserate. I wished him good luck and told him that I had played under him before with no problems, and was looking for- ward to doing so again.

As it turned out, the 1989 series did not go at all right, for Allan Border's side was absurdly undervalued before the Tests – because we had won the Ashes in 1985 and 1986/87 – and turned out to be a well-balanced, fiercely competitive team. A captain is only as good as his team. Look at Clive Lloyd. He had one of the best teams of all time when he was captain of the West Indies. But with four fast bowlers as good as he had, almost anyone could have skippered them in the field. It's true he was a great motivator and he really got them going. But he was nowhere near as successful when he captained Lancashire.

I seriously wondered in 1989 if I had come to the end of the road as far as Test match cricket was concerned. If I had done so, I would have departed the scene as having been, okay, a pretty good Test player on his day, but an inconsistent one who left a bit of spare promise unfulfilled. Around 4,500 Test runs, with eight centuries and an average of about 36 wasn't too bad, but by history's standards it was fair-to-middling ordinary. As far as any more bites at Test captaincy were concerned, I was certain that my name was out of the hat altogether, but it still rankled that, having had a taste for the two Tests in the summer of 1978, and having been chosen as captain of the aborted tour of India, I wasn't given another chance to prove to myself, or to 'them', if I could make a prolonged go of it.

I started the season well enough. John Stephenson and I put on 234 for the first wicket against Michael Holding and Derbyshire in early May, and, when we had our pipe-opening one-day jousts against Allan Border's touring Australians, I was made 'Man of the Series'. Then everything began to fall apart. The first Test at Leeds heralded the debut of the 'new management' firm of Ted Dexter and David Gower. David put the Aussies in, but we bowled woefully – for which no captain can legislate – and they declared at 601 for seven. We made 430 but after they declared at 230 for three we collapsed spinelessly, all out for 191, and lost by 210 runs. Although I easily top-scored with 68 on that last day, I was dismissed, lbw b Hughes, the same way I had been out in the first innings to Alderman. The lbw saga had begun.

I went straight from Headingley to Chelmsford, where I made an unbeaten century against Leicester. I was reasonably pleased with my form, so I suppose the penny hadn't dropped yet. At Lord's in the second Test I hit another 60 before I was caught behind but then, in the second innings, Alderman had me lbw again, for a duck. Alderman was a good bowler: smooth, accurate and thoughtful. His comparatively long run-up would make you think he was faster than he is. He had a good foil in Lawson, more noticeably aggressive, and, of course, in Hughes who is all heart and spirit as well as a bowler with the ability to conjure up something unplayable.

I could now see how Allan Border might have profited from those partnerships we had together for Essex. As Bill Morris had spotted (but left well alone), everyone knew by now I was one of the famous 'right-arm' batsmen who liked to hit the straight ball through mid-on or wider, or when in very good nick, hit hard across the line and sometimes uppishly through mid-wicket. So Allan at once put fielders in blocking as well as catching positions in those areas just to sow seeds of doubt in my mind. Alderman has a good late swing and is very 'wicket-to-wicket' straight; he seldom gives you much width. After the Lord's duck, things really began to prey on my mind and I asked Geoffrey Boycott, who by then was a broadcaster, if he could try to put me right.

Geoffrey gave me a 'masterclass' in the Edwardian players' bathroom, behind the dressing-room at Lord's. Basically, he said my technique had unconsciously fallen to pieces, with the emphasis on the word 'fallen'. He said I was noticeably falling away to the offside, especially when trying to work the ball to leg. 'You just aren't batting the same as when we played together,' he said. 'Your head's not right, so your body's not right, so your feet aren't right; they're shuffling across the crease.' He said that, when we used to bat together, I never moved my feet very much, either forward of back, but when I did it was always in a straight line, back or forward, never across the crease at all, however fractionally. 'You're not a "big" forward player, nor a "big" back-foot player, but just make that little half-step, either forward or back, in a straight line, never across the crease, then your head won't begin to fall away and your whole body will be more still. That'll stop all these lbw's and you'll stop wafting around in front of your pad and being a sitting target for any outswing bowler's "nip backer".'

So I went away and worked very hard at my technique. It was later that the former Essex batsman, my good friend Alan Lilley, became the county's Youth Development Officer, and he took me under his wing when he could and became a sort of personal coach. It was a very rewarding partnership. Back in 1989, however, there were no immediate benefits from that first session with Geoffrey. It was one thing knowing about possible technical faults, another to iron them out at once, so ingrained was my habit of 'falling away'. Later in the year, I had another 'in depth' session with Boycott in the indoor nets at Headingley which helped to begin solving the problem.

Meanwhile, my whole season was also falling away. The tension and worries about technique were, in themselves, exacerbating the flaws. My Essex runs dried to a trickle, and in the third Test at Edgbaston it was Lawson who got me for next to nothing – lbw again, playing across the line. No offence to umpires, but I now had the black spot on me – the 'lbw candidate'. Then at Old Trafford, Lawson got me cheaply both times (in fact, through the summer and including the tourists' match against Essex, Lawson dismissed me the same number of times, four, as did Alderman). I asked David Gower and Micky Stewart not to consider me for the next Test, the penultimate one of the rubber at Trent Bridge. In no way was I being selective about my England place, but my confidence was drained and I knew I didn't merit selection. I thought I would be doing myself as well as England a service if I went back to the drawing-board with Essex and sorted out my batting.

Both David and Micky asked me to have another think. In the end I stuck to my decision. In hindsight I think I should have played when they asked. I remember, back in 1986, I was having another grump and a glitch of poor form and confidence against India. I then suggested to Mike Gatting that I should make myself unavailable for the following Test, the first against New Zealand. 'Nonsense,' he said. So I stuck with it, and made 183 at Lord's. This time I did get my form back into a reasonably good groove with Essex – I averaged over 60 in the end – and in my place England chose Martyn Moxon, at twenty-nine no spring chicken and himself not in very good form either.

During the Old Trafford Test, the story broke of another unofficial tour to South Africa. But not for me this time, thanks very much. Of those who had been playing in the series against Australia, Broad, Robinson, Barnett, Foster, Dilley, Jarvis and John Emburey had all signed up – but the big shock to me was that Mike Gatting decided, at the eleventh hour, to go as captain. Micky Stewart tried to warn him against it right up to the last minute. Micky and Mike had worked well together when Mike was captain. But Gatt was still more than somewhat disillusioned with the powers-that-be, who had sacked him so unceremoniously and then turned him down when Dexter and Stewart proposed he take the job again at the beginning of the 1989 season. Had Mike publicly turned down the offer to go to South Africa – and, of course, the tour was cut short when all the amazing political developments began to overtake everything out there by the day – I am convinced it would have represented a full hand of brownie points at Lord's to give him the captaincy back on a plate once David, after this calamitous series, got the chop.

As the series proceeded, David became more and more detached. I felt sorry for him; England bowled like drains, and never scored enough runs to put Border's side under any sort of pressure. On the field, David stood at cover and, more and more, seemed to let the game drift, seldom trying to make things happen. He was on his way now to losing 14 out of 15 Tests in three successive series, and he knew that he would be walking the plank before too long. He and Micky Stewart were two completely different characters. One thing which was plain to see during the English depression of that series was how fast disillusion can set in for a badly beaten side.

I could sense that there was surprise around the land – in Fleet Street anyway! – that my name was not among those who had signed up for South Africa. I was not going to put myself or my family through all the hassle again; and also, in spite of my depression over certain technical aspects of my batting during that summer I still hoped desperately that, if I could solve those, I might, even at thirty-six, have a couple of Test-playing seasons left in which to improve my Test record and leave something for 'posterity' of which I could be proud – say, an average of 40 and 12 Test centuries, up there with the likes of Peter May, John Edrich, and Tom Graveney. As it happened, there was a public way of telling everyone I was not going to tour South Africa this time. I had sued for libel the *Daily Mirror* for announcing that I had already signed for the tour when I hadn't even been approached. The paper settled out of court for £18,000. It was important to me that they didn't get away with it.

With Gatting so surprisingly out of the frame, and David Gower under severe pressure and seemingly fed up with the job, I wondered suddenly if I might be in with a chance of a 'second coming'. I played under David in the final Test at The Oval, but my continuing nightmare with the bat – lbw b Alderman 0, and c & b Alderman 10 – must have made most commentators wonder if I would be on the West Indies tour in any capacity. At the NatWest final the week after the Test there was a radio discussion during the lunch interval devoted to the captaincy for the tour. The three national newspaper journalists on the panel each came up with their 'favourite' for the job. The names brought up were Ian Greig, Peter Roebuck, and Phil Neale. I didn't even rate a mention.

But by the following Saturday, after being summoned to a meeting in London on the Friday night, lo and behold! I had been handed the captaincy – perhaps again I was the only choice – and charged by the selectors with a difficult, awkward, and embarrassingly unpleasant task.

So by the end of 1989 Dexter had made me captain again. The irony of the appointment would have been relished by readers of the *Sunday Mirror*. On the Sunday of the Oval Test against the West Indies in 1988, Dexter had written in that newspaper that my captaincy had the effect on him of a 'slap in the face with a wet fish'. He was entitled to his opinion, but it is curious that, despite it, he felt able to offer me the captaincy again only a year later. He has never said a word about that article and I don't suppose he ever will.

He's not the only one, though. There are some cricket writers I find it very hard to get on with. They have a job to do and they are entitled to write what they like and voice whatever opinions they wish, even if I don't always agree with them and sometimes find them hurtful. What I find amazing is that they can write such critical remarks one day and expect me to buy them a beer and have a friendly chat with them and give them more quotes the day after. They really can't have it both ways. Their most annoying habit is when they lay down the law about tactics and captaincy and batsmanship when many of them have never played the game at any sort of level. I'm not saying that if you haven't played cricket at professional level you can't have sensible opinions about the game. But whenever they start to pontificate with an air of infallibility

I wonder what real experience and knowledge they are basing it on. Moreover, they often write one thing one day and something totally contradictory the next. And one old drunk once accused me of not getting into line against Patrick Patterson or Malcolm Marshall in Jamaica. He couldn't even have got into a straight line to walk out to the wicket!

I resolved to begin as captain as I intended to continue – by being upfront, straight, and totally honest. By a fluke, Essex's final Championship match of the season was at Leicester. When I arrived at the ground on the morning of the first day, I asked Leicestershire's captain if I could have a quiet word in the privacy of the club's committee-room. And I broke the disappointing news to David Gower that, not only had the selectors reinstated me as captain for the tour of the West Indies, but that he was not even in the team that would be going.

It was not pleasant at all. I felt rotten. But captains have to do these things. Though David might have imagined he would lose the captaincy, he fully expected to go as a senior batsman. Not even being in the squad came as a bombshell to him. I attempted to explain the reasons to him and that, having been given the job after just a bit of experience at it before, I was now determined on a fresh, dynamic attitude, else England would just go on failing.

On top of that, having done the deed, both of us had to go out and toss up. We batted, and on a bitterly cold, showery autumn day poor David had to attempt to direct operations as Mark Waugh and I both hit big centuries and put on 272 together. By the time the team had been announced publicly there was at once a beeline made for Grace Road by every scribbler and TV reporter within range. It was a difficult time for both of us. David then had to go in and bat; and Pringle got him lbw, fifth ball, for a duck. But in the second innings, when Leicester followed-on, David played one of his most beautifully crafted innings against us and his 109 in 130 balls must have satisfied him a lot in the circumstances.

The media fuss was, in fact, blowing double-hurricane force that weekend. For not only David Gower, but a certain Ian Botham was not in the tour party either.

Ian had played three Tests that summer, but achieved little, and had missed the last two with a broken finger. Nor had he set the

Severn on fire for Worcester – not one century and just 50 wickets. Nor had he any big or consistent form against the West Indies, the one blot on his dazzling record. I telephoned him with the news and said, same as with David, that of all people a former captain must know that a skipper on tour must have the squad he thinks is right for that particular job. And I said I had set my heart on changing losing attitudes, and needed concentrated single-mindedness without any non-cricketing distractions. Ian brayed and blustered a bit, said fair enough, but if he hadn't broken his finger he could have proved his indispensability and then – good for him and typically – he vowed he would fight his way back into the team and prove me wrong. Which he ultimately did, and it delighted me to have him back. And so, of course, did David. He came back a year later to play some important and enchanting innings for England.

But that 'Saturday, bloody Sunday' at Leicester in September 1989 was the first act of a long-running soap opera that was to embroil the England side for more than a few years yet.

The fixtures' calendar this time happened to work in our favour. Before the West Indies tour began after Christmas, Micky Stewart and I had over a month in India playing the Nehru tournament of international one-dayers. Many derided this as a 'nothing' competition, just another slog on the world cricket merry-go-round. But we saw it as a lucky boon and bonus to be able at once to foster a brand new spirit in our new team and to see how our inexperienced players coped in front of the passionate and volatile crowds. Also, in India, social distractions, unlike in Australia or the West Indies, are not as evident so, as well as playing some good cricket – we lost in the semi-final only after an innings of utterly one-off splendour from my future Essex colleague Salim Malik – we could 'bond' together, talk cricket and plan and discuss every aspect of strategy for the upcoming trip to the Caribbean.

Together, Micky and I put it to the team that fitness now had to be possibly the most vital consideration in any top-class sport. It always used to make me smile that, in my early days of touring with England, you would say cheerio to the players after the final Test of the summer at The Oval with a, say, 'See you in two months' or whatever, which was when you would meet up on the day before flying off for the winter tour. And then you'd be expected to go straight out into the tropical sun and immediately take on an acclimatised side.

So this time we not only had an invaluable three-day coaching session for batsmen at Headingley under Geoff Boycott – one of the game's genius players of fast bowling – which was mighty rewarding, but also a full week's intensive, live-in, physical fitness regime in Shropshire at the National Sports Centre at Lilleshall.

Cricket in India and winter practice at home were not only invaluable at getting the competitive team spirit fired up, but also gave Micky Stewart and me 'space' and time to work out our own relationship and how it would function. I know David and Micky had often not seen eye to eye nor been sympathetic to their respective roles. Very soon I found what a pleasure it was for me to be in tandem with Micky. I was wholly responsible for the team on the field and the general playing strategies, and Stewart took on all the peripheral jobs, very important and often crucial ones, which can divert the captain's concentration away from the main job in hand. He was a good link – or, rather, a buffer – with the press, which annoyed some sections, and his whole working day was devoted to the good of English cricket and its progress. Even in his most famous sergeant-major style, he was a tremendous encourager. We debated and discussed things endlessly and never seriously fell out about anything.

The 1980s suddenly became the 1990s. We were ready to go.

The run-up to the first Test match at Jamaica's Sabina Park went reasonably well, although rain ruined both the preliminary one-day internationals in Trinidad. We needed some quality time in the middle. Remembering the notorious 'terror track' at Sabina in 1986 – when Gatting had his nose smashed and I spent that uneasy, frightening morning – I was very keen to see what the new relaid pitch looked like. In fact, they all look the same in the West Indies – marble-hard, greenless, and glassy, with tiny cracks which could widen later – but it is how they play that matters. The Test pitch was scarcely a couple of yards from the track on which we were to play the pre-Test game against Jamaica. In this, I did myself the world of good by 'booking in' and hitting 239. I paced it just nicely enough so that the whole side had a bat and we still had seven overs left to bowl before close of play. Of course, their slow bowlers bowled a lot, for Jamaica had rested their two pacemen, Patterson and Walsh, but in many ways I figured that served us well, too, because we all got the vital practice warm-up we needed as well as the confidence booster for the Test. If anything, the ball had kept low. Thankfully, there was going to be no repeat of 1986.

We bowled Jamaica out for 331, and then Ned Larkins hit a fine tuning-up hundred and the other batsmen all had a knock. Although the match was dead as a dodo, I made sure that we used our last fourteen overs entitlement to give Devon Malcolm and Angus Fraser a final workout. Gus had been having some problems through the tour so far and we all exhorted him to 'let the handbrake off'. Whether this had done the trick, we would see in a couple of days. En route to this first Test, at St Kitts, Allan Lamb, the vice-captain, and I had taken just the bowlers out to dinner where we chewed over all aspects of their job and what was expected of them. Our insistence, and their determination, amounted to the same thing – don't let the West Indian batsmen tuck in with their favourite leg-side strokes, but 'bore' them to death with the tightest of tight off-stump line, Micky's famous 'corridor of uncertainty'. Like Ian Botham thinking bowling maidens is 'boring', so the majority of West Indian batsmen consider that patiently playing out a few successive maidens is an insult to their manhood. Thus they can try to break out wildly with, sometimes, unfortunate consequences.

The Jamaica cricket board hosted a celebration dinner before the match in memory of the West Indies first-ever victory on English soil in 1950 at Lord's, three years before I was born. The guests of honour from England who had played in that match were flown over: Sir Len Hutton, Godfrey Evans, Geoffrey Parkhouse, Hubert Doggart and Alec Bedser. I don't think any of these luminaries of history gave us a cat in hell's chance this time. England's last victory against the West Indies had been way back on the 1973/74 tour captained by Mike Denness. Geoff Boycott had set it all up with two superb innings and then Tony Greig had bowled them out with off-spinners.

But sixteen years was a long time ago.

10

CHALLENGING THE CHAMPIONS

FK

Gooch asked Sir Len at the celebration dinner preceding the first Test at Sabina Park in 1990 about his double-century on the same sweltering field thirty six years ago. Hutton replied: 'I was batting for nine hours. Not against pace but spin, Ramadhin and Valentine. We won the match and drew the series. Trevor Bailey never bowled better in his life.'

Cricket is richer for such diversions and comparisons. Sir Len Hutton was knighted on his retirement in 1956. He died in September 1990, thirty-seven days after watching Gooch score 333 in the Test match at Lord's against India, 31 runs short of England's individual Test batting record of 364, which Hutton himself had set in 1938. 'I always knew he was the one modern English batsman remotely to challenge my score,' he remarked when Gooch came in.

Figures can prove or disprove anything, but there is a neat and tidy relationship in *Wisden's* small-print between England's captain-openers, Hutton and Gooch. In September 1994, Gooch became only the 15th batsman in history to reach 40,000 first-class runs, and in his last innings of the season he overtook Hutton's career total to stand in this list of immortals at 40,174, just 34 ahead but, to all intents, two peas in a pod. The thirteen legendary names above them all completed 1,000 innings. *

In his career, Hutton scored 129 centuries; by the end of the

---

* In order of runs made: Hobbs, Woolley, Hendren, Mead, Grace, Hammond, Sutcliffe, Boycott, Graveney, Hayward, Amiss, Cowdrey, Sandham. Hutton needed 814 knocks to post his 40,000 runs, Gooch 888.

English summer of 1994, Gooch had logged 112, and was still determined to be going strong for some while yet. Hutton's 19 Test match centuries in 79 Tests is a better ratio than Gooch's 20 hundreds in 112. As well, Hutton hit 33 half-centuries, Gooch, to date, 45. Gooch, of course, is England's heaviest run-scorer of all time in Tests with 8,655 at the end of the 1994 home series.

Hutton captained England 23 times (W11, L4, D8); Gooch on 34 occasions with a record, when he handed in his badge, of W10, L12, D12. Only Peter May, captain in 41 matches, led England more often than Gooch.

No batting-captain has ever responded to leadership with such guzzling potency as Gooch. When he became captain his batting average was 38, with eight centuries. In his next 34 matches as captain, Gooch scored 3,583 runs, with a phenomenal 11 centuries, at an average of 58. In his 23 Tests as captain, Hutton hit 1,825 runs (average 52) with five hundreds.

If one were to attempt a book on 'The Fifty Greatest Test Match Innings of All-Time', Gooch and Hutton would be sure of at least three nominations. Both their triple centuries, of course. Hutton twice carried his bat through an England innings – for 202 against the sparkling West Indians in 1950, and for 156 (out of a total of 272) in Adelaide the following winter. Gooch's undefeated 154 (out of 252) against the West Indies at Headingley in 1991 was a genuine epic, arguably the best English 'captain's innings' of the century; he almost matched it twelve months later on the same ground against an electrically charged Pakistani attack; earlier in his career, two or three innings in the Caribbean might also qualify.

Hutton, of course, lost six prime years to the war, while Gooch forfeited three for his South African adventure. But what Hutton also missed was the regular perspiring punctuation, some would say distraction, of one-day cricket. At every form of one-dayer, Gooch's prolific diligence bestrides English record books with far and away more runs than any other batsman since the first Gillette Cup competition in 1963. No batsman has scored more centuries in limited-overs internationals (9), the Sunday League (12), or the Benson & Hedges Cup (11), although in the NatWest Trophy – the former Gillette Cup – Gooch's six centuries stand second to Hampshire's Chris Smith's seven. In the 40-overs Sunday League his record 176 in 1983 must have been an extraordinary innings, to be sure; and Gooch's highest ever Benson & Hedges Cup score, 198 in 1982, also stands mountainously challenging for some future record breaker. In the World Cups, Gooch's 897 aggregate (average 44) is head and shoulders above that of any other Englishman.

As captains of England, neither Hutton nor Gooch could quite see the point of pre- or post-match press conferences – 'You get cliché answers because you ask cliché questions'. There were many years between their 'reigns', and although neither was quite as brusque as Douglas Jardine (Reporter: 'Could you give us names of the team you'll be leading out this morning, Mr Jardine?' Captain: 'Mind your own business'), both Hutton and Gooch are credited with the line, on returning from an elongated innings of heroism and being asked 'How do you feel?', 'All right, thanks'. One time, after a couple of dropped close catches the match before, Gooch was asked a rambling pseudo-technical question about field placements which ended aggressively, 'so how will the slips be lining up for this match, captain?' Answered a lugubrious Gooch, 'Alongside the wicket-keeper, I should think.'

GG

I had convinced myself that this first Test at Sabina Park, starting on 24 February 1990, was the most crucial of my life. At the team meeting I reiterated the positive over and again. We knew we were up against it. We went to bed early. And all got up early. This was it. Vivian Richards won the toss. The coin flew 'miles' and I had to go over and look at it and say, 'Your choice, Viv'. He said, 'That's good,' but then kept us waiting till he had a head-to-head with, I presume, his manager Clive Lloyd and his bowlers, before saying, 'Graham, I'll bat'.

During the Nehru tournament in India, we had a dressing-room which had no privacy so that the world and his wife, let alone the opposition, could hear any last-moment strategies or exhortations I needed to voice. It was the same this time at Sabina. With the rebuilding going on there was only a flimsy partition between the teams' quarters, so as soon as we went on to the field we gathered into what became the famous 'huddle' – like a rugby team at half-time – where I reminded everyone what was expected of them: 'C'mon, bowlers, this-that-the-other, you know what we've determined to do; and fielders, c'mon, these bowlers are there to be encouraged, and what encourages them most is good, snappy, clean and aware fielding ...'

Those who ducked into my 'huddle' that day were Ned Larkins, Alec Stewart, Allan Lamb, Robin Smith, Nasser Hussain, David Capel, Jack Russell, Gladstone Small, Gus Fraser, and Devon Malcolm.* Two of them, Stewart and Hussain, were playing in their first Test, and Malcolm, back in the island of his birth, in only his second.

Had I won the toss, we would certainly have batted. The wicket was playing low. The old firm of Haynes and Greenidge booked in. Their opening partnership is the rock on which the foundation for so many West Indian victories has been laid. Their basis is security, but they never miss a scoring opportunity. We were keyed up, taut, but they survived our first thrusts.

When they had reached 62, Greenidge tucked a ball from Fraser off his hips to long-leg, where Malcolm was fielding. He got down and behind it, but on the bobbly hard outfield he missed it with his hands and the ball hit his knee and bounced away from him. As he was turning at the bowler's end, Greenidge saw his chance and, ignoring the age-old maxim 'never run on a misfield', called Haynes for a second run. By this time Devon had recovered, retrieved the ball, and hurled it with a thrilling, fast, flat and arrow-straight return smack into Russell's gloves at the stumps. Greenidge was run out by a yard. That dramatic first-blood encapsulated all the hard work Micky and I had put in because Devon's reputation as a fieldsman has been none too good, mainly because of his poor eyesight. On one famous day, playing for Derby, he had misfielded on the boundary, rather similar to this time, and as the ball bounced off his body his glasses had fallen off. And as he scrabbled around on all fours trying to find his specs, the batsmen ran five! Now he was in contact lenses, and at practice we had concentrated long at sharpening his fielding. Greenidge obviously knew of Devon's reputation but he forgot that the Derbyshire bowler's throw is like a tracer.

It is usually ridiculous to say that one moment turns a match. But

---

* The remaining members of the touring party were Rob Bailey, Phillip DeFreitas, Eddie Hemmings, Chris Lewis and Keith Medlycott. David Gower also played in one match after Gooch was injured.

not this time. As Jack broke the stumps from Devon's throw, we were allowed to take a grip. West Indies went into lunch at 72 for one, but the most telling figures of the morning had been Gus Fraser's application of 'the handbrake' with a spell of 11 immaculate overs for 11 runs. Our insistence on bowling those 'meaningless' fourteen overs at the end of the Jamaica game had 'grooved' Gus to perfection.

After lunch, David Capel bounded in to have Richardson and Best caught, both wafting airily. Gladstone Small reacted superbly to take a return catch from Haynes and 62 for no wicket had become 92 for four. Viv Richards survived two raucous appeals, both 'turned down' by the noisy full-house at Sabina of 13,000 as well as the umpire and then, as he does, Viv tried to hit himself imperiously out of trouble. He hit five fours in the next twenty-odd balls but always looked slightly uneasy and I was not too surprised when Malcolm trapped him plumb in front – which opened the hutch for Angus, gloriously and deservedly, to mop up the middle and end after tea with a spell of 6–3–6–5. West Indies were all out for 164, their lowest against England for thirty years. Fraser's full figures were five for 28 in 20 overs.

Ned Larkins and I had two hours to establish our reply that evening. The bowlers steamed in, as you can imagine. We survived almost one hour when, with the score on 40, I played an authentic leg-glance off Patterson, got a decent lot of bat on it, but the wicket-keeper, Dujon, swooped like a goalie at the bottom of his left-hand post and came up with a stupendous catch. After a promising start to his Test career, Alec Stewart was caught at slip fending off a fearful lifter from Ian Bishop, but when bad light stopped play we were almost halfway to their total with eight wickets standing. There was a long way to go, sure, but as the team coach took us back through Kingston and to the Pegasus Hotel that night it was full of players mighty pleased with themselves.

The next day belonged, simply, to Allan Lamb. He was proving a grand vice-captain in every way. In the field the day before he had been a tower of strength – chivvying, cajoling, geeing up, encouraging his troops. Now he set about batting the West Indies out of the game. Has he ever played better? Before he went out to bat, he fixed a new grille attachment to his helmet. 'They'll never get me now that I'm behind bars,' he cackled. Nor did they – or not until six hours

later by which time he had hit a wonderful 132. He had staunch support early on from Larkins, and then he and Robin Smith put on 172.
After Allan had saluted the crowd applauding his century, the scoreboard workers obviously had a re-think and the old thing slowly and
rather ominously cranked back his score to 99. Lamb saw this. 'No
problems,' he said, and the very next ball whistled square to the
cover-point boundary. More applause, more acknowledgement of
it. 'Blimey,' said Allan to Robin, 'that's two centuries in a day, the last
one the fastest in all history!'

The surprise was that it was Lamb's first Test century overseas.
But of his ten centuries it was his fifth against the West Indies. He was
not only a batter, but he never failed to 'carry' the fight. 'Not bad for
a one-day player, eh?' Allan chided one of the previously sarcastic
journalists at the close-of-play press conference – when we were still
batting, thanks to Jack Russell's courage and stickability, and were
178 ahead. Ideal. The West Indies surely had nothing else to do but
bat to save the match. What pleased Micky and me most was that
England had had their hands around the West Indies' throats for two
days on the trot. Usually we had the odd good day, but seldom two
in a row.

And then it was three. After Russell and Fraser had valuably
extended our lead in the morning to exactly 200, I knew we would
be in for a much more determined display from the West Indian batsmen. This was a new scenario for them. When did they last start a
second innings 200 behind?

I opened with Gladstone Small, who settled at once into his
groove, and Malcolm's 'wild card' explosiveness. The latter struck
in his fourth over when Haynes, having hit Devon for two blistering
fours, played over a fast full-toss from the same bowler which
cannoned into the base of the stumps.

Thereafter we kept nipping in exactly at the moment the West
Indies thought they had seen off the worst. From 112 for four, for
example, Best and Richards carried them to 192, with Viv fidgety
but threatening to cut loose, when Devon produced a full-length fast
break-back which hit the leg-stump as he tried to play it through the
on-side. First Devon's throw, now that, and he had contributed two
of the decisive moments of the match. By the close the West Indies
were only 29 ahead with Marshall and Walsh batting and only

Patterson to come. There was a rest day, then two days left. Surely we had them now?

But we had forgotten one thing. Rain. On the rest day it poured. We stayed cooped up in the Pegasus and prayed. When we got down to Sabina first thing next morning, the ground was under water. The rain had stopped, but the bowlers' run-ups were in a terribly soggy state and the ground staff were not exactly busy or even bothered about trying to get them dry. They seemed to knock off for a forty-minute 'refreshment break' on the hour, every hour. One of them said to me when I badgered him to get a move on – I think he was joking – 'No, ma-an, we're waitin' for a real flood of rain to come by, to save the West Indies faces'. I was getting in a real state. David Gower had arrived, writing for *The Times*, and we had a good chat. By mid-afternoon we agreed that, at home, we had played on worse, but to be honest you would have to risk injury if you let your bowlers plough through it, or they would have to bowl round the wicket and away from the footmarks. Knowing that even half an hour's play would be a bonus to us, I told the players to stay around ready to go out. But at around five o'clock the umpires had a final look and abandoned play for the day. Another overnight storm and victory could still be snatched from us. The forecast said 'changeable'.

I woke up at five past six and, with trepidation, pulled back a corner of the bedroom curtains. The sun was just glinting over the ridge of the Blue Mountains. Surely our day had dawned? Micky, next door, had been up since five but for half an hour hadn't dared to look out. Then he went straight down to the ground just to keep a 'weather' eye on the ground staff. No offence, but just in case – and, to be sure, as they were pulling off the overnight tarpaulins a huge puddle of water accidentally ran off to soak the edge of the square. Any nearer and it might have caused another delay.

As it was, the morning forecasters had got it right. It was a bliss-ful day and everything was dried for a start on time. Now it was our turn to mop up – and in no time Small pinged out Walsh's off-stump and Capel coolly ran out Patterson. We needed 40 runs to win, a for-mality, and although, disappointingly, I was caught at square-leg off Bishop when we were six short, Ned Larkins knocked them off in his first Test for all of ten years. Viv Richards sprinted to catch up with him as he ran, arms aloft, from the field. Viv shook his hand warmly, and then came in to do the same with me. (We had agreed before the match that, throughout the series, the batting side would pop into the other's dressing-room for a beer immediately after close of play each day, so that the heat of battle was not allowed to compromise cricket's friendly and sporting philosophy.)

So we had done it at last, 30 Tests and 16 years after England's last defeat of the West Indies. We did our duty by Tetley, toasting their canned product for the cameras, then the British press posse sent down a case of champagne and the party began. 'Is this the greatest moment of your sporting career?' I was asked at the press conference. 'One of 'em, certainly,' I remember saying; but I noticed it still came out the next day as 'THIS IS THE SWEETEST MOMENT OF MY WHOLE LIFE,' SAYS GOOCH. I lavished praise on the whole side. So, generously, did Viv Richards – 'We've had a kick up the arse in our own back yard and we deserved it and perhaps we needed it. But we'll be back, I promise, by the end of the series, we'll be back.' The West Indies manager, Clive Lloyd, told the press, 'Gooch had really done his homework on every one of our men and knew exactly what fields to set for them – and then his bowlers carried out the strategy to the letter.' I felt proud.

It was only lunchtime. A feeling of utter relief swept over me. I had a quiet hour, feeling absolutely whacked. Then the party began. It went on past midnight, as the empties outside Room 175 of the Pegasus Hotel testified. Every English supporter in the Caribbean seemed to be there, and David Gower, who had been captain during the awful dramas of 1986, proposed a gracious toast to the team, and after the champagne bottles had all gone from my bath full of ice, one or two of the victors themselves jumped in to cool down!

Next morning, a pile of messages and telegrams from home were delivered to my door, including one from the Prime Minister, Mrs Thatcher. There was also a copy of the *Jamaican Daily Gleaner*. Its front page had a photograph of Ned Larkins hitting the winning boundary. The headline read, 'SLAUGHTER AT HIGH NOON'.

The rains hadn't finished with us yet. As we were coming through Guyana airport to prepare for the second test, a Customs officer said to me, 'Cricket? Goochie ma-an, you'll be lucky'. What was he talking about? He explained that the full moon in March invariably signalled a full week of rain. He was dead right. And how. I sent a postcard home to the girls saying, 'It has only rained twice in Georgetown this week; once for four days and next time for three!' The same had happened ten years before, the time of the 'Robin Jackman palaver' when Boycott had told us of Cooke's South African plans. The upshot of that fateful meeting had been Guyana cancelling their leg of the 1986 tour. I was yet to play a Test on the famous old Bourda ground. Nor would I this time, for the Test match was abandoned as early as the rest day.

Some people were saying that skipping a match in the series in this way suited us, as we were already one-up. I thought that was nonsense. We were on a high and keen to press home our advantage. Ten days playing one-dayers or watching a flooded field in Guyana was not only depriving us of serious cricket but also of the razor-sharp momentum and impetus we had gained in Jamaica. Would it still be there in Trinidad?

We had a warm-up game against the Trinidad President's XI at Pointe-à-Pierre, a nice enough pitch, but in another way a real 'stinker' because it is placed slap in the middle of the world's third largest oil refinery. Nasser Hussain had sprained his wrist playing tennis in Guyana (weeks later it turned out to be broken and it wasn't right till the middle of the summer) so Rob Bailey did well to make a half-century forty days after his last first-class knock. Rob, who had been a marvellously efficient and helpful twelfth man at Kingston, fully deserved his Test chance now. Robin Smith also batted himself into form and we won well. I made a couple of 60s. The President's XI included a twenty-year-old local left-hander who scored 134 and glistened with promise: he was like quicksilver with his wristy strokes all round the wicket. I remember thinking at the time that he looked more like one of those magical little keen-eyed, fast-footed Pakistani batsmen than a typical West Indian who likes to 'hurt' the ball more. His name was Brian Lara.

At Port-of-Spain the Queen's Park Oval pitch looked greenish, so I called 'Heads' when Desmond Haynes tossed the coin (Richards was ill) and put them in. 'A good guess in anyone's cuppa tea,' as Kenny B might have said – for in no time the West Indies were 29 for five. But Carl Hooper (32) and, especially, little Gus Logie (98) came to the rescue with help from the tail, and they were all out for 199.

Logie is another untypical West Indian bat – no bludgeon, just an ingenious placer of the ball and a good improviser. At breakfast I would have been delighted at bowling them out for 199, but in the event I was annoyed because at one time they were 103 for eight. Might we yet rue those extra 90-odd runs and more than two hours? Our chairman of selectors, Ted Dexter, flew in from London that day. At Trinidad airport, he heard the score '120 for eight' and sighed. But he was almost doing cartwheels after hearing it was the West Indies batting!

It was a difficult pitch, even more so after we'd lost over two hours to rain on the second day and it sweated under the covers. But Larkins and I put on 112 for the first wicket. I was not out 83 at the close, one of my more dogged efforts, particularly as I had two boils on the inside of my thigh and a sty in my right eye. On the third day, West Indies bowled themselves back into the game, skittling us from a healthy 214 for three to 288 all out. Their openers had eight overs to negotiate in poor light before the close. Without thinking, I gave Devon Malcolm the new ball. He bowled a couple of dangerous looking bumpers, the umpires conferred, and off we came. With the slower Small and Fraser we might have picked up a valuable wicket – and as it was next morning the two master openers put on 96 to head us – and, of course, we were batting last and the cracks were getting wider.

Devon Malcolm turned the Test again, just as he had done at Kingston. Blisteringly fast, he pocketed three quick wickets and suddenly the West Indies were, to all intents, in their second innings 12 for four. They dug in nobly from that but by the close were only 145 ahead with just one wicket standing. One day to go. Unless the pitch goes completely, it must be in the bag, fingers crossed.

The morning sun was as perfect as the weather forecast. In no time we were going out to bat, needing 151 for victory and an unassailable 2–0 lead in the series. At lunch we were 70 for one, and looking good. Well, not as good as that seems – because both openers were back in the pavilion. Or rather, Larkins was, having been caught behind off Ezra Moseley; and I was having my hand x-rayed at the nearby St Clare's Medical Centre. Is it lightning that always strikes twice, in exactly the same place? Moseley had bowled me a pacy enough ball, on a length, which flew off a crack in the pitch. As I stood on tiptoe, the ball hit the top of my left hand, on the smallest knuckle. It dropped down harmlessly in front of the wicket, there was no 'bat-pad', and we took a quick single. It hurt all right, but I could still grip the bat okay, and presumed the pain would soon disappear. The very next time I got down to the other end to face Moseley, I played slightly back again to another decent-length ball. I am convinced it hit the very same crack in the pitch at the identical angle. Certainly it smashed into exactly the same knuckle. And that was that. I could not grip the bat any more. Some of the press immediately filed off stories about 'GOOCH, THE VICTIM OF DESPERATE WEST INDIES BUMPER WAR', but both Moseley's deliveries were perfectly good-length balls.

I didn't know quite what had happened – because in seventeen years of first-class cricket I had never before broken a finger. When our physio, Laurie Brown, ran on with his bag of tricks, I told him I thought it must be a dislocation. That's why those pictures, which immediately went round the world, of me in excruciating agony (which I was), show Laurie attempting to 'put back' the 'dislocation'. So off I came, retired hurt, and on my way for an x-ray. I was none too bothered – 81 more runs to get and eight wickets, plus me if needed, to fall.

At the medical centre as I waited for the x-ray, all of a sudden it seemed as though some nutter had opened up on a tin-roof with continuous machine-gun fire. 'What the hell's that?' 'Only a thunderstorm,' said the nurse. What? Only? I could not believe it. When I left the ground the weather had been sublime and sunny.

Then they told me the bottom of my finger had been badly broken in two places and I probably wouldn't be fielding again on the tour, let alone batting. That was my secondary worry, because, outside, the rain continued to pelt down, every continuing minute of it robbing us of the chance of history.

I went back to the ground, promising to return in the evening for an operation which meant them putting wires through the broken bone and the adjoining finger to lock it tight like a splint. At the Queen's Park Oval it was still raining, but not so hard. I said to put the word around that my hand had only been badly bruised, but I would be quite all right to bat if needed. Under no circumstances did we want to give any sort of fillip or a glimmer of a chance to the opposition if the game was resumed. I told the same to the press box. They would make up anything they fancied anyway.

The rain stopped. The mopping up began. The umpires announced that thirty overs were left, but we knew that in the increasing gloom nothing like that would be bowled before the light closed in. Perhaps twenty overs at the most. An hour and a half? A bit more? Only 81 needed. Easy. Desmond Haynes was under pressure in his first Test as captain. He contrived to bowl just 16 overs in all of two hours. There was an English outcry. But in fairness, in the same position, what England captain wouldn't have tried the same?

In the end, alas, we had to surrender our chase at six o'clock with 30 runs needed and five wickets down. It was my decision alone. It was almost (and literally) pitch dark. From the middle David Capel couldn't even see any of our signals from the pavilion. The umpires had already 'offered us the light' but we stayed on. A couple of quick wickets in the gloom and we might not be offered it again. It would have been irresponsible to have risked defeat, even from the jaws of victory. A draw.

So far anyway it had been the most gripping fifty-fifty sort of Test match I'd ever played in. But what a sad ending, not only to an enthralling game but also to my whole tour. I stayed with the team, of course, but Allan Lamb took over as captain to direct matters. The injury list got longer and longer. The final two Tests were back-to-back at Barbados and Antigua. We put up a hell of a scrap in the first, till running out of luck and succumbing on the last day, but were soundly beaten in Antigua because, by then, it was steam we had run out of and Fraser had had to go home after the third Test.

We had given it a 'go'. We set out as a 'together' unit, bonded and utterly determined at least, and at last, to show the world champions they could be faced down, challenged to the hilt, and that they would have to play mighty good cricket to retain their title. Which is what they had to do.

For us it was a start. Now to stay there.

11

ESSEX MEN AND A WORLD XI

FK

Gooch stayed in Antigua for a week's sandy holiday with Brenda and the three girls, Hannah, now six, and the twins, Megan and Sally, three. He returned home almost a hero. Certainly to prolonged applause. In spite of the lost series, the Jamaican victory and the dramatic draw in Trinidad had been two swallows that made the winter warm for the British public who were able, for the first time with a Caribbean tour, to watch coverage on Sky TV, edited highlights on BBC TV, and hear regular live coverage on BBC radio. Listeners also enjoyed the sounds – snap, crackle and seeth – of critics eating their words. A few months before, almost to a man, they had written off Gooch's inexperienced team. As for the captain, he had not only pleaded to be dropped for loss of form only the August before but, on return from his previous two overseas trips with England, had said he was so disenchanted that he would never be touring again. Fellow journalists who sent off the team had queued to agree with Matthew Engel's waspish comment in the *Guardian* that Lord's dispatching the unwilling tourist Gooch as leader of the Caribbean mission was itself 'like hiring a Sherpa with vertigo'. Ian Botham had said cheerio to Gooch's men with the scarcely encouraging, 'In my heart I wish the boys well, but my brain tells me five-nil'. David Gower, now briefly of *The Times* of course, and captain during the previous tour's 'blackwash', was in a vantage position to write 'that captaincy in the Caribbean reminds me of the Spike Milligan poem:

The boy stood on the burning deck ...
Twit!

Gooch and his four girls arrived back at Gatwick from Antigua on Saturday 21 April. He had telephoned to tell Essex he hoped his wounded hand would be all right for him to begin the season on the following Tuesday in the Benson & Hedges zonal Cup tie against Nottinghamshire. But on the Sunday morning, his hand still sore but no longer painful, he was early in the Chelmsford nets. Then Keith Fletcher gave him some fielding practice – and he announced himself fit to play that afternoon in the summer's opening Sunday League game against Kent. He even bowled five overs for 28, but when he batted he was at once caught off another familiar West Indian 'quick', Tony Merrick. On the Tuesday, in the Benson & Hedges Cup tie, against another, Franklyn Stephenson, then of Notts, he led Essex's stiff winning run chase with 102 in 132 balls. He was up and running.

There is no secret about Gooch's appetite for pacy West Indian bowlers as opposed to nagging medium-pacers with late swing. He likes the ball to come on to the bat and to hit it hard. Gooch may have returned from the West Indies with his reputation gloriously enhanced, but in fact he was already Test cricket's most prolific batsman against the world champions through the eighties, as the table below demonstrates. His might be the technique and style which enjoyed tucking into such bowling, certainly, but these figures are also testament to his skill, courage, determination and staying power. One of his adversaries throughout the decade, Malcolm

Best batsmen v West Indies in the 1980s

	Tests	Completed innings	Overall Runs	100s	Average	Average v WI
D B Vengsarker (I)	17	26	1119	4	44.50	43.03
A R Border (A)	21	35	1479	2	53.37	42.25
G A Gooch (E)	21	41	1717	4	45.98	41.87
S Gavaskar (I)	11	18	745	3	45.73	41.38
Javed Miandad (P)	10	18	688	2	57.09	38.22
A J Lamb (E)	14	25	864	4	34.04	34.56
D I Gower (E)	19	35	1149	1	43.42	32.82
M Amarnath (I)	11	20	655	2	42.50	32.75
R J Shastri (I)	17	28	847	2	34.19	30.25

(Qualification: 10 Test matches)

Marshall, saluted his achievement: 'His record against us at our peak proves Graham is fit to be ranked with the best batsmen of all time.'

Overall, through the decade, Gooch also scored more runs in first-class cricket (21,174) than any other batsman in the world. In 269 matches, he averaged 49.01 from 465 innings, and his 59 centuries were exceeded only by Vivian Richards, who had a slightly better average but, of course, never had to face his own bowlers!

For Essex in 1990, after that first Benson & Hedges Cup hundred against Notts, Gooch showed just how his broken hand was mended. Two days later, in the first Championship match against Middlesex, he firmly planted his battle standard at Lord's (137 off 157 deliveries). The orders from the TCCB this season were for better wickets and a ball with less 'seam'. It was a gloriously sunny summer, and batsmen were making hay long before harvest time. Not least Gooch. In early May, against Lancashire, he and Paul Prichard put on 403 for the second wicket, the highest-ever for any Essex stand. Gooch made 215 of them (28 fours and a six) and he reckons there was only one appeal against him when the ball nicked a pad just before he was out. By June, when the Test matches began – two short, three-match rubbers against New Zealand and India – in six first-class matches for Essex Gooch had scored a double-century, four centuries and 72.

Essex were on a coldly keen mission this summer, for they still felt unfairly denied the previous year's Championship trophy after Lord's had docked them 25 points for an inadequate pitch for the match against Yorkshire at Southend. It rankled with the whole team – a fine, yes, but the players themselves had no control over the wicket and, anyway, they did not need the pitch's help to beat the woebegone Yorkshire side of that time, who finished four points from the bottom of the table. The 25-point forfeit allowed Worcestershire to win the title by default, by just six points from Essex.

Earlier that summer, of course, Essex had also been beaten at Lord's in the Benson & Hedges Final off the last ball when Gooch's England colleague, Nottinghamshire's Eddie Hemmings, needing four to win, slid John Lever's last delivery dramatically to the fence at deep backward point. It was good for Hemmings but a traumatic moment for the sterling JK, who was in his final season for the county he had served so admirably.

Gooch blamed himself. As captain, he and Lever consulted and adjusted the field prior to the final delivery. JK said he would bowl a leg-stump yorker. An over or two before, Gooch had noticed with surprise that Hemmings, even more of a county veteran than Gooch and Lever (he first played for Warwickshire in 1966), had agriculturally lolloped a couple over mid-wicket, not one of his usual strokes. A leg-stump yorker might just feed this new clout in Eddie's batting locker. So JK, a supremely cool and experienced last-over operator, agreed they post a mid-wicket, a move which meant bringing up their man from deep cover-point on the fence to backward point on the edge of the square.

Like a switch being turned off, the din of the Lord's throng becomes a pin-drop silence. Hemmings is on guard. Lever is up, bowls his spot-on leg-stump yorker. As JK is in his unchangeable act of delivery, the wily Hemmings takes a large stride to leg – and slides the ball off the bat to the non-existent deep cover-point and victory for Nottinghamshire. 'I agonized for weeks afterwards,' says Gooch years later. 'Had I let Essex down? Had I let JK down?' Of course he hadn't: a captain has only nine men to deploy on a huge field. But what the incident did manage to do, for any unbiased romantic that is, was to square some sort of heightened dramatic unity; for was not this bowler to whom his younger captain had now supplied a deep mid-wicket instead of a cover-point in his last big match for Essex, the very same fellow who allowed his clapped-out silver-painted Vauxhall Victor to explode near the Rayleigh Weir roundabout when transporting Gooch to his own first big match for Essex all of sixteen summers before?

While the broiling summer of 1990 may have been draining in terms of stamina, it was glorious in terms of personal achievement. Essex may have been only runners-up to Middlesex in the Championship but, that disappointment apart, this thirty-seventh summer of his life was, quite simply, Gooch's annus mirabilis. In 11 matches for the county, he never failed to record at least 50. Only another hand injury, this time a broken thumb suffered while fielding early in the match against Kent in the penultimate county fixture, cost Gooch the opportunity (with a possible four innings left) of being the first in thirty years to post 3,000 first-class runs in the season. Gooch ended with 2,746 runs at an average of 101.70; only one other, Boycott twice, has averaged three figures in a summer. In all forms of cricket in 1990, Gooch hit 18 hundreds. 'Cash in when you can. Tomorrow it could all end,' as Gooch likes to say.

He also found a stable new opening partner for the Test matches, a young one, who possessed the calm of a Boycott and the bottle of a Gooch. But his and Atherton's first two opening partnerships were 0 and 0!

GG

After our shaky start against New Zealand in 1990, it was tremendous to forge a new opening partnership with Mike Atherton. Our styles and temperaments, I believe, perfectly complement each other. When I failed Mike was doubly determined to hang in there and make runs, and vice versa. From the first time I saw him bat I rated him highly and reckoned he could make it to the very top. He is technically very organized, proficient and unflurried; he does not panic. Moreover, he gives nothing away.

For Essex, John Stephenson was now my settled partner but, sadly for all of us, my old long-time opening 'mucker', Brian Hardie, retired at the end of the 1990 season to take up a splendid job as coach at Brentwood, one of the county's leading public schools. We all wondered how long it would be before we would see a generation of his former pupils growing up to bat in Brian's inimitable style.

Brian played his first game for Essex in 1973, the same summer as I began. He was a marvellous character: a great team man much loved by everyone and a top player who made regular and crucial forties and fifties, and important big scores too. And if he was having a bad run with the bat, as everyone does from time to time, he was still fully worth his place as a fearless fielder at bat-pad. In fact, he took over 400 catches for us.

Within a fortnight of coming down from Scotland to join us, Brian was nicknamed 'Lager'. He was popular throughout the whole county circuit, but he had an unorthodox batting technique in which his body would go one way and his bat the other. His legs would be all over the place. It looked shocking, almost primitive. But it was massively effective. He used to infuriate bowlers, especially the pace merchants who couldn't believe why they didn't dismiss such an 'incorrect' batsman. He would plunge his leg down the wicket, play and miss, play and miss, and then crack the next ball through the covers like a bullet. Next delivery he would hook savagely – and the ball would get a top edge and fly down to third-man for a one-bounce four. Then he would cut, and the ball would whistle to the fine-leg boundary. Unbelievable. By now the bowler had a real 'hump', and decide that a yorker should settle this nutter – and Brian would smash it back straight, nearly breaking the bowler's ankle on the way to the sightscreen.

I'm reminded of the old Scottish broadsword, the claymore. When our man from Stenhousemuir was on the rampage the word would go out 'Lager's claymoring him!' and everyone would rush out to watch. It was like the January Sales: 'Everything Must Go!'

The first year we won the Championship in 1979, we went to Bournemouth to play Hampshire. This raw young West Indian called Malcolm Marshall had arrived to terrorize everyone. Our all-rounder, Norbert Phillip, had been on the West Indies tour with Malcolm that winter and reported back: 'He's quick, he's bloody quick all right'. So JK runs through Hampshire on a fast green bowler's wicket, and then Marshall gets me, Kenny McEwan and Fletch. Hardie comes in at no. 5, and from the very start he begins to 'claymore' Marshall to every point of the compass. He would back away and smash him over extra-cover's head, or plunge that leg down the pitch, then swivel and clock him over square-leg. Marshall was hit all over Hampshire that day! Every time he was hit, he took a longer run and came in even faster. Hardie made 146 not out to ensure we won the match. Ever since, whenever Marshall played against Essex, he would arrive on the first day and enquire, 'He's playing? Hardie playing today? He open? I bowl very fast today if Hardie open. Have to get rid of Hardie.' And usually he did. Malcolm never forgot the day Hardie hit him out of sight for 146.

Another bowler whom Brian infuriated was Surrey's paceman Sylvester Clarke. The way he played him, in that almost nonchalant style of his, convinced Clarke that 'Lager' was taking the mickey. Clarke could be a very dangerous bowler indeed on his day. Once, our spinner and tailender, David Acfield, came in at The Oval to join Kenny McEwan. Clarke was in full cry. David announced definitely and positively, 'Kenny, I'm not coming down that end, this ball, next ball, or any effing ball! And you make sure that I don't.' Another time, in 1983, on a humid evening at Chelmsford when the ball was swinging like a boomerang, Sylvester was soaking in the bath after his long bowl, when they told him another wicket had fallen. Thinking his Surrey mates were trying to wind him up, he continued relaxing. When he finally got out of the bath, he saw it was no joke and that, as no. 10, he was next man in. He went out still buttoning up his shirt, and hit the only four of the innings to save Surrey the humiliation of recording the lowest first-class total in history. They were bowled out for 14!

As well as wielding his magnificent 'claymore', Hardie was for years the Essex 'travel manager'. He would work out the routes and take the van with the kit, plus a couple of other players, while the rest would come in two or three cars. Most county sides do the same, although Lancashire have usually taken a coach for the whole team. A few seasons ago when we had a one-off Sunday League game against Yorkshire at Scarborough, Derek Pringle, our off-beat gourmet and real ale expert, suggested it would be fun to make a weekend of it and all go up by coach on the Saturday afternoon.

So the kit is loaded into the hired coach at Chelmsford, and we are due to rendezvous with 'Pring' himself and young Nick Knight on the M11 flyover roundabout at the Junction 11 turn-off for Cambridge. When we get there, they are nowhere to be seen. We cruise around in the rain a few times but to no avail. I ring both their homes on my mobile phone. They had left base in good time. Finally someone spots an old, seemingly abandoned golf umbrella on the grass bank of the roundabout. Pringle and Knight are huddled under it. A bad start. We are already late.

Then Pringle announces, 'Right, we're going to the Blue Bell at Wentbridge. Driver, turn off the motorway at Doncaster. Top-class and genuine Yorkshire ale and food.' Wentbridge village – I had been there when we played at Leeds – might be all right for beer and for cars, but it is not suitable for coaches, and of course ours gets stuck in the narrow street. Then we had to wait three-quarters of an hour for the pub to open. The beer and the meal did make up for it – when we finally got it. So, at last, when we arrive in Scarborough it is far too late, even for the night-owls. Everything is closed.

Next morning, we get to the ground and unload the kit. Pringle's kit isn't there. Nothing. He says he'd left it at Chelmsford and asked me to load it. Well, perhaps he had, and I presumed I had. Had he left it in the right place? He hadn't. It's now one o'clock and we're starting at two. It's a Sunday, and borrowing kit is not all that easy when the man you're lending it to is 6ft 6in and takes size 13 boots. And I need him to play. We are very much in contention at the top of the table.

I go up to the Secretary's office to ask if any sports shop just might be open in town. It is a holiday resort, after all. Yes, there's one. I ring him up. 'Any size 13 cricket boots?' 'Sorry, lad, best I can do you is a size 12 in Reebok trainers. I'll bring them down to the ground for you.'

So I pay £35 for them, and Pringle goes out looking like Worzel Gummidge with a borrowed untucked shirt, half-mast trousers six inches too short, and no socks to cover up his hairy shins because he can't get the shoes on as well as socks; and anyway his toes are all crunched-up inside them, it's a damp field and he'd slip all over the place, so he doesn't bowl anyway. He just stands at mid-on and mid-off looking foolish all through the Yorkshire innings. So I have to bowl – and I get Moxon and Kellett, their two openers. Just to rub it in for Derek.

Pring bats and gets a good 20-odd just when we need it. I overtake Dennis Amiss's all-time Sunday League aggregate number of runs and we win by three wickets.

Back in the coach, we cannot get out of Scarborough for hours what with the traffic jams and windy little hills that are too small for the bus. Everyone is hungry and thirsty. We ring the Blue Bell at Wentbridge. They'll only serve us if we are there by 10.30. We arrive with five minutes to spare and eat and drink merrily. Well past midnight we drop off Pringle and Knight, first stop in Cambridge – and Pringle has long been fast asleep by the time we unload at Chelmsford and then have to drive ourselves to our own homes. I get to bed nearer four than three-thirty.

It would be Essex CCC's last-ever coach journey. And I've still got those £35 size 12 Reeboks in my cupboard at home.

In my first years, when Kenny McEwan was given the 'perk' of that old team van with a kitchen chair in the back, there was often great haste to get to an 'away' hotel as soon as possible the evening before a match started, even by teatime, so we could all be ready to meet up and go out on the town together. I suppose the younger ones still do that sometimes, but I never liked beer as a kid – much too bitter, literally – so I used to have cider a few times. I never was a heavy drinker, but in South Africa I really began to enjoy a couple of glasses of good red wine. In the middle years on the circuit I used to have a few beers. Say I'm at Headingley for a Test match, and we're staying at Bramhope, as we often do – after a long day in the field a couple of pints, even three, up the hill at the Fox & Hounds obviously does more good than harm. But that's what, 12–15 pints over a six-day stay at the most? That would certainly be my limit now. Too much affects me, and I do know what a hangover is like!

As a captain, I understand the value, not only of the need to unwind but of the social side of the game. So I've never told anyone not to drink; I just occasionally say to a player, 'Look, I've been through it, most older players have, we've all done it and might do again, but just be sensible and don't let it affect your performance tomorrow.'

Normally, I get down to the hotel for a county match around nine o'clock the previous day, and I'll like to meet up with the players, especially at places like Taunton or Worcester or Canterbury, old traditional cricketing 'county towns' with genuine character. J K Lever was always the master at identifying the best Indian restaurant in the vicinity. On tours abroad we mostly stay at hotels with all the facilities, like the Hilton or the Hyatt, but they often are so alike and 'soulless' that you would never choose to spend an evening in the cocktail-bar. And although a week or two under the palm trees might be enviable enough, when it becomes three or four months that feeling of enjoying the cricket but longing for home can become very wearing.

But you don't have to be abroad to get that particular feeling. For matches at Lord's, for years and years, many Test and county teams would regularly stay at the Clarendon Court hotel on the Edgware Road, just a quarter of a mile down the hill from the Grace Gate. Then what was first the Westmoreland, then the Regent's Park Hilton and the Swiss Cottage Marriott were built, so there was a greater choice of places to stay near Lord's. I remember at the end of play in one Test when Derek Randall popped into the Cornhill sponsors' tent before returning to the hotel, doubtless practising his 'forward-defensives' as he ambled along the pavement. He gets to reception, asks for the key to his room, takes the lift up, opens the door, goes in – and has a ten-minute row with the fellow in there who is none too pleased at being disturbed. They each insist it's their room, until a bolt out of the blue hits Derek and he realizes he's in Room 416 of the Clarendon Court hotel, not the Westmoreland where he spent the night before.

Typical Randall, head in the clouds. A law unto himself, at the crease as in life. I shared a room with him on the 1978/79 Australian tour. Every night he would come in, fill our bath to the brim, jump straight in and the bathroom and half the bedroom would be flooded. 'Hey, hang on, Arkle,' I'd say, 'don't fill it so ruddy full!' 'All right, son, all right, son, sorry,' he'd say in that Retford way of his. But next day he'd do exactly the same. Every night the place was like a lake.

So I was pleased to say farewell to 'Arkle' when Derek's wife Liz and their little son Simon came out for a visit in the middle of that tour. He was so named, after the racehorse, for obvious reasons. What helped make him such a superb fielder was his hyper-activity. I remember watching him playing with Simon, who was about three or four. Normally, when a father plays with a son it's the adult you hear saying after a while, 'Hang on, son, give me a break for a minute, just let me have a little sit-down then I'll play with you later.' But not in the Randall household. There they were, playing around together, and suddenly it's Simon saying, 'Okay, Daddy, that's enough, just let me have a little rest for a minute.'

On that tour, at Adelaide, once we'd both got out, we put on our blazers and took a stroll round the ground. We were going along that grassy bank on the opposite side to the old pavilion and press-box when two Australian girls asked us for our autographs. So we obliged and, to pass the time of day, asked them how they were enjoying the cricket. One of the girls' boyfriend came back from the bar with a drink. Derek says to him, in typical matey manner, 'How y'doing, all right, then?' The Aussie bloke just looks the famous England cricketer up and down and says, 'Clear off, Randall, I've seen better heads on a crab!'

The Adelaide Oval is a super venue with long, straight boundaries and numerous seagulls. It's a ground steeped in history. Melbourne and Sydney are great cricket stadiums but, down my time, 'improvements' have changed them. The Sydney 'hill', for instance, is now all covered with plastic seating, and the famous old, evocative scoreboard-building is almost hidden and used as a groundsman's junk shed. At Lord's, by far my favourite ground, the new stands – the Mound with its distinctive vanilla-ripple roof awnings, and the Compton and Edrich stands at the Nursery end – even enhance the 'feel' of the place.

In my early days with Essex, Lord's was officially one of our 'home' grounds. Our Contract of Employment stipulated that 'matches at Lord's, The Oval, and Cambridge University shall be deemed home games'. In other words we had to go home and back each day of a match. I even used to do that for Test matches, but these days you cannot confidently drive up and down to Lord's or The Oval each day of a match. The traffic and the 'cones' make it a nail-biting lottery.

During long journeys on the summer circuit most players listen to their car music tapes, and who shares journeys with whom can well depend on a mutual taste in music. Although not in one particular case: of all the Essex regular pairings and sharings, the most eccentrically and diametrically opposed duo must be that of Derek Pringle and our old scorer Clem Driver. Pring lives where he studied, at Cambridge, and Clem lives en route in Langley in Essex. They say Clem is slightly deaf – and I'm not surprised, because all that travelling with Pringle means his ears have been bombarded by Derek's self-spliced banks of sound from such bands as the 'DB's', 'The Flaming Groovies', 'Half Japanese', 'American Music Club', and 'Lee Perry and the Upsetters'.

I'm more of a Radio 4 or Radio 5 man. I prefer listening to current affairs or 'talk' programmes as I find music can be too 'soothing' and can sometimes make me drowsy. I find it easier to concentrate when someone's talking. I also really enjoy audio books, but best of all are those books and plays on tape which have been dramatised by the BBC, with a cast of actors and sound effects. At the moment I'm listening to John le Carre's *Smiley's People*, an audio book on *Inspector Morse*, and two BBC tapes of the *Best of Steptoe & Son* and *Blackadder*. I have also one of our exclusive Essex cassettes, an interview of about an hour with one of our players 'in conversation with' the broadcaster, Ralph Dellor, who for ages has been a good friend of the Essex club.

One of these is an interview with Neil Foster. Neil played 29 Tests for England, but it could have been many more. I was interested to hear him say how he often seemed to be brought back for the second Test of a series, at Lord's, 'to bail England out after they'd lost the first'; but he would always be made to bowl from the 'wrong' end to use the famous 'ridge'. He would have little success. So, inevitably, he would then be dropped for the third Test.

Like many new-ball front-line bowlers 'Fozzie' was always a bit of a moaner, especially in his days under Keith Fletcher, because his early entry into the England team had made him ambitious to hang on to his place. As he matured he became less insecure and began to realize how much the club valued him. He would have played more for England if he had not been so wracked by injuries. For Essex he fought through thirteen operations, nine on his knees and four on his back, and always returned to give it his wholehearted effort, even when his captain had first diplomatically to ignore the colourful flak and whinges from 'Mr Angry' about being over-bowled. I remember, in his last season for Essex, when Neil was bowling a tremendous spell against Lancashire at Old Trafford. It's quick – the ball bouncing and darting this way and that and batsmen nicking it anywhere – but what's worse, we're not fielding well for him. The final straw is a flukey inside-edge from the batsman that sends the ball rattling down to fine-leg, where the fielder gormlessly allows it through his legs for a boundary.

Neil looks at Barry Meyer, the umpire at the bowler's end. 'Barry, old boy,' Neil announces calmly, 'sorry, but you're not going to like this at all.' At which point Neil takes a run at the stumps and, with a follow-through as if he's taking a penalty at rugby, CRACK!, he sends two of them flying out into the outfield. Barry, of course, had to report him, and he was fined £250. 'For how I was feeling at that moment,' said Neil, 'it was cheap at the price.'

Neil did a grand job for the county when he stood in for me as captain and we won the Championship in 1991. He was elected the Championship's Player of the Season that year.

With Foster and then Pringle retiring one after the other, the county found themselves in a transition period. Promising batsmen don't seem hard to come by, but in English cricket there is a real dearth of potential top-class bowlers. When JK was our spearhead, with Foster and Pringle alongside, we must have had the best front-line attack in the country.

Pringle had a different sort of competitive cussedness to Foster. He used to play Devil's Advocate just for the hell of it. It used to disconcert some of the club's younger players because they felt that this 'scholar' was talking down to them. There was always something of the 'perpetual student' about him. Pring was a far better bowler than many thought, and could have been a better bat than he realized. When he played for England in his maturity he was so important a part of the set-up that I was always surprised when he attracted some 'stick' from crowds around the country mostly concerning his ungainly, beanpole build, or about his unconventional taste in music. But he was a thinking cricketer, very bright tactically, and on his day a marvellously nagging bowler with disconcerting bounce. In one Test match, going out to toss with Viv Richards, I mentioned that Derek was unfit and wasn't in our XI. Viv looked delighted and paid Pring a genuine compliment: 'He's matured into a high-class bowler who's never quite there for the drive'.

Viv Richards, of course, is one of cricket's all-time legends. I could never consider myself in that sort of bracket, but I am proud to have done well with the talent I have. I know I have a real ability and that I have worked hard to make every ounce of it pay off. I am immensely warmed that, as the end of my career became imminent, I could see myself riding high in the record books. Although I am no 'legend' of the game, when I look back I get a real buzz and satisfaction that I am up there near the top of the list, with Sir Gary, Sir Len, Sir Don, and Sir Jack, just as plain 'Graham Gooch'. Of my contemporaries, Sir Richard Hadlee is rightly labelled a legend, so was Viv, and Ian Botham, and possibly Sunil Gavaskar. Brian Lara doubtless will be one day. One of the genuine regrets of my career occurred when I was picked in 1973, the year of my first-class debut, to play a Sunday League game against Nottinghamshire at Trent Bridge. Sobers was going to play for the opposition, and I was so excited about that. But it rained all day. When my grandchildren ask, it's a pity I won't be able to say that I played against 'The Greatest'.

In my early days I played against Barry Richards towards the end of his Hampshire career. Just once, I also walked out to open the innings with him. It was in one of those festival matches in Jesmond in the late eighties. They invited me to play, and I was saying I would think about it when they told me who else was playing: '… and also Barry Richards'. 'Right, count me in,' I said without hesitation. It wasn't a huge partnership but we did put on a few runs, which was very satisfying because he had been 'The Hero'. At the crease, Barry had so much time, and such a correct technique; he was a wonder-fully clean striker of the ball, with unlimited strokes, superb shot selection and everything in place. On top of that, he was a spectator's delight. What a tragedy that the South African ban scarcely allowed him a chance to display his qualities at Test level.

Whenever I think of putting together an all-time World XI made up of those I've played with and against, Barry Richards takes first strike. As for my own Test opening partners, Geoffrey Boycott would be my favourite to bat with, no doubt about that, and second would be Mike Atherton; but neither of them will walk out with Barry Richards to open my World XI innings. Nor will either of that stupendous duo, Gordon Greenidge and Desmond Haynes, who have represented the most glittering and consistent opening part-nership not only of my generation but of many before. To stride out with Barry for my team I must choose the 'little master', Sunil Gavaskar. There was near genius about the man. Neither Haynes nor Greenidge ever had to face their own West Indies bowling, while Gavaskar made thirteen centuries against the West Indies when they were dominating world cricket, including two in the same match twice. His feet were never out of position, but what struck me most about him was that, in spite of his monumental concentration and patience, every time you bowled a fractionally poor ball at him he was ready for it, and it would go for four.

To follow my openers, Barry Richards and Gavaskar (if ever they got out) I would have a no. 3 and a no. 4 who were chalk and cheese; two top-order men, a right-hander and a left-hander, who have dom-inated my career in their totally different ways. My man at first-wicket down would not so much walk in as strut. It would, of course, be Vivian Richards. Viv is a very proud man, he looks it, too, and not only as he approaches the wicket. Once down at the business end and ready to go, he exudes the pride and command of an emperor. It never leaves him. He looks at bowlers and fielders as if to say, 'I'm Vivian Richards, I'm the main man out here, I'm the boss, and you're not going to forget it either'. So he puts the eye on the bowlers and, as often as not, reduces them to quivering wrecks. Viv had presence, power, strokes, everything – but most of all he had a burning self-belief.

At no. 4 or no. 5 I need to balance my side with a left-hander. My South African sojourns allowed me to witness Graeme Pollock batting at close quarters. Even if he was not in the full bloom of his wonderful prime, it was a privilege to see such a genuine left-handed hall-of-famer. As it was a pleasure on many occasions to share partnerships for England with another blond left-hander, David Gower, who had bravery, instinctive class, and elegance beyond measure. But my no. 4 just has to be Allan Border, a man with determination, guts, character, and a massive amount of technical skill. Allan is the man I would ask to bat for my life in a pressured situation on a bad wicket. He is Mr Dependable. When he played briefly for Essex he showed a tremendous capacity for application and going about his job as if it was a Test match, which was heart-warming and a very meaningful example to the club's young players.

What about my no. 5? I could put up a good case for a number of batsmen of my time; for instance one or other of the Chappell brothers, or Martin Crowe. The latter has played some splendid innings for New Zealand, none better than his century on a gammy leg against England at Old Trafford in 1994 (when he also had the flu). His footwork then was absolutely brilliant, a model for any player, young or old.

But even that does not allow Martin to do more than 'nudge' this selector. In view of probably the most brilliant innings I have ever witnessed, my no. 5 has to be Javed Miandad. Of course, I have seen Javed play many a superb knock for Pakistan in Test matches, but his innings for Glamorgan against Essex at Colchester in September 1981, on a broken, turning pitch, was nothing short of miraculous. He scored 200 not out in Glamorgan's 311. Only three other men got to double figures in that innings, with the next top score 36. Keith Fletcher had declared on the last day to leave Glamorgan (captained then by our former team-mate Robin Hobbs) to get 325 at a run a minute. When Javed took guard they were 7 for two. In no time that became 44 for four.

As well as John Lever and Stuart Turner, we had David Acfield and Ray East, two gifted and high-class spinners. The ball was turning square and we were crowded round the bat. Javed played every stroke known to man, and then some more, with quite astonishing improvisation. He never played a false shot. His partners hardly needed to play a ball, so precise and mischievous was his farming of the bowling. Glamorgan needed less than 100 runs to win when the seventh wicket fell at 227; and then came the most fantastic passage of all. For Robin Hobbs himself was next man in – only to be out first ball. But he had come in at 227, and was out for his duck at 270, all of eight overs later. Javed had contrived to face every single one of those 48 balls! When the last man came in, 34 runs were needed. Javed organized 20 of them before no. 11 was lbw. Javed was on 200 not out; he had failed by 13 runs to reach the winning target. It was a breathtaking performance.

So with a batting order of Barry Richards, Gavaskar, Viv Richards, Border, and Javed Miandad, the balance of my side now needs an all-rounder. There have been no end of true greats in my time – even though Gary Sobers is disqualified because it rained that day at Trent Bridge. When this lone selector thinks about it, funnily enough, the choice seems reasonably easy: Mike Procter, Imran Khan or Kapil Dev. I'm tempted to think again of the first of those, but the overpowering choice above either of these has to be Ian Botham, a much better bat than the others and, at his peak in the late seventies and early-to-mid-eighties, totally irresistible. Even in a line-up such as this one he would still attempt to dominate the dressing-room, supremely confident in his own ability and making sure, in the most rumbustious way, that everyone knew he was. He would be full of beans and honest bravado, especially when burning the candle at both ends. It's the way he has always lived his life and played his game – and it is impossible to fault his blazing career at its peak.

At no. 7 I will play my wicketkeeper. With respect to everyone else (and there have been some brilliant men with the gloves in my time), to me there is only one possible contender. Alan Knott was truly a one-off all-time great, besides being a one-off eccentric as well –

different foods would have to go on different plates, even different toothbrushes used for different teeth! When helmets came in, he contrived a sort of pulley gadget with a weight on the end which he hooked onto one of those little leather, old-fashioned cyclists' hats. He would use this in exercises to build up his neck muscles because, he said, the helmets were so heavy. Alan was almost a genius as an inventive batsman and a fantastic wicketkeeper. In the end, England didn't play him because he was fed up with touring, but he was so good that they should have let him play in any Test he chose.

So with Knott at no. 7, I need three pace bowlers and (with Viv and Allan Border able to turn their arm as well if necessary) a spinner. I know I played Tests against Dennis Lillee and Jeff Thomson, against Imran Khan and Kapil Dev and Richard Hadlee, not to mention the splendid battery of West Indians like Andy Roberts, Michael Holding, Colin Croft, Joel Garner, Courtney Walsh, and the tremendous Curtly Ambrose. So how do I separate, say, the different attacking styles of Lillee and Holding and Hadlee? First, though, I must quickly put down my absolute ace man on the list and that, without a doubt, has to be Malcolm Marshall. He was simply the most brilliant fast bowler of my time: terribly awkward for me to play and very quick. He was always wonderfully aware and intelligent, always plotting and probing. He could swing the ball late either way or cut it back off the pitch. He was a true, thinking bowler, a schemer who would look to manoeuvre your batting technique into insecure and vulnerable corners. His strike-rate is proof of his greatness. And he can bat a bit too.

I need two more pacemen, then, to fight over the new ball with Malcolm. I'm ruling out Lillee because I only faced him in my early days. Nor, however much I try to convince myself, can I quite squeeze in Holding or Hadlee. And is there room for Garner's yorker? Alas, no. I know I personally had particular trouble with Terry Alderman's style of bowling, but on a general all-time level he would not make my top ten. I'm also resisting the romantic idea, which one can be prone to in games such as this, and hark back too much into the past, to one's youth, and think that everything in the old days was better. I am seriously tempted to have as my two other pace bowlers – in their case they can fight over the old ball – both of those brilliantly hostile Pakistanis, Wasim Akram and Waqar Younis. But that would mean leaving out Curtly Ambrose – and no selector in his right mind would do that – so Wasim sneaks in ahead of Waqar.

Up to my final tour, the very best spinner I ever faced was another Pakistani, the demon leg-break bowler Abdul Qadir. It really says something about the impact Shane Warne has had on the game, since he so dramatically burst upon us, that the Australian who calls me 'Mr Gooch, sir', must have Qadir's place.

So my World XI, those all-time greats against whom I played, reads: Richards B, Gavaskar, Richards V, Border, Javed Miandad, Botham, Knott, Wasim Akram, Marshall, Warne, Ambrose.

I am privileged to be the team's manager and baggage-man. All we need now is a twelfth man. Not to be drinks' waiter (that could only be J K Lever!), but to be an ace fielder if needed. Another difficult choice. The South African Jonty Rhodes is a tremendous performer. In their time, Derek Randall and David Gower dazzlingly patrolled the fringes of the square for England, with Derek truly outstanding, although the most 'classic' English cover-point during my career has probably been Paul Parker. Near the wicket, in that crucial deep gully or shortish backward-square position, Chris Lewis and Nasser Hussain are as good as any I've ever seen. Then Roger Harper would be a lethal fielder anywhere, close in or out deep. So would Viv Richards in his prime. And if we are talking of slip fielders, I would be happy to open the bowling myself if my slip cordon comprised Mark Taylor, Ian Botham, and Graeme Hick. But for my twelfth man, for old time's sake as well as for genuine reasons that he was the best, I would bring back from his native Barbados Keith Boyce, to thrill the crowds at Essex again. Keith was the first genuinely great fieldsman I ever played with, so wonderfully athletic, and with a throw from the farthest boundary which was as arrow-flat as it smacked into the wicketkeeper's gloves as when it left Keith's hand.

In the meantime, there were some quality players to face up to in the forthcoming 1990 summer series. Would I be able to make my mark?

12

ALL RECORDED ON PAGE 333

FK

Gooch followed the Trinidad carnival of broken bones, floods and time-wasting by taking guard in a Test match in early June 1990 at Trent Bridge against New Zealand and Richard Hadlee. And at once came another personal record – the first 'golden' duck of his Test career, lbw to Hadlee's first ball. It was not an auspicious start for his brand new opening partnership with the young Lancastrian and Cambridge blue Michael Atherton, who went on to make 151. In the second Test at Lord's the partnership again failed to register, this time Atherton going for nought. In the second innings the two of them opened with a substantial enough partnership of 68, and in the third at Edgbaston they established England's victory from the first with a stand of 170: Gooch 154, Atherton 82. This was Gooch's ninth Test century. Since his last in 1988 he had scored seven Test fifties, plus 75, 84, and 85. This time he took forty minutes to move from 95 to 100. It was England's first series win at home for five years.

Atherton's Lancashire colleague, the dashing middle-order left-hander Neil Fairbrother, had managed only 40 in four innings against the New Zealanders, and so, for the opening Test at Lord's of the three-match rubber against India, David Gower replaced him. Gooch had been disappointed with Fairbrother's lack of runs in those two matches, but in Essex's match against Lancashire at Colchester on the eve of the Test, Fairbrother had illustrated his class in a beguiling stand with Atherton of 220 which set up an almost ludicrously stiff last innings run-chase for Essex of 348 in only 54 overs which they got, Gooch heading the charge with 177 from 152 deliveries. And so to Lord's for the first Test against India.

India's captain, Azharuddin, won the toss and, although the pitch was fresh and there was some morning humidity in the air it was a surprise when he asked Gooch and England to bat. It nearly paid off, however. Atherton went for 8, bowled through the gate by Kapil Dev; the returning Gower, playing his record seventeenth Test at Lord's, was sent dubiously on his way, bat-pad, when he was 40. With his score at 35, Gooch completed 30,000 runs in his first-class career. One run later, off the fourth ball of the seamer Sharma's fourth over, Gooch 'followed' a delivery, nicked it, and the wicket-keeper, More, spilled the most comfortable of waist-high catches. More grimaced, picked the ball from the turf and, with apologies, lobbed it back to the bowler. Nine and three-quarter hours later, More was slapping his gloves together in chivalrous acclaim for Gooch as he returned to the hundred-year-old rose-pink pavilion – bowled by Prabhakar for 333. In the second innings, to set up England's victory, Gooch hit 123 in 113 balls.

It was obviously the first triple-century by a man in a helmet, the first by a man wearing red-white-and-blue sweatbands on his wrists and wielding a 3lb bat, perhaps the first too by a man who had not shaved that morning, and certainly the first by a man who can imitate Bob Willis's bowling action to a 'T'. (For further such trivia, and plenty more besides, statistical enthusiasts should consult the 1991

Records broken by Gooch at Lord's in 1990

- Match aggregate of 456 a new world record (previous best, 380, Greg Chappell, 1973/74).
- First player to score triple-century and a century in any match (four had previously scored a double and a single hundred).
- Highest first-class score ever at Lord's (previously: 316, Jack Hobbs, 1925).
- First to score five Test centuries at Lord's in career: 1,582 highest Lord's Test aggregate by any batsman (previously: 1,241, David Gower).
- Highest score in any Lord's Test (previously: 254, Don Bradman, 1930).
- Highest Test score ever v India (previously: 280, Javed Miandad, 1982/83).
- Highest score by an England captain (previously: 258, Peter May, 1957).
- Highest score by any Test captain (previously: 311, Bobby Simpson, 1964).
- Third-wicket partnership of 308 with Allan Lamb (139) highest for any England wicket v India.
- Highest series aggregate record at home against India, in one match (previously: Ian Botham, 1982).

---

edition of *Wisden* where, by a delicious fluke, the full details of this epic Test are given on page 333!)

Brian Lara has since, of course, become the thirteenth Test-match triple centurion. The astonishing little West Indian who broke both the all-time first-class record with his 501 in 1994 only a matter of weeks after breaking Sir Garfield Sobers's world Test record of 365, had his twenty-fifth birthday between the two feats. When Gooch became the twelfth triple Test centurion, he was thirty-seven. The previous eleven had all been in their twenties, with one notable exception. After Sobers, who set the record at the age of 21, came Len Hutton (364 at 22), Hanif Mohammad (337 at 23), Walter Hammond (336 at 29), Don Bradman (334 at 22), Andrew Sandham (325 at 39), Bobby Simpson (307 at 25), Don Bradman (304 at 26), and Lawrence Rowe (302 at 25).

There have been two scores posted of 299. Between his two 'triples' in the early 1930s, the young Bradman was on 299 against South Africa at Adelaide when the last man in, 'Pud' Thurlow, ran himself out attempting to scurry home for the Don's 300th. And in 1991 the New Zealander, Martin Crowe, was on 299 against Sri Lanka with three balls of the match left. He was caught off the last of them.

What was in no doubt on the evening of 27 July 1993 was that Gooch's 333 had batted him into an awestruck public's affections. As a player and leader, he was now as nationally pre-eminent as Leonard Hutton. Ironically, it was exactly a year to the day when Lawson had clean bowled Gooch for 11 in the Old Trafford Test, at the end of which Gooch, in his despair, had asked Gower and Stewart to drop him for the following match. That was back-page news. The triple-century made the front pages.

'GOOCH ATTAINS GREATNESS AT LAST' was the headline in *The Times*, and the rest of the public prints, in their varying ways, echoed that sentiment. The *Independent* had the good idea to get the editor of *Wisden*, Graeme Wright, to watch from the 'bleachers':

'Regular Gooch-watchers would have known that he was aware of his achievements. When he reached a century, his thirteenth in all cricket this summer, he acknowledged the applause with no more than a raising of the bat before scratching his mark with his right boot and resuming his innings. When he passed 200, and again when he reached 300, he removed his white helmet and, for a moment allowed the capacity crowd to share his satisfaction. By spending Thursday and Friday away from the press box, away from the record books and the statisticians, I followed Gooch's innings as most spectators did. So many of the milestones had been passed before the public address system brought them to our notice. Nevertheless there were clues. Those listening to the radio on headphones became noticeably more tense and attentive as another landmark approached. Others sat enjoying the warm weather and the slaughter of the Indian bowlers, content to let the tide of history wash over them until even history could no longer be ignored. There, before us, the captain of England was approaching 300 and everyone took on board the awesomeness of his achievement.'

Paul Weaver of *Today* also left the press box, to seek out Alf and Rose, still the hero's most faithful supporters, and he sat between them as the 300 was posted:

'"Please don't write a gushy piece," Gooch senior implored. "We're not gushy sort of people you see – just the same as Graham. Today was a great day for us. But for me it doesn't match up to that hundred he scored in the 1979 Benson & Hedges Cup final, or his first Test hundred the following year, against West Indies at Lord's. I was so excited then. There weren't any tears, but I had to leave my seat and go out the back to keep my emotions bottled up. My stomach still churns around when he's batting, but it gets less over the years as he scores more runs. I suppose I get a little blasé." Rose did not agree with her husband. "Oh, I think this is the best day of all. I mean, 300, it's so special isn't it? I won't forget this day ever ..."'

In all, Gooch batted for 10 hours and 28 minutes, facing 485 balls, and was just 32 runs away from equalling Gary Sobers's world record. He hit 43 fours and three sixes, which means that he had to run 143 of his runs – and then there were also those of his partners to run. Under the headline 'BEYOND THE BOUNDARIES OF BELIEF', Matthew Engel wrote in the *Guardian*:

'In a nutshell we are all flabbergasted, Gooch's innings was remarkable not only for its quantity but for its quality as well … Gooch batted sensationally. In its middle period, in particular, his on-driving was of a quality that I have never seen surpassed. Later, when he must have been mentally and physically exhausted, he was able to step down the wicket and hit Shastri into the Nursery. But he must have found not so much second, as eight, ninth and tenth wind. When he was finally out, even Gooch – the ultimate businessman/cricketer – may have been able to savour the romance of the moment. The crowd rose; it would have bowed to him. In his career he took one dreadful turn-off to South Africa, but history will concentrate on his path to glory. This year he has saved the honour of England's cricket.'

In the *Independent on Sunday*, Tim de Lisle wove the innings into the fabric of the unhistrionic Gooch's dramatically undulating career:

'In Gooch's case, character is not destiny. His Test career has been a saga, a soap opera, a fifteen-year switchback ride, on and off the field; an unlikely mixture of success, failure, joy, heartbreak, acceptance, rejection, leadership, self-doubt and political intrigue on four continents. Every cricketer has his ups and downs; none has had quite such violent ones as this placid, modest, even-keeled man. Nobody has made more runs in a single Test match than Gooch, and nobody has made fewer.'

Even those with time to reflect went on pinching themselves: 'Sunlight pierces the curtains. The eyes blink open. My angel asks if I have been dreaming. Yes, I reply. I was at Lord's, and Graham Gooch scored over 450 runs in a Test match', wrote David Frith in his *Wisden Cricket Monthly*. In *The Times*, Alan Lee noted: 'If Ian Botham, the people's hero, had achieved such a feat, there would have been instant and insistent demands for nothing less than a knighthood'. In fact, a year later Gooch was awarded the OBE at Buckingham Palace. Hannah dropped the medal on the gravel afterwards as Graham and Brenda and she (only two guests allowed) posed for the cameramen. Brenda had missed seeing the 333 in person, but when a pressman telephoned she said, 'Don't worry, he won't get too ecstatic, he's not your over-excitable Essex Man'.

But one of all cricket's asterisk scores was something to gush about: 333, its numerical-alliteration was, somehow, pluperfect. And 333 light years away from good Bill Morris's indoor nets; from Fletch asking 'Does it speak?'; from the 'pair' at Edgbaston and the empty bar and misery of a hotel in Droitwich; from the tedium and homesickness of touring; from the wretched 'on-off', 'bold-funk' insecurities of deciding on South Africa; from a humiliating ban for a law-abiding man; from voluntarily forfeiting an England place, as well as the honoured captaincy of your beloved county; from 'lbw b Alderman'; the denial of even an interview for the job as England captain (which he held anyway), compounded by the jibe about a wet fish's charisma.

Well, here was vindication and, to Gooch much more to the point, English cricket had suddenly rediscovered a strut and sunny self-confidence. And someone nicely remembered the verse, written by another reserved and modest Essex man, Clement Attlee, about himself after he retired as Britain's most improbably successful Prime Minister:

There were many who thought themselves smarter
Few thought he was even a starter
But he ended PM
PC and OM
An earl and a Knight of the Garter.

GG

I muttered 'Okay, I suppose', at the press conference when they asked me how I felt about scoring a triple-hundred. However thrilled and proud of myself, it hadn't all sunk in and I was still in a bit of a blank – and, anyway, I wasn't going to destroy my reputation among the media people for being a dour old misery-guts. Perhaps they imagined that this time at least they might have got me tap-dancing on the table. I often enjoyed gently winding up the press by playing everything down. It was safer that way, too.

The first thing to say about my 333 is that one single man, first and foremost, has to be thanked for presenting me with the opportunity of scoring it – the Indian captain Azharuddin for putting England in when he won the toss. Apparently he made the decision totally off his own bat and when he got back to the dressing-room the Indian coach, Bishan Bedi, was furious. Any batsman knows it's not so much an 'ability' to get a big score that's the crucial thing, but the opportunity.

To be fair, it was a humid morning and the ball did swing around early on, and if the wicketkeeper had taken that easy catch off me England would have been 60-odd for two and it might have been a different story, with the Indian captain taking the plaudits instead of the English one. Funny, I felt much more tired after the first day than the second. I doubt if it helped much that I had a nasty ear infection. Or perhaps it was some sort of fatigue hangover from the 177 in 152 balls in the Colchester run-chase against Lancashire two days before. I went out to dinner up at Primrose Hill – Doug Insole had booked a table – but I could hardly keep my eyes open from the first course onwards. I was on 194 at the end of that opening day but, once I had got into the 200s next morning, I seemed to be carried along by the momentum as Alan Curtis on the public address loud-speaker kept everyone informed of the various milestones I passed on the way.

Irrespective of my part in it, I reckon it must be the best Test I have ever played in. Allan Lamb and Robin Smith both played magnificent innings, and Gus Fraser, 'the captain's dream', bowled superbly. Then Shastri replied with a rock-solid century for India and Azharuddin's own hundred off 88 balls was a stupendous answer to his critics for putting us in. It was the wristy knock of a classical Indian master especially as he was batting only to save the game – or so I thought at the time! And Kapil Dev's four successive sixes to save the follow-on was the most astonishing assault under pressure that I've ever seen in my life, just as the seventeen-year-old Tendulkar's running catch in the deep to dismiss Lamb in the second innings was not only straight out of the top-drawer but clear proof of India's competitiveness almost to the end.

It had been especially good to have dinner with Doug Insole between two such memorable days. Insole, not only a former Essex captain, but manager on my first senior England tour, has always been a major influence and a wise counsellor. It was satisfying, too, the next morning, to be walking across the ground for an early net with Micky Stewart and seeing the scoreboard showing England 359 for two and me on 194. Since becoming captain I had of necessity been working much closer with Micky and my batting form was correspondingly going from strength to strength. Much of this I owed to Micky for all the time and effort he put into sharpening and honing my technique as well as, of course, taking a lot of the off-field captain's administrative and organizational slog off my shoulders. Geoff Boycott's expert help had also been invaluable, but Micky's contribution in the nets went almost unnoticed in terms of publicity, as did Alan Lilley's back home in Essex.

It was already a very sticky, sultry day when we finished practice. Then came a very important time for me. Always if I'm batting, half-past ten to eleven o'clock brings an exact and very important ritual. Get a cup of tea, get stripped off, towel down, and put all my gear on pretty smartly – 'box-briefs' (underpants with a pouch for your box which Stuart Surridge Ltd 'invented' and now successfully markets), thigh pads, regular pads etc. At Lord's for Tests (we're in the other dressing-room for Essex), I always change in exactly the same position. If you look in from the outside it is to the left and against the far wall at the back. Most England regulars have their favourite place and then, as teams chop and change and people come and go, new regulars assume their place as of right. For instance, if you're looking in from the balcony, there are two little windows at the side of the French windows; that's where Ian Botham's permanent 'throne' was, so he could keep one eye on the cricket by peeping out, but also another on the television and the horseracing. At the time of that India match in 1990, Lord's still had the old deeply snug armchairs in the dressing-rooms, but since then they've put in modern benches. These are more practical, but without the armchairs I feel the place has lost a bit of its Victorian 'gentleman's club' character and charm.

Once I'm ready to go out, I like to spend the last twenty minutes or quarter of an hour sitting alone on the balcony, composing myself. What does the team need from me? Who are the bowlers (have I played them before?) and particular fielders? Can I recall past innings and re-visualize that success I had against them? One of the major reasons why I gave up the Essex captaincy that brief time in 1987 was because I found I wasn't able to organize this 'space' for myself before batting.

So, that morning, Lamb and I went out to continue the assault on India. Ideally, we were looking for around 600 and a declaration before the close. Robin Smith and John Morris (winning his first cap as Alec Stewart had an injured back) would follow us. The Indians had the new ball at once. I remember very carefully playing out two maidens – 'Don't go charging out to get it, let it come to you' – before middling Prabhakar square to the boundary to pass my previous best Test score of 196. Two balls later, an on-driven three and I'd made my first Test 'double'. I was delighted. That would do for me.

Now, four years later, the rest of the innings comes floating back in a lovely jumble of recollections. After about an hour's play it began to drizzle and there was a stoppage of about twenty minutes. Allan and I posted our 300-stand, which was a record for any England wicket against India, and took us both by surprise. Then Allan was well caught in the gully just before lunch. It was his twelfth Test century and also his highest; oddly enough he had never before got beyond 139.

I was much less tired on this second morning than the previous day, and the ear infection, responding well to the antibiotics, was no problem. At lunch, I had a good wash, towel-down, and threw a sopping shirt and vest into the drying-room near the boilers – most other grounds now have a dressing-room tumble-dryer – sorted and organized my kit for the afternoon, put my feet up, had a couple of slices of breast-of-chicken and a bread roll, before it was back on with the now-dry shirt and time to go out again. To a county game I'd probably take three shirts, say five to a Test match, three pairs of flannels and four or five pairs of socks. By and large, most players just keep rotating their stuff and drying it as they go along. With some of them it can get quite smelly!

After lunch, the Indians kept going with their medium-pacers as it was still humid and overcast. There was some thundery rain around too. Just before the lunch interval, Alan Curtis announced that I had overtaken Wally Hammond's best-ever English Test score at Lord's (240) which made me feel proud. Immediately after, they said I'd passed Boycott's 246 at Headingley, the highest by any Englishman against India. I could relate more readily to that and wondered with a bit of a smile how old 'Fiery' was explaining that away up there in his commentary box.

Because I reached 250 in the first over after lunch, I'd obviously already changed my left glove. I suppose people think that's my one big superstition, changing my left glove at every 50-mark, but where I grip the bat with my left hand, when it's hot the glove gets sweaty and slippery. Only the left hand, never the right. In my bag I'll always have seven or eight left-hand gloves and just two right-hand ones, one for the match and the other for practice. I number all the left-hand ones, so the twelfth man knows which to bring out when I signal. Recently there's been a spray on the market which squash players use to stop their hands getting sweaty. Changing my left glove is done for practical reasons but, at every fifty runs as well. Another of my 'superstitions' is that, if I go out in my helmet, I stay in my helmet fair weather, fast bowling, or fine. In the superstitions game, my glove-changing is mild compared to some. Jack Russell, the wicket-keeper, is almost as finicky as Alan Knott used to be; he's worn the same patched-up, battered old hat since his Gloucestershire debut in 1981. And Neil Taylor, of Kent, has worn the very same shirt to bat in for eight years.

When Alan Curtis's PA boomed out that I'd passed 254 and the highest score in any Lord's Test, it consciously hit me how momentous the day was becoming. I thought of being down on the grass all those years ago with Dad and Mum doling out the sandwiches in the tight crowd where the Nursery end curves into the Mound Stand. That was a Gillette Cup final and Ted Dexter was batting for Sussex. Now, in front of a packed house, here was Graham Gooch of Essex.

I have never been one to set actual specific 'targets' each day or match – like Richard Hadlee was said to do – I just concentrate on 'this 20' and then the 'next 20'. But when I heard that 254 figure had been passed I realized that 20 more runs would get me to that 275 I had made against Kent, when I so annoyed myself by not trying to go on to 300. I thought then if the time and opportunity ever did present itself again, I would make sure of it.

I levelled my 275 with a four and then pushed the single to overtake it. The spinners, Shastri and Hirwani, were wheeling away now. Earlier the umpire, Dickie Bird, had a quiet word with Azharuddin about bowlers scratching the ball. 'Leave the ball alone,' he said. They were probably getting desperate. I admit it was a very good pitch to bat on and that this Indian attack was not one of the world's strongest, but I hoped people wouldn't dismiss or write-off the innings because of that. The runs still had to be made.

I on-drove a two to get me to 291 and then, for the first time, I did get a flutter of nerves – but with them an overpowering determination not to make a mistake. I was very patient and I must have played about the equivalent of three overs as I edged through the 290s. In the last over before tea, I could see Robin Smith, at the other end, looking urgently for the extra run. I signalled him to calm down.

At tea I was 299 not out. It made for an apprehensive twenty minutes. I didn't take off my pads. I just towelled down, had a cup of tea and nothing else, and put on a clean shirt. I said the plan still was to declare and to have a charge at the Indian batsmen before the close.

I was facing the first ball after tea. The left-armer Shastri bowled it. I tucked it gently down towards fine-leg and Robin and I ran the single. I was on 300. Only the third Englishman to score a triple Test hundred at home. It was a very satisfying moment. Records themselves will come and go, but the magic 300 itself will always be there in my mind. Brenda was not coming to the match till next day, Saturday, but she had been keeping an eye on the TV and she told me later that the BBC had not shown the vital single live because they were at a horse-race at Ascot, but she knew I'd reached it before the TV got back to the cricket because the Press Association rang her up for a quick 'quote'.

Now there was the little matter of Sir Gary Sobers's all-time Test record of 365. Of course, I was aware of it. What cricket-loving schoolboy wasn't? He made it in 1958 in Kingston against Pakistan. I was five. Oops! Shastri nearly caught-and-bowled me when I was on 306. It was getting more and more overcast and murky. Robin and I had sailed into the 600s now. I was wondering about the declaration. I hit Shastri for four and, at 316, they announced that I had passed Sir Jack Hobbs' record in a county match and mine was now the highest-ever score at Lord's. I celebrated by hitting Shastri for a big six into the building site at the Nursery end where they were erecting the Compton and Edrich stands.

It began to drizzle again and we were off for another twenty-odd minutes. I thought of declaring then, but the light was now so poor that, had we opened our bowling attack with Devon Malcolm the umpires would have needed to look at only one of Devon's express deliveries and they'd have had us off straightaway. So we batted on. I was on 324 at the break and I thought I'd try one last rush for the record; but on 333 I played a lazy, airy sort of drive at Prabhakar and was bowled. It was over.

For a shy man, the standing ovation from the pavilion and the whole ground was a very moving moment. I will remember it always. My bat, one of Stuart Surridge's 3lb 'Turbo Test Selection' range, chosen and signed personally by me, was handed over at once to Jack Russell, our wicketkeeper who doubles as an artist, and later he painted the Lord's scoreboard showing 333 on the front of the bat in oils. The finished painting was loaned to Lord's and is now displayed in the Long Room for all to see. I've never been obsessive about a favourite bat. Some players get attached to a bat or a pair of gloves that they will go on using them until they are damaged antiques. I've never had a problem about having a knock-up in the nets and then taking a brand new bat out to the middle.

Just before I was out, the rain had freshened the thundery air and the light had improved enough to allow Devon to have a bowl at the Indians. As soon as Robin got his century I declared (at 653 for four), but their openers Shastri and Sidhu, survived the evening. Next day, any thought that the Indians were going to counter our big score by sitting on the splice behind the sandbags and grinding out a stalemate reply was soon scotched. Ravi Shastri held things together with a good, sound hundred and at the close of the Saturday they were 376 for six, the whole innings adorned by the quite marvellous Azharuddin. His hitting area is so exact and he is such a beautiful timer of the ball. If you pitch a fraction short and a half-inch outside off-stump he smashes you through the covers on the up. The same line, but six inches fuller length and his wrists whip the ball past square-leg or mid-wicket. It was still muggy, so I bowled a few overs myself, got a bit of swing and had Sanjay Manjrekar caught behind for my only wicket of the season.

On the Monday morning India needed 78 to save the follow-on. They were still in headline-making mood. However, Kapil Dev was lucky to still be there. In Angus Fraser's first over of the day, I caught Kapil low down at second slip, both my hands cupped right underneath, between the ball and the turf. No doubt about it, it was a fair catch. Kapil just stood there and waited, which he is entitled to do. Nigel Plews was at the bowler's end and he looked uncertain. He went over to Dickie Bird at square-leg and asked, 'Did it carry?' Said Dickie, 'Can't help you there, sorry'. So Kapil was given 'in'. I was not too happy. It's a bit 'disappointing' when two umpires don't want to give a perfectly straightforward catch, and there was also an implication about my honesty in claiming a catch from a bump-ball.

When Hirwani came in, as 'genuine' a no. 11 as you can find in Test cricket, he survived one ball from Gus, the last of his over. India needed their 24 to make us bat again. I knew Kapil was a good striker of the ball, but also knew he could be impetuous. In 1979 at The Oval, when Gavaskar hit a magnificent double-hundred in an all-day run-chase, Kapil had come in and, instead of pushing it around and continuing with the decent momentum which could have meant India winning, he panicked himself into a slog, skied a catch to me, and a collapse set in and we won. Then at the World Cup semi-final in Bombay in 1987, he did exactly the same thing: victory was in the palm of his hand. Mike Gatting put himself out at deep square-leg, Eddie Hemmings tosses one up, and Kapil knocks it straight down Gatt's throat.

Now my bowler was the same Eddie Hemmings and I figured that Kapil would again have a rush of blood and adrenalin and sky up a catch. In one way I was right. The adrenalin was cascading like Niagara. And they were catches all right, but only to the hard-hat workers high on the building-site scaffolding at the Nursery end. Kapil blocked the first two balls of Hemmings' over, then sent the next four, on the trot, for sixes in among the construction workers. It was magnificent hitting. The follow-on was saved. And Kapil's dramatic boldness was proved totally necessary because Hirwani was leg before to the very next delivery from Gus. We would have to bat again.

So what Kapil's sixes allowed was me to get another century, this time 123, and the record aggregate for a Test of 456. When Sharma

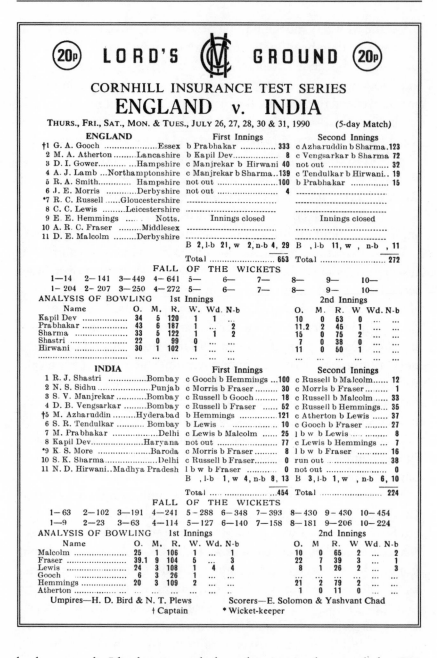

LORD'S ⓂⒸⒸ GROUND
(20p) (20p)

CORNHILL INSURANCE TEST SERIES
ENGLAND v. INDIA
THURS., FRI., SAT., MON. & TUES., JULY 26, 27, 28, 30 & 31, 1990   (5-day Match)

ENGLAND

	First Innings	Second Innings
†1 G. A. Gooch ....Essex	b Prabhakar 333	c Azharuddin b Sharma.123
2 M. A. Atherton ....Lancashire	b Kapil Dev.................8	c Vengsarkar b Sharma 72
3 D. I. Gower............ ...Hampshire	c Manjrekar b Hirwani 40	not out 32
4 A. J. Lamb ...Northamptonshire	c Manjrekar b Sharma..139	c Tendulkar b Hirwani.. 19
5 R. A. Smith............ Hampshire	not out 100	b Prabhakar 15
6 J. E. Morris ....Derbyshire	not out 4	
*7 R. C. Russell .....Gloucestershire		
8 C. C. Lewis ....Leicestershire		
9 E. E. Hemmings .... Notts.	Innings closed	Innings closed
10 A. R. C. Fraser ....Middlesex		
11 D. E. Malcolm ....Derbyshire		
	B 2,l-b 21, w 2,n-b 4, 29	B , l-b 11, w , n-b , 11
	Total 653	Total 272

FALL OF THE WICKETS
1—14   2—141   3—449   4—641   5—   6—   7—   8—   9—   10—
1—204   2—207   3—250   4—272   5—   6—   7—   8—   9—   10—

ANALYSIS OF BOWLING   1st Innings   2nd Innings

Name	O.	M.	R.	W.	Wd.	N-b	O.	M.	R.	W	Wd.	N-b
Kapil Dev	34	5	120	1	1	...	10	0	53	0	...	...
Prabhakar	43	6	187	1	...	2	11.2	2	45	1	...	...
Sharma	33	5	122	1	1	2	15	0	75	2	...	...
Shastri	22	0	99	0	...	...	7	0	38	0	...	...
Hirwani	30	1	102	1	...	...	11	0	50	1	...	...
				...	...	...	...	...	...	...	...	...

INDIA

	First Innings	Second Innings
1 R. J. Shastri ....Bombay	c Gooch b Hemmings ...100	c Russell b Malcolm...... 12
2 N. S. Sidhu ....Punjab	c Morris b Fraser 30	c Morris b Fraser......... 1
3 S. V. Manjrekar ....Bombay	c Russell b Gooch 18	c Russell b Malcolm...... 33
4 D. B. Vengsarkar ....Bombay	c Russell b Fraser 52	c Russell b Hemmings... 35
†5 M. Azharuddin ....Hyderabad	b Hemmings 121	c Atherton b Lewis 37
6 S. R. Tendulkar ....Bombay	b Lewis 10	c Gooch b Fraser 27
7 M. Prabhakar ....Delhi	c Lewis b Malcolm 25	l b w b Lewis 8
8 Kapil Dev.................Haryana	not out 77	c Lewis b Hemmings ... 7
*9 K. S. More ....Baroda	c Morris b Fraser 8	l b w b Fraser 16
10 S. K. Sharma...................Delhi	c Russell b Fraser......... 0	run out 38
11 N. D. Hirwani..Madhya Pradesh	l b w b Fraser 0	not out 0
	B , l-b 1, w 4,n-b 8, 13	B 3,l-b 1, w , n-b 6, 10
	Total 454	Total 224

FALL OF THE WICKETS
1—63   2—102   3—191   4—241   5—288   6—348   7—393   8—430   9—430   10—454
1—9   2—23   3—63   4—114   5—127   6—140   7—158   8—181   9—206   10—224

ANALYSIS OF BOWLING   1st Innings   2nd Innings

Name	O.	M.	R.	W.	Wd.	N-b	O.	M	R.	W	Wd.	N-b
Malcolm	25	1	106	1	...	1	10	0	65	2	...	2
Fraser	39.1	9	104	5	...	3	22	7	39	3	...	1
Lewis	24	3	108	1	4	4	8	1	26	2	...	3
Gooch	6	3	26	1	...	...	...	...	...	...	...	...
Hemmings	20	3	109	2	...	...	21	2	79	2	...	...
Atherton	...	...	...	...	...	...	1	0	11	0	...	...

Umpires—H. D. Bird & N. T. Plews   Scorers—E. Solomon & Yashvant Chad
† Captain   * Wicket-keeper

had me caught I had apparently been batting in the match for 774 minutes. Mike Atherton and I put on 204 for the first wicket. We set India 472 for victory and I was well content reducing them to 57 for two at the close, with one day left. By the middle of the morning session next day they were out of steam and losing wickets regularly. At lunch they were 158 for six and the end came about an hour later – when an arrow-straight direct throw from mid-on uprooted and sent cartwheeling the middle stump at the bowler's end with the batsman, Sharma, well out. Fielder's name? G. Gooch. I don't think I've done anything so theatrically dramatic in the field since practising in my daydreams all those years ago down in the playground near the bicycle sheds at the Mills Court council flats. A memorable end to an unforgettable five days' cricket.

The summer got hotter, the wickets flatter, and even more runs piled up for batsmen in England. After Lord's Essex played Nottinghamshire at Chelmsford and I continued tucking in with 87 and 65 not out – and 136 in 103 balls in the Sunday match in between. The next Test at Old Trafford was another high scorer, but a draw this time when a few dropped catches and a resolute not-out century by the child-prodigy Tendulkar thwarted us on the last day. Mike Atherton and I had put on 225 in just about even time and my 116 was my fourth century in five Test innings and the first hat-trick of hundreds since Boycott did it nineteen years before.

At The Oval, Azharuddin won the toss and didn't make the same mistake twice in London – so it was India's turn to pile up the runs – 606 in the first innings. I made 85 and 88, having a partnership in the second innings with Atherton of 176, during which I passed Bradman's all-time record of 974 for an English summer series. I had never been in such nick in my life. I was 'cashing in'.

To secure the draw against India and our series win, David Gower made an understandably cautious start and then blossomed out as of old with a sumptuous century, 157 not out, to book his place on the plane to Australia. This had been in some doubt for he had not till then taken advantage with everyone else of the summer's general run-spree – there were 428 three-figure innings in English first-class cricket in 1990, 180 more than in 1989, but David had averaged only a mediocre 34 for Hampshire with just one century. But now I was pleased that I was going to have his experience on board against the Aussies.

13

OPENING TIME

FK

Gooch and Boycott had, as an opening partnership, just failed to total 2,000 runs, but they nevertheless stood, when divorce was imposed on them, third in the England first-wicket aggregates behind only Hobbs and Sutcliffe, and Hutton and Washbrook. With total partnerships of, respectively, 3,204 and 3,079, those two famous old firms stand astride England's mighty plinth – and not only for accumulation, but as well for romance, poesy, and the attraction of opposites.

The 'opposites' theory down the century has endured as tried and, literally, tested. Before setting up home with Gooch, for instance, Boycott had fruitful partnerships with Bob Barber and John Edrich. Boycott much preferred the former – Barber fluently, even languidly, got on with it and the scoreboard was always on a hum. Edrich was a fine player but too much like Boycott himself – gritty, patient, a porer. Thus the tyro recruit, early-Gooch, was ideal for Boycott; the poring scholar and the lusty blacksmith.

After Hobbs and Sutcliffe last opened an innings together for the Players XI at Lord's in 1932, the writer Ronald Mason acclaimed 'a legendary technique and repute unequalled by any other pair; the lean, active, quizzical Hobbs and the neat, wiry, imperturbable Sutcliffe, who together set a standard that can serve as a guide, but defied all attempts at emulation'. In 1994, the nonogenarian, R E S Wyatt, who also rewardingly opened with Sutcliffe in the 1930s, told me, 'Of all the great players Herbert was the least selfish, he was a grandly inspiring partner and absolutely fearless.' Which, as it happens, is almost word-for-word what Mike Atherton said of his senior partner when Gooch handed the younger man the reins of England some sixty years later.

Cyril Washbrook, aged eighty in December 1994, said that his partnership with Len Hutton – which embodies England's highest opening partnership, 359, against South Africa, in 1948/49 – was, 'and like any worth it salt should be, based on technique, composure, mutual encouragement, and firm friendship'. And attraction of opposites? 'I suppose so. Perhaps I was in more of a hurry to take off the shine. I was a hooker, you see. I was the pugnacious one, if you like, to Leonard's calm. But all based on a perfect understanding between the wickets. Which made for a real partnership, didn't it?'

By the time of the separation, perforce self-inflicted, of Gooch and Boycott, a new opening partnership had not long begun. By the weight of its runs in tandem the pairing was to break all the world opening partnership records, most likely for all time. The West Indians, Gordon Greenidge and Desmond Haynes, patiently ruthless plunderers, were to post, together, 6,483 runs before Greenidge made his curtain call in 1991.

No one has better described the arts and science of opening the batting than one of its most stupendous practitioners, Bobby Simpson, who walked out, and in, with his friend Bill Lawry, a gum-chewing crag with a nose almost as large as his concentrating powers. Simpson and Lawry head Australia's opening aggregates with 3,956 runs, and they were only overtaken by Haynes and Greenidge in the later 1980s. This is what Simpson told me.

'Bill was a remarkable man; hard as nails, ruthless, detached and determined at the crease – but wonderfully, immensely generous to bat with. Off the field he had a marvellous jokey, hilarious nature, but on the field he was grim and grinding and obviously never able to project his real personality on the crowd. But we had a tremendous opening partnership because, even if it didn't look it to you, we both knew the secret of relaxing totally between deliveries ...

'As a definite plan and policy we would rotate the singles, share the strike as near to 50–50 as we could; to keep giving the bowler a different target, give him as few chances as possible even to bowl a full over at you so he could never work out his game-plan with any consistency, never get a prolonged shot at you. The singles and threes are the vital scoring shots in cricket, not the twos, and fours.'

Gooch, in his maturity, swears by the Lawry–Simpson creed. In addition to Boycott, Gooch has opened for England with seventeen others (see page 306) including his long-time Essex partner, John Stephenson, who played one Test only for England. Stephenson said, when he first went in with Gooch, 'the great man would score so quickly that it would sap the bowlers' hearts and confidence. When he was on 50 and I was on eight, it felt like batting on another planet. In the first seasons of our partnership, if Graham wasn't hitting the ball for four all the time he would get annoyed with himself, but as we went on he became increasingly keen on quick singles and fast threes. He says strike-rotation is crucial. Not much calling goes on, he just looks up and we go.'

GG

When Keith Fletcher, back in 1977, pushed me up the order to open the batting, I joined Mike Denness, who had been captain in my first Test match at Edgbaston in 1975. The experience of Denness, then thirty-six and for many years previously the captain of Kent, was a telling factor in my taking to the position like a, well not that species perhaps, say, a seagull to water! Mike was invaluable during that initiation period; a high-class batsman, a very good influence on all matters cricketing. Technically, he was a classic driver of the ball. At first, he thought I was a bit of an overweight 'sloppy 'erbert' and too much of a chancer, but I learned a great deal from him.

After that brief apprenticeship, I opened with another Scot, Brian Hardie, who was unselfish and confidently versatile enough to move up and down the order to accommodate whatever strategy or my Test calls imposed. Often in the 1980s I opened with Chris Gladwin, ten years younger and a good bat, who had been a toddler with whom, in the mid-1960s, I would lark about with a scruffy old tennis ball on the boundary edge when both our fathers were playing at weekends for East Ham Corinthians. But as a Test opener, it was Geoffrey Boycott with whom I enjoyed batting best.

In my earlier Test days, I used sometimes to try and lighten up a dead match on the last day, and if I happened to be bowling I would go in for impersonations of other people's bowling actions – Bob Willis tearing in, all arms and wonky knees and intense eyes, like a gander trying to get airborne off a runway; or injury-prone Chris Old, collapsing and holding his back in the middle of his run-up. Once in India, I put a handkerchief on my head in the middle of an over and did my 'Bishan Bedi' and although Sunny Gavaskar was in fits of laughter at the other end, the umpire no-balled me 'for not informing the batsman I was changing from right-arm to left in the middle of an over'. But the most popular bowling-action send-up of all was my 'Geoffrey': cap reversed like a dustman, the wonky grin, a curving three-pace run-up and then, in the delivery stride, he falls down in a panic and scrabbles around the grass, blindly looking for his lost contact lens!

When I do public speaking engagements now, the most frequent questions I am asked concern batting with Boycott and his running between the wickets. In fact he was a very good judge of a run, and he ran me out only once, whereas I 'sawed him off', as we put it, at least three times! Anyway, to forestall the questions nowadays, I have my answer ready in my speech. It's not true, it's an embellishment, but gives the audience what they want, for it unfailingly goes down a treat.

I set my story at Lord's in the late 1970s. England v New Zealand:

Down the Pavilion steps, opening with Geoffrey, first day of the Test, a huge crowd, all anticipation. On to the turf, and Boycott says 'Nice morning for it, young Graham', as if it's the first time he's spoken to me for weeks. I get to the middle and go on down to face Richard Hadlee, bowling from the Pavilion end. And so we proceed, cautiously. Ten minutes, twenty minutes … and then it crosses my mind that this Lance Cairns must be bowling pretty decently from the other end because Boycs can't get a run off him. He's taking Cairns and I'm stuck with ruddy Hadlee. I hit a handful of twos and then a couple of fours and then, after about forty minutes, I get a thick inside edge off Hadlee that runs down to Richard Collinge at long-leg and I think 'Thank heavens for that I've got a single'. I amble up towards the Pavilion-end crease when suddenly there's this urgent Yorkshire voice from the Nursery end, 'Two! Two!' So I touch-in, turn, sprint back, and just get home, and think to myself 'Well, okay, fair enough, old Boycs made me a nice two there'.

But I'm still facing Hadlee, aren't I? Five minutes later, I push a ball to deepish point for a strolling single – and at last, after three-quarters of an hour Geoffrey is finally facing Hadlee. First ball, just like me previously, Boycs inside-edges Hadlee's inswinger, although to Geoff it's never an inside-edge is it, it's always a genuine leg-glance, and it goes down to Collinge at long-leg exactly the same as mine. Collinge is none too quick and I think 'Boycs gave me a two to Collinge, so I'll return the compliment'. I dash down the wicket, touch-in and shout 'Two, Boycs, Two!' and I turn and am into my stride when I look up – to see that Geoffrey, having contentedly completed his single, has followed through twenty yards past the stumps and umpire at the Pavilion end. In panic, I jam on the brakes in mid-pitch and swivel back round, only to see Hadlee ready to gather Collinge's throw and clatter down my stumps. Run out.

As I pass Geoffrey on my slow march back to the Pavilion, he shouts out commiserations, 'Great sacrifice, Graham lad, great sacrifice'.

For the 1990/91 tour to Australia, we were due to fly from Heathrow on a Thursday in the middle of October, but we were told to assemble at the Excelsior Hotel near the airport early the evening before. I took a bit of hump at that, losing my last evening with the kids at home because Micky Stewart and Ted Dexter wanted an inaugural team meeting to get the tour off on the right foot. So I hugged and kissed the kids and my Dad drove me down to the hotel. At once I saw Allan Lamb in the bar and, as he was never the promptest of people, I was pleased that my vice-captain was out to show me up for punctuality. Dad stayed for one drink, then we went along the corridor into one of the hotel meeting-rooms and before I could wonder why everyone in the team was looking so dolled-up and smart in their ties and blazers, Michael Aspel jumped out and said, 'Graham Gooch – This is Your Life!'

So that was why Brenda and the kids at home hadn't seemed too worried that I was leaving for four-and-a-half months. And why Brenda's mum was there with a brand-new hair-do and dress.

I was whisked down by a chauffeur to the ITV studios at Teddington, with everyone following behind. John Emburey did the honours, so did Lamb and the three B's – Boycott, Border, and Botham. There were faces from the distant past – my old teacher Douglas Kemp, my schoolfriend Graham Hammond, and 'uncle' Bill Morris from the Ilford indoor school, who had come down specially from Kilmarnock. It was a grand evening, and really good of the team to give up their last night at home to come and wish me well.

That night might have represented a happy and convivial send-off in October; for, having made our point in the West Indies the winter before, and having won both our summer series in pretty good style, I really thought an assault on the Ashes was more than a viable proposition. How wrong could I get?

At the end of the summer my broken finger had mended but, at practice as soon as we arrived in Perth, I stuck out my hand instinctively in trying to take a return catch from a Robin Smith drive. It split my 'ring' finger open like before. It was to heal but then become very badly infected. The injury ruled me out of the first Test at Brisbane which we lost with some poor batting in a low-scoring match.

Then Lamb, the vice-captain, missed the next two Tests with a calf injury. I came back for the second at Melbourne in a vain attempt to hold the breach when possibly I was not ready; we competed well enough for half the match and then subsided disastrously. Then, with the beginnings of his severe hip problems, our one world-class bowler, Gus Fraser, missed the drawn fourth Test as well as the fifth where we again folded turgidly and spinelessly at the last. At Perth I worried myself into a state and I blew my top in the last match. I wondered if it was all my fault, and whether it was worth going on. What was more, between the Tests there was a 50-overs one-day World Series Cup competition. Humiliatingly, we allowed the New Zealand team, in a very transitional state, to stop us even making the final stages.

How much my hand injury affected things is hard to tell. It necessitated me taking it off the tiller at the very beginning, which is always a crucial stage of any tour, and when the poison set in, it could well have affected my general morale and well-being more than I realized at the time. The original stitches were certainly healing okay when we arrived in Adelaide a couple of serious weeks into the tour, and well enough to have a morning net with Micky Stewart prior to announcing I was ready to play again. Afterwards, although I hadn't taken any sort of knock on the hand, I suddenly felt the blood 'pumping' in it, a nasty feeling, rather like one time when I got an infection on the back of my knee.

In no time I was flat on my back in St Andrew's Hospital on an antibiotic drip and about to slip into a serious fever. A fast and angry mystery virus was taking over. Suddenly, people weren't worrying about me playing in the upcoming Test, but whether I'd ever be playing first-class cricket again. By immense good fortune, the top specialist in hand surgery, Randall Sach, had remained in the city that weekend and was there to be called in straightaway to operate. He withdrew all the poison at once, but my fever was still none too comfortable for a day or so. The infection, they reckoned, was a rare but lethal organism which became sealed in my hand just as the original cut had closed. Dr Sach was tremendous. But this time he had to put thirty stitches in my hand once all the poisoned puss had been totally eradicated.

Meanwhile, the team had gone to Hobart en route to Brisbane and preparation for the first Test. I stayed in St Andrew's for over a week, and rejoined the boys in Brisbane. I felt wretched about it. Only eight months after Trinidad and here was the same scenario – myself sidelined, a captain only in name, and knowing that I had to be careful not to get too involved because, as vice-captain, it was now Allan's 'show'. The etiquette of cricket is that the captain on the field is the one to make the tactical and selectorial decisions that matter as well as being the one to rally the troops and keep their spirits up. I had to stay in the wings.

From that low point, and a ten-wicket defeat, things simply got lower. The second Test at Melbourne immediately after Christmas had also looked pretty good for us during the first couple of days, when David Gower scored a lovely and typical hundred with an injured wrist. But we folded tamely at the end to lose by eight wickets. At Sydney David made another entrancing century, so did the rock-solid Mike Atherton; Alec Stewart unluckily missed his maiden Test century by nine runs and we made 469 for eight declared in reply to Australia's 518 in the first innings. We needed to bat well, if only for our self-respect, because the second day, as the Australian lower order piled on the agony, was up until then the most shaming day of my cricketing life. We fielded so poorly that the crowd began laughing at us.

In the end, we pulled ourselves together enough to look reasonably good in getting a draw. On the final morning, I was seriously at fault in bowling our two spinners, Hemmings and Tufnell, too long and not allowing Devon Malcolm to wrap the Aussies up. Which meant an impossible winning target for us of 255 in 28 overs. Over nine an over. But David and I went in first and managed at least to put a couple of extra furrows in Allan Border's forehead by racing to 84 at seven runs an over before we obviously ran out of time. At least that retort put me in a slightly better mood. Slightly. In reality, we could not win the Ashes now, but the final two Tests gave us a chance to display an attitude and collective commitment that had become so transparently threadbare.

Between the Tests, mercifully, we registered our opening first-class win of the tour against Queensland. That was the good news. The bad was that, when Robin Smith made his first century of the tour, two of our batsmen who were already out, David Gower and John Morris, having left the ground and gone to the nearby airport, buzzed the ground in a hired Tiger Moth. The unwritten rule in cricket is that if you are playing you ask the captain (or manager) if you can leave the ground. I assumed that, as David hadn't asked, he expected me to say 'no'. And I would have. The press took the manager Peter Lush by surprise when they asked him about the prank soon afterwards, and when Peter came back to the pavilion to ask David about it, we found that he and Morris had actually returned to the airport to pose for press photographs in the cockpit, dressed up in 'Biggles' outfits. In some newspapers back in London next day, the pictures shared the front pages with the coverage of the Gulf War! That let us down badly, I thought. What if the rest of the team, especially the younger ones, thought that sort of behaviour was par for the course? Lush, Micky Stewart, Lamb and I decided to fine them both £1,000. David thought it exorbitant.

As far as I was concerned, once the 'disciplinary committee' had imposed the fine, the matter was closed. It was nothing 'personal', and I'm sure that if I had done the same thing when David was captain, however thoughtlessly, he would have been on the committee to fine me. And, once done, there would be no hard feelings or recriminations on either side. Which is as it should be and how, in this instance, it was.

But that Tiger Moth scenario became for the press yet another contretemps to use against us. We had begun our 'face-saving' fourth Test at Adelaide well enough in the field before once again letting Australia somewhat off the hook and after being, at one stage, 124 for five they ended with 386 thanks to a superb 138 by my young Essex team-mate, Mark Waugh, his first in Tests. In our reply, we immediately lost Atherton and Lamb for ducks and then Robin Smith not long before lunch. I was going well enough, but it was crucial that David and I dig in and then consolidate through the afternoon session. Off the final ball before lunch bowled by McDermott, however, David airily swatted to wideish long-leg – and hit the ball straight down the throat of Merv Hughes who had been placed there for the purpose. A lot has been made ever since of the significance of it being the last ball before lunch, but I was more disappointed that David had so palpably fallen for the trap which he knew they always set for him. Someone said the shot was more worth the £1,000 fine than the Tiger Moth escapade.

I walked in slowly to lunch after David and the Australians had gone in, and people read into that another censure for David with my body language. Inside, he was obviously even more disappointed than I was. Nothing was said between us. There is no point in those circumstances. David is a one-off law to himself; he can be absolutely stupendous and unmatchable, just as he can so carelessly fall for the three-card trick.

Needless to say, we collapsed, the last seven wickets falling for 69. I ended with 87 out of 229. Then Boon and Border held their innings together so they could declare at 314 for six and have just over a day to bowl us out. The target was 472. Mike Atherton and I began really well and at lunch we were 115 without loss. Lamb agreed we should seek the victory, and as we walked out for the afternoon session I said to Mike, 'Don't let's do anything daft, but we'll just crank up a gear.' Then Border put on the spinner, Matthews, and I said to Mike, 'We'll go for him'. It worked, for a time. In the first hour after lunch we really pushed the score along. I made my first century in Australia – fully a dozen years after that 99 in Melbourne – and Allan Border was certainly looking worried. We passed 200, but then

Geoff Marsh brilliantly caught me in the gully off Bruce Reid. Atherton and Lamb kept up the momentum for a while, but once Mike went for 87, David and Alec Stewart were gone inside three overs and we called off the chase and put up the shutters for a comfortable draw. It was fun while it lasted. We ended at 335 for five, a goodish effort. Mum and Dad had flown in for their first trip to Australia and I was especially pleased they had seen not only my century but also a reasonably valiant contest by England.

At Perth, however, we had another disaster. We were only 63 behind on the first innings, in spite of a disastrous lower-order collapse, and in the second our last six wickets crumpled for 102, so the Australians were never remotely extended and they won by nine wickets. By now I was more and more convinced that commitment and attitude were essential ingredients for a Test side. Border's Australians had it in abundance. In Essex we had it for many years – it fosters a team spirit which insists on a collective will to go for the jugular when you have played yourself into a promising position, and gets you fighting for each other desperately when the team is in a tight corner. On this tour England, taking each day of the series as a separate entity, had any number of good periods when all we needed was a tight and committed follow-up. But each time we blew it.

At Perth I was mortified. I blamed myself, and rightly, because I had been given the team I wanted before we set off. Through the tour I had muttered the usual platitudes to the press and media, but after the Perth match, without naming names, I said frankly that the attitude and commitment of some of the team had upset me, and that went for both experienced tourists and inexperienced ones. The players themselves took umbrage when they heard what I had said. I told them I was delighted they were upset. It showed me they cared. At last. I said I cared enough about it because I was seriously considering my future as skipper. But if I did stay on, if some of them wanted to continue with their Test careers they would have to show me they were willing to put in a big commitment too – from the moment the new season started back home. Because, by then, the West Indies would be among us again.

I also felt particularly sorry for Micky Stewart. Our philosophies gell. Our views on life and cricket are very similar. Call it 'work ethic' or any other fancy name you like, if it is going to squeeze out some results we're going to continue with it. English cricket more often than not has been synonymous with beer and drink. The English are fond of cricket because we are most fond of its social life, and feel that the pavilion and the bar are almost more important than the wicket. That's all very well, but too much of our 'top' young talent is lost in a forest of mediocrity. Micky and I are fired with the same determination. If anything is worth achieving, it is worth working hard for. And it is hard work. If there's no pain, there's no gain. Neither of us likes being beaten. What's the point of playing top sport unless you want to win? In international sport, the enjoyment is the success, surely?

Or was it me? Was I too gloomy and introspective to be a real leader? Was my 'black dog' about our performance contributing to our bad cricket? Should I try and be more relaxed and carefree myself? Was I taking it all far too seriously?

Did Brian Taylor, my first captain at Essex, ever brood like me, or take things as much to heart as I do? Taylor was a beaky, padded yeoman and a born leader of the sergeant-major variety. He had the growler's voice to match. Even on our worst days he insisted that we young charges were well turned out and fielded like furies. We did not win many games, but when Tonker's wit broke through, he had his lads rolling on the floor. Once, after a leather-chasing day at Headingley, the team went to the Leeds City of Varieties. A dismal, in fact embarrassingly awful comedian was on the bill. He ended his string of limp gags with a crooning rendition of 'I May Never Pass This Way Again'. In the stalls Tonker stood up and shouted, 'Can we have that in writing?'

When Essex cocked things up and even became a bit of a laughing stock, did 'Tonker' become depressed like I do? How did he feel when in 1969, Essex created a batting record which can be equalled but never beaten? The Essex opener Brian Ward, against Somerset at Yeovil in a Sunday League match, played out the full quota of Brian Langford's eight overs, incredibly, as maidens. The spinner's analysis was 8–8–0–0. In the Sunday slog! Not only that, Essex's rampant hitter, Keith Boyce, was watching from the other end. When Ward finally hit his own wicket (facing Roy Palmer) he came in to be asked 'What the heck were you doing?' He said, 'Saving Boyce from Langford, the danger-man'.

That would have infuriated me as captain. I bet Tonker shook his head and smiled a little at the dottiness of man.

On the other hand, the military-man in him could get ratty. One day Ray East's orthodox left-armers, pushed in, were keeping the opposition quiet on a somnolent county afternoon. Over after over of the same tightly accurate stuff. Out of the blue, suddenly, the mischievous East tossed down the wrong-'un – the 'chinaman'. Behind the stumps, Taylor went one way, the ball the other. Four byes. Taylor did not even turn to watch the ball vanish under the sightscreen, but marched up the pitch loudly berating the bowler who, with the rest of the field, was merrily convulsed: 'East, you turned that ball on purpose, didn't you, just to make me look like an effing twat, didn't you?'

Perhaps what I needed with this England side was a fierce, barking no.2. If Tonker Taylor's leadership was, simply, the making of modern Essex, his heir, Keith Fletcher, had learned from Taylor although by the end of his reign Taylor himself was learning many a new wrinkle from the crafty countryman. Fletcher would study the opposition. He might not have remembered their names, but he knew their technical idiosyncracies. He logged them in close-up from bat-pad where he was a fearlessly composed fieldsman. Then, tongue shoving his chewing-gum to the other side of his mouth, he would sidle alongside Taylor at the end of the over, head furtively cocked towards his captain, and whisper, 'Slip 'Obbsie at this joker, skip', or 'Give JK a couple of darts at this geezer', or 'Tell Boycie, a few up his throat, eh?', or 'A couple of gullies will do this bloke, easy'.

I once asked Fletch what his regrets were, if any. He chewed his gum and stroked his chin and thought long. 'Yes,' he said, 'just one thing. I've never ever been any good at making gravy.' He pronounces that 'gwavy'. He has always had difficulty with his 'r's, yet he called his daughters Tara and Sara!

While Fletch was England's captain we played in Sri Lanka's inaugural Test match in Colombo. Fletch had played on the island, of course, when it was still Ceylon. Thus his unconscious compromise every time: 'How happy we are to be in SRI-LON.' When Derek Pringle first joined Essex from Cambridge, Fletch vaguely knew there had been a promising player at the university the year before,

Alistair Hignell. Somehow he thought they were one and the same, and through Pring's first county summer he was addressed by his captain as 'Ignell'.

On the 1982 England tour of India, Fletcher as captain had to introduce his blazered team before play began to the Prime Minister, Mrs Indira Gandhi. It was the third Test match at Delhi and the tour was already six weeks old. Halfway down the line was England's Surrey wicketkeeper, Jack Richards. Jack bowed slightly, offered his hand to India's famous First Lady and waited to hear his skipper do the honours. There was dead silence, until the unfazed Fletch – it possibly happened to him all the time – muttered, 'Sorry, cock, I've forgotten your name, better ruddy-introduce yourself'. Fletch and the First Lady moved on along the line. Two or three places further on was Paul Allott, proudly on his first tour. 'This, ma'am, is ... er,' said the skipper. He peered at Allott as if for the first time. 'Allott,' whispered Paul. 'Oh yes, ma'am,' said Fletch, 'this is Arlott, John Arlott.'

On that one tour of his as captain of England did Fletch brood about it as much as I was doing as we left Australia for home? I doubt it. He was disappointed, yes. But not as paranoid as I can get. Still, we were at least coming home to Essex. In the *Independent* Martin Johnson once remarked on my twin loyalties 'with England, a team Gooch is extremely fond of, and Essex, a team he is totally besotted with'.

Fair point, perhaps. But now, not only was Essex waiting for me, so were Viv Richards's West Indians.

14

THE BEST-EVER TEST INNINGS IN HISTORY?

FK

Gooch's new England side came up against against the still relent-lessly formidable West Indies at Headingley in early June 1991. It was four months since the nine-wicket defeat at Perth and, as threatened then by the captain, the England team was a changed one. Five new men were in the XI – Graeme Hick, Derek Pringle, Mark Ramprakash, Jack Russell and Steve Watkin – the changes reflecting Gooch's mood after Australia (no David Gower, for instance), and including one fresh face which had long been pined for, so much so that the back pages could almost let Gower's absence pass as they heaped their lip-smacking hyperbole on to the shoulders of the young Zimbabwean, Hick.

Still only twenty-five, but already with 54 first-class centuries and an astonishingly precocious career average of 64, Hick was acclaimed as the prodigy around whom a disillusioned Gooch could overnight rebuild his team. There was also a place for the young Middlesex player, Ramprakash, who had been singled out as a special talent since his mid-teens and was home from scoring a big century for England's 'A' team in the 'Test' against Sri Lanka on the winter tour. Of all the England six Test arenas, none is more a 'horses for courses' ground than Headingley, so England also called up Gooch's Essex colleague, Derek Pringle, whose bowling style – 'He's never quite there for the drive', Viv Richards had said – suited the traditional Leeds flavours.

And typical Headingley it was – a flat enough wicket, but damp and difficult, lying under pewtery-grey cloud cover with rain always in the murky air and regularly interrupting the action. Richards won

207

the toss and asked England to bat. The West Indian pace quartet was just as formidable as when Gooch had first met its predecessors eleven summers and winters before. The legendary platoon of Roberts, Holding, Croft, and Garner had retired to become, well, legends. Their heirs, now in their pomp, also comprising an Antiguan, two Jamaicans and a Bajan were, respectively, Curtly Ambrose, with the same skyscraper arm and steep bounce of 'Big Bird' Garner, but with an even more venomous mien and just as terminal a yorker; Patterson, the epitome of the old slogan 'pace like fire'; Walsh, accurate and unrelenting, with the propensity of Croft to 'inslant' dangerously from a height; and Marshall, senior pro and for some years acknowledged as, quite simply, the best in the world. Headingley suited the West Indies. England had last beaten them in a Test match at home way back in 1969, also at Headingley, when Illingworth's side faced the far gentler attack of Sobers, Grayson Shillingford, Vanburn Holder, and John Shepherd, as well as Lance Gibbs, the off-spinner.

In four of their last eight innings – that is, once a match – England had failed to reach 200 against the West Indies. They failed again on this miserable Thursday, only Gooch, Robin Smith and the debutante Ramprakash contributing more than 20 runs in an all-out 198. But in a dramatic reply, England's slower, steadier seam attack of DeFreitas, Pringle, and the new boy Watkin of Glamorgan, found conditions even more to their liking and, backed up by some exciting fielding, surprised even themselves by bowling England to a first-innings lead of 25. Richards made 73, oddly his highest Test score at Leeds, and the rest of his side just 100 runs between them.

On the third morning, Gooch knew that the very minimum required to put the West Indies under any sort of pressure in the fourth innings would be to repeat their opening score of 198. By lunchtime, that already looked a forlorn and distant mirage – Ambrose, with avenging fury, had dismissed Atherton and Hick, brutally, for just 6 runs apiece, and Lamb for a duck. England were 38 for three, only a perilous 63 runs ahead. The match could be over by close of play and if so, with wretched humiliation, the TCCB would have an empty stadium on the next day, the first ever Sunday scheduled for a Test match in England.

Courageously sustained in a partnership of 78 with deadbat

defiance by Ramprakash, Gooch batted on past tea and towards the evening with phlegmatic control. During the day, there were three breaks for rain; short, but long enough for the West Indies bowlers to change, refresh themselves, and put their feet up.

Fortitude and concentration, applied technique and placement; the sharpest single never spurned, ones daringly turned into crucial twos. The knowing throng rapt, admiring, pent up, mostly silent ... a smatter of applause for a well-run two, even for a ball watchfully 'well left'; certainly for a fizzing yorker skilfully dug out; eruptive relief which could be heard down in the city square to celebrate a boundary. Against this attack 'boundary balls' come rarely, yet Gooch was never too locked-in to the defensive mode to miss one; in all he was to hit 18 fours.

With bat held high, head turned, as if squinting down a gun-barrel at the enemy, and hands cocked, Gooch repeats to himself, 'Don't give it away; don't give it away'. Battle standards, flashes of old campaigns, colour splice and blade – bold, capital 'SS' for Stuart Surridge, and '333' and Turbo. For once he bats in a long-sleeved sweater, testament to the grim weather and, in a way, the grimness of the vigil. A crown and three lions for England. White T-shirt undervest at his collar. Unbadged white helmet. Moustache bushy, black. White gloves, piped in red and blue and, aptly, bearing the legend 'ULTIMATE' across the knuckles – and at every single, or at over's end, he is biting at the velcro at his left wrist and tearing off that single glove, which he either carries in his hand or hangs on his bat-handle, a limp flag on a pole on an airless day. Once, in mid-afternoon, the twelfth man comes out with two or three left-hand gloves from which to choose, and he pokes and prods at the selection on offer like a housewife at a fruit stall ... Then he settles back to his audacious task, two feet four-square at the crease, and heart of oak.

He lost Ramprakash at 116 for the mighty Ambrose's four-out-of-four. Only eight runs later it was six-out-of-six, with Smith wiped out first ball and then Russell for 4. Good cousin Essex, Pringle, comes in. Only four wickets are left, and still not even 150 ahead. Another stop for rain. On return, the lentil-soup gloom is worse. The umpires offer the light. 'We'll stay out,' Gooch says. They do, and survive until rain drives everyone in for the night, with England 143 for six, still only 168 ahead, Pringle not out 10; Gooch not out 82, having faced 189 of 330 balls bowled. He enjoys his bath, a pint at the Fox & Hounds, an early supper and bed. As normal, he sleeps soundly and is up early for loosening callisthenics.

Next morning, rain interrupts a proper outside net. No play is possible for fifty minutes. But with Pringle resolutely pushing his long left leg down the pitch and digging in, there is time enough before lunch for Gooch to go to his century – a famous hundred, not only in the context of the match but in Test history, for only the three 'Bs', Barrington, Boycott, and Botham, have reached three figures on each of England's Test grounds. Some locals said that the standing ovation, rare at Headingley, matched that for Boycott's one hundredth century in 1977.

The applause was almost as warmly acclaiming for Pringle when he was finally prised out by Marshall – like Ramprakash for only 27 – but, crucially, he had lasted for almost two-and-a-half hours in a seventh-wicket partnership of 98 runs.

DeFreitas and Watkin went at once, but Gooch nursed the last man, Malcolm, away from the strike for six more overs before Marshall bowled the rabbit. England all out 252, Gooch not out 154. West Indies, needing 278 to win, lost a wicket (Simmons) that night and folded next day for 162 (Richardson 68, Dujon 33). England had won, famously, by 115 runs.

In *The Times*, John Woodcock, with the experience of watching over four hundred Tests in forty years, pronounced: 'Since the Second World War, no innings by an England captain has surpassed Gooch's. It stands out, not for artistic merit, but for skill and courage against a very formidable attack in awkward conditions at a crucial time'.

Wisden was to go further: '... as fine a captain's innings as there has ever been'.

And editorials in both the *Independent* and the *Guardian* topped even *Wisden* by suggesting it was, in the circumstances, the best Test-match innings ever – the latter newspaper attracting a follow-up letter:

'You are right in nominating Graham Gooch's heroic innings against the West Indies last week as the finest this century. But you missed an important fact which underlines the innings' greatness even further. Gooch not only "set himself the sternest of tasks and carried it out", but as captain of England was expected by the nation to do so. Many captains have wilted under this type of pressure, but not Gooch. To perform well is great, to perform well when expected to is greatness.' (Malcolm Tait, Maidenhead, Berkshire)

In the *Sunday Times*, Robin Marlar wrote:

'Carrying his bat for 154 in a total of 252 puts Gooch on a pedestal above anything he or any of his contemporaries have done. Church bells have been rung and sermons preached for less. At least we can put the man's name in lights. Which is more than Gooch himself will have been doing, and in that modesty he shares one of the principal characteristics of another England opening batsman, Jack Hobbs, The Master. It is a feature of cricket that when something happens like this, the nation gets a share of the glory too.'

To carry his bat was historic feat enough. To do so in fashioning, almost singlehandedly, a victory was unique for an Englishman. In the present century, only Len Hutton, twice, and Geoffrey Boycott had carried their bat from beginning to end of a Test innings, but in doing so neither secured a victory. Hutton made a first innings 202 out of 344 at The Oval in 1950 against the West Indian spinners, Ramadhin and Valentine, but England ended up soundly thrashed, as they were when he did it again, only seven months later, at Adelaide (156 not out, out of 272). Boycott, interestingly, is one of a dozen Test-match openers in this century to have carried their bats for less than 100, which does not deny infinite skill on the day, certainly, but an innings collapse forfeits the marathon ingredient. Boycott was undefeated on 99 (out of 215) at Perth in 1979/80, when the last man, Willis, was caught in the slips off Dymock for a duck.

When Gooch became the twenty-third Test opener of the century to carry his bat, as well as Sir Leonard three others had done it twice – two Aussie Bills, Woodfull and Lawry, and Glenn Turner, the high-achieving New Zealander. At the end of this particular summer, the West Indian opener Haynes also completed his second bat-carry, 75 not out, at The Oval.

At a percentage of 66.11, Gooch's score was the highest by far of a side's total of any bat-carrier of the century. In seven-and-a-half hours, from first to undefeated last, Gooch's runs made up exactly two-thirds of those made from the bat – 154 out of 231 – against one of the most potent attacks in history; in poor light, and interruptions for rain, with 27 the next highest score. In the whole match only five of the 22 players passed 30 runs, but Gooch did so twice.

Romantic cricket lovers may swoon at Gilbert Jessop's dare and genius at The Oval in 1902, or at Victor Trumper's first-in-and-last-out (74 of 122) in 1903/4. But what coldly drawn-up qualifications should determine 'the greatest Test innings of the century' – in context, that is, and taking account of the quality of the opposition, the relative difficulty of the pitch and elements, the state of the game and how the innings altered it, and the comparative performances of those around you? Similarly, a truly great innings must surely be 'against the odds' and one which inspires such words as valour, defiance, resolution, technical mastery, and fortitude, both physical and cerebral. 'Greatness' can be displayed in sheer beauty of batsmanship, certainly, but it will be even greater for the bearding of the lion in his den. Nor can sheer weight of runs be conclusive.

Brian Lara's accumulative genius which delivered him the record 375 in Antigua against England in 1994 (as well as, not long afterwards, his 501 at Edgbaston for Warwickshire against Durham) was undoubtedly a 'great' innings, but where does it rate in the all-time pantheon when judged by the objective criteria just mentioned? Was, for colourful display for instance, Stan McCabe's 232 at Trent Bridge in 1938, or Graeme Pollock's 125 at the same place in 1965, the greater? Or Derek Randall's 174 in the Centenary Test of 1977? Did Martin Donnelly or Bert Sutcliffe (or Herbert Sutcliffe, for that matter) play *the* great Test innings which nobody recognized as such at the time? Or Zaheer Abbas, or Javed Miandad? Or one of the 'Three W's'?

The young Bradman's 309 in a day at Leeds in 1930 must surely be in the top frame somewhere – but many witnesses have sworn that his 254 at Lord's in the same year was even greater. The greatest? Four years earlier, same place, and Hammond's 240 against Australia is still enthused about, just as George Headley's two innings (106 out of 277, and 107 out of 225) against England in the

Lord's Test of 1939 would be put up still by many, especially taking every factor into account.

At the beginning of the century, Jessop's furious glory at The Oval can only have been matched, historians insist, by another merrie Englander when Ian Botham struck his unbeaten 149 at Headingley in 1981. But the purists say Botham's century at Manchester in the same series was a far better innings. So where does that leave the 149 for 'greatness'? Level with Gavaskar's 221 at The Oval in 1979, perhaps, or Greenidge's 214 at Lord's in 1984, or Sobers's counterattacking 132 in the tie at Brisbane in 1961? And where do you fit in Viv Richards's 56-ball century against England in Antigua in 1986? As the best-ever Test innings in history?

Or was that Graham Gooch's match-winning 154 not out at Headingley in 1991? It could well have been.

GG

I couldn't be anything less than proud of myself, could I? But as I drove home that Monday night to get ready for Essex's Benson & Hedges semi-final against Worcester on the Wednesday, I honestly felt an even warmer and more satisfied buzz inside me at a victory for the England team, especially after our disappointments in Australia.

An obviously good century, even when you lose, can still be rewarding on a personal level. But it is nothing to compare with a good performance which makes the difference between the team winning and losing. Also, as any batsman knows, however many runs are against his name on the board, it takes 'two to tango' and the men who stay in with you play just as crucial a part. The concentration and application of Ramprakash and Pringle (and Robin Smith in the first innings) had therefore been as vital to the victory as my part in it. This is not false modesty. In the end, in cricket, if they go, you go. Also, the solid nagging consistency and understanding of the particular necessities of the Headingley pitch of the bowlers, DeFreitas, Pringle again, and Watkin (five wickets in his first Test), made our match. And I was particularly proud of our fielding.

But why is it that only when you are losing, like in Australia, that everyone criticizes our 'joyless work ethic' which makes all the players 'dull, jaded, and overtired'. Do the critics think good performances happen by accident?

One thing I have to agree about with the critics, is that this 154 was my best Test innings. We just had to keep battling on, grinding out each run knowing that there was one more for them to make in the last innings. To do your best against the best, and to succeed at it, is the point of competitive sport. So in difficult conditions and against this sort of opposition, it was stupendously rewarding to carry my bat. Yet I have to add that, if I timed perfectly eight shots in all the seven-and-a-half hours, I would be overstating it. It was just a question of gutsing it out. I hadn't been in particularly good form, and there were not many red blotches on the sweet spot of my bat after that innings.

Looking back, I recalled one of the crucial psychological strokes late on the third, Saturday, evening. It had been a damp and murky day, and, after tea, even more so. Since the interval we had lost Ramprakash and then Smith and Russell in quick succession, all to Ambrose, and we still only had a puny lead. But Derek Pringle settled in capably and calmly enough; in fact, I could really feel Pring concentrating. I didn't know, till I was told afterwards, that it had been the coldest Test-match day for twenty-six years – when, at a drinks interval at Edgbaston, apparently, the England and New Zealand teams had called for hot soup! But I could sense that the West Indians in the field were mopingly fed up with being out there and that their two-sweatered bowlers had begun to go through the motions, just longing for the close.

It began to rain harder. I told the umpires, Dickie Bird and David Shepherd, that we'd stay on. We didn't want the bowlers to get a rest. This got them a bit more down, I think, and, tactically, it threw down another little moral gauntlet to Viv Richards, for although we were only about 150 ahead and nowhere near out of the wood, it showed them that we were being really positive and aware that runs in the bank, any runs, were our priority. Especially as, at exactly the same time and conditions the night before, and alarmingly for us, Viv himself had been counter-attacking with typical verve and dash.

As he reached 73 not out, the umpires offered Viv the light, and to our massive relief, as we were wilting after the long day, Viv marched off to the pavilion at a rate of knots. I knew that next morning we would be fresh and he'd have to play himself in again – and, sure enough, Pringle had him caught at slip off his third ball at the very start of play. The night before, had he stayed out there, the way Viv was going he could easily have scored another 30 runs.

Still, that's Viv Richards, always doing his own thing. He is generally tough out on the field, and leads by example. His players respect him and do what he says. He is a proud man, but he is also generous and gracious in defeat. (Not that he has had much experience of that!)

It struck me more than a few times during my innings that if we could only keep grinding on, then a victory here at Leeds would be (and I agree I'm cheating slightly by claiming the 'moral' victory at Trinidad when I broke my hand before the rainstorm that snatched it from us) my personal hat-trick of three wins in succession when I'd been playing. It's these little challenges that keep you determined and concentrating in a big innings. In Jamaica, as he was here, Richards was never grudging in defeat.

As a captain, he made the occasional error, for instance when he seemed to let us off the hook that Saturday afternoon. Richards suddenly decided to share eight gentle overs with himself and Carl Hooper instead of going for our jugular. With us still groggy and insecure, that half-hour or so allowed Mark and me to organize ourselves much more comfortably, though still cautiously, while four of the world's finest bowlers were resting in various parts of the field. Curtly Ambrose, who had taken the first three wickets – and was soon to come back for the next three – must have been pawing the earth during that little diversion. And I could sense Malcolm Marshall snorting in the outfield.

It just shows how powerful the West Indies have been all through my career, and before it, when you realize this was going to be England's first victory at home against them since 1969 – the year when I was setting out on my dear old 'L-plated' Vespa to my apprenticeship as a toolmaker. Which all made the Sunday morning at Headingley, not long before lunch, a nicely rewarding one to hear English Test cricket's PA 'voice', Alan Curtis, announce my sixth century so far against the West Indies. As I say, the definitive challenge is to pit your skills against the best in the world. In fact, it was my fourteenth Test hundred in all – not bad considering that I had only notched up eight when I began my reign as captain eighteen months before.

I have never been a great follower of records or statistics. But when you are told over the tannoy about certain landmarks or achievements, they are usually nice to hear. So when Curtis also announced that I now shared a record with three others – my friends Boycott and Botham and also Kenny Barrington – who all scored a century on each of England's Test grounds, I did come in to lunch thinking fondly of Kenny, of much he had done for me, and wondering whether he'd be looking down on Headingley from somewhere with that old beaky-nosed, proud-as-Punch grin of his, as well as offering a friendly wisecrack about how come I was batting so well in my old age. In a month I was going to be thirty-eight. Kenny had played his last-ever Test here at Headingley in 1968, when he was also thirty-seven. He had hoped to go on too, but in the following winter he had been forced to give it all up after he'd had the first of his heart attacks in Australia. Dear old Ken.

Our famous victory on the last day was clinched dramatically when Mike Atherton sprinted miles from gully to cover-point to poach a skier off Courtney Walsh which had been going straight down Ramprakash's throat. It had been a heart-stopping moment. I wasn't locking myself into what the press say is my monosyllabic, tight-lipped mode, when I made a point of saying after the match that our fielding had been vital to the outcome.

For Hick and Lamb had flypaper hands at slip, and young Ramprakash had set up not only his debut but our whole keenly competitive stall in the West Indies' first innings with two stupendous strikes out of the blue – a goalkeeper's full-length dive for a catch in the covers to dismiss Simmons, and a quicksilver direct-hit run out of Hooper. Those two brilliant bits of fielding put the West Indies under pressure at once.

I remarked that this vindicated our insistence on serious fielding practice. Of course, some smart idiot then retorted that Ramprakash had not played in Australia and was new to the team, so how could I claim that the Stewart–Gooch heavy-practice regime had anything to do with him?

Hadn't 'Ramps' been in our one-day Texaco squad at the beginning of the season, I replied, and hadn't he been practising here at Leeds with us for the days before the match? Taking catches at practice is a different matter from being under pressure in the match itself, but the value of practice catches is that they can send you on to the field with confidence to take anything that might come your way during a match.

Confidence is vital in fielding. I should know, for the older I was getting, the less confident I felt. I wasn't putting myself permanently in the slips any more – it's important for a captain to get a perspective away from the concentration of the close-up field. In this match I clung on to one diving left-hander in the slips to get rid of Gus Logie – the sort photographers love but, in truth, it's a matter of going for the ball and hoping it sticks – and held on to two steepling swirlers, one from Walsh in the first innings, and then a running over-the-shoulder job to dismiss Richards in the second which turned the match our way. They were both extremely good examples of why we practise fielding – and 'open-and-shut' evidence against our critics.

Of course, you can practise until you're blue in the face, but what you cannot legislate for in cricket is luck. Some of the players whose counties had been knocked out of the Benson & Hedges stayed in Leeds to continue the party, but as I drove contentedly back down the motorway that evening I realized that I might easily have been doing the same journey a day or two earlier, and in a less happy frame of mind ... if two slices of good fortune had gone against me.

In any big innings you need luck. Not often can a batsman look back and genuinely say, 'Great, that was chanceless'. In truth, at Headingley, off the very first ball I faced I didn't move my feet decisively and hesitantly push-drove Patterson's first 'sighter', which might have been slower than I expected, just fractionally wide of Marshall at mid-off. If 'Maco' had been a stride nearer I could have gone first ball. Then, soon after lunch on that first day, I prodded forward uncertainly to a great delivery from Walsh which cut back and whistled between my groping bat and the top of my pad-flap, just brushing the latter as it went on to smack into Dujon's gloves. All the West Indians went up for it.

Mercifully, Dickie Bird's finger didn't. But it so easily might have, as obviously there had been a noise and a fractional deviation. I don't blame the fielders or the bowler for appealing with a song and a dance. Nor could you have blamed Dickie if he had given me out; the ball must have been just a blur to him. But he was proved right on the TV slow-motion replay, which showed that my bat never touched the ball. Not long afterwards, when I reached 50, a number of the West Indians pointedly did not applaud, thinking I should have 'walked'.

On the subject of walking: would I have walked without even waiting to see what the umpire's decision was, if that ball had nicked my bat instead of my pad?

If it had obviously hit my bat and deviated a mile, of course I would have. But in any close decision I believe it is much better to wait for the umpire's decision. So many batsmen want it both ways – they don't walk for obvious dismissals, and then kick up a fuss when the decision is close. I am sure it is best simply to wait for the decision, and if it goes against you, get off promptly. That way there need be no moans or complaints, and the umpires' authority is maintained. Since I've been captain I have always instructed my players, whether batting or fielding, to wait for the umpire's decision and, once it's been given, to comply without hesitation.

I may be a bit more phlegmatic than most, but I get decidedly annoyed when some of our own players question umpires' decisions. Ask those competitive, hot-under-the-collar firebrands like Nasser Hussain, Alec Stewart or Phil Tufnell. Once I had to tell Essex's brilliant overseas batsman, Salim Malik, to apologise to the umpire, David Constant, for theatrically grabbing at his own sleeve, to show where the ball had hit, after he'd been given out caught behind. Salim did apologize, but he was still reported by Constant.

Then, at The Oval three years later against Australia, I was facing Shane Warne and went to cut him just outside the off-stump. I was pretty sure I got a tiny nick to wicketkeeper Ian Healy. The Australian fielders all appealed. Umpire says 'not out' – and I stay there. Warne dances around seething and strutting at how hard done by he is, but there's no abuse aimed at me personally. Perhaps he was a respecter of old age! After the match, I mentioned to Shane that, in truth, I thought he was right and that I had got a nick, but that my system was to leave it to the umpires as sole arbiters so, either way, right or wrong, you do not undermine their authority. 'That's fine with me, no worries,' said Shane. 'That's the way I play it too.'

The batsmen who are out of order, however, are those who stand and wait for the umpire's decision, like I did at The Oval, and if it goes in their favour, fine, but when they get a bad one, they stomp around as if the whole world is against them. They can't have it both ways. If your philosophy is not to walk but to leave without complaint if the umpire's finger goes up, then the same applies even if the decision might seem incorrect.

The case against those who think batsmen should try and help the umpire by walking every time is simply that human nature just doesn't allow it. Ken Barrington used to tell me that waiting for the umpire was right, because in his day people like Colin Cowdrey and Peter May were known in the game as definite walkers, but in tight situations in top Test matches they would suddenly decide to wait for the decision and so, because of their reputation, they would perhaps inadvertently sow a seed of doubt in the umpire's mind.

So, suppose I get a millimetre of wood on the ball. Everyone appeals like a dervish. I stand there. The umpire says 'not out'. Fair enough. Then repeat almost the same scenario, except that I know, and the fielders and the bowler know, that I haven't got a touch. But they still all go up. And this time, so does the finger. Off I trudge. They know I haven't hit it; nevertheless they all go into a huddle of self-congratulation.

And I've never had one of them calling me back.

Only once have I called a batsman back myself after he'd been given out. Allan Warner, of Derbyshire, was given run out at Chelmsford, quite correctly, but there was some doubt about whether our bowler had accidentally got in his way as he was running and I thought it fair to ask the umpires to call him back. Eight or even nine times out of ten, a batsman will know when he's out lbw, or at least that it's very close; he knows where his feet are and before he looks up he's saying to himself, 'That's pretty plumb'. With run outs, however, it can be more of a lottery.

At Headingley the 1991 Test, for instance, when Robin Smith took on Ambrose's arm and went for a second run just after he'd got his fifty, and was given out. He came in seething, saying he was sure he'd made it. But we all had to shake our heads and say, 'Sorry, Robin, you were out by a good few inches', because we'd already seen the incident from every conceivable angle on the television slow motion in the dressing-room.

Luckily Robin's dismissal did not alter the result of the match. I once tried to do exactly the same and backed my 'speed' in going for the extra run against a throw from, of all people, Michael Holding in the Antigua Test on my first West Indies tour in 1981. There was a shortish mid-on and a nice open space behind him. I firmly on-drove Colin Croft's in-slanter down there and set off, presuming a comfortable three, and telling Geoff Boycott exactly that as we crossed. Holding had to give chase and make a lot of ground from mid-wicket. But I had forgotten that Holding, if he had not taken up cricket, could have been an Olympic 400-metre champion. As we turned for the third, Geoffrey said 'No! Stay!' But I signalled 'C'mon', even though I was going to the danger end. With Michael's arrow-like throw on the turn, 60 for no wicket and going well became 60 for one.

Such things can turn an innings, a match, a series – even a career. As I drove back down from Headingley, for instance, I reflected how such a fine match with bat and ball had obviously changed the course, for the immediate future anyway, of the Test career of Derek Pringle. Derek very nearly didn't play in that match. First, he had a stiff back and might have cried off anyway. Then Chris Lewis dropped out on the morning of the match, so 'Pring' had to play.

Even so, he might not even have been picked in the first place, except for someone else's injury. In the three pipe-opening Texaco Cup one-dayers which preceded the Test (and which England had won 3–0), Derek had been hit for plenty, while in the first of them at Edgbaston our bowling star had been the 'comeback kid' himself, Ian Botham, who with his little swingers and seamers had shot out the heart of the West Indies batting order. But then, when he was batting with Mike Atherton, Ian badly pulled a hamstring going for a sharp single, and so he missed the Test. Derek, as an all-rounder, came in and his stout performance was warmly acclaimed by the Headingley crowd which had hitherto been jeeringly suspicious of his 'southern softie' and 'varsity toff' persona.

I was delighted for him, of course, and mighty grateful, too, for what could well be the most influential innings of his whole career – but what was gloriously pleasant to hear, as Fred Trueman mentioned Derek's name when he was presenting the match awards at the end from the pavilion balcony, was the whole crowd singing in unison, 'God Save Our Gracious Pring, Long Live Our Noble Pring'.

Derek milked the moment, while pretending to take it all in his stride!

It had been good for us to have Ian Botham challenging again for what he obviously regarded as his rightful place. Ian had begun the season meaning business with a typically swashbuckling 161 against the West Indies at Worcester (passing his century off 80 balls), and he followed that with five-wicket pickings against both Gloucestershire and Lancashire – also hitting the latter's attack, which included Wasim Akram and Phil DeFreitas, for another century. So he was seriously in our minds for the Test series, until that hamstring went in the first Texaco one-dayer. Back at Chelmsford for the Benson & Hedges cup semi-final against Worcester, I enquired about his fitness for the next Test at Lord's but he told me

---

ENGLAND v WEST INDIES (First Test)
Played at Headingley on June 6-10, 1991. England won by 115 runs. Toss: West Indies.
Debut: G.A. Hick, M.R. Ramprakash, S.L. Watkin. Man of the Match: G.A. Gooch.

ENGLAND

		Balls	Mins	4s	6s			Balls	Mins	4s	6s
G.A. Gooch*	c Dujon b Marshall	34	49	61	6	–	not out	154	331	452	18	–
M.A. Atherton	b Patterson	2	16	22	–	–	c Dujon b Ambrose	6	33	38	–	–
G.A. Hick	c Dujon b Walsh	6	31	51	1	–	b Ambrose	6	20	25	1	–
A.J. Lamb	c Hooper b Marshall	11	37	55	1	–	c Hooper b Ambrose	0	1	1	–	–
M.R. Ramprakash	c Hooper b Marshall	27	103	142	4	–	c Dujon b Ambrose	27	109	142	2	–
R.A. Smith	run out	54	88	135	7	–	lbw b Ambrose	0	1	1	–	–
R.C. Russell†	lbw b Patterson	5	29	45	1	–	c Dujon b Ambrose	4	12	14	1	–
D.R. Pringle	c Logie b Patterson	16	73	111	–	–	c Dujon b Marshall	27	94	144	2	–
P.A.J. DeFreitas	c Simmons b Ambrose	15	34	43	2	–	lbw b Walsh	3	27	41	–	–
S.L. Watkin	b Ambrose	2	9	14	–	–	c Hooper b Marshall	0	5	6	–	–
D.E. Malcolm	not out	5	31	41	1	–	b Marshall	4	11	28	1	–
Extras	(lb5, w2, nb14)	21					(b4, lb9, w1, nb7)	21				
TOTAL	(79.2 overs: 13.0ph)	198					(106 overs: 14.1ph)	252				

WEST INDIES

		Balls	Mins	4s	6s			Balls	Mins	4s	6s
P.V. Simmons	c Ramprakash b DeFreitas	38	62	77	6	–	b DeFreitas	0	1	2	–	–
D.L. Haynes	c Russell b Watkin	7	38	55	1	–	c Smith b Pringle	19	51	84	–	–
R.B. Richardson	run out	29	62	97	2	–	c Lamb b DeFreitas	68	141	195	11	–
C.L. Hooper	run out	0	5	8	–	–	c Lamb b Watkin	5	25	32	–	–
I.V.A. Richards*	c Lamb b Pringle	73	98	129	7	2	c Gooch b Watkin	3	8	9	–	–
A.L. Logie	c Lamb b DeFreitas	6	15	25	1	–	c Gooch b Watkin	3	7	7	–	–
P.J.L. Dujon†	c Ramprakash b Watkin	6	13	14	1	–	lbw b DeFreitas	33	62	72	5	–
M.D. Marshall	c Hick b Pringle	0	5	8	–	–	lbw b Pringle	1	7	4	–	–
C.E.L. Ambrose	c Hick b DeFreitas	0	3	4	–	–	c Pringle b DeFreitas	14	26	33	3	–
C.A. Walsh	c Gooch b DeFreitas	3	16	23	–	–	c Atherton b Malcolm	9	23	31	–	–
B.P. Patterson	not out	5	14	18	1	–	not out	0	–	2	–	–
Extras	(lb1, nb5)	6					(lb1, nb6)	7				
TOTAL	(54.1 overs: 13.8ph)	173					(56.4 overs: 13.9ph)	162				

WEST INDIES	O	M	R	W	O	M	R	W
Ambrose	26	8	49	2	28	6	52	6
Patterson	26.2	8	67	3	15	1	52	0
Walsh	14	7	31	1	30	5	61	1
Marshall	13	4	46	3	25	4	58	3
Hooper					4	1	11	0
Richards					4	1	5	0
ENGLAND								
Malcolm	14	0	69	0	6.4	0	26	1
DeFreitas	17.1	5	34	4	21	4	59	4
Watkin	14	2	55	2	7	0	38	3
Pringle	9	3	14	2	22	6	38	2

FALL OF WICKETS				
	E	WI	E	WI
1st	13	36	22	0
2nd	45	54	38	61
3rd	45	58	38	77
4th	64	102	116	85
5th	129	139	116	88
6th	149	156	124	136
7th	154	160	222	137
8th	177	165	236	139
9th	181	167	236	162
10th	198	173	252	162

Umpires: H.D. Bird and D.R. Shepherd. Overall over rate: 13.69

that the injury was nowhere near ready to stand up to a five-day match, and he wasn't even sure about it lasting even for a one-dayer. And then, of course, we went in first and Ian helped confine us to a miserable 104 all out, with superb figures of 11–6–11–3.

At Lord's, as it happened, the second Test against West Indies was ruined by rain; we were outplayed in the third Test at Trent Bridge, and lost a competitive match at Edgbaston when Richards steadied his side before steering them home at the last. So we had to win at The Oval to square the series, which after a tremendous contest and a highly evocative five days we did. It was Viv's final Test and the crowd gave him an emotional send-off. At the beginning of the tour, Viv had said to me, 'Graham, let's make it all sweetness and light, no aggro', and I was happy to comply with that. I was more than chuffed when their manager, Lance Gibbs, named me Man of the Series and said, 'Gooch deserves it, not least for making this the happiest and most sporting of series I can remember'.

Who hit the winning boundary for England? None other than I T Botham. 'IT AIN'T OVER TILL THE FAT MAN SWINGS', was one headline. Robin Smith again showed the value of all the concentrated dedication he puts into his batting by setting us on our way with a century. Then Phil Tufnell induced an astonishing collapse to finish off the West Indies' reply – and I wasted no time in asking them to follow-on for the first time against England since 1969.

After the disasters in Australia, Tufnell knew that our failure to select him for England all through the 1991 series (when we did pick a spinner it was Worcestershire's Richard Illingworth) was intended to make him pull his act together. I had been keeping in touch with John Emburey, who told me that Tufnell was bowling well and consistently, and was the most dangerous spinner in England. I accepted that, on his day, he almost certainly was, but what was still worrying me was his general attitude. How Tufnell could have so complacently accepted the derision poured on him by the Australian crowds for his shoddy fielding – and it really was atrocious on a couple of occasions – mystified me. If that had happened to me on my first tour I would have curled up with shame. They even unfurled banners proclaiming his uselessness and he took this notoriety as a sort of fan-club hero-worship. Ian Chappell publicly advised me to put him on to bowl more often, 'That way, at least he won't be fielding'. There was even a comedy cartoon of a plane with the England team landing at Sydney airport, and the stewardesses coming down the aisle, as they do, with the aerosol spray to get rid of any incoming bugs and pests. Then they cut to me in my seat, saying, 'Oh good, that's got rid of Tufnell anyway'.

Perhaps Phil and I will never quite relate to each other. His carefree flippancy had me seething. Phil has a marvellous natural talent for bowling, but his mental toughness seemed suspect to me. When you're bowling you have to take the good times with the bad and still stick to your task. Phil is very, very good when everything is going well for him, but when the batsmen are dominating he makes me feel he doesn't want to know. And if he loses out on one or two decisions he throws a tantrum and appears to want to give up.

The reason that John Emburey is such a fine bowler, is that when things are not going well and the batsmen are in the ascendant, 'Embers' will dig deep, guts it out for you, and never lose his line or length or his cool. Perhaps it has to do with age?

As time went on and I gave up the captaincy, I became more mellow and began to think that perhaps it was my fault for not handling Phil better. Certainly, as he matured, his fielding really improved. And, on his day, he continued to be a fine and original bowler. That spell at The Oval, when he took six wickets in 33 balls to send the West Indies into a tailspin, was memorable. In a way, it showed that our proverbial 'kick up the backside' had paid off.

Ian Botham, of course, had missed out on Sabina Park and Headingley, so this was his first win against the West Indies in twenty Tests. I heard that more than a few 'swift halves' slipped down the big man's throat that evening. Alas, Allan Lamb, who had for so long been a courageous battler against the world champions, missed out at The Oval. He had had a miserable season in 1991, the most barren of his career, and he'd been dropped for the final Test – but there was no way I was going to be without him for the World Cup in Australia in the following winter.

Unfortunately I had fallen out with Allan earlier in the summer, as anyone who eavesdropped on our exchange on the dressing-room balcony at Lord's during the Texaco match would tell you. It was to change a relationship and a friendship which I had long valued.

Basically, it was my mistake. When I was put in charge, I was happy to have Allan as vice-captain, a job he filled on both the tours when he stepped in for me in the Tests following my two hand injuries. In between, in the summer of 1990 for the two home series, he had also been named as my vice-captain, which was a departure from tradition as, for home series, we never usually named anyone officially as vice-captain.

So now, when we met to pick the team for the Texaco one-dayers, we reverted to that system. Nothing sinister in it, just basically because, with Allan being almost a 'senior citizen' like me, we thought we'd leave any official post of vice-captain open so we could start thinking of some of the younger players as likely candidates – Alec Stewart or Michael Atherton, for example.

It did not seem too big a deal to me; doubtless Allan would have taken over had I been injured during a match. Nor was the decision, as some of the more mischievous journalists suggested when the story broke, anything to do with Lamb being 'caught' out late at a casino with David Gower and Kerry Packer at the beginning of the Australian tour. But what I should have done is either to have rung Allan as soon as we made the decision, or taken him aside when we arrived at Edgbaston for the first one-day game. As it was, we had dinner together at Birmingham when rain meant the game going into a second day and Allan said the press were wanting to know if he was still vice-captain. I said, 'Well, no, we've simply decided not to have one, but it was no reflection on you personally'. But, of course, he did take it personally – having had the position one year but not the next, he took it as a demotion. Then at the Lord's game, he decided to have it out with me on the balcony after he'd bumped into Ted Dexter, the chairman, who'd told him the position was 'fluid' and that in the event of me being injured he 'could' be asked to captain the side.

So the whole matter was a total misunderstanding, and I still regret my lack of diplomacy. Allan issued a statement to the press saying he was bitter and hard done by and that, even if asked, he would never consider captaining England again. That was particularly upsetting because Allan was a very good person to have around, both as a player and a vice-captain.

Then, the following summer of 1992, Allan was dropped from the

The oldest swinger in town. As the years wore on the more I worried about maintaining my fielding standards, although this skier from Steve Waugh at Lord's in 1993 (right) stayed in the hands.

Above: Nothing can beat a good personal performance when it makes the difference between your team winning or losing. Carrying my bat in making 154 against the West Indies at Headingley in 1991 has to be my best of all.

Below: The Cup that cheers – yet again. Essex celebrate the 1992 County Championship, our sixth victory since 1979 and eleventh trophy in all. When I joined the club, the trophy cabinet had been pretty bare.

Middle for diddle ... bowled by Malcolm Marshall for 45 at Edgbaston in 1991. Marshall was the very best of my time – a thinking bowler, fast and cunning with it.

The media and the message, 1992. I often enjoyed winding up the press by playing everything down. It was safer that way, too.

Left: Devon Malcolm, ten years younger, fails to out-sprint the veteran. To me, fitness has always been crucial.

Below: Adelaide, 1991. A smile at last after a century and a fighting England performance in the middle of a generally grim trip.

We watch Pakistan receive the World Cup at Melbourne in 1992. They deserved it on the night. We had done everything right till this final hurdle.

Above: The 1993 tour to India and my hundredth hundred at Cuttack. Or was it? My century at Cambridge the following season made absolutely sure.

Below: Announcing the end of my captaincy in the summer of 1993 alongside Ken Lawrence of the TCCB. I had done my best, but in the end the poor results outnumbered the good.

Above: This boundary off Paul Reiffel, during our victory against Australia in the Sixth Test at The Oval in 1993, helped me to 8,235 Test runs – the most by any Englishman in the history of the game.

Below: My last home Test was a victory, celebrated as Mike Atherton and I put on 48 in 23 balls against South Africa at The Oval in 1994, which some said was the 'most explosive Test start in memory.

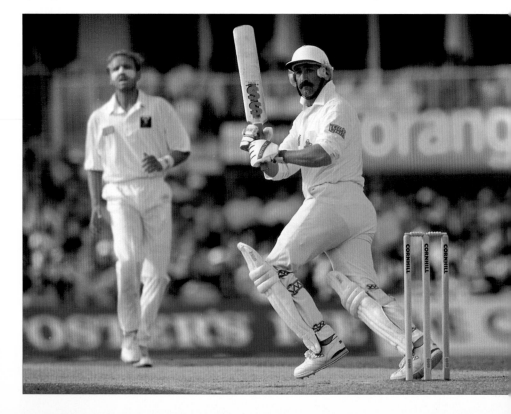

Above: Dad's pride and joy … Hannah (centre) and the twins Megan and Sally.

Below: Old boys' reunion at Edgbaston, 1994, with Keith Fletcher, long-time captain and mentor, and Alan Knott, the finest wicketkeeper I ever played with.

The end of the road – caught by McDermott for 4 in my final Test innings in Perth. England's future is now in Mike Atherton's capable hands (below left). Walking off to a standing ovation (below), I've time to reflect on the ups and downs of my 20 years in Test cricket.

team when we recalled David Gower to play against the Pakistanis, and he seemed to become even more bitter towards me, thinking his services had been dispensed with too soon. I understood his displeasure at being dropped, but I could only pick eleven players for a match. When David replaced his friend against Pakistan, at least Allan came out with the excellent line: 'Good luck to David. He's back and I fully realize there's no room for both of us in the cockpit of his Biggles's Tiger Moth!'.

Face to face there was no animosity between Allan and me. It was just that a close working relationship, especially on tour, had now become strained. After the great victory at The Oval against the West Indies (before which Allan had been dropped for the first time), by a fluke in the fixture-list I had to go straight to Colchester for Essex's match against Lamb's Northamptonshire. Essex were mounting the final assault for the County Championship in a contest in which Warwickshire had been making all the mid-summer running. I fear Allan felt his nose even more put out of joint by me because, on a dry and turning pitch, after David Capel had hustled three of us out cheaply, Nasser Hussain and I switched into overdrive and put on 287 for the fourth wicket. In just the afternoon session we put on 177 off only 39 overs. We declared on 403 and then bowled Northants out twice.

That 173 of mine was my 86th first-class hundred (and during the summer I had also equalled Gordon Greenidge's record of eleven Sunday League centuries). My 87th and 88th came before the end of the summer: the first in that one-off Test against Sri Lanka at Lord's – a record sixth Test hundred by anyone at headquarters – and the second when, to clinch the Championship in a dramatic and satisfying manner at Chelmsford, I hit 259 against Middlesex, the champions of the year before, and we won by a huge innings margin. The players drowned me in champagne, I received the trophy and grabbed the microphone to say that the string of six victories in our last seven matches had been due to our determination to avoid the ignominious record of being runners-up three times in succession – the deducted 25 points in 1989 being one of the causes! I also said it had been 'the best year of my career' and that 'Essex cricket meant the world to me'. And I really did mean that.

We were approaching the next World Cup. At the last one in India and Pakistan in 1987, Mike Gatting had been the England captain. He was still serving his ban for his rebel tour to South Africa, but we had a good discussion about England's plans for the 1991/92 contest which was being staged in Australia and New Zealand in February/March 1992. Gatt had finished the season as the top England batsman (2,057 runs at 73.46 to my 1,911 at 70.77) and I told him we would be missing him!

Earlier in the summer, with Nelson Mandela freed from jail and plans for the multi-racial democratic elections announced in South Africa, the International Cricket Council had readmitted South Africa to world cricket and I had written to the TCCB to ask that, in view of the new political situation, surely there could now be an amnesty for the 'rebel' cricketers. Besides anything else, I wanted to be able to choose my best England team. I asked the TCCB to forward my letter to the ICC. Whether it was ultimately to do any good, I didn't know, but as yet nothing had happened and Gatting was still *persona non grata* as far as playing for England was concerned.

As I said, there was no way I was going into the World Cup without Allan Lamb, probably the most brilliant one-day batsman England have had, and the best in the world at pacing the run chase. But David Gower, sadly, was never in the frame.

At the end of the Australian tour in 1990/91, we had played three one-day internationals against New Zealand. One night at Wellington, David and I had found an empty restaurant and settled down for a heart-to-heart. I said that I was going to put my cards on the table. Looking back now, with four years of hindsight, I consider I might have got it wrong and that I should simply have accepted David for what he was – a big-match player of great natural ability, touched with genius – and simply regarded him as an automatic choice for England. But some of our performances and our general commitment on the tour had disappointed me so much that I was determined, as captain, to keep doing things my way. So at our Wellington tête-à-tête I said I was looking for more evidence of David's commitment to cricket generally and to his setting a better example to the younger players who looked up to him. I said to him, 'Give me evidence, not words, that you mean business'. David, as languid and charming as ever, said his ambitions certainly took in playing many more games for England and that he would prove that intent to me with his scores in the upcoming season with Hampshire, whom he had joined in 1990.

But by the beginning of the summer, the runs had dried up for David. In 1990, he had hit only one century, in his home debut for Hampshire, and throughout 1991 he did not hit one. So even his strongest supporters – and there were plenty of those in the county and elsewhere – could not make out much of a case for his Test comeback. They just said he was a 'big-match player' and we should pick him so he could prove it to us once again. They may well have been right.

The World Cup of limited-overs matches, however, was not David's scene. His antipathy to one-dayers was well known, and his bad shoulder injury had left him with no throwing arm. I have to confess, however, that my hangover after all the tribulations in Australia might still have had a bearing and that, during the 1991 West Indies series, I did find myself more at ease with the leadership without David in the squad. I have no personal animosity towards David, it's simply the truth about how I felt at the time, and I want to be honest about it.

However, I fought hard to make sure that I got Ian Botham to the World Cup. The old lion had been a breath of fresh air during the Oval Test against the West Indies. He revelled in his comeback, practised seriously and keenly, jollied and jockeyed up the youngsters and put them on a keen Test match 'edge'. They relished his presence. His bits of advice and encouragement to the bowlers were invaluable – after all, he was the man who has taken more Test wickets than any other Englishman in history. He batted responsibly in the first innings, just when we needed him to, with a two-hour 31; he bowled decently, and caught anything he could reach. Most important, with our winter in mind, he relished the big occasion and was always looking to be centre stage.

So Micky Stewart and I made it our business to get Ian available for the World Cup. Since his disappointment over the last West Indies tour, Ian had not left his winters free for the possibility of cricket. He had signed on to play in a pantomime in Bournemouth over Christmas and was also booked to continue his long-running and ongoing television quiz programme *A Question of Sport*. The

BBC kindly agreed to reschedule their recording dates for that, and the pantomime producers were happy for Ian to get out to New Zealand as soon as possible in January so he might even be competing for a place in the third and final Test – certainly in time to be fully keyed-up for the World Cup.

When he arrived, Ian did look rather overweight, although he assured me he had kept himself fighting fit. The press tried to get up a head of steam about 'The Podgy Panto Prince', but in no time they had to change tack to 'No stopping the Demon King' when he played well in the Wellington Test, stepping in when both Pringle and Lewis were injured, and then in the last one-day international at Christchurch. He went in first and blazed 79 at a run a ball. It was just like the old days – outrageous. The opposition just didn't know where to bowl at him. And that one innings convinced us in dramatic fashion that Ian had proved his point, because all along he had been asking Micky and me to consider him as opening bat for the World Cup.

As Ian was going mad out in the middle, Micky and I had looked at each other and nodded, 'Well, why not? What have we got to lose?' We agreed that Ian batting at no. 6 or no. 7 might be a bit wasted. If we bat first and bat well, he's not going to be involved that much apart from a last mad flurry when he might smash a few runs. But to my mind he wasn't by nature a great operator in a run-chase situation, unlike Allan Lamb. If, say, you have 50-odd to get in the last eight overs, you'd back your mortgage that Lamby would get them for you, with the winning hit coming in the last over. He will play it calm and work out what's required, take the runs he's given without a fuss, and hit a four when he needs to. If Ian needs 50 in eight overs, his nature is to try and get them in three or four overs.

Another possible bonus of Ian going in first in the World Cup was that a number of the matches were being played in New Zealand, in the All Blacks rugby stadium, ringed by concrete terracing like our old soccer grounds. I had noticed how a well struck boundary had the cricket ball rebounding sometimes from the concrete right back to the middle – which did the ball plenty of harm. It would be very user-friendly terracing if Botham could pepper the fours early on and so make the new ball 'old' in no time.

Funnily enough, this was my first tour to New Zealand. I found it a lovely place; I enjoyed the cricket and the people very much, not that they actually thronged to the Test matches. On the first day of the Christchurch Test, we took our two team minibuses from the hotel to the ground to arrive at about 9.30 for an 11.00 start.

There's not a soul in sight. No caretaker, no groundsmen, no anybody. And certainly no atmosphere. The gates are locked. To me, the first day of a Test is all buzz and expectancy – Who's going to be left out? Who'll win the toss? Will they bat or bowl? What's the wicket like? Everyone is hyped up.

Not in Christchurch, however. The gates aren't even open! Finally, one man wanders across. I think he'd just woken up. 'What's the problem? he asks. 'We've come to play in a Test match in an hour-and-a-half,' we say, 'and the gates aren't even open.' 'Oh, okay,' he says, 'no problems,' and he opens the gates for us. In we go, and of course we are the only ones there.

We won the three-Test series handsomely along with the one-day rubber. I was delighted with everyone, including Phil Tufnell who had obviously worked hard at his fielding in the summer. We had arrived in January and hit the ground running, thanks, I am sure, to a good rest at home in the autumn and then to serious training work at the Lilleshall centre in Shropshire. I tuned up with a century in the opening game at Hamilton – so did Graeme Hick, his sixty-first hundred, and he was still only twenty-five. At his age I'd only scored eight! In the event Graeme again struggled in the Test matches. He was having a very uncomfortable baptism, but he was such a good, sensible and hard-working fellow that I knew, with his innate talent, it would all come good for him if he persevered.

I hit a painstaking century in the second Test at Auckland to wrap up the series 2–0, but early on I knew I had infuriated the Kiwi bowlers by playing and missing. It was a green damp pitch which seamed a lot, and only two other batsmen in the whole match passed 50: Lamb with a glorious daredevil 60 and Martin Crowe with 56. I dropped into my 'dangerous wicket' mode – playing the line of the ball but playing it late; in other words reaching out too far in order not to fetch the ball or play it too early. As long as I played the ball late, if it seamed laterally the odds were that the movement would take the ball past the edge of the bat. So I was, in fact, consciously 'playing' to play-and-miss.

But the despairing New Zealand bowlers didn't quite see it that way. It was my sixteenth Test century and, considering the conditions, one of my best. It was my eighth in 16 Tests – the previous eight had taken 77 Tests, so I must have been doing something right in my old age!

The third and last Test in Wellington put a dampener on the whole trip. The match was petering out for a draw on the last day after I had declared to leave New Zealand to get 230 in 32 overs. They never even attempted to mount any sort of chase. David Lawrence, the popular Gloucestershire fast bowler, was playing his first Test for England abroad. There is only one way David knows how to bowl – with all-out effort and wholeheartedness. He was galloping in for his first ball of his third over when, in his delivery stride, as he put all his considerable weight on it, his left knee buckled with a crack accompanied by an appalling scream of pain from David.

His kneecap had simply cracked in two. The pain must have been excruciating. It was the worst sports injury I have ever witnessed and I still wince for poor David's agony whenever I think about it. As it turned out, he was never able to play serious cricket again. It was nothing less than a harrowing and upsetting tragedy. David was twenty-seven. He had played in the last two West Indies Tests of the summer, and the game against Sri Lanka. He was a worker and great team man. It was going to be intriguing, I thought, to nurse him into a regular Test match career and push him to the limit of his talent and see if he could go all the way. After that frightening moment in an already dead match at Wellington, we will never know.

The accident threw us all a bit, but once we had seen David over his operation at the Wellington Hospital and knew he would soon be okay to undertake the long flight home and more treatment, we agreed that the New Zealand passage, despite that, had been rewarding beyond expectations and settled down to plan our World Cup strategy.

I was convinced we could win the World Cup this time. I had played in two finals, and been presented with the runners-up medal in both. I did not relish a hat-trick of them. In 1979, in England, we had played above ourselves up to the final against the West Indies at Lord's. Viv Richards had made a trademark century, batting first, and I have never forgotten how, off the last ball of the innings, he imperiously swatted a fast full-toss outside off-stump from Mike Hendrick into the packed crowd on the square-leg boundary just to throw down the gauntlet. We opened with an unbeaten century stand by Boycott and Brearley, but by the time the strokemakers were in, the task was not so much too daunting as too difficult. So 130 for no wicket quickly became 180-for-six, and death. The lesson is, pacing is all. I am not blaming Boycott and Brearley but, in hindsight, they should not have opened together.

The World Cup final of 1987 could – and should – have been won by England. We were firm favourites going into that match. We had well beaten India in the semi-final at Bombay when I made a deliberate decision on a worn pitch to sweep the left-armers, Ravi Shastri and Maninder Singh, as much as possible. I must have swept or pulled five balls out of six every over. I made 115 and was well past 60 before the Indian captain, Kapil Dev, plugged the holes he had left on the leg side.

The day before, in the nets, I had planned and practised this tactic. After an hour one of the Indian net bowlers we had hired came up to me sorrowfully. 'Please, Mr Gooch, I now realize you treat me with total disdain as a bowler, because you sweep every delivery of mine to leg-side.'

In that 1987 final, Australia batted first. At the time, I was used as England's fifth bowler in the one-dayers. Australia were getting bogged down when Border sent in the fast bowler, Craig McDermott, at no. 4 to hustle the score along. Up until then, I had bowled seven tidy overs for 20 runs. When Craig came in with obvious orders to hit, I said to captain Mike Gatting, 'Do you still want me to carry on?' He said, 'Yes, one more at least'.

I was hit for 20 in that over and, although I did clean bowl McDermott, the flurry had put them back on course. Chasing 250, we were well in the hunt at 135 for two at 30 overs. I cursed myself for getting out, lbw b O'Donnell, for 35, after doing all the hard work. Then Border put himself on and, first ball, Gatting mistimed his reverse sweep and was caught behind. Then Bill Athey ran himself out going for a third run, and after that we were always chasing our tails. They beat us by seven runs. And those seven runs, I am convinced, marked the beginning of Australia's Test renaissance. Allan Border had showed his team what rewards hard work, commitment and a belief in themselves could achieve, and they have never looked back.

Now at Melbourne in 1991/92, in front of 90,000 people, we are favourites to be third time lucky. In a qualifying round we had bowled Pakistan out for 74, but after that they pulled themselves together and improved all the way to the final. After the success of the New Zealand tour, we continued in like vein until injuries and the hassle of travel began to sow tiny seeds of doubt. The experiment of opening with Botham only half worked. He bowled well throughout the tournament, and he did a pretty good job with the bat too, but he only provided the vintage fireworks once – against Australia in Sydney.

In the final, Pakistan batted, and started badly. Imran Khan and Javed Miandad steadied them. I dropped a high swirler from Imran, which proved costly. They accelerated brilliantly in the last half of the innings. Even though no World Cup final had ever been won by the chasing team, I still thought 250 eminently gettable if we batted decently. Unfortunately, we started badly. Ian Botham and Alec Stewart went cheaply, and I got out for 29. A dashing innings by Neil Fairbrother, in partnership with Allan Lamb, brought us back in with a chance, but two successive and quite brilliant deliveries from Wasim to bowl Lamb, and then Chris Lewis, did for us. We finished 22 runs short.

I was choked. Gutted. So was Botham. We all were. But the better team on the day won, no doubt about it. Perhaps we had just come off the boil?

Imran's team had the makings of a very fine one. But so, I reckoned after a tour of mainly plusses, did mine. And a chance to avenge the Cup final disappointment was imminent. Imran himself may have signed off with his famous victory, but his side would be touring England in the summer of 1992, and playing five Tests and five one-dayers.

15

THE REVERSE SWING OF FORTUNE

FK

Gooch returned to Headingley in July 1992 to make again a century of epic and steadfast dominance, as English as Big Ben, against the Pakistanis on another of Leeds' damnably awkward pitches. England's resulting victory by six wickets squared the series with one match to go. At the age of thirty-nine, Gooch's stock as a national totem and public icon can never have been higher. The *Guardian's* resident laureate, Simon Rae, hymned Wordsworthian approbation:

> 'Gooch, you should be batting at this hour!
> What's more you were – and you were truly great.
> E'en though some thought your declaration late?
> England had need of you and all your power.
> The rhyme-scheme here insists on David Gower –
> But leaving him aside, let's contemplate
> Your imperturbable majestic state.
> Above mere mortals at the crease you tower.'

It proved a bad-tempered, tabloid-driven series, but was full of rich and fascinating cricket. Pakistan prevailed to settle the rubber 2–1 in the final match at The Oval, their resplendent pair of strike bowlers, Wasim Akram and Waqar Younis – who together took 43 wickets in the series not to mention batting England to defeat in the thrilling second Test at Lord's – making the difference. David Gower was restored to the England side for the last three matches in which he averaged 50 and overtook Geoffrey Boycott's Test aggregate record of 8,114 runs. But as Mike Gatting's ban for his unsanctioned tour of South Africa was now rescinded, the one batting place up for grabs on the following winter's tour of India went to him, for he was regarded as the better player of spin bowling. So the 'Roundhead' Gooch v 'Cavalier' Gower theme song was played again, this time more vociferously than ever. Even a former captain, Mike Brearley, found himself torn:

'Gooch and Stewart err on the side of solid, puritanical virtues such as hard work and visible endeavour, and have little time for a more cavalier approach even when suffused with class. What impresses them is certainly not Dionysian intoxication, but sobriety. The question is: Were the selectors right to set their stall so rigorously on rigour? My view is still that the insistence on such qualities was too absolute; the presence of a left-handed, curly-headed minor genius inclined to the ill-timed facetious remark (or flight), not over-keen on physical training, would hardly have undermined the steadfast discipline of the team. Gooch's influence has been crucial. Not tactically ingenious, he inspires his players through his determination, personal skill and straightforwardness. As Atherton said, you feel you would like to do anything for him.'

Gooch now feels that he should have stepped down as England's captain at The Oval in 1992. But his Essex mentor, Keith Fletcher, had just taken over from Micky Stewart as England's manager. So one last foreign expedition to help 'play in' his old friend might be fun, Gooch thought, and besides Fletcher would be pleased, for Gooch's batting was still not being affected in the slightest by the responsibilities of leadership.

Before leaving for the tour, Gooch surprised his parents, his closest friends, and indeed the cricket world by announcing that he and Brenda were to separate after sixteen years of marriage. Never a man to carry his emotions on his sleeve, he nonetheless carried his heartache to the subcontinent.

If sickness, injuries and palsy, not least to the captain himself, might have been mitigation for the bad defeats suffered in India in the 1992/93 series, the memory could well have been wiped from the slate as mere aberrations had the following summer produced revival and restoration. Because another reason behind Fletcher's hopes that Gooch would take the team to India as captain, was that Allan Border's Australians were due to tour England in the summer of 1993. Gooch was keen to have one last tilt at them. How better to bow out, not long after your fortieth birthday, than having regained the Ashes for England?

But it was not to be.

After a defeat by 179 runs in the first Test match at Manchester, in which Gooch scored 65 out of 210 and 133 out of 332, no other Englishman in the match passing 43 – he was talked out of resignation by Fletcher and the chairman, Ted Dexter. But England's hopes were soon in tatters. After another defeat, this time by an innings, in the next Test at Lord's, Ian Botham, not long since a team-mate, announced publicly and cruelly, 'No way England can save the series while Gooch continues as captain. With Gooch at the helm they look like a bunch of men condemned to walk up Tyburn Hill before being publicly hanged one after the other.' Certainly, in his now obviously terminal despair, the slope of Graham's shoulders and his moustache were resembling King Charles's as he opened (and closed) the innings on the Westminster scaffold.

A good enough draw at Trent Bridge was celebrated with rapture by England. But another abject surrender at Headingley in the fourth Test pushed Gooch over the edge. On the second day of the match Graham celebrated his fortieth birthday. By way of bearing gifts, Australia lost just one single wicket on their way to 653 for four declared. It led to another gruesome innings loss for England and Gooch, touchingly near to tears, formally at last resigned from the captaincy and returned to the ranks. 'I am very sad,' he said. 'At least, whenever and however long I look in the mirror I can only say that I did nothing but my best on every single occasion. Now the Ashes are gone, I feel the best way forward for England is a fresh approach. Someone else to look up to. We have not been doing well under my leadership and it is only right and proper to go. Whoever takes over will have all my support and, if selected, hopefully my expertise with the willow.'

Border took time out from his own understandable euphoria to say that he was sad to see Gooch go. 'We are good mates, and he is one of the great cricketers England has produced. He prepares for a game of cricket as well as any man I've ever seen, but he's forty years of age, and he can't do everything. I fully understand his reasons, because the side he's leading is not responding. If you are losing, you cop it. That's the way it is. I know. I've been there.'

Border shook his head as he described arriving at the ground to find Gooch, already changed, running around the square in his batting pads. 'Graham has his own way of preparing,' Border said, 'and some of it may be pretty strange for a forty-year-old. But what he cannot bear is to see others less committed than he is.'

In the *Daily Telegraph*, Christopher Martin-Jenkins wrote: 'A good name is more precious than fine perfume. When Graham Gooch resigned in a mood of deep disappointment at Headingley yesterday afternoon he could and should have consoled himself with the fact that his has been an honourable reign. Like Charles I (although not only in the moment of his departure), "he nothing sordid did nor mean". In the end that is more important than the record of success or failure because a Test captain, apart from doing all he can to win, is also a steward of cricket's character and reputation. In Gooch's case, sadly deflating though the last seven months have been, not only has the decline in the standards of behaviour been firmly arrested but the playing record has been better than some might guess. Gooch never lost the respect of his players. Who could not respect such a decent man, dedicated professional and steadfast trier, or so courageous and classy a batsman.'

In fact, when he looked in the mirror, his captaincy record had, in the circumstances, been a noble one. Only Peter May (41) led England more times than Gooch (34). As captain, Gooch won 10, lost 12, and drew 12. As a player in the ranks in the 1970s and 1980s, in 128 Test innings, Gooch hit eight centuries and 27 fifties to average 36.45. As captain, astonishingly, in less than half that number of innings (63) he hit 11 centuries and 16 fifties. No England captain in history has scored more centuries (the next best was May's 10).

But if he had, as he puts it, 'jacked in' the captaincy of his country, he had not finished with batting records. In the sixth and last Test at The Oval against Australia (which England jubilantly won under the new leadership of Michael Atherton), an off-driven four off Reiffel took Gooch's score to 21 and past David Gower's all-time record

Test aggregate by an Englishman of 8,231 runs. At the beginning of that summer, Gooch had joined the game's 23-strong elite band to have scored a century of centuries. That was when, in the grand manner, at 99 he took a stride down the wicket at Fenner's and hit a Cambridge University bowler, Richard Pearson, high into the trees over long-on for six.

In fact, that might have been his 101st century – because immediately prior to the one before, at Cuttack on England's tour of India, the International Cricket Council, in their dotty wisdom, had suddenly announced, eleven years later, that Gooch's century for the England 'rebel' team against South Africa in 1982 should not be deemed 'first-class'. If that pronouncement was some sort of spite, Gooch was unfazed, for he simply muttered when he came off at Cuttack, 'Don't worry, I'll be going up to Cambridge in early May'

Gooch stayed at home for England's tour under Atherton to the West Indies, but he greeted the touring New Zealanders in the first Test of 1994 with a massively mature and relentlessly unerring 210. Hitherto, only four forty-year-olds – the masterly Jack Hobbs, the super stalwart Patsy Hendren, and the doughty South Africans, Dudley Nourse and Eric Rowan – had ever scored a Test 200.

Later in the summer, Gooch was moved and delighted to be playing in the three-match series on South Africa's return to the Test brotherhood after their twenty-nine-year banishment for apartheid, happily now itself banished. He felt that playing in an 'official' Test against South Africa somehow vindicated at last his tour there as a 'rebel' all those years ago. To set up England's win and series-levelling run-chase at The Oval Gooch and Atherton put on 48 in the opening 23 balls , perhaps the most explosive Test start in history. This was Gooch's 204th innings for England, and another all-time record. After which, the match won, England's venerable national treasure drove home to his happy heath at Chelmsford and, laconic and expressionless as ever, clumped and clobbered soon after elevenses, an 86-ball 79 against Sussex during which, when he had reached 54, Gooch became only the fifteenth man in cricket history to pass 40,000 runs.

After Essex's two acclaimed and successive County Championships, in 1991 and 1992, under Gooch's leadership, he announced his retirement as captain. He would play on, of course, in 1993. But was he perhaps steadying himself to achieve, as his last task, new glories as an elder statesman? He wanted to help, surreptitiously and behind the scenes, to build a brand new team for his county, as successful as those he had played in and with for two decades.

Among those comparative toddlers he had seen nervously come and then swaggeringly go was Derek Pringle, whose finely observed analyses and literary talents had been hired by the *Independent on Sunday*. So, freed from his 'no-tell' county contract, he could now appraise his famous and longtime general:

'Gooch is a difficult man to get to know. Few, outside a very tight social circle that rarely goes beyond his immediate family, could claim to know him well. Even playing with him in the same side rarely affords any insights other than a few obvious weaknesses, like a craving for jam doughnuts and real ale with a creamy head. The only time the Essex dressing-room had seen him in a flap is when he forgot to leave tickets for his mum and dad on the gate. Few things have ever seemed to ruffle his impassive exterior, for he is an organized man with the tidiest cricket case in England. He has even rationalized his approach to batting, taking fewer risks than he used to. In the mid-1980s, if Essex had been in the field and were about to bat, all the bowlers would hurriedly towel themselves down just to go and watch him take on the opposition's fast bowlers. In those days, he liked to dominate and it occasionally led to his downfall. Now players just get on with the crossword, for they know that Gooch will look to bat for at least fifty overs, taking as few risks as possible, in order to get a hundred. The discipline has been the cornerstone of his success since 1990.'

One morning during the 1994 summer, a BBC Radio 5 commentator remarked how he had seen Gooch having a private practice in the nets soon after an early breakfast and before the rest of the England team arrived on the ground. 'If only,' he said, 'Gooch's batting disease was infectious; then the rest of the England batsmen might catch it.' Then, he wondered what name you would call the disease? In no time, two listeners had telephoned. 'Bowlimia,' suggested one; 'Willowitis,' the other.

GG

I realize hindsight usually makes for a boring know-it-all but, looking back from this distance I should have given up the England captaincy at the end of the 1992 series against Pakistan. Certainly, if I had, my captaincy record with England would have been staring out of *Wisden's* all-time records' page in a much healthier state. And if not my sanity exactly, then my general demeanour for the following twelve months would have been less fraught.

We had come from a successful winning series in New Zealand and, apart from the disappointing night of the final itself, we had made all the running in the Fifth World Cup. Since I'd begun my run as captain, we had done ourselves justice in series against the West Indies both away and home, and beaten India at home. Now we had a highly committed scrap against a fine Pakistani side.

In truth, I had, early in 1992, happily resolved in my mind that I would not tour again, but as the Pakistan series progressed and I continued to be pleased with my batting – inside a week in two innings against the tourists at the end of July I hit 135 in the Headingley Test and then 141 against them for Essex at Chelmsford – I thought, well, why not? You are a long time retired and, with England competing with a measure of consistency at last, what immense satisfaction to gell together the side even more in the three-Test series in India and then to go out and win back the Ashes in 1993 against the Australians and my old friend and foe Allan Border.

There was another factor too: Micky Stewart had been promoted by Lord's to take more general charge of English cricket's development, and the new England manager was to be Keith Fletcher. The tour to India would be his first in the hot seat.

However, it is not true that I stayed on just to accentuate the 'Essex mafia', as the media called it, or help nurse Keith through his first tour. Nor did Keith put any pressure on me to stay on. I knew he wanted me to stay, but there was nothing that resembled arm-twisting. It was certainly a bonus having Fletch at the helm, but staying on as England captain was my decision totally, and one based on the team's generally wholehearted and competitive showing against the Pakistanis.

And Pakistan were a great side, no doubt about it. Ultra-competitive, too. Perhaps even more so with Javed Miandad taking over as captain from the more 'stabilising' Imran Khan. I bow to no one in my admiration for Javed as a supremely gifted, improvising batsman, but as a captain the little man is a streetwise stirrer and high-tension hustler who never misses a trick. His batting-order lieutenant was Salim Malik, another highly talented all-round batsman. We at Essex had been delighted when we signed 'Sali' as our overseas player in 1991.

It is crucial for a captain to 'bond' with the team's overseas star and, early on in that first summer of his, Salim and I arrived at the moment when we had to put our trust in each other and hope we both came out on the other side with the relationship intact. He seemed to be fitting in really well, but it was still only June when he asked if he could go home to Pakistan for a brief visit. He had not long been married, and his wife was sitting her exams at university and was worried about them. Not only that, he was missing her tremendously. There was a short gap between Championship fixtures and it would mean him missing just one Sunday match, so he asked if I could see my way to allowing him his one flying visit home.

It was against my better judgement, but already I had grown to like him (and, more than that, he had just scored an exquisitely played double-century against Leicestershire at Ilford which had all Essex purring with delight). So I said, 'Okay, Sal, you can go, as long as you promise to be back for next week's Championship match against Sussex at Horsham: so don't let me down, please'. 'I won't let you down,' he said.

I knew I had put my head on the block because we certainly needed him for the Sussex match as Derek Pringle and I were playing in the second Test against the West Indies at Lord's. But when the Essex team assembled at Horsham on the eve of the game, there was no sight of Salim. Had he taken me for a chump? That night and early next morning, the club checked all the flights coming in from Pakistan – and no 'S. Malik' was registered as a passenger. But when the Essex players arrived at the Horsham ground to begin practising after breakfast, there was Salim, changed and ready to play. No one has any idea how he made it back, but there he was.

With Javed and Salim providing the solidity in Pakistan's exciting young batting order, it was the Pakistani bowling attack which had now become about as hostile and well balanced as any I had faced in recent times. Waqar Younis had not played in the World Cup because of injury, but by the second Test at Lord's he was back in harness with the left-hander, Wasim Akram. Throw in the aggressive Aqib Javed and the expertise of the googly bowler, Mushtaq Ahmed, and no batsman could ever afford to relax.

England's five Test matches against Pakistan that summer was as good a cricketing series as it was niggly and controversial. The first Test at Edgbaston was a high-scoring draw marred by rain, but the second at Lord's was a thunderously compelling low-scorer from first to last. In their final innings, Pakistan needed only 138 to win. We were short of two bowlers, with injuries to DeFreitas and Botham, but Malcolm, Salisbury, and Lewis had them 18 for three, 68 for six, and 95 for eight. But then, at the 'kill', I had nobody else to turn to and deliver the coup de grâce, and it was Wasim and Waqar, with the bat, who bravely carried them home for a famous victory.

That injury to Botham meant he had played his 102nd and last Test match. What a career he had had – and at least he was able to end with two typically instinctive slip catches to come level with Colin Cowdrey's and England's all-time catching record of 120. Cowdrey needed 114 Tests for his 120 – and the measure of Botham's stupendous catching is that he also had to bowl some 22,000 deliveries to take 383 wickets at the other end. Lord's was also Allan Lamb's last Test of his grand career, although both he and Ian came back for a final curtain call in the Texaco one-dayers which followed the Test series.

For the third Test at Manchester, David Gower returned and he delighted all of us by scoring a fluent 73, during which he overtook Geoff Boycott's record English Test aggregate. Then, at the end of England's innings, a good enough 390 in reply to their 505 for nine declared, it all turned sour. Devon Malcolm was batting and Aqib Javed, an excitable competitor at the best of times, peppered Devon with a few short balls and then 'ran through' the crease and bowled a vicious delivery at him – that is, a deliberate and extravagant no-ball which means he was aiming and letting go from 17 or 18 yards, not 21, and intending to hit the batsman. Umpire Roy Palmer warned Aqib for intimidation. Aqib became abusive and then, when Palmer was handing back the bowler's sweater, it stuck momentarily in Palmer's belt, so the gesture seemed to be more emphatic than it was meant to be. So now the captain himself, Javed Miandad, was strutting around and kicking up more of a fuss, instead of doing his captain's duty of calming down his bowler. It was disgraceful behaviour.

To cap it all, at the end of the drawn match, the referee, former West Indian opening batsman Conrad Hunte, issued a statement which, after fining Aqib half his match fee, stated:

'Both captains must be more mindful of their responsibilities to their teams and the spectators and should insist in future that their men conduct themselves more in the spirit of the game'.

I was infuriated. To bracket both teams as guilty after the disgraceful performance of one of them was unfair. I took it up with Clyde Walcott (who would have been refereeing instead of Hunte, but he had been called to Lord's that day for an ICC meeting) and said I took it as a total insult that the England team had been bracketed with Pakistan in being censured about our conduct. What had we done? The answer was: absolutely nothing.

For a fast bowler to 'go through' the crease is an accepted 'no go' area in cricket in the first place; so was Javed Miandad's 'orchestrating', as *Wisden* put it, a five-minute exchange on the pitch with the umpire. So England get censured as well as the culprits – for me, that was too much to bear, and I said so in no uncertain terms. I've always prided myself, and always will, on how my England teams have behaved and conducted themselves.

Even before the match-referee system came in, I used to tell our team before every Test that, although the official rule was that umpires gave two cautions before reporting a player, I was telling the umpire to dispense with the second one. A single caution would be enough for any team of mine. Step out of line once and be cautioned; do it again, be reported and take the consequences. Once the referees came in I told them, as well as the umpires and my players, that the same would apply.

I am proud of the way my teams have played the game – for England and for Essex too. England teams have never been given any thanks for it, but some in the cricket establishment look at other international sides and say 'Oh dear, the state of players' behaviour in the game is sinking to terrible depths', and then collectively include England as well. Just like Hunte did that day at Old Trafford. In my view, it's not right.

On the field, it is up to the captains to come down hard even before the umpire or referee gets involved. As skipper, you can have a quick little talk with a player, a short, sharp ticking-off, and get him back into line – but then that's it, over and done with. I learned that under two of the best captains I have played with, Mike Brearley and Keith Fletcher. Mike could really fly off the handle sometimes, but his secret was this: there would be no grudges and nothing would be left to fester. Make your point, short and sharp, and, once he gets the message, leave it at that.

So we went to Leeds for the fourth Test, where my first innings of 135 out of 320, in reply to Pakistan's 197, gave me enormous satisfaction against such a high-quality Test attack. That innings (415 minutes and 301 balls) also meant I had now scored a century against every Test-playing country. Strangely enough, I had only played five times against Pakistan before this series. I was obviously enjoying that low, slow Headingley wicket in my old age although this time the pitch was less difficult and the light not as bad as it had been against the West Indies the year before. Thanks to my first-innings century and some valuable contributions from Mike Atherton and Robin Smith with the bat and new boy Neil Mallender with the ball, we ended up winning by six wickets on the fourth day.

It was 1–1 and all to play for in the decider at The Oval. We made a solid enough start – 182 for three before Wasim blew away our batting with six for 67. We finished on 207 all out, and in the second innings, after limiting them to 380 all out, we were well and truly 'Wasimed' and 'Waqared' on the last day and only saved some face with Robin Smith's heroic, four-hour undefeated 84 out of 174.

That was when I should have given up the England captaincy.

I should have let either Mike Atherton or Alec Stewart prepare for the Indian tour by taking charge of the side for the remaining Texaco trophy one-day matches. But I didn't, and in the fourth one-day international at Lord's the lid of the simmering kettle finally blew its top.

I was rested from that match with a sore wrist so Alec Stewart did take over the captaincy. A close contest was decided in favour of

Pakistan by 3 runs. But more newsworthy than the result were the notorious incidents that occurred during the match.

Pakistan won the toss and had reached 139 for five. Allan Lamb had picked the ball up and shown it to the umpire, Ken Palmer, just before lunch. Apparently, one side was shiny, the other very much 'worked on'. During the interval we were told that the ball had been 'interfered with' and the Pakistanis were being offered a choice of two balls of 'inferior' quality. So that suited them fine, didn't it?

The umpires should have given the Pakistanis a brand new ball if they wanted to censure them. Does this incident suggest that the umpires or authorities did not quite understand the aerodynamics of reverse swing with an old ball?

What was never in doubt through the summer was that the Pakistani pace bowlers were getting better as each of our innings progressed. They had been blowing away our tail almost at will, because by then the old ball was swinging far more than the new one had been at the start of our innings. And not only swinging, but *reverse* swinging.

The older the ball gets, the more it loses its shine but, it stands to reason, the fielding side will also have more time to 'work' on the ball. Every team knows this and duly polishes one side of the ball and keeps it dry while legitimately letting the other side get scuffed and dulled with natural wear and tear. The charge around the world of cricket, which remains unproven, is that once the leather starts cracking up the Pakistani team goes into a concerted 'working-over' of the ball, accentuating the cracks on one side with their fingernails (or, as Imran Khan has admitted doing once, even with a bottle-top) so that after 40 or 50 overs one side of the ball still retains a dull shine, while the other is scuffed and rough, almost as if a dog has been gnawing it like a bone.

Whether the Pakistanis are just twice as good as anyone else at having perfected the art of legitimately working on the ball, or whether there is something more sinister going on , I do not know. What I do know is that in the hands of Wasim and Waqar, the old ball can suddenly start swinging late in an almost unplayable banana-like curve. With a fast left-arm swing bowler like Wasim this late swerve with an old ball can be devastating – witness the successive deliveries which dramatically accounted for Allan Lamb and Chris

Lewis in the World Cup final. Then, at the other end, Waqar's inswinger with the old ball is even more awesome.

As a batsman, I can tell when his inswinger is on the way because Waqar puts much more into the delivery to get that extra yard of pace he needs for the inswing, but by the time you realize it's on its way, primed for its dramatic late curve, you are already set-up for your shot – and then, suddenly, vroomf!, it's either an instep-crusher or it yorks you all ends up. If your eye is in and you're well set, you've got a chance. But lose a wicket when the old ball starts to 'go' and, with these two bowling, a new batsman is in all sorts of trouble. A new tailender has virtually no hope at all.

How have the Pakistanis come to perfect this reverse swing with an old ball? Possibly they might have needed to more than we did because, in their first-class game in Pakistan, they only get a new ball every 120 overs.* In the English county game, we now hand the ball to the umpire for inspection after every over. Perhaps that should be the rule in Test cricket too, except that I am not sure whether some umpires quite know what they are looking for. If the fielding side is just roughing up and accentuating the natural wear and tear of the ball, who is to arbitrate on when it's been done with malice and is therefore tantamount to cheating? What I am saying is that if one side is doing it and being allowed to get away with it, then so should the other side. A level playing field is all anyone wants.

When Lamb wrote in a newspaper column about how a former Pakistani bowler who used to play for Northamptonshire, Sarfraz Nawaz, had once shown him the methods he used to tamper with the ball, and was then sued for libel by Sarfraz, I was surprised when I received a letter from the Sarfraz camp asking me to speak up for him in court. Their request was based on my press conference statement at the end of the game at Lord's in which I had, I admit, gone through the usual platitudes of 'the best side won fair and square, no sour grapes that we lost, and we'll be trying harder next time'. Through my solicitor I told Sarfraz in no uncertain terms that if he called me as his witness, then I would get up in court and happily air all my personal suspicions about how reverse swing came about.

---

* The English system is that a new ball is available after 100 overs, or after 85 overs in tourist matches.

Of course, I never heard another word. Apart from that ultimately aborted court case, the ball-tampering story faded away with the return home of the Pakistan side at the end of that 1992 summer at Lord's – until it returned in dramatic fashion two years later, and at the same place.

By the time of the 1994 Lord's Test against South Africa, I had already given up the England captaincy and was fielding at deep third-man in front of the Lord's pavilion and under the England dressing-room balcony. The tea interval was approaching and as I glanced up I noticed Keith Fletcher, the England team manager, signalling that he was sending a message down via the twelfth man at the end of the over. The gist of it appeared to be, 'Tell the captain [Atherton] when he comes off at tea that he must ignore any posse of pressmen in the Long Room and come straight up to the dressing-room, because there's some fuss brewing about ball tampering.'

So next over, I'm at mid-off and Mike's at extra-cover, and I relay the message – 'Steer clear of the press, there's a fuss about the ball or something' – and I add with a caustic laugh to Mike, 'it must be something to do with the ball the South Africans were using in our innings because, sure as heck, this ruddy ball of ours isn't doing much, is it?' Mike chuckled in agreement and went to his fielding place.

And so was set in train the accusations and allegations over Atherton's 'dirt in the pocket' incident, which came close to losing him his job.

The TV pictures certainly made it all look suspicious. No question, Mike seemed to be putting something from his pocket on to the ball. My reading of it was that he was putting dirt on his fingers to dry them so he would not get any sweat or moisture on the shiny side of the ball. I had never heard before of anyone putting soil or dust in their pockets, but whether it is legal or not depends on how you interpret a rather fuzzy law in the first place. Spin bowlers often unconsciously rub a hand or a couple of fingers on the worn footmarks on the pitch in order to get a better grip on the ball. And in practical terms, Mike was not altering the condition of the ball in any way, a fact that was acknowledged by the umpires. To the uninitiated, though, it certainly looked odd and out-of-the-ordinary on the TV pictures.

With the match referee, in this case the Australian Peter Burge, ready to make an example of any offenders, it appeared that England chairman Raymond Illingworth's immediate heavy fine of Atherton saved the day in extracting the sting from any further sanctions Burge might have had in mind. If that had included a ban from even one match, it would have made Mike's position as captain untenable. So he was lucky, especially as he admits he had been foolishly 'economical with the truth' when Burge first called him in to discuss the matter.

The questions you have to ask yourself are these: is drying your hands with a bit of dirt in your pocket – however unusual – just allowable gamesmanship? Or is it cheating even if it didn't alter the condition of the ball? And is drying your hands on dirt and then rubbing one side of the ball any different from putting sweat from your brow on the other side?

Down the century in cricket there has always been a fine line between accepted gamesmanship and cheating. Gamesmanship has been part and parcel of county cricket since the championship began. For instance, what batsman hasn't 'inadvertently' scuffed the pitch with the studs on the soles of his boots when he's batting just before a declaration? Or what wicketkeeper hasn't 'accidentally' made a practice of running down the track to take a throw from the boundary and so scuffed up the pitch 'on a length' for his bowlers? As for ball tampering, perhaps the answer is for the umpires to throw the new ball to the fielding side at the beginning of an innings and say, 'There you are, it's yours for 100 overs, shine or mutilate it as much as you want'.

At the end of that 1992 series against Pakistan, one other reason made me change my mind about staying on as captain and taking the team on the tour of India. It was a selfish one. Simply, I was enjoying my batting for England and Essex as almost never before. For the county that summer I averaged 83 as we stormed towards our second successive Championship. In all cricket, I averaged 71, with eight centuries and seven fifties. Good old Mike Gatting was the Englishman to dog me all the way in the first-class averages, and he finished on 66, with six hundreds and ten fifties. Obviously I was delighted that the responsibility of captaincy was continuing to make me concentrate and knuckle down at the crease, and my success with the bat in turn was making me ever more comfortable and confident as a leader. By the end of the summer, I was averaging 62 for every Test innings since I had assumed the England captaincy, compared with just 37 when I played in the ranks. Apparently, Imran Khan, with a batting average of 52 as captain and 26 as an non-captaining player has a comparable record. Of course, Imran was mainly a top-rank bowler. I was not bowling much in those days, although, as it happens, in that 1992 series against Pakistan I did top the England bowling averages with five wickets for 94 at just under 19 apiece!

As for Essex in 1992, we won the Championship with two games to spare after defeating Hampshire by eight wickets at Chelmsford. This meant that since that first famous Championship of ours in 1979, when I was just twenty-six, we had won six times.

We celebrated this latest title in style against Derby in the second week of September. I handed over the captaincy for this match to Paul Prichard and allowed him to drop me down the order to no. 6. Incidentally, it had nothing to do with a hangover after the party which followed the Hampshire match. I wanted merely to give some of our young batsmen, like Nick Knight and Nadeem Shahid, the chance to build an innings and establish their credentials. Unfortunately, I chose the wrong day.

In answer to Derby's 226, the hostile West Indian Ian Bishop shot us out for 96. I went in at 18 for four and managed 53 of them. Derby then made 309 and set us a most unlikely 404 for victory. Amazingly enough, we got them, the first time Essex had ever scored over 400 to win a match on the fourth innings. It took us nearly two days and everyone contributed, especially Stephenson, Shahid, and Garnham; and, in a grafter's knock, I made 123 not out as we lost only one wicket on the last day. Because it was part of a real team effort and put a glittering seal on our Championship, I will always treasure that innings for Essex. It was almost on a par with my 154 at Headingley against the West Indies.

Some cynics might have said that the reason I batted so long (373 minutes) in that innings on the Racecourse ground was because I was safer out in the middle than facing the press. For on the first day of that match the news had broken of David Gower's omission from the England side for the tour of India. Once again, it was Gower the 'Shining White Knight', and Gooch the 'Baddie in the Black Hat'.

I might have made a misjudgement, but after we picked the side for the tour, I made a conscious decision not to telephone David or any of the other 'near misses' until just before the team was officially announced from Lord's. I knew that if I had rung David a few days before, the news would have leaked inadvertently to the press ahead of the official announcement, and a great row would have erupted.

So when he didn't receive my call immediately after the selection meeting, David may well have assumed that he had made the touring party. I was sorry for that misconception on his part, and I think it did come as a bombshell to him as I phoned him on the way to Derby. David was understandably upset, and he asked me if we had chosen the team on Test runs already made or on county form. At one point my mobile cut out and we lost contact; I was worried that David might have thought I'd hung up on him. Fortunately, I got him back on the line and tried to explain our reasoning for giving the last two batting places to Mike Gatting and the left-hander Neil Fairbrother. David was not best pleased. His performances had been exemplary during the three Tests on his recall against Pakistan and we had got on really well. I was genuinely sorry that he was to be the one to miss out.

In a way, I think he must have sensed the writing on the wall once the International Cricket Council announced, earlier in the summer, that the ban on Mike Gatting's South Africa rebels would be cut short because of South Africa's readmission to international cricket. So Mike, a proven player of spin bowling on Indian wickets, and a prolific English batsman all down the years in the Championship, was obviously in the frame. And in the three Texaco one-dayers at the end of the Pakistan series we had included, instead of David, the left-handed Fairbrother, who scored 62, 33 and 15 and, it goes without saying, fielded like a quicksilver demon. David had admitted his throwing arm in the field was now a liability in the one-day game, and on the upcoming tour of India and Sri Lanka there were to be four Tests and all of eight one-day internationals.

Even so, it had been a very difficult decision. David was a proven Test player of undoubted class. So he had to be judged on his Test record, not what he did for his county. Bob Willis was another who was seldom consistent for his county Warwickshire. The tension between David and me on the 1990/91 tour of Australia, when I felt he was not setting the right example, had long passed. On reflection, I might have got things out of proportion then, and in my gloom about the wheels coming off the tour after my injury I undoubtedly pushed the practice sessions too hard and neglected the relaxation side. But times had changed now. All I was looking to do was pick the best side for the job in hand.

So in the end the decision was made totally for cricketing reasons. But the flak flew and so did the hate mail. It was upsetting of course, but at no stage was it a personal problem between us.

Perhaps, in hindsight, we did get that selection wrong for India. Certainly, England would not have done any worse had David come with us; who knows, we might well have done a lot better. Of the three Tests against India, we lost the first by eight wickets and the next two by an innings. We drew the six one-day internationals 3–3 (Fairbrother batting very well in four of them) and then, when I had come home as planned and handed over the captaincy to Alec Stewart, we lost the Test match and the two one-day matches to Sri Lanka. You could say that all my hopes had turned to dust.

It was not only the cricket which made it a most upsetting passage for me. In fact, you could even say that the cricket was the last thing on my mind. For as we left for the tour, Brenda and I announced that we had separated, would be living apart, and that our marriage was over.

In India my touring jinx continued The serious hand injuries picked up in the West Indies and Australia on my first two overseas expeditions as captain were now compounded by two debilitating bouts of illness.

In the match before the first Test, I had scored what I and everyone else thought at the time was my one hundredth first-class century, against India Under-25s at Cuttack. Mike Atherton scored a brave 80 not out, but he and a couple of the others England players had picked up a virus. Mike couldn't play in the Test, and by the time we arrived in Calcutta I wasn't fancying my chances either. Not only was I laid out in bed with the blinds drawn, I felt dizzy, I couldn't breathe properly and was continually throwing up. Even walking fifty yards in an attempt to shake the bug left me gasping for breath. But I was determined to play, for the first Test is always an important game in any series. So I raised myself from my sick bed on the morning of the match.

I lost the toss and at one stage we had them at 93 for three, but then the Indian captain, Azharuddin, made 180, and from there our fortunes took a disastrous downturn for the rest of the series. My personal demeanour was no better. The Calcutta smog is fairly thick at the best of times, and in my present state it was like breathing in metal filings. I spent the whole time inhaling Vick and smothering it all over my handkerchief, so all I could smell and taste was the stuff. I felt groggy right through the match. In retrospect, I reckon I did really well to make 17 in the first innings, and 18 in the second after I just lifted my foot and was out, stumped. Most uncharacteristic. I just wasn't my normal self.

Another victim of the smog was the England and Essex scorer, Clem Driver. Well built and in his seventies, Clem was climbing a flight of stairs to his post at the top of the pavilion, when he collapsed suddenly and had to be rushed to a nearby clinic (and was soon on his way home). 'Angina and Exhaustion' was the official diagnosis, but I knew it was the dreaded virus compounded by the smog. At the end of each day's play, I took a taxi to the clinic to check whether Clem was all right. It was an unbelievable journey through the clogged-up rush hour traffic, with buses and lorries pumping out evil, thick black exhaust fumes. There was I on every journey sat with my Vick-infused handkerchief clamped to my nose. Must have been quite a sight for the locals.

My mind was taken back to eleven years before, when Geoff Boycott had been ill in Calcutta and dropped out of the Test, but had then got up from his bed to take in a round of golf. None of us had any sympathy for him. He had just broken Sir Gary Sobers's record Test aggregate and, we reckoned, was just looking for an excuse to be sent home. After my experience, I wonder now if we'd been too hard on him. If he had been feeling like I was now, then poor Geoffrey would have been very ill indeed.

On previous tours to India before I had experienced the usual odd bad bouts of illness – twenty-four hours feeling rough and shut up in the toilet or being sick to clear your stomach. But this was something else altogether, and it was to hang around. In fact, I don't think I ever really shook it off throughout the trip. Not that that can be an excuse for my cricket – or indeed the cricket of the England team. Simply, we played terribly.

Once on the slippery slope, we only slid further. Our defeat in Calcutta was followed by an even more comprehensive one in Madras; but to suggest, as many members of the press did, that we were unprofessional in eating prawns for supper on the eve of the Test is a bit steep.

In fact, we had eaten prawns often during the tour and had no problems. This was just a rogue portion. Half-a-dozen of us were in the hotel's Chinese restaurant that night. The joke from journalist Martin Johnson of the *Independent* was that once Mike Gatting came down to join us the number of dishes increased so rapidly that when the hotel management came to try and identify the guilty dish 'they could only narrow it down to one of the twenty-eight that Gatt had ordered'. In retrospect, you have to laugh, but at the time it was far from funny.

I felt really queasy as soon as I woke the next morning. By the time I was at the ground I was having dizzy spells and waves of nausea. I couldn't concentrate, not on anything. I knew that if I won the toss, I simply wouldn't be able to bat and if we'd fielded I'd have had to send out the twelfth man. So I handed over to Alec Stewart, and retired to my bed. The TV was showing the cricket in my room, but I was just fading in and out of a dreamy sort of sleep. Mercifully, it was just food-poisoning and it cleared up within seventy-two hours, by which time, unfortunately, we were well on the way to losing by an innings.

The third Test which followed at once in Bombay was just as mortifying, with my two innings of 4 and 8 gloomily setting the tone. In Madras and Bombay, respectively, Chris Lewis and Graeme Hick had at least scored the maiden centuries we had been looking for from them since they were first selected. Those hundreds were about the only two crumbs of comfort on a desolate trip.

After my sympathetic reassessment of Boycott's malaise in Calcutta, I could only think of our chairman Ted Dexter and offer penitence for my smile at his being laid low on our previous trip to India in 1989. We were in Kanpur for the Nehru Cup, my first in charge of England abroad. Ted came out, bristling with that public school vigour of his and said he'd take half a dozen of us to dinner at the none-too-salubrious restaurant at the top of the Megdhoot hotel. 'C'mon, you chaps,' said Ted, grabbing the menu, 'when in Rome and all that. You fellows are too finicky about your food, always go for the local nosh and you can't be wrong'. At that time, I was still a bit unsure about curries and the local food, but seeing Ted was our chairman we all did as we were told and piled in to the food, which was very tasty. Full marks to Ted, the man of the world.

The only trouble was, none of the others saw him again for the whole week of his stay. Confined to his room with severe food-poisoning. Judging by the way he looked – gaunt and immobile, his face staring into thin air from his pillow like a death-mask – he must have felt like I did four years later. He lay there for a week, and at one point Micky Stewart and I were genuinely concerned whether he'd make it home at all.

On returning home from that depressing series on the Indian subcontinent, I found our admittedly horrendous four-out-of-four Test defeat by India and Sri Lanka being blamed unaccountably, not on our poor cricket (which our succession of illnesses could not mitigate, and quite rightly), but on our wearing sun-block cream, or tracksuits at the ground instead of blazer and tie, and on one or two of us – me, particularly – wearing 'designer' stubble. The letters of complaint from cricket supporters are mostly fed to Ted so he reacted by announcing in the press, 'There is a modern fashion for designer stubble, and some people believe it to be attractive. But it is aggravating to others and we will be looking into the whole question of facial hair on our cricketers.'

The English can be perverse. Why should the short, tight-cropped beard I like to wear have anything to do with my form as a batsman or captain? Nobody seemed to get in a lather about it when we were beating the West Indies or when I scored 333 with it! Same with my 'gloomy over-practising regime'. England was proud when we knuckled down and practised hard and defeated the West Indies under a captain wearing a short beard. But when we lose, it's these very things that are given the blame. Later, when Raymond Illingworth took over from Ted, he too was inundated with letters from around the country about 'designer' stubble and he decreed we all had to be clean-shaven on Test match mornings. As a result of this, for a bit of amusement, the players instituted the 'credit-card' test, which involved holding a credit-card flat on your face and checking that no bristle was growing above it.

There were more letters sent to Lord's about this subject than the situation of our actual cricket in England.

When David Gower was captain and things weren't going well it was all because the team was being headed by a band of 'good-time boys', the free-and-easy 'Champagne Charlies'. Nobody minded about that when we were beating the Aussies in the mid-eighties.

What got up my nose most of all on coming back from India, was that one or two of us had been really quite ill. Of course, we were outplayed by a home side on top of their game. But what do the press and certain elements of the cricket establishment concentrate their post-mortems on? Not only on our cricket, or our technique against spinners, but on the design of the tracksuits we were wearing and the sun-block or the stubble on our chins.

What seemed to enrage the cricket public was that we were not wearing shirts, ties, jackets or black lace-up shoes in the heat. But in the last five years of Test cricket around the world the England team, in my view, has unquestionably been the best turned out.

Of more serious concern in that summer of 1993 was the return of Allan Border's Australians. But first I had to resolve finally the issue of my hundredth hundred in the Lord's statisticians' books. After I had attempted to put the memory of India behind me with 88 and 32 not out against England 'A' at Chelmsford, I finally reached my milestone at Fenner's against Cambridge University. It wasn't a case of milking joke bowling as I reached the coveted three figures with a six. The University had been bowling quite well and I'd been on 99 for about a dozen balls as they brought in the field to stifle a quick single. So when a fuller-length delivery came down, a slog into the trees seemed the best, if rather dramatic option. But someone did wonder afterwards in the pavilion if any other of cricket's 23 'Centurions of Centuries' had passed the mark with a six. No matter now but, yes, I felt good about joining that distinguished list begun by the bearded W G Grace. (What if Lord's had told him to shave daily?)

It looks as if the next to manage the feat will be Mike Gatting, Allan Lamb, or Javed Miandad, all with over eighty centuries; then, presumably, will come Graeme Hick, and after him there will be a long wait – perhaps for Mike Atherton? Brian Lara, for sure, and Mark Waugh will one day break the 'ton' assuming they continue to play in county cricket.

The week before the first Test match of the 1993 series I was keen to work more on my technique so I turned out for Essex 2nd XI against Somerset at Colchester. I found it quite valuable to stick around for a while in both innings and make some technical adjustments, like making sure my head was still as I struck the ball, and my feet were moving along the plane of the crease – but the real reason is that quality time in the middle for a batsman who might be feeling insecure is crucial practice. So the wheel had turned full circle: *Wisden 1994* would now record, 'Essex 2nds: Also batted G. Gooch 25, 23', just as it had almost a quarter of a century before, when the 1970 almanack noted, 'G. Gooch played in one match but did not bat'. That was the day Johnny Welch drove this quite happily petrified fifteen-year-old to Northampton in his 'Roller'; but I don't think I was as nervous that day as before I went out to bat in the first Test of this new Ashes series at Old Trafford in 1993 when I was almost forty. I fancy I was even more calm, clear-thinking, and philosophical in that first-ever Test match against Lillee and Thomson at Edgbaston in 1975. This time it was an immediate hangover from India where, in two Tests, I had averaged only 11, and felt some inner doubts about the effectiveness of my captaincy. If I couldn't motivate the team by example, what else had I to offer?

The series started really well at Manchester when we bowled Australia out for 289 in their first innings. My premonitions and fears began to dissolve, and as Mike Atherton and I comfortably reached 71 for the first wicket in reply, I thought to myself, 'We're okay, this is going to be a competitive series after all'. Then Merv Hughes had Atherton caught behind. Mike Gatting, our acknowledged champion against spin, strode in – and, give him his due, Allan Border immediately threw down the gauntlet and summoned up the young leg-spinner Shane Warne, whom the Australians been keeping comparatively under wraps during their build-up matches to the Tests.

First ball from Warne – would it be a loosener? No chance! Warne

255

flicked it out of his hand on the line of Gatting's pads and then it hung and dipped in the air even further towards the leg-side. If Mike had been set, and not just arrived at the crease, most days of the week he would have treated it like a full-toss leg-side cheese-roll, put his left leg down the pitch and whacked it unceremoniously over mid-wicket, one-bounce and over the ropes for four. But quite correctly, in a Test with a new bowler, he wanted a good look and was happy just to push out, cover up and either block it or let it continue floating down the leg-side. Then the ball pitched. It turned a good foot, almost at right angles; in a blur it ripped across Gatt's body, and whisked away the off-bail.

Gatt could scarcely believe it and stood there transfixed. I was at the other end, poking and prodding and pretending nothing extra-ordinary had happened. But in my mind I was thinking it was one hell of a delivery. The Australians went potty with glee, and more so immediately afterwards, when Warne had Robin Smith caught at slip groping vaguely. From 70 for no wicket, we collapsed and were eventually all out for 210, Warne having taken four for 51 in 21 overs. He also got my wicket, for 65, caught at mid-on off a full-toss. It was a careless stroke.

We still could have saved the match and gone on from there – but for two deliveries from the dogged Merv Hughes. Border had declared the Australian first innings at 432 for five, leaving us to bat a day and a half for a draw. Atherton and I began with another solid partnership of 73, then Gatting joined me and, just minutes before stumps, we were very comfortable at 133 for one. I was confident, with nine wickets standing, that we could bat out all the fifth day. (And if Gatt and I had mastered Warne the next day, then it might perhaps have been a different series.) Five balls of the last over before stumps were safely negotiated. More often than not, the final ball of the day from an aggressive fast bowler like Merv Hughes would be a bouncer just to warn you what to expect the next morning. Perhaps that was the delivery Gatt was expecting. To his credit, and with a final triumphant snort, Hughes arrowed down a fast yorker. It worked – an in-off via his pads, and Gatt was bowled.

It was a crucial strike. So was Hughes's delivery the next after-noon, when we had reached 223 for three and were again going com-fortably. I was on 133. It looked as if we could hold on for a draw.

Then Hughes dug one in, looking for a bit of bounce. It took me slightly by surprise, popped up behind me, and for a moment I sensed it was going to fall vertically down on to my leg-bail. By sheer instinct, I flapped it away with my gloved hand. The umpire Dickie Bird had no doubt at all – and I became the first Englishman in Test history to be given out 'handled the ball'. Needless to say, I trudged off feeling very cross with myself. England were all out for 332 only nine overs short of safety and a draw, and Australia won by 179 runs. (At The Oval in 1951, Len Hutton apparently had an almost similar dismissal against South Africa. He tried to turn the off-break bowler Athol Rowan to leg, got a top edge and the ball popped up. Thinking it might fall on to his stumps, Hutton took a second swat at it – not realizing that the wicketkeeper was poised to make the catch. He was given out for 'obstructing the field', another Test match 'first'.)

We were beaten badly by an innings at Lord's in the second Test, before which, against my better judgement, I agreed to be named as captain for the rest of the series – 'as long as I could begin to motivate the side to be more competitive' was my rider to Ted Dexter. We were, briefly, in the third match at Trent Bridge, which we drew, and where I went in at no. 5 to accommodate Mark Lathwell of Somerset on his Test debut. I made my eleventh century as captain, and also passed 8,000 Test runs. We had been very close to calling in David Gower for the Lord's match – he had scored what was his first vintage hundred for a year for Hampshire at Trent Bridge on the very first day of the Old Trafford Test – but then he injured his shoulder. So for Nottingham we selected the Surrey left-hander Graham Thorpe, who had done well on several 'A' tours – and Graham's fighting century on his debut to all intents made the left-hander's spot his own for the series.

Before Australia completed an even bigger innings victory at Headingley, I knew for certain that the time had come for me to stand down. Nobody would talk me out of it this time, although Keith Fletcher tried. I was in a gloomy depression, banging the same old drum, but the players weren't reacting. Nobody was following my tune. It was time for a fresh, younger bandleader with a new approach and brighter ideas. Once I'd made the irrevocable decision in my own mind on the Saturday evening – the Australians' victory

by an innings and 148 runs came soon after lunch on the Monday –
I telephoned Ted Dexter to ask him to be alongside me when I made
my announcement at the end-of-match press conference. I had got
on well with Ted and thought his general contribution to English
cricket as a whole during his period of office will one day be seen to
have been beneficial. I was sad when he said he could not make it to
Leeds on the Monday.

So I was on my own. I repeated my feelings about having lost the
knack of motivating the team and the need for a new broom, and
that I had simply done my best. I knew I had failed, though, and was
close to tears.

Mike Atherton took over the captaincy. I soon perked up, feeling
quite relieved I had done the right thing. Mike's approach *was* fresh-
er than mine. I felt relaxed under his leadership, and he encouraged
me to offer any advice I thought would be useful. We lost at
Edgbaston in his first Test as leader but then, quite joyously, we won
a famous victory (for England's self-respect if not for the long-gone
Ashes) in the finale at The Oval, where I quite happily found himself
doing the juniors' honours and wearing the hard-hat at bat-pad. I
even took two catches! And I contributed 56 and 79 to the victory
(by 161 runs), during which I passed Gower's England record total
of 8,231 runs. When I got home later that day there was a telegram
waiting for me from David which read: 'Many congratulations.
After all these years you must be immensely proud of your new position at short-leg in the helmet. Very well caught and, by the way, very
well batted too.'

For the winter of 1993, Mike Atherton took his first touring team to
the Caribbean, just as I had done mine. I missed out on that tour,
specifically asking not to be considered. My marriage split with
Brenda had now lasted a year, but it continued to be a strained and
painful time for us and I believed that a winter in England, seeing as
much of the three children as I could, was the best possible thing for
the family. I had moved into a modern bachelor flat at nearby
Ingatestone so, apart from an enjoyable series of speaking engagements with Fred Trueman and David Lloyd, I was regularly on hand
to help Brenda take the girls to their various school outings and
activities. Hannah, Megan and Sally mean the world to me, and this

rare opportunity over the winter to be fully and regularly involved with them was, I feel, rewarding for all of us.

I did go to the West Indies for a week during the first Test in Jamaica to cheer on the team and do a bit of broadcasting for the BBC Test Match Special team. Apparently, during one of the commentaries I referred to Jack Russell as 'a batsy guttler' instead of a 'gutsy battler', but even the one-and-only Brian Johnston had his slips of the tongue! They asked me if I missed the cricket. To be perfectly truthful, more than once or twice I regretted not being out in the middle, padded up, and facing the West Indian 'chin music'. I still get a sensational buzz at the memory of how I went out to pit my skill against the very best the game has offered.

'What?' they asked incredulously. 'You mean to say, Goochie, that you are up here in the commentary box, in the shade with cool men and cool drinks all around you, watching the cricket – and you're telling us that you'd rather be out there on a blinding white-light tropical midday, batting on a pitch of corrugated concrete, and facing up all alone to a relentless relay of very dangerous fast bowlers? Bowlers who, one after the other and from each end, gallop in to bowl with seemingly murderous intent, with you surrounded by a circle of slipfielders and short-legs in maroon caps?'

'Sure,' I said, and truthfully. 'I'm up here in front of a microphone, and in many ways I long to be out there, with Mike Ath at the other end, as Curtly begins another over, and bears down at me with another six-ball selection of surprises – his meaningful little leap at the crease, in the middle of which he momentarily waggles his wrist with the threatening ball in his hand as if to say: "See this here, man, this is my explosive hand-grenade, pin out, primed, and unplayable". Then if you hit the ball, say for a single or a two, and you run towards his end, there he is, pouting, and looking at you with his stare. Glaring at you, no words, but eyeballs wide like undipped headlights as if to say, "How did an ordinary fellow like you get a bit of bat on a ball like that?" Then his lips curl into a half-friendly half-smile which insinuates, "Okay, you had no right to be still there after a ball like that, ma-an – but you just wait for my next surprise, ma-an!"' Against the West Indies, batsman against bowler, both of us know that the bigger the contest, the better the satisfaction for whoever does the business on the day.'

After that stint behind the microphone, I returned home and enjoyed, for once, the English winter. Aside from the speaking tour with Trueman and Lloyd, I watched West Ham and even went to a couple of rugby internationals. It was a relief to be missing out on the helter-skelter of a cricket tour, and the daily phonecalls home to ask Hannah, Megan and Sally what they did at school that day. Now I could scrape the ice off my windscreen and run them to school, and pick them up again afterwards. Or take them for a swim, or to brownies or girl guides. First and foremost, I am a family man and always will be.

In the summer of 1994, the three-Test series against New Zealand was followed by three matches against South Africa, which put a famous seal on that country being allowed back into the Test match fold. I was particularly happy about that and was more determined than ever to win back the England place I had 'abdicated' by not going to the West Indies. Mike Atherton's team had rallied with heartening grit after a bad start in the early Tests, which included being bowled out for 46 in Trinidad, to defeat the champions in Barbados, Alec Stewart scoring a century in each innings.

So with Alec and Mike forging a good opening partnership, I knew I had an added incentive to begin the season in some style. So in the first New Zealand Test at Trent Bridge, I went in first-wicket down – and started off with a very satisfying knock indeed. Just six weeks before my forty-first birthday, I made a double century – apparently only the fifth forty-year-old ever to score 100 in a Test. Another pleasing little record – because it said something about the consistency which I had been aiming for so long to graft on to my game – was notching my 65th Test score of 50 or more and so beat Geoff Boycott's 64. Coincidentally, it was in my 108th Test, just as Geoffrey needed 108 Tests to post his record. Statistics can be made to show almost anything, but in this case I was happy they proved that I might, in my old age, have become as consistent as my old Yorkshire mentor.

At lunch on the third day at Nottingham, I had come in with 210 not out after six-and-a-half hours at the crease. I laughed when I heard that somebody said Ladbrokes suddenly had shortened my odds from 12–1 to 5–1 to pass Brian Lara's Test record of 375 which he had set seven weeks earlier in the Antigua Test against England.

Steady on, I thought, another 160-odd is an awful lot of runs. Sure enough, my present to the bookies was to get out to the first ball I faced after lunch!

New Zealand were below par at Nottingham, but they picked themselves up and drew the next two Tests. At Lord's I was smartly brought back to earth when the highly promising young Kiwi seamer, Dion Nash, had me lbw in both innings, for 13 and 0, my first duck in 60 Test innings. Then in the first innings at Manchester, Nash had me at once, caught at second slip for another duck, my first consecutive Test noughts since my debut match nineteen years before. This represented a mini-crisis for me, and I began to brood.

Generally, I was more than happy with my form. Before the middle of June I had become the second player to pass 1,000 runs after Warwickshire's Brian Lara. And at Worcester that month, in a Championship match, I made 101 and 205, only the fifth man ever to score two separate hundreds in a match five times. Worcester had set us 405 to win in 107 overs. Young Ronnie Irani and I put on 245 for the fourth wicket as we made the winning total with four wickets to spare. Scoring over 400 to win a Championship match had been done only six times since the Second World War – and now three of those feats belonged to Essex, and in successive years: the famous run chase against Derbyshire to celebrate our title in 1992; then a summer later at Hove when we made 412 for three, with centuries from John Stephenson and Nasser Hussain before I came in to blast 74 and finish the match with a six; and now this success at Worcester in the championship.

So there was no need for my confidence to be low. But the fact remained that with the three poor scores in the spotlight of a Test match, the whispers would be flying around that my eye had gone for Test-level bowling. This, of course, tenses you up, and when that happens it works against you: you try too hard, fret about making a fractional mistake so that you might, say, over-compensate and perhaps get into position for the stroke too early. Tiny insignificant things, yet crucial when your mind is a fraction insecure.

The South Africans had a pretty good attack – three persistent, nagging seamers and a quicker strike bowler in Allan Donald, who is always dangerous. It was a tremendous occasion at Lord's for their return and I bumped into many old friends from Cape Town.

Somebody gave me a scorecard of the last time they played at Lord's, way back in July 1965, and like a schoolboy, I asked the likes of Peter van der Merwe and Peter Pollock to sign it. It was good to have them back for the sake of all cricket but, of course, the real joy for that country was that their return signalled the end of the apartheid system, to be replaced with free elections and the installation of Nelson Mandela as president.

I am not a political animal, but I know what's right and wrong. I could personally share in this joyful celebration of political freedom and a happy reunion at Lord's with my friends from South Africa, many of whom – like the team coach Mike Procter, my old hero Barry Richards, Eddie Barlow, and the Pollock brothers – had put their cricketing careers on the line many years before by demanding multi-racial sport in their country.

In the match itself, we were well beaten by 356 runs, although the South Africans' achievement was partially obscured by the fuss over Mike Atherton's 'dirt in the pocket' affair. I had made 20 and 28. In many ways I have always been more disappointed at getting out in the twenties than for noughts. Being out for a duck can happen to anyone, but once you get to 28 you should be confidently thinking of Kenny Barrington's 'booking in for bed and breakfast' philosophy. Still, those runs at Lord's were enough for me to pass 2,000 Test runs in Tests on that most famous ground in cricket and, in fact, to be the first to log 2,000 runs on any one Test ground.

In the next Test at Headingley, where we easily had the best of the draw, I was pleased when Mike restored me as his opening partner (although we only put on 34 and 39 together). Going to The Oval for the last of the three Tests, England managed to seal a dramatic victory. And I do mean dramatic. In our first innings, I pushed a single and Mike faced Fanie de Villiers. This was the cue for more controversies to erupt.

It was Mike's first delivery. The ball jagged back at him as he covered up but in my view, no question, there was an element of bat and pad about the sound I heard. Yet up went umpire Kenny Palmer's finger. Mike had to go, adjudged lbw for 0. As he started to walk, he brought his bat up momentarily, studying it carefully. It's a common gesture by any batsman who is disappointed at being given out, and you will see it no end of times any summer. Okay, however brief, it is a pointed mime, but even Test opening batsmen are human in their disappointment.

I looked away. I did not want to catch Mike's eye, but I felt sorry for him. Kenny Palmer is a good umpire and I asked him about the incident afterwards. He said he hadn't heard a thing – that is, he didn't think the ball hit Mike's bat – and so that should have been the end of it. The umpire can only give the decision as he sees or hears it. Mike knew that too.

I batted on uneasily for about an hour, before Donald had me caught behind. In mid-afternoon, the new chairman of selectors, Ray Illingworth sidled up to me.

'Graham,' he said, 'could I have a private word?'

'Right', I thought to myself, 'this is it, the chop at last.' Certainly I reckoned he was going to tell me something I didn't want to hear – like I'm too old and past it, and they weren't going to allow me one last chance to take on the Aussies and win back the Ashes. I knew I'd had a lean Test mid-summer with the bat, and missing Kepler Wessels at deep gully the day before could well have made Illy think my time had come. I followed him to a quiet corner feeling like a schoolboy without an excuse.

Contrary to my expectations, Illingworth tells me that the Australian match referee, Peter Burge, is going to discipline Mike Atherton for showing dissent by looking at his bat and shaking his head after he was given out. Illy wanted to know what I thought. I say it's ridiculous; it was an honest enough decision, but a debatable one nevertheless; 'Mike hit the cover off the ball', I added, and, while he had looked at his bat, he had in no way overstepped the mark with his gesture. I did agree, however, that it might have been more dramatic in the TV close-ups which Burge had at his disposal

In my view there was no possible case to answer. If a player shows dissent he should be punished severely – but there was no over-reaction by Mike in this instance. So was Burge doing the over-reacting by making an issue of it? To fine Mike so exorbitantly that he even contemplated resigning the captaincy was, in the view of many observers, somewhat over the top. Perhaps Mike was a marked man after the 'dirt in the pocket' affair at Lord's.

The upshot, of course, was that Atherton was fined heavily for 'dissent'. The press then began to get all excited about it, but even they soon realized it was an unfair storm in a teacup. However, I was concerned about Mike and worried that he might be thinking, 'First Lord's, now this. I can do without this hassle, so let someone else have a go'. I could sense that Friday night that Atherton might be on the brink of resigning. And who could blame him?

With all the headlines flying around on the Saturday morning, Fletcher said to me after practice, 'Have a word with the boys'. I agreed with him that someone should. I asked Alec Stewart, who was vice-captain, his opinion and he said, 'That's fine, as senior pro you speak to them'. So Fletch took Mike into the physio's room on the pretext of a discussion on different field placings for various South African batsmen, and I gathered the team around and, for a moment, felt transported back to those early days of my captaincy in India, Jamaica and Trinidad and our famous 'huddle'. I told the players, 'Ath is really down and, I reckon, close to jacking it in, and as none of us wants that the very best way to show him is to go out and play today as if our lives depended on him staying as our skipper. So let's really get behind him; he's been very good for us and to us, so let's show him we can be good for him when he so desperately needs proof of it.'

Whether it was the strong words (which I very much meant) that did the trick, or Fanie de Villiers's bumping of Devon Malcolm, we will never know. Perhaps it was a combination of both. Anyway, the South Africans have to mop up our tail. Immediately, no. 11 Malcolm is hit on the helmet. De Villiers couldn't have known what a whirlwind he was uncorking. Devon readjusts his helmet and mutters to the fielders, 'You guys are history'. And of course, very soon they were.

De Villiers is an aggressive but fair cricketer. My view about tailenders being bounced, however, is that whoever bounces them must expect tit for tat when they come to bat themselves. Mind you, it should never be done brutally if a batsman obviously cannot defend himself, like what happened to Devon himself in Jamaica the winter before against Courtney Walsh. I always remember Andy Roberts's simple and highly philosophical analysis of the situation: 'If he gives me one, I give him one back.'

What also fired Devon up was the row he'd had with his captain at close of play on the Thursday night. Mike had taken the new ball to polish off the South African tail, but Devon would not bowl anything short to disconcert their tailender and fast bowler, Allan Donald. Mike kept cajoling Devon to bowl a few hostile rib-ticklers to Donald, but he kept pitching it up, trying to hit the stumps. I'd said to Mike quietly, 'Try my old trick. When I was captaining Devon, I'd tell him to pitch it up. Then he'd bowl short and sharp. In other words, tell him one thing and he'll always do the opposite.' Mike didn't believe me, but that has always been a private joke between myself and Malcolm. There's a lot of truth in it too. Anyway, Mike bawled out Devon when we got back into the dressing-room on the Thursday night and that might still have been rankling with the bowler on the Saturday.

Some might say that, as captain, I overbowled Devon on occasions. Perhaps I did, but I was always praying for him first to find and then to settle into his groove when he's firing on all cylinders and following-through. He can then be almost unplayable. In a five-Test series, he might only find it in two matches, but if he does you'll win them. He has raw pace all right, but what is so disconcerting about him for batsmen (as the South Africans found out at The Oval) is his terrifying unpredictability. You never quite know with Devon Malcolm where the ball is going to land or at what speed. And rule number one is: never face him in the nets. I always refuse to. It's like being in a coconut shy.

I have never forgotten when Mark Waugh first came to Essex in 1989 and we were playing Derbyshire. Mark strolled into the nets. Devon was hanging around, but wasn't playing for Derbyshire that day so said he'd have a bowl at this new Aussie kid of ours. Mark wasn't even in a helmet. First ball hit him on the shoulder, the next was within an inch of tearing his ear off, another almost broke his toe, while a couple in between hissed down the side-netting or even finished in the adjoining net. Mark came out of the net looking as white as a ghost.

But he's worth his weight is Devon, if he gets it right and is fired up, as he was this time at The Oval. Off his third ball, which reared up, Gary Kirsten turned away and the ball popped up from his bat handle and Malcolm followed through to take the catch himself almost on the batsman's crease. 'It's one of those days,' I thought contentedly down at long-leg. 'Devon's following-through, so he's on song.' It's when he falls away towards short extra-cover in his delivery that you know he's not going to get it right. But not this time.

The South Africans were routed. Devon took nine for 57, the best-ever Test figures in The Oval's history and the sixth best Test return of all time. We knocked off the 200 runs required to win in no time after Mike and I had set the tone in the second innings.

Yet, amid all the England euphoria, I was distraught on that Saturday night. I cannot remember being so distressed about a personal aspect of my game. It was a very different feeling to the year before when I had handed over the captaincy. This time, I convinced myself the time had come to pack in Test cricket – because my fielding had become a serious liability to the England side.

After Devon had taken the first three South African wickets in nine balls, we kept up the pressure with a really tight and committed display in the field. South Africa attempted a gutsy fight back and were 40 for three at lunch, but then, at 70-odd for four, we were poised to break through seriously when Brian McMillan top-edged a hook down to me at fine-leg on the boundary. I had only to move ten yards to my left and wait for it – a regulation sitter. Because I was well in position as the ball dropped, I prepared to catch it in my usual way in front of my face, baseball-style, palms facing outwards. I settled under it, in front of the new pavilion stand. No problem, I thought to myself.

In the last couple of years I had been working very hard at my fielding, not only at practice, but during the play, always concentrating on the assumption that 'the ball will come to you every single delivery'. I wondered whether my catching had deteriorated since that hand injury in Australia, but I felt that the work I'd put in was reaping its rewards in the field – against New Zealand I made a couple of good catches, and at Old Trafford, when I just held on to a catch at mid-off against Ken Rutherford, it was my one hundredth Test catch in 110 matches (only the fourth Englishman to hold a century of catches after Botham and Cowdrey, 120, and Walter Hammond 110). Then at Lord's, in the first Test of this South African series, I judged and held a difficult swirler on the run at deep fine-leg under the new Nursery stand.

Now at The Oval, with the game dramatically on edge, up comes this far easier chance. I'm in position, hands ready. Easy. But I've miscalculated a fraction – and instead of dropping in front of my face, the ball's three inches ahead of me. If I'd had time to adjust my hands I'd have taken it comfortably in front of my tummy-button. But, too late, I don't have time. It hits the 'heel' of my outwardly-cupped hands – and drops to earth.

Not having been a regular fielder anywhere near the boundary all through my career, I cannot remember such a loud collective groan from a packed crowd. Miserable? I felt worse than miserable. I was stunned with depression. That's it, I decided, I should pack in Test cricket here and now. My fielding had dropped to unacceptable standards. I was a forty-one-year-old liability.

I was more sorry for myself that evening than I can remember. I spoke to Keith Fletcher and to Illingworth and said I thought the time had come. 'Sleep on it,' they each said. We were staying at the Conrad in Chelsea Harbour, and that evening I sought out Mike Atherton in the bar. He came out with all the right things and said how dropped catches happen to everyone and the only thing is to put them behind you. I told him straight, 'I'm seriously thinking the time has come. That spilled catch was the signal, the sign that everyone gets that this is the end.'

'Whatever you do, Goochie,' he replied, 'we still need you, so don't make any hasty decisions.'

Mum and Dad came to supper at the Conrad. I told them my England career had to finish soon, but I wanted desperately to make the decision for myself, to get out at the top, not have it forced on me by the obvious lowering of my standards. Dad said I only had to look at my first-class batting average for 1994 to realize my powers weren't on the wane – and Mum, good old Mum, was just Mum. I'm not a publicly emotional person, and never have been, but sometimes it just wells up and the tears boil over. Like then.

Could I do it any more? Was it still there? If I went to Australia, might it be one tour too far?

16

A SERIES TOO FAR?

FK

By Christmas time, most of wet, windy faraway England was sighing that it was 'a tour too far' for every single one of its cricketers. By the end of the year, the England team's limping early progress around Australia had presaged two quite terrible beatings in the opening two Tests at Brisbane and Melbourne. England was cowering and the rampant Australian team was crowing. One of the banners in the first-day crowd at the vast, packed Melbourne arena had proclaimed, 'If the Poms win the toss and bat, keep the taxi running'.

In mitigation, the injuries to the England side were running at a level Gooch could not recall on any of his previous ten tours anywhere. Even the team's physiotherapist broke his hand when helping out at fielding practice. Not surprisingly, the team photograph taken on the bright first morning at Perth in October bore little relation to the group taken on the same WACA bench in February.

Ironically, the oldest man in the side was the only one of the original party to remain free of injury. In fact, Gooch had begun the tour in quite excellent form. In all types of cricket, he began imperiously with 129, 38, 68, 50 and 101, the latter century at his favourite ground abroad, Adelaide, being his 113th first-class century. During that initial sequence on the tour, Gooch passed 25,000 runs since his thirtieth birthday, a post-war figure only exceeded by Boycott. In the first Test at Brisbane, batting beautifully against the wiles of Shane Warne, Gooch left Allan Border behind as the most prolific scorer of Test runs since the age of thirty. Feted around the country as a visiting eminence, Gooch seemed set on a serene course to figure as prominently and profitably as he had ever done in an Ashes series.

But at Brisbane, batting at no. 5, he as good as dismissed himself in both innings with totally uncharacteristic cross-batted strokes as he attempted to impose himself and break the spell that the spin bowlers were having on his colleagues. Even though he was to re-assume his favourite position (on Stewart's re-broken finger) at the top of the order, and though he practised assiduously as ever each day – colleagues hurling balls at him in the nets from about forty-five feet for at least an hour – the half century he made in Brisbane's first Test was, unbelievably had one known it at the time, to be his last fifty in Test cricket. In his ten innings of the series, his scores were 20, 56; 15, 2; 1, 29; 47, 34; 37 and 4. His scores in the international one-day competition were no better.

After Warne's 11 wickets and big centuries by Slater and Mark Waugh had laid England to waste at Brisbane by 184 runs, Australia's second Test win at Melbourne was even more crushing – by 295 runs. This time both Waugh brothers ransacked England's attack in the first innings and, after a century by Boon in the second, England were bowled out in their last innings for a paltry 92. Warne and McDermott shared 17 wickets in the match. No team can have looked more bedraggled than England in an Ashes tour this century. Their performance, as well as his own cricketing (and, back home domestic) trough depressed Gooch immensely.

The third Test at Sydney began on New Year's Day and, with it, England's fortunes changed dramatically. They batted first and scored 309, then young Darren Gough's exuberant six wickets, fol-lowing his explosive 51 with the bat, helped bowl Australia out for 116; Atherton was then able to set the shaken home side a target of 449 to win, and although the first wicket put on 208 Australia were left desperately hanging on for the draw at 344 for seven with England unable to use their pace bowlers because of the bad light. So England's sudden momentum carried on to the fourth Test at Adelaide and a famous victory when Atherton asked Australia to get 263 in 67 overs and they wilted in the face of some hostile bowling from Malcolm.

England thus had the chance to square the series at 2–2 in Perth – although Gooch, for one, knew that such a result would be a phoney one for the tour had shown that no amount of papering over the cracks would permanently sort out English cricket's general malaise – which was at once illustrated by some appalling catching by England which left them always chasing the game forlornly and another last innings collapse had them thunderously routed by 329 runs.

Some Test match opening batsmen might be more than reasonably satisfied with his ten innings in a series producing a 50, a 40, two 30s, and two 20s. Not Gooch. Those sort of scores to him had, through his whole career, only been numerical prophecies for what was to come, just first-course tasters. He was distraught. It was time, he now felt, to leave the Test match arena for good. It was fully twenty years since he tremulously entered it.

GG

I was on my fifth tour of Australia and the team had to report to the Excelsior Hotel, Heathrow, the evening before the flight to Perth on 17 October. Because of our marriage split, the goodbyes had seemed harder to take than ever that afternoon at Brenda's house; Hannah, Megan and Sally looked puzzled as I hugged them and I could see them wondering why their Dad couldn't make it back to spend even Christmas Day with them. Christmas! It would be the second week in February before I saw the three of them again, and I would miss them.

At least Perth – a fresh, open city with fine practice facilities – is a super place to settle in at the beginning of a long tour. To Mike Atherton's squad of thirteen which had been selected for that dramatic final Test of the summer at The Oval against South Africa – Atherton himself, Stewart, myself, Hick, Thorpe, Gatting, Crawley, Rhodes, DeFreitas, Gough, Malcolm, Benjamin and Tufnell – was added the Hampshire off-spinner Shaun Udal, and two players who had been brought up in Australia: Craig White, the Yorkshire allrounder and Martin McCague, Kent's quick bowler. The non-selection of Angus Fraser was really the only surprise.

Being away so regularly on winter tours – and don't forget, six days in a hotel at a home Test match is, to all domestic intents, so far away from home it may as well be abroad – obviously contributed to the break-up of my marriage with Brenda. We had been together sixteen years. Initially, we were extremely happy, then we settled into a contented enough married state. But by the late 1980s (I felt anyway) Brenda and I were seriously growing apart.

When something like this happens, you try hard to work at it and seek ways to rectify the relationship. But in my case the cricket, and the concentration and intensity I always put into it, seemed only to place the marriage on an even sharper edge. Brenda never wanted the split, and she fought hard to patch up the cracks. At the same time, I felt more and more wretched.

When I did finally move out and the break-up became public knowledge, Brenda understandably was very upset at the misleading conclusions arrived at by the press which implied that she had given me an ultimatum to the effect that, 'If you go off on another cricket tour, we cannot stay married'. Nothing was further from the truth, and never had it been a factor, even remotely – although I suppose when they mischievously put such words into Brenda's mouth the journalists were only reflecting the long-held and general perception of our marriage in which I was the henpecked sportsman forever wanting to opt out of touring because my wife didn't like it. This was nonsense. It had been my decision every time to miss any tour.

So in her distress and outrage at these scurrilously fabricated quotes, Brenda went public in the *News of the World* in an attempt to put the record straight. The story appeared not long after we had arrived in India for the 1992/93 England tour. Brenda told how she had realized fully two years before that I had been increasingly unhappy at home – 'A wife can always tell', she said – and that 'much as Daddy loved his children, he didn't love their Mummy any more'.

That was the sum of it. It was Brenda's right to give that interview and it was obviously important for her to do so. But I could never have done the same. I have never felt the need to share my personal and intimate feelings with newspaper readers. To me a private life should be just that – *private*.

Nevertheless, I want to tell the whole truth about myself – although at the same time I am desperate not to re-open personal wounds. The break-up and my ultimate unhappiness in the marriage was somehow the more wrenching because I was all too aware that Brenda had been an extremely loyal and supportive wife to me as well as a very loving and caring mother to the children. It took me a long time and much heartache even to envisage leaving the children.

I never thought I could do so. Yet, finally, I reasoned that, however harrowing the decision was, a miserable father at home was even worse for them than a happier father away from home. So I left.

Brenda remains upset and bitter, but she has handled the situation probably better than I have, and with her strong integrity it is testament to her character that we have managed to remain on amicable terms, both of us determined to do the very best for the children. We still have occasional family holidays together and when I am in England I probably get involved with the kids (and spoil them!) more than when I was living in the family home at Shenfield.

Although I didn't leave home to live with another woman, the truth is that while I was still brooding over my dilemma at home in the late stages of our marriage, I had already met Julia. We saw each other occasionally as friends, then as better friends; and as time went by (and I left home) things snowballed and our feelings became stronger and stronger for each other.

Once I had moved into my bachelor-pad at Ingatestone, Julia and I saw more of each other and were able to make no secret of our relationship – and my friends and those on the cricket circuit got to know her so, mercifully, we soon became a stale item for the gossip columnists and newshounds. As I get on with my cricket, I still feel remorse about the pain I have caused to all those who have been close to me.

It had been a long time since I was a bachelor. I had never lived on my own before – if you don't count the single hotel rooms on the international circuit, that is – and certainly this 'new' bachelor was not much good at 'doing for himself'. (Opening a tin of soup is about the limit of my culinary skills, or bringing home a ready-prepared meal for the microwave from Marks & Spencer.) In a reverse sort of logic I reckon it's done me good because on the cricket circuit you can get into the habit of eating too much and my fast metabolism means I put on weight far too easily. Certainly I eat far less red meat than I used to. Nine times out of ten in a restaurant I'll go for the fish or chicken. At the cricket, during lunch, I'll enjoy a nice pasta salad if there's one available. At breakfast on match days, I'll have a mixture of cereal and yoghurt, toast and tea and, once a week, usually as a brunch before the Sunday game I'll allow myself a real treat and go through the hotel 'card' – sausages, fried bread, bacon, eggs, and all the trimmings.

If I was not exactly lonely in my modern 'yuppie commuter' two-up, two-down mews 'pad', I found I had become increasingly rest-less. Getting myself to relax was difficult enough when I was living with Brenda. Not that I'm one to come home and flop in front of the television all night. Nor am I a real reader of books, though I really enjoy those book audio tapes for long car journeys. At night, my head hits the pillow at around 10–10.30, and I don't need an alarm-clock – I'll wake up on the dot at 6 o'clock. Then even on days-off in the summer, and if I'm not going to practice, I'll have a run before perhaps driving over to the old house and taking the children to school. Then I'll keep myself busy by catching up on things that accumulate – paperwork, letters, no end of phonecalls. I'm not the type to potter about. I'm more of a doer. But I wish I could relax more.

When Mike Gatting and I went out for our first practice together at Perth, the photographers were obviously keen to get shots from every angle of England's two veterans – and although Gatt is far greyer around the jowls and head, at thirty-seven he is four years younger than me. We go back a long way. I had already played for England, of course, but in fact Mike toured before I did – he was on Mike Brearley's tour of Pakistan in 1977/78, which I was disap-pointed to miss. Mike's cricket has always been charged with enthu-siasm for the game. He was the last England captain to retain the Ashes, in 1986/87. We sensed some Aussie surprise at two such emi-nent old codgers being selected this time round, but I told Gatt they only had to look at the summer's first-class averages to see we deserved to be chosen. Mike had scored 1,671 runs with six cen-turies, and I made 1,747 runs also with six hundreds. Only Warwickshire's phenomenal young West Indian, Brian Lara, had a higher aggregate, and his 2,066 runs only bettered both of us once he had decided to chalk up that little matter of 501 in Warwickshire's match against Durham.

After morning practice, most of the England team continued their acclimatization with afternoon golf, a game which I do enjoy. I used to play pretty regularly, especially on tour, but I've never been as keen as some cricketers, who would even skimp on nets to rush down to the golf club at every opportunity. On that fateful tour of

India in 1981/82 – can it really be all of thirteen years ago? – I made a hole-in-one at the old British Raj colonial course at Tolleygunge, near Calcutta. However, as I've got older, I've played less and less golf. Certainly not eighteen holes – unless I'm provided with an electric buggy! Perhaps I'll hit a few and have an hour's stroll, but on the whole I feel it's more beneficial to lie down and have a little sleep and rest, preferably in the shade, for sunbathing can sap your strength.

On the previous tour in 1990/91 Perth, of course, was where I cut my hand which subsequently became badly infected, and that injury threw the whole trip out of kilter. Now on this last tour during practice, poor Alec Stewart, one of the linchpins of our side, had his finger broken by Craig White. Then, in the first competitive match in the middle, a friendly against the Australian Cricket Board Chairman's XI at Lilac Hill, Shaun Udal had his thumb broken attempting to take a return catch. The two of them would be out for three to four weeks. The injuries were bad omens.

I was delighted with my own form, however, moving my feet well and striking the ball sweetly. My confidence was high that I could make a really telling contribution to this assault on the Ashes. I made 129 at Lilac Hill. My old friends Dennis Lillee and Jeff Thomson opened the bowling against us while Rodney Marsh kept wicket. (How I would have liked that score when I first came up against them at Edgbaston in 1975!) It was really great to see them back in action again – Thomson 7–1–30–0, Lillee 10–0–32–2, and the wickets of Atherton and Hick. Lillee bowled me two bouncers, which I would have been hurriedly ducking only a few years back; this time I hooked them for four. His marvellous bowling action is still intact, and so is his competitive edge – when Gatt came in Lillee complained, 'Gatting, you're so fat I can't see the stumps!'

In the opening first-class match against Western Australia at the WACA ground we had the upper hand all through. With my 68 in the second innings I felt in fine fettle, and continued to do so when we moved on to Adelaide to play South Australia. We were set a target of 260 in 76 overs in the last innings and got them with 12 balls and four wickets to spare, with me leading the charge with 101. It was my 113th first-class century. Apparently, I'm just one behind Viv Richards now; it would be an honour to get level with him. We all felt happy that night. It's crucial when you are on tour to stamp your authority in the state matches, it shows you mean business and it breeds confidence. In the first innings (when I made a half-century), Hick hit 101 and Thorpe 80, while our emerging pace bowlers, McCague and Gough, took five wickets apiece in each of the state's innings.

The team had a hiccup against New South Wales at Newcastle – allowing the Australian Test batsmen Mark Taylor, Michael Slater and Mark Waugh each to warm up with some runs – and we lost by four wickets. Afterwards we drove down for a stopover at Sydney where I was privileged to take our young all-rounder Darren Gough with me on a visit to Harold Larwood at his Sydney bungalow home. It was very moving to meet the man who had won the Ashes for England in 1932/33 and I know Darren was touched by the experience as well. Harold will be ninety in November and he is almost blind. He chuckled proudly in telling us about his clashes with Don Bradman all those years ago; he still calls Bodyline 'leg theory'. I asked him if he ever pitched it up when he was practising leg-theory. 'No, never,' he said. His little front room is almost a museum, with photographs lining the walls and mementos of his great past. He showed us his most treasured item – a silver ashtray given to him by his captain on that celebrated tour, Douglas Jardine, and inscribed simply 'To Harold, from a grateful skipper'. I know I'm getting a bit old myself, but I didn't laugh as much as Darren did when Harold said to me, 'You must have seen Hedley Verity bowl.'

Our final warm-up game before the first Test at Brisbane was against an Australian XI at Hobart, Tasmania, which is an extremely pleasant city – almost like being in New Zealand – but a far chillier and breezier one than boiling hot and humid Brisbane, so it might have been okay for practice but not necessarily for acclimatisation. We continued our loss of momentum at Hobart, unfortunately, and although we recovered from a disappointing first couple of days to get a draw, the really dismal news was confirmation that poor Devon Malcolm, whom we had been nursing up to full throttle for Brisbane, had gone down with chicken-pox. The first match of any Test series is always a vital one; if you lose it's a long way back, a point rightly emphasised by Mike Atherton at our team meeting. We just had to compete in every department – skill, awareness and character, plus non-stop commitment.

I had been delighted with my fitness and my form so far, and I was in good spirits and keen as mustard for the Test to begin. It has always thrilled me and put me on edge going in to a big match. I had particularly enjoyed opening the batting in the run-up to the Test, but Alec's finger seemed to have healed when he scored a second-innings century at Hobart and so we reverted to Plan A, with him opening with the captain and me at no. 5 followed by Mike Gatting. Australia seemed certain to play their two spinners, Tim May and the prodigiously talented Shane Warne, and one of the ideas was that the experience of Gatt and myself against the turning ball would help bolster our middle-order batting.

It goes without saying that I would bat anywhere England want me to, but the truth is I prefer by far to open the innings. I've done it for so long now; I'm in the habit and groove. In the 1993 home series against Australia, for the third and fourth Tests, we picked young Mark Lathwell of Somerset to open. Everyone insisted he was the up-and-coming prospect and I went along with that although I'd not seen him bat for any length of time. I agreed that he should bat in his normal county position and, as captain, I dropped myself down the order. Mike Atherton and I had three opening partnerships of over 70 in our first four innings of that summer and I remember Mike was horrified ('Goochie, you're not splitting us up are you?'). Anyway, the experiment with the promising Lathwell was not successful and after two matches I reverted to opener.

I don't particularly mind batting at no. 3 – at first wicket down, you are padding up with the openers and know you have to be ready to go out at any time. But adjusting to no. 5 is much more difficult, certainly for an old hand like me who is set in his ways. I never have really scary nightmares, but since that 'experiment' of my batting at no. 5 in 1993, I have had this nasty, sweat-inducing dream perhaps a dozen or so times.

I dream I'm due in at no. 5, but am 'caught short' when the wicket falls and cannot get back into the pavilion to change. My mind is in a terrible fret and panic and when I do get back in everything is in a mess. I cannot find my pads, then when I do I put them on the wrong way round. Where's my box? I can't find my bat or helmet, my gloves aren't laid out. They're all waiting for me out there, but I simply can't get ready in time. I'm going to be given out before I even make it to the wicket (weirdly Freudian, you might say) ... but then I wake up in a cold sweat.

Okay, call it a nightmare if you want. But this nightmare does more than hint at how fretful I have found it adjusting to batting down the order. When exactly do I begin to change and get ready? When do I sit down to compose myself into my pre-batting mood – which is easy when you are opening – and meditate on past achievements or encounters? At no. 5, do I sit and just watch the opening overs, or do I keep walking around so as to keep light on my feet? Batting down the order, you cannot sit there in your corner, changed and ready and padded up, in a completely fully-focused state of mind, because you could be there all day long if the top order makes a bucketful of runs. But then if you totally switch off until the wicket before yours falls and then start to get ready, what happens if the batsman before you is out first ball? If that happens, the nightmare could – just – become a horrible reality.

As it turns out, at Brisbane, in the first Test, I am not kept waiting in my no. 5's quandary for too long. First Mike Atherton loses the toss, then Slater smacks Phil DeFreitas's first ball for four and he and Mark Waugh go on to get big hundreds. We bowl badly with the new ball, but later pick up our game somewhat and restrict them to 426 all out. But on a still good batting surface, we are bowled out for a lamentable 167. Craig McDermott takes six wickets, Warne three, and May one – me. I join Atherton at 83 for three. Mike is going steadily after the early alarms, but the feeling between us is that with Warne and May settling into a groove we should not let the innings get bogged down. In this first meeting with the two contrasting spinners, who bowl so well in tandem, it is crucial to take the attack to them. I am feeling keyed up and in great nick, the ball coming on to the meat of the bat. I smash Warne one-bounce over mid-on, then sweep him high over the square-leg fence for six. From the other end, Mike nods his approval and then, between overs, we agree I should keep the momentum going and go for my shots, as long as I don't do anything too rash.

After the Warne assault, I feel May deserves a bit of tap. He switches to bowling round the wicket to me, I shape to hit him high over mid-wicket, mistime it minutely, and top-edge a catch to the wicketkeeper, Ian Healy. I am furious with myself, and for leaving

Mike on the burning deck. I determine to leave the sweep-shot in my pavilion locker in the second-innings.

The Aussie captain Mark Taylor surprised us all by not enforcing the follow-on (they were 259 runs ahead), for Atherton and Stewart were already padding up when the Australian captain told us. We bowled and fielded much better this time, and restricted them to a declaration score of 248 for eight, which left us to bat five full sessions and a final hour for the draw (and a technicality of 508 for victory, over 100 more than any team had managed in a fourth innings to win a Test).

We also batted much more resolutely second time round. The skipper and Alec Stewart put on 50 for the first wicket, Alec looking at his particularly skittish best. He had seen off McDermott and, as soon as Warne came on, cracked him to the fence at deep cover. 'Watch out for the flipper, Alec,' I thought to myself on the balcony. 'He often bowls that delivery after he's dropped short and been hit for four.' Sure enough, as Alec pulled back in anticipation of another short one, the ball hissed through at a lick and took out his middle stump. It was brilliant bowling. Then almost at once Mike was leg-before, playing back to the top-spinner. England 59 for two.

Graeme Hick and Graham Thorpe came together and batted really well to see out the day, but Warne struck again first thing on the final morning and at 220 for four I was joined by Gatt and we two old soldiers and former captains, last survivors of the 1970s, attempted to dig in for the duration. Gatting lasted well over the hour till, not long before lunch, McDermott took the new ball and he touched one to Healy. 'Billy' McDermott is one of those players who makes things happen. It was an important wicket for Australia.

Steve Rhodes went immediately in the same manner with the ball still shiny after lunch. I was with the tail as Warne and May came back. I was playing with a good rhythm and momentum. My job was to upset theirs. I reached my fifty and at the day's half-time 'whistle' we were 300 for six.

I raise my bat perfunctorily and Warne says to me with a grin, 'Well played, Mr Gooch'. He always addresses me as 'Mr Gooch', he says as 'a mark of respect of skill and age', but I think he overdoes it a bit. Nevertheless it is a marvellous challenge batting against him. When Warne said 'Well played', I said to him, 'Thanks, you've got the others (he had already dismissed Stewart, Atherton, Hick and Thorpe), but I'm damned if you're going to get me'. Alas, scarcely said and it was done – an over later and I'm on 56.

I can only say I had a mental block. Down comes a 'legger', which I misread for a top-spinner. I do what I'd sworn after the first innings I would never do again in this series unless I was already over a big hundred. I go down for the great hoiking sweep-slog to clear mid-wicket, but instead get a bottom-edge to Healy. I am as dumbfounded with myself as I am mortified. 'Aberration' is the only word I can find to describe what I did. It was quite out of character, especially as I had determined to cut out the sweep-shot. Warne had somehow led me into it.

I was distraught. I knew I had let England down. I had to go up to Mike Atherton to apologise to him, I was so full of grief about the incident. I was still in a daze of self-recrimination long after Warne had joyously wrapped up the match for Australia – he took eight for 71 in 50.2 overs, a quite remarkable performance by a very special operator.

That shot still upsets me as I write about it now.

Coincidentally, it was here at Brisbane that I first wore a batting helmet in my career. It was 1978 and Kerry Packer's World Series was in operation and had already instituted changes in how cricket was being presented to the public. It was my first overseas Test and, probably unused to it, I was hit on the 'hard hat', on the very flag of St George, by a Geoff Dymock bouncer. (The sight of me being hit made Ian Botham go to war when we bowled!) The point now being, who would have thought, when we were trying on those helmets for the first time all those years ago and realizing the way cricket combat was heading, that seventeen years later England would be bowled out by an Australian leg-spinner in his mid-twenties who was not only good, but probably the best there has ever been?

Before Warne, the Pakistani Abdul Qadir was the best 'legger' I had ever played against. He was a superb bowler, but already the Australian has the edge on him. Warne can spin the ball more, and still control the flight superbly. His line of attack makes it terribly difficult to hit where you would expect to hit any other leg-spinner. Warne's very tight line, on middle-and-leg or even leg-stump, has him hardly ever being driven through the covers or, confidently anyway, hard through mid-off. He imparts such a spin on the ball that his 'drift' in the air is also very disconcerting, and the ball you have very much in your mind each time he approaches is his flipper. It is a quite astonishing delivery, and he produces it at pace. Hit him for a boundary and expect the flipper next ball! Shane Warne is already, and deservedly, in the all-time bowlers' hall-of-fame.

So we lost the first Test by 184 runs, and then went to Melbourne for Christmas and lost the second by 295 runs after Warne and McDermott bowled us out for 92 in the fourth innings. We felt humiliated. In the match, McDermott took eight wickets and Warne nine. I was at no. 5 again and 15 not out overnight in the first innings. McDermott's opening delivery to me next morning was a full toss. Surprised, I smashed it straight back at him ... caught and bowled.

I had practised diligently in the nets for an hour after breakfast – and received every possible type of delivery except a full toss! Perhaps he played for it, because McDermott has caught-and-bowled me a few times down the years with the same delivery, beginning at The Oval in 1985 – but not before I had made 196 that time. I was beginning to think I could do with some of those runs on this particular trip.

I opened the batting in the second innings – and would do for the rest of the series – because the same finger Alec Stewart broke at Perth was smashed again in the first innings here when he was facing McDermott. It was a tragedy for Alec as well as for the team because he is not only a fine player but an imposing bold-as-brass influence. This further piece of wretched luck meant our injured were queuing up for treatment like a throng of extras on the set of *MASH*. Truly, I had never known anything like it; as the injury crisis worsened it seemed I was the only one keeping a clean-sheet on the injury-list and I joked, 'I might not be playing too well, but at least I am *playing*.

I felt sorry for all of them. Joining Malcolm on the absentee list was Joey Benjamin; and at different times McCague, White and Hick were sent home with serious injuries; but I felt for no one more than young Darren Gough as he collapsed in a heap in his first over in the one-day international following the Sydney Test, when his flamboyant all-round performance had begun to restore our shattered pride. When Darren had to fly home with torn ankle ligaments, a sparkle left our dressing-room. He is a vibrantly engaging character with a bounce and commitment reminiscent of the young Ian Botham. If he is even half as good as Ian, Darren will be some cricketer all right, but the strut and smile and the attitude is already there. Like Beefy, he just wants to get out there and make things happen. Such players boost a team no end. If he keeps improving and steers clear of serious injury, Gough should have a long and successful Test career in front of him.

The spurious one-day competition in which Darren was injured was a distraction and although it pulled in the crowds, I was not at all happy with the concept of the Australia 'A' side being included. In a way it even took the mickey out of us – why should we help develop young Australian cricketers? Then when the 'A' side and the senior Aussie team began to interchange players it made any form of real competition a complete farce. As for ourselves, we did not play consistently well enough, and losing to Zimbabwe was a low point, but by the end we were more concerned with our wounded and whether we could have enough fit players to contest the final two Test matches.

Unfortunately, my reverting to opener again did not bring me a dramatic change in fortune. Enter Damien Fleming on his home ground at Melbourne for the second Test. He had me caught behind for two, and then at Sydney he dismissed me in the same way, for one in the first innings, and lbw for 29 in the second. Fleming is a good, medium-paced swinger of the sort who has given me more trouble through my career than the out-and-out paceman or spinner, although I have scored no end of big hundreds against countless top-class medium-paced swing bowlers. What was beginning to nag away at me after Sydney was not that I was out for one in the first innings, but that I was out for 29 in the second. Caught behind for one or two can happen to any opener. Getting out after having 'got in', however, was becoming very worrying. Once in, I should have been going on to really big scores. Making thirties or fifties was not my game and never has been. England is entitled to expect more from a senior batsman. I was becoming depressed enough about it to give serious thought to Test retirement. Had the time come at last? I hoped not, but I was not confident. The next, and fourth, Test at Adelaide would tell.

As it turned out, I got 'in' both times … and then got out, for 47 and 34. No excuses now, for the stark issue in my mind was not highlighted any longer by England's dismal displays of the first two Tests. We could have won the Sydney Test but for the weather at the very last, and at Adelaide we won famously. But 47 and 34? I was unable, as of old, to convert good starts into major innings as of old. Thirties and forties may be good enough for some. Not for me. It was definitely time to call it a day.

As soon as I made the decision, I knew it was right. For myself, and for England as well, I had done my bit down the years – I remain proud of that – but suddenly it was patently obvious to me that for the team to progress at a pace under Mike Atherton and his vice-captain, Alec Stewart, other batsmen in the side must be encouraged to take charge, to pick up the gauntlet and rally to the challenge of establishing themselves as fully-blown international cricketers on the world stage – players like Graeme Hick who, even though he does not look the most permanent or solid of batsmen, was sumptuously striking the ball as well as ever before his back injury; or Graham Thorpe with his boldly positive approach and already admirable teak-hard Test match temperament.

So I did the deed at last. I made my announcement – with a sad heart, but a proud one. Playing cricket for my country meant a tremendous amount to me.

And so, with one last match at Perth, I would take my leave of Test cricket fully twenty years since I first nervously walked out at Edgbaston in 1975. I was upset that, on this last expedition, I could not achieve what all my preparation and motivation had been geared towards for six months; namely to be at the forefront of a side which brought back the Ashes to England. But I was going to Perth for this final emotional Test fling to do what I had always promised myself I would do – to go out, graciously, and at the top.

After being two-down, to be going into this final Test with the chance of squaring the series 2–2 was in itself a minor triumph for Mike Atherton and those of us who were still comparatively fit in his injury-wracked band. Both Mike and I knew 2–2 would only have been papering over the weaknesses in our domestic cricket but we were confident, nevertheless, after the Adelaide victory.

But at once at Perth we began indulging ourselves in a terrible spate of dropped catches. No cricket team can be so profligate and still hope to win. It proved yet again how inconsistent England teams had been down the years; we've won solitary Test victories in one-off dramatic style, but seem unable to string a row of successes together. Unfortunately I set the tone for our butterfingers in Devon Malcolm's first over. With Graeme Hick on his way home with an injured back, I took his place in the slips – and put down Michael Slater. It wasn't an easy chance, but if I'd clung on as I dived to my right there's no telling how the script might have been rewritten.

So it was hardly an auspicious start to my final Test, but it made me doubly motivated to atone with the willow and, when we batted, I could not have been more pleased with my form. I was moving well and timing the ball sweetly enough into the thirties, repeating to myself my 'mantra' of old, 'Don't give it away now, don't give it away and you could be "in" for a big one'.

Then Mark Waugh comes on to bowl to use the last remnants of shine. The ball hits my pad. No, that must be a fraction too high? Up goes the umpire's finger and I'm on my way, out lbw for 37. It could have gone either way. You get the disappointing decisions when things aren't quite happening for you. But it's part of the game. I've benefitted more than a few times down the years from marginal decisions, so I've never been one to complain when the rub of the green goes against me. If the finger goes up, you go.

From 77 for three the innings closed at 295, thanks mainly to a stand of 158 between Thorpe (123) and Mark Ramprakash (72), who had been summoned hastily from India where he had been playing for our 'A' team. That left us 107 behind Australia who now, and despite being 123 for five at one stage, made 345 for eight declared.

In the second innings, I was quite overwhelmed.

I felt a warm buzz of gratitude for the crowd and their generous standing ovation but also, somehow, for everyone who has helped and encouraged me all along the way, from my very beginnings in cricket. Then, when Mike Atherton and I got to the middle, the Australian captain Mark Taylor summoned his men in a farewell 'three cheers' for me, and that was extremely gratifying too.

We were facing a huge target of 452, and forty-five minutes' batting that evening plus the whole of the next day. I dearly wanted to go out on a high note. Mike and I agreed there was no point sitting on the splice, we must be positive and if the ball was there to hit, then we must hit it.

You must show the bowlers you mean business. When you are in that frame of mind, even early on, you tend to look for balls to go for if it's in the hitting area. So McDermott at once bowls this short one, and I'm quickly in position and shape for the hook. Off the pitch it seams wide of off-stump, then even wider – but I'm still committed to my shot and go through with it. I wallop it like a two-handed over-head smash at Wimbledon and I get enough 'wood' on it to spoon up a gentle dolly just over shortish mid-on's head where Jo Angel only needs to take a couple of paces back for a sitter of a catch. But now he's panicking as much as I was, and he goes into reverse, trips over his own heels, and falls into an ungainly heap just as the ball hits the ground a yard behind him. General hilarity all round – except for Angel – and relief for me. Chance number one.

But I wasn't finished. I was not aware that the emotion I'd felt at the ovation from the crowd and the players had affected my concentration. Now McDermott bowls a full length ball, I get a thick inside-edge and it flies straight to David Boon at short-square and hits him on the box at a rate of knots … then falls gently to earth. Chance number two.

Third time round I was not so lucky. Next over, McDermott bowls a straight 'four' ball and I crack it back very hard and really off the meat. As the bowler follows through he has no chance of getting out of the way and, travelling at a lick, the ball hits him on the front of his shoulder – and pops up into the air. Give him his due, McDermott has the agility and presence of mind to stop, turn, and wait for the ball to drop into his hand.

Gooch c & b McDermott 4. The End. I had faced 12 balls. Not quite the finish I wanted, to put it mildly. But a final confirmation for me, if one was needed, that the time had been exactly right to retire from Test cricket. The breaks weren't coming and I was not achieving anything like the standards I had always set myself.

My departure from the Test arena for the last time was accorded another standing ovation from the over-generous cricketing people of Perth. I was very moved. It was shared by Mike Gatting, who followed me to the crease and also received three fully deserved cheers of farewell from Taylor's Australians.

Was this 'hip-hip-hooray' the Australian captain's secret weapon? I had not even taken off my pads before Gatt was back in the pavilion. There has always been a bond and firm affinity between Gatt and me; but, on this last occasion, we had both set in train another England collapse and at close of play we were a perilous 27 for five. We rallied somewhat next day to 123 all out, thanks to Mark Ramprakash again and Steve Rhodes, but that evening I looked across at Mike Atherton, who had carried his bat in for eight not out during the early clatter of wickets, and my heart went out to him. He looked drained.

It was at Perth, of course, at the end of England's last tour in 1990/91 that our performances and lack of commitment had got me in such a state as to read the captain's riot act. I guessed Mike was feeling something like I had, reckoning that the attitude of one or two might have let him down. Certainly nobody could accuse him of not leading from the front. Since being made captain, his batting had gone from strength to strength, which is what happened to me in the job. Mike has great patience and determination at the crease, and with his good, correct technique he sells himself very dearly. He is tough all right, and fiercely patriotic about playing for his country. He was a good choice as captain, and I hope desperately that England under him can graft some steely competitiveness and consistency in to their game for Mike has many years of Test cricket ahead of him.

Before the chairman, Ray Illingworth, came over midway through the tour there was a media controversy about him and the captain being at odds, and on some days it seemed that the two of them were conducting conversations from thousands of miles away solely through journalists. Illy, of course, said he was being regularly 'misquoted' and he probably was. For myself, I'll stick to my old philosophy of being careful and guarded about what I say out loud. I know the press thought I was a monosyllabic old misery-guts, but it kept me out of headline-hotwater. Raymond is an affable 'chatter' about cricket, just as Ted Dexter was a ruminating 'thinker' who thought aloud. Both can be fatal – for if something is said as a passing jest or unconsidered throwaway line, the next morning, while not being a factual misquote, it can appear isolated, highlighted and headlined, and a massive emphasis is being put on it that was not given to it the day before. Suddenly, throwaway lines can be set in stone ten feet high!

Just as I had a good relationship with Dexter when I was captain, so I got on well with Illingworth once I was back in the ranks. Ted was generally a 'hands-off' chairman, allowing the captain his say and, mostly, his way. Raymond has far stronger views over selection, and it is obviously different now with the captain and chairman each trying to get their own preferences on board. But with any luck, this sparking off against each other by two very positive Northern characters will be just the thing to force a dynamic, forward thinking, philosophy for English cricket. Heaven knows, we need one.

Raymond knows his cricket from A to Z and then some more. 'Aye,' he mutters approvingly as he watches Atherton bat, 'the lad's got a good sound Northern technique.' He is particularly fond of players from the North, especially east of the Pennines. I have found it both fascinating and rewarding to listen when Raymond is in full spate on all matters cricketing. I will miss those conversations. He was, of course, captaining Leicestershire when I made my first firstclass hundred in 1974. 'Yes, I remember,' says Raymond quick as a flash. 'I got three for 60-odd that day, didn't I?' He has an amazing memory for the detail of matches he played in, particularly ones he featured in strongly. In the summer of 1994, rain stopped play one day in the series against New Zealand and BBC TV re-ran edited highlights of an old Test in which Raymond was batting. Suddenly Dennis Lillee has him lbw. 'Illy, what sort of shot was that?' we rib him. 'Ah, but I'd got 51 when he did me,' he retorts at once, 'and what's more it was easily top score.' Mention any county ground, seemingly at random in the conversation, and Illy can recite you his best batting and best bowling, chapter and verse. Drop the White Cliffs of Dover into a sentence and he'll fall for the bait without a flicker of a pause. 'Dover? Once against Kent I hit 135 and took 14 wickets in the match, 1964 it was.' But he knows the game inside out, for which he is much respected by the players, and he mixes with them very well.

My sincere hope, as I packed my England 'trunk' for the last time, was that Illingworth and Atherton would stick together, and forge a victorious young squad – with Alec Stewart as dynamic first-lieutenant and wicketkeeper batsman. And make sure you only pick genuine English players, or rather British players. In these days of dual-passports anyone seems to be able to drift in, qualify for a county, and then get a game for England as if it was any old team. Surely there needs to be a show of commitment to their country and its society; not just a commitment to their sport and a means of making more money out of it.

Patriotism is a vital ingredient in international sport – personally I wish we'd line up before each Test to hear the National Anthem played like they do at soccer and rugby. That would help a captain motivate his players – and both under my charge and under Mike Atherton's some of our men have been very difficult to motivate.

In the end it all comes down, perhaps, to self-motivation. Every squad in county cricket has players just resting on past laurels or promise, just going through the motions. Squads should be combed regularly and even harshly to get rid of dead wood. Players must be ambitious and take a real pride in their own performance and never stop working or asking questions about their own game. Daley Thompson, our great Olympic decathlete, told me in 1994 that what he wanted all his rivals to know was that he was famous for being the first to arrive in the morning for training and the very last to leave. For all that, I have sometimes been sneered at by those who have a more laid-back, laissez-faire approach to their sport; but those are the sort of standards that have dominated my approach to a career in professional sport. Call it 'dull work-ethic' if you want, but I didn't go running, or walk up six flights of hotel stairs when I could have stood in the lift, or carry around permanently in my bag my dumbbells just to keep myself (and others) amused. I did those things because throughout my career I never saw a fitter, healthier and stronger cricketer ever become a worse cricketer.

It has required sacrifices all right, and in my personal domestic life, too. Certainly all the time and effort I have put into keeping my cricket at the highest level has had a detrimental effect in that regard. I missed the children desperately on this last tour with England. But being away from the three of them at least gave me some space and a determination to reflect on my whole domestic situation. The children's contentment and well-being means everything to me.

Brenda says she would like me back, although I am happy she is spreading her own social wings again. It has been a traumatic period and, as I write this at the end of a long tour, I have to confess that these personal matters have weighed heavily on my mind. This time I have not coped well with my cricket. I have worked at my game as diligently and conscientiously as ever, but I know I did not deliver the goods to Mike Atherton and the team as I wanted. To say my last England tour was a disappointment would be an understatement.

So I came in with Essex and Keith Fletcher and I went out with England and Keith Fletcher.

I was sad when the decision was made to sack Keith from the manager's position after our disappointing Ashes tour – although when Ray Illingworth came onto the scene it was obvious to me that there would be changes within the England set-up. I think Keith found that managing England was a completely different ball-game to managing a successful and closely-knit county side. Success on the international field proved more elusive.

Keith will always remain a diligent enthusiast with the true values of the game at the forefront. Just as he was with me as a young up-and-coming player, he is still brilliant with players on a one-to-one basis. Not that some of the new young Test recruits want that – on this last tour, as the very senior pro, I was there ready and willing to offer any help or advice, technical or even psychological, if asked. Scarcely anyone asked a thing, which was disappointing in the extreme.

Even in Fletcher's over-pressured, high-profile, necessarily press-placating job on tour, one of his famous and treasured one-liners will be cherished. In Australia there is a popular and well-known men's clothes chainstore called 'Country Road'. One day Fletch was looking for me. 'Anyone seen Goochie?' he asked. 'He's gone down "Country Road",' he was told. 'What, the blighter's not out running again, is he?' exclaimed Fletch.

For me, it is literally back to the country road. Round the shires exclusively with Essex all through the 1995 summer, my testimonial year. I will savour the journey with relish. As I will still need challenges to aim for and heights to attain, my motivation for 1995 – as an ordinary working county pro again – is, simply, to walk out and demonstrate that I am the best batsman playing county cricket. And the very same will be my intention if I play on in 1996. But once my

own standards begin to drop – which they will one day, obviously –
I will apply the very same principles as I did between the Adelaide
and Perth Test matches of 1995, and I'll bow out and take my leave,
quickly and, I trust, gracefully.

Then I will be able to say the very same as I did both when I gave
up the captaincy of England and when I came in from batting in a
Test match for the very last time at Perth – 'It's a sad occasion, but for
the rest of my life I think I will be able to look myself in the mirror
and say "If I did nothing else, I know I always did my very best".'

Leading Test Batsmen

Runs	Batsman	Tests	Avge	100s	HS
11174	A R Border (Australia)	156	50.56	27	205
10122	S M Gavasker (India)	125	51.52	34	236 *
8900	G A Gooch (England)	118	42.58	20	333
8832	Javed Miandad (Pakistan)	124	52.57	23	280 *
8540	I V A Richards (W Indies)	121	50.23	24	291
8231	D I Gower (England)	117	44.25	18	215
8114	G Boycott (England)	108	47.72	22	246 *
8032	G StA Sobers (W Indies)	93	57.78	26	365 *
7624	M C Cowdrey (England)	114	44.06	22	182
7558	C G Greenidge (W Indies)	108	44.72	19	226

Looking to the future, I would like to continue to do my best for my
country and work with promising young players – both on a technical and a mental level. If the immediate need in English cricket is to
unearth match-winning bowlers, there is also the necessity for
talented players to come through who are ravenously hungry to
achieve the consistency that would allow them to compete with, and
beat, the very best. This in no way excludes fun and laughter and
camaraderie at close of play. On the contrary. But it does include
concentration, dedication and unrelenting commitment to the cause
during the hours of play. That is the way forward for English cricket,
and I would be honoured if, with the experiences I have had and the
knowledge I have gained, I could be part of it.

Meanwhile, if never again for England, there are still runs to be
made, catches to be caught, and comradely laughs to be had with
Essex County Cricket Club – the enduring and longest love of my
cricketing life.

POSTSCRIPT
by Frank Keating

The stern moustache seemed more bushily Lord Kitchener than ever, the gait more ploughman-plodding, the shoulders more drooping – body language, perhaps, indicating the genuine surprise of a shy man receiving a suddenly thunderous massed acclamation from all round the jam-packed stadium. So he went forth to bat at Perth in a Test match for the final time. By a happy accident (or, possibly even, design?) it was his 118th Test match, one more than any English cricketer has ever played.

The afternoon sun still blazed. His long sleeves were down, and the badged crest of St George and the Dragon was embroidered at his breast. He wore his trademark white helmet, red and blue flashes on his gloves, and his bat handle was of the brightest of azure blue to match the cloudless southern skies.

He had, it goes without saying, been the earliest of his team to rise that morning, putting in his routine five minutes in his room with a pair of 7 ½ kg dumbbells. After a breakfast of cereal and yoghurt, he was first down to the ground and in the nets to face, oh, easily a hundred balls thrown at him, not bowled, from around fifteen yards. Then 200 sit-ups, some regimented callisthenics, a loosening jog, and fielding practice.

Much later that day came his and England's turn to bat. Down in the shade of the concrete pavilion, he is fast into his armour, but nevertheless meticulously and fussy like a jousting knight, and in enough time to allow himself minutes of meditation and reflection on past encounters against these bowlers and opponents. A final check on the left-hand gloves, laid out and numbered 1 to 4, a glance at his bold young skipper, and out they go.

He faced only a dozen balls, batted abberantly, nerve-janglingly, like a reticent man overwhelmed by the multitude's reception. A couple of times, when a delivery beat his bat, there was the characteristic and momentary nod of 'well bowled' to the bowler that had been a feature of his batting two decades and many hundreds ago. At the Test match crease, a Hobbs or a Hutton would never have indulged in that almost pastoral, village-green nod of chivalry. Still less a Bradman.

In his last Ashes Test, Hutton made 6 at Sydney; in his, Hobbs made 9 at The Oval, the same London arena where Bradman made his farewell with a duck after the England captain, Yardley, had (like Taylor this time for Gooch) called for three cheers of farewell.

Gooch c & b McDermott 4. The throng applauded him all the way back again. Shyly, he hoisted his bat in thanks. Then he was gone from the clamorous scene, with grace, and forever. Roll credits.

Perth's ovation echoed round the world. In London, the *Daily Telegraph* ran an editorial: 'We shall see him for a couple of seasons yet in county cricket, where he will not fail to entertain. For now, though, we salute his departure from the international stage as befitting, in its dignity and good grace, the career that preceded it.'

So did *The Times*: 'Certainly, he must not be lost to the national team, for his influence has been remarkable. Gracious in victory as in defeat, a protector of etiquette and imposer of discipline, he ends his career commanding the respect of opponents worldwide.'

The sports editors demanded more space for their eulogies. Let just three cricketers turned journalist with whom Gooch played down the years speak for all:

'Gooch has been a remarkable cricketer, playing innings of rare genius and unshakeable tenacity which for a time made him the best of all the batsmen in the world. He did not seek the England captaincy and he did not flaunt it but, while he had it, he quite typically gave it his best shot.' (Mark Nicholas, *Daily Telegraph*.)

'Masterful against spin, courageous against pace, he could shuffle so agonisingly against swing that the enduring image is of a large and drooping figure dragging himself from the crease – an image of frailty and majesty which is also inaccurate. After all he is England's heaviest scorer ever in Tests. It has been a marvellous career. Gooch was honest and humble. He could be mournful. But he was never half-hearted.' (Peter Roebuck, *Sunday Times*)

Mike Selvey in the *Guardian* emphasized the grandeur of an enduring twenty-year span of batting, 'from the destruction of his youth to the bravery of his dotage'.

That last point is well remarked. Sport's major players could be said to fall into two categories in the public's perception: the flamboyant overpowering naturals who cavort and entertain with colourful swash, brio, and buckle; and the more sober-sided, quietly craft-versed high achievers of diligence, technical merit, and calm. Graham Gooch has been both. In the course of the twenty-two years since he first trod the fresh grass of an English spring for his beloved county Essex, the bonny adventurer has turned not only into conscientious accumulator but into eminent national treasure.

'A working class hero is something to be,' sang John Lennon. The apprentice Gooch assertively celebrated the fact with a series of youthful innings which had all the grandeur of a gale. If the day was right any bowling attack in the world could be brutally knifed and scissored into shreds. But those were only touchstones, inconsistent markers and signposts for the mature, composed and priceless glories which were to come as he crossed the divide which separates cricketing men from immortals.

And the nation gave thanks and applauded.

CAREER STATISTICS
by Wendy Wimbush

Milestones in First-Class Career

1973	Debut v Northamptonshire at Westcliff-on-Sea (18 July)
1974	First first-class hundred v Leicestershire at Chelmsford
1975	First representative match – MCC v Australians at Lord's
	Test debut v Australia at Edgbaston
	1000 runs in season (1) at average 27.30
1976	5 wickets/innings first time – Essex v West Indians at Chelmsford
	1000 runs in season (2) at average 42.43
1978	Recalled to Test team – England v Pakistan at Lord's
	1000 runs in season (3) at average 41.80
	Passed 5000 f.c. runs during season
1978/79	First overseas representative tour to Australia
1980	1000 runs in season (4) at average 47.90
	1st player to 1000 runs on 19 June
1981	1000 runs in season (5) at average 43.38
	Passed 10000 f.c. runs during season
	100 before lunch v Leicestershire at Leicester
1981/82	1363 runs at average 54.52 in India, Sri Lanka & South Africa
1982	Best f.c. bowling analysis – 7–14 v Worcestershire at Ilford
	1000 runs in season (7) at average 44.10
1983	1000 runs in season (8) at average 40.02
	100 before lunch v Cambridge University at Cambridge
	Passed 15000 f.c. runs during season
1984	1000 runs in season (9) at average 67.34
	1st player to 2000 runs on 18 August
1985	1000 runs in season (10) at average 71.22
	1st player to 2000 runs on 12 September
	Hit 30 off an over bowled by S R Gorman (Cambridge University)
	Passed 20000 f.c. runs during season
1986	Appointed Captain of Essex
	1000 runs in season (11) at average 38.15
1987	1000 runs in season (12) at average 38.88

1988	1000 runs in season (13) at average 64.55
	Captained England for first time v West Indies at Oval
	100 before lunch v Surrey at Chelmsford
1989	1000 runs in season (14) at average 41.86
1990	1000 runs in season (15) at average 101.70
	Scored 18 hundreds in all cricket in season
	100 in each innings twice – England v India & Essex v Northamptonshire
	Opening partnerships 227/220 with J P Stephenson in both innings v Northamptonshire at Northampton
	Passed 30000 f.c. runs during season
	403 partnership 2nd wicket with P J Prichard v Leicestershire at Chelmsford – record partnership for any Essex wicket
1991	1000 runs in season (16) at average 70.77
1992	1000 runs in season (17) at average 71.15
	100 in each innings v Sussex at Southend
1992/93	100th first-class hundred at Cuttack – 23rd player, 19th England batsman
1993	1000 runs in season (18) at average 63.21
	1st player to 2000 runs on 20 September
	100 each innings v Hampshire
1994	1000 runs in season (19) at average 64.70
	100 both innings v Worcestershire
	Passed 40000 f.c. runs during season

Milestones in Test Career

1975	Test debut at Edgbaston – pair v Australia
1978	Recalled to Test team – England v Pakistan at Lord's
1979	First Test wicket – S M Gavaskar
1980	Reached 1000 Test runs in 21st Test
	Scored first Test hundred in 22nd Test, 38th innings
1981	Reached 2000 Test runs in 35th Test
1985	Recalled to Test team, having missed 32 Tests – England v Australia at Headingley
	Reached 3000 Test runs in 48th Test
1986	Took 50th Test catch (K R Rutherford)
1988	Reached 4000 Test runs in 63rd Test
	Captained England for first time v West Indies at Oval
	Dislocated third finger of left hand attempting a catch in the second innings, so D R Pringle deputised as captain
1989	lbw b Alderman 0 at Lord's, giving the bowler his 100th Test wicket
1989/90	Resumed captaincy of England v West Indies
	Left hand broken by E A Moseley in second innings at Port-of-Spain
1990	Reached 5000 Test runs in 78th Test – 11th England player
	Scored 1264 Test runs (av 79.00) in calendar year (9 Tests)
	Scored highest Test score – 333 v India at Lord's
	Scored a record 752 runs in a series England v India
1990/91	Reached 6000 Test runs in 83rd Test

1991	Carried bat in second innings v West Indies at Headingley – 154* (total 252)
	1040 Test runs (av 65.00) in calendar year (9 Tests)
	Reached 7000 Test runs in 91st Test – 13th player
1992	Best Test bowling – 3–39 v Pakistan at Old Trafford
1992/93	100th Test at Calcutta – 14th player
1993	Handled ball 133 v Australia at Old Trafford – 5th instance in Test history
	Reached 8000 Test runs in 104th Test – 8th player
	Resigned captaincy three days after 40th birthday
	During Oval Test passed D I Gower's record highest aggregate 8231 runs for England
1994	Second innings 0 at Lord's (109th Test) – the previous 0 was in 76th Test in 1990
	Took 100th Test catch (K R Rutherford – as 50!) – 11th player 100 Test catches
	Played 200th Test innings v South Africa at Lord's on 41st birthday
1994/95	Announced retirement from international cricket at Adelaide, to take effect at the end of the tour
	Perth – 118th Test – record number of appearances for England

First-Class Summary by Age

The first ten years – debut five days short of 20th birthday until 30th birthday, 23 July 1983

M	I	NO	HS	Runs	Avge	100	50	Ct
249	420	35	205	15126	39.28	34	78	223

The second ten years until 40th birthday, 23 July 1993

M	I	NO	HS	Runs	Avge	100	50	Ct
250	422	33	333	22348	57.44	69	109	266

Aged 40 to end of Australian tour, 7 February 1995

M	I	NO	HS	Runs	Avge	100	50	Ct
36	65	4	236	3385	55.49	10	16	24
TOTALS 535	907	72	333	40859	48.93	113	203	513

Summary of all First-Class Matches

Season	Venue	M	I	NO	HS	Runs	Avge
1973		1	1	0	18	18	18.00
1974	/	15	25	3	114 *	637	28.95
1975		24	42	0	100	1147	27.30
1976		21	34	4	136	1273	42.43
1977		23	37	6	105 *	837	27.00
1978		21	33	3	129	1254	41.80
1978/79	Aus	13	23	1	74	514	23.36
1979		17	25	2	109	838	36.43
1979/80	Aus/Ind	7	14	3	115	639	58.09
1980		19	35	5	205	1437	47.90
1980/81	WI	7	13	0	153	777	59.76
1981		16	31	0	164	1345	43.38
1981/82	Ind/SL	13	21	3	127	967	53.72
1981/82	SA	4	7	0	109	396	56.57
1982		23	38	1	149	1632	44.10
1982/83	SA	9	18	3	126	597	39.80
1983		26	38	1	174	1481	40.02
1983/84	SA	7	13	1	171	615	51.25
1984		26	45	7	227	2559	67.34
1985		21	33	2	202	2208	71.22
1985/86	WI	9	18	0	53	443	24.61
1986		19	32	0	183	1221	38.15
1987		24	41	6	171	1361	38.88
1987/88	Pak	3	6	0	93	225	37.50
1988		21	37	1	275	2324	64.55
1989		18	31	1	158	1256	41.86
1989/90	WI	6	11	1	239	616	61.60
1990		18	30	3	333	2746	101.70
1990/91	Aus	8	14	1	117	623	47.92
1991		20	31	4	259	1911	70.77
1991/92	NZ	7	10	1	114	379	42.11
1992		18	29	3	160	1850	71.15
1992/93	Ind	5	8	1	102 *	278	39.71
1993		19	35	3	159 *	2023	63.21
1994		17	29	2	236	1747	64.70
1994/95	Aus	10	19	0	101	685	36.05
TOTALS		535	907	72	333	40859	48.93

100	50	Ct	Balls	Runs	W	Avge	BB	5wI
–	–	1	–	–	–	–	–	–
1	2	4	336	153	3	51.00	1–17	–
1	7	16	216	113	2	56.50	2–32	–
3	6	17	658	334	10	33.40	5–40	1
1	5	11	657	345	8	43.12	4–60	–
2	9	23	216	90	2	45.00	2–33	–
–	3	13	208	80	1	80.00	1–16	–
1	6	28	468	201	4	50.25	1–10	–
1	6	9	270	113	3	37.66	2–16	–
6	2	17	864	367	15	24.46	3–57	–
4	1	4	252	108	1	108.00	1–14	–
5	5	11	468	243	6	40.50	3–47	–
2	6	10	349	150	2	75.00	2–12	–
1	3	6	198	114	4	28.50	2–45	–
3	12	25	1380	541	22	24.59	7–14	1
2	1	10	320	86	5	17.20	4–15	–
4	7	35	1272	572	11	52.00	3–40	–
2	1	5	255	89	3	29.66	2–34	–
8	13	27	1927	850	38	22.36	4–54	–
7	9	25	1706	773	29	26.65	5–46	1
–	5	10	102	56	1	56.00	1–21	–
3	5	22	958	398	9	44.22	2–46	–
3	7	20	1503	687	21	32.71	4–42	–
–	2	3	12	4	0	–	–	–
6	15	28	912	401	10	40.10	2–29	–
3	9	25	408	245	1	245.00	1–30	–
1	4	6	18	6	1	6.00	1–6	–
12	8	16	396	220	1	220.00	1–26	–
1	5	7	198	90	2	45.00	1–23	–
6	6	22	379	215	4	53.75	2–16	–
2	1	3	162	85	3	28.33	2–14	–
8	7	19	804	305	9	33.88	3–39	–
1	1	4	30	2	2	1.00	2–2	–
6	14	13	216	110	0	–	–	–
6	5	15	189	50	3	20.00	1–0	–
1	5	3	162	79	2	39.50	1–5	–
113	203	513	18469	8285	238	34.81	7–14	3

Test Match Summary

Season	Opp	M	I	NO	HS	Runs	Avge
1975	A	2	4	0	31	37	9.25
1978	P	2	2	0	54	74	37.00
1978	NZ	3	5	2	91 *	190	63.33
1978/79	A	6	11	0	74	246	22.36
1979	I	4	5	0	83	207	41.40
1979/80	A	2	4	0	99	172	43.00
1979/80	I	1	2	1	49 *	57	57.00
1980	WI	5	10	0	123	394	39.40
1980	A	1	2	0	16	24	12.00
1980/81	WI	4	8	0	153	460	57.50
1981	A	5	10	0	44	139	13.90
1981/82	I	6	10	1	127	487	54.11
1981/82	SL	1	2	0	31	53	26.50
1985	A	6	9	0	196	487	54.11
1985/86	WI	5	10	0	53	276	27.60
1986	I	3	6	0	114	175	29.16
1986	NZ	3	5	0	183	268	53.60
1987/88	P	3	6	0	93	225	37.50
1988	WI	5	10	0	146	459	45.90
1988	SL	1	2	0	75	111	55.50
1989	A	5	9	0	68	183	20.33
1989/90	WI	2	4	1	84	128	42.66
1990	NZ	3	5	0	154	306	61.20
1990	I	3	6	0	333	752	125.33
1990/91	A	4	8	0	117	426	53.25
1991	WI	5	9	1	154 *	480	60.00
1991	SL	1	2	0	174	212	106.00
1991/92	NZ	3	5	0	114	161	32.20
1992	P	5	8	0	135	384	48.00
1992/93	I	2	4	0	18	47	11.75
1993	A	6	12	0	133	673	56.08
1994	NZ	3	4	0	210	223	55.75
1994	SA	3	6	0	33	139	23.16
1994/95	A	5	10	0	56	245	24.50
TOTALS		118	215	6	333	8900	42.58

100	50	Ct	Balls	Runs	W	Avge	BB	5wI
–	–	2	–	–	–	–	–	–
–	1	2	60	29	0	–	–	–
–	2	1	–	–	–	–	–	–
–	1	9	48	15	0	–	–	–
–	2	6	150	49	1	49.00	1–16	–
–	2	1	114	36	2	18.00	2–16	–
–	–	1	24	3	0	–	–	–
1	2	5	150	59	3	19.66	2–18	–
–	–	–	48	16	0	–	–	–
2	1	3	84	36	0	–	–	–
–	–	1	60	28	0	–	–	–
1	4	4	199	77	2	38.50	2–12	–
–	–	1	–	–	–	–	–	–
1	2	4	248	102	2	51.00	2–57	–
–	4	6	42	27	1	27.00	1–21	–
1	–	5	78	31	1	31.00	1–19	–
1	–	6	114	38	1	38.00	1–23	–
–	2	3	12	4	0	–	–	–
1	3	6	–	–	–	–	–	–
–	1	3	–	–	–	–	–	–
–	2	4	186	72	1	72.00	1–30	–
–	1	2	–	–	–	–	–	–
1	1	3	78	25	0	–	–	–
3	2	4	108	70	1	70.00	1–26	–
1	4	6	138	69	2	34.50	1–23	–
1	2	6	48	14	0	–	–	–
1	–	–	–	–	–	–	–	–
1	–	–	–	–	–	–	–	–
1	2	2	306	94	5	18.80	3–39	–
–	–	1	–	–	–	–	–	–
2	4	2	150	66	0	–	–	–
1	–	3	42	26	0	–	–	–
–	–	1	18	9	0	–	–	–
–	1	–	150	74	1	74.00	1–20	–
20	46	103	2655	1069	23	46.47	3–39	–

County Championship Summary

Season	M	I	NO	HS	Runs	Avge
1973	1	1	0	18	18	18.00
1974	15	25	3	114 *	637	28.95
1975	18	30	0	100	784	26.13
1976	19	31	4	136	1189	44.03
1977	21	34	6	105 *	723	25.82
1978	13	22	0	129	867	39.40
1979	10	15	2	109	535	41.15
1980	11	20	5	134	766	51.06
1981	9	17	0	164	1091	64.17
1982	22	37	1	149	1597	44.36
1983	24	35	1	111	1227	36.08
1984	23	40	7	227	2281	69.12
1985	11	17	2	202	1368	91.20
1986	13	21	0	151	778	37.04
1987	20	34	6	171	1100	39.28
1988	14	23	0	275	1631	70.91
1989	12	20	1	158	994	52.31
1990	11	18	2	215	1586	99.12
1991	11	16	1	259	996	66.40
1992	11	18	3	160	1246	83.06
1993	10	18	2	159 *	991	61.93
1994	10	18	2	236	1343	83.93
TOTALS	309	510	48	275	23748	51.40

First-Class Summary by Team and Venue

	M	I	NO	HS	Runs	Avge
England	74	131	3	333	5917	46.22
Essex	346	569	54	275	26719	51.88
MCC	5	9	0	117	328	36.44
D H Robins' XI	1	1	0	57	57	57.00
International XI	1	2	0	66	84	42.00
UK/HOME	427	712	57	333	33105	50.54
England XI						
in Australia	37	68	4	117	2404	37.56
in India	17	28	5	127	1202	52.26
in West Indies	22	42	1	239	1836	44.78
in Sri Lanka	2	3	0	47	100	33.33
in Pakistan	3	6	0	93	225	37.50
in New Zealand	7	10	1	114	379	42.11
SAB English XI	4	7	0	109	396	56.57
Western Province	16	31	4	171	1212	44.88
OVERSEAS	108	195	15	239	7754	43.07
CAREER	535	907	72	333	40859	48.93

100	50	Ct	OV	Runs	W	Avge	BB	5wI
–	–	1	–	–	–	–	–	–
1	2	4	56	153	3	51.00	1–17	–
1	3	14	3	11	0	–	–	–
3	6	14	63	202	2	101.00	1–23	–
1	4	10	82.3	230	4	57.50	4–60	–
2	5	17	2	4	0	–	–	–
1	4	14	24	75	1	75.00	1–21	–
4	–	10	85	247	8	30.87	3–57	–
5	4	8	63	181	5	36.20	3–47	–
3	12	25	225	510	22	23.18	7–14	1
3	6	33	187	514	8	64.25	3–40	–
7	11	22	288.1	756	36	21.00	4–54	–
6	4	17	155.3	432	18	24.00	5–46	1
1	5	11	127.4	329	7	47.00	2–46	–
2	5	16	212.3	584	18	32.44	4–42	–
5	9	19	135	342	9	38.00	2–29	–
3	6	21	30	124	0	–	–	–
7	5	8	35	125	0	–	–	–
3	3	11	42.1	155	4	38.75	2–16	–
6	4	17	69	149	3	49.66	1–4	–
3	7	8	5	30	0	–	–	–
5	5	10	19.3	24	3	8.00	1–0	–
72	110	310	1910	5177	151	34.28	7–14	2

100	50	Ct	Balls	Runs	W	Avge	BB	5wI
15	26	66	1844	728	15	48.53	3–39	–
79	129	345	13855	6368	192	33.02	7–14	3
1	2	6	174	103	1	103.00	1–46	–
–	1	3	60	24	0	–	–	–
–	1	–	–	–	–	–	–	–
95	159	420	15933	7223	208	34.72	7–14	3
3	19	31	814	359	8	44.87	2–16	–
3	7	14	403	155	4	38.75	2–2	–
5	10	20	372	170	3	56.66	1–6	–
–	–	1	–	–	–	–	–	–
–	2	3	12	4	0	–	–	–
2	1	3	162	85	3	28.33	2–14	–
1	3	6	198	114	4	28.50	2–45	–
4	2	15	575	175	8	21.87	4–15	–
18	44	93	2536	1062	30	35.40	4–15	–
113	203	513	18469	8285	238	34.81	7–14	3

Test Match Results During Captaincy

1988	Aus 5	Oval	Lost by 8 wickets
	SL	Lord's	Won by 7 wickets
1989/90	WI 1	Kingston	Won by 9 wickets
	WI 3	Port-of-Spain	Drawn
1990	NZ 1	Trent Bridge	Drawn
	NZ 2	Lord's	Drawn
	NZ 3	Edgbaston	Won by 114 runs
	Ind 1	Lord's	Won by 247 runs
	Ind 2	Old Trafford	Drawn
	Ind 3	Oval	Drawn
1990/91	Aus 2	Melbourne	Lost by 8 wickets
	Aus 3	Sydney	Drawn
	Aus 4	Adelaide	Drawn
	Aus 5	Perth	Lost by 9 wickets
1991	WI 1	Headingley	Won by 115 runs
	WI 2	Lord's	Drawn
	WI 3	Trent Bridge	Lost by 9 wickets
	WI 4	Edgbaston	Lost by 7 wickets
	WI 5	Oval	Won by 5 wickets
	SL	Lord's	Won by 137 runs
1991/92	NZ 1	Christchurch	Won by an innings & 4 runs
	NZ 2	Auckland	Won by 168 runs
	NZ 3	Wellington	Drawn
1992	Pak 1	Edgbaston	Drawn
	Pak 2	Lord's	Lost by 2 wickets
	Pak 3	Old Trafford	Drawn
	Pak 4	Headingley	Won by 6 wickets
	Pak 5	Oval	Lost by 10 wickets
1992/93	Ind 1	Calcutta	Lost by 8 wickets
	Ind 3	Bombay	Lost by an innings & 15 runs
1993	Aus 1	Old Trafford	Lost by 179 runs
	Aus 2	Lord's	Lost by an innings & 62 runs
	Aus 3	Trent Bridge	Drawn
	Aus 4	Headingley	Lost by an innings & 148 runs

Test Match Hundreds

For England (20)

				Test No
123	West Indies	Lord's	1980	22
+116	West Indies	Bridgetown	1980/81	28
153	West Indies	Kingston	1980/81	30
127	India	Madras	1981/82	40
196	Australia	Oval	1985	48
114	India	Lord's	1986	54
+183	New Zealand	Lord's	1986	57
+146	West Indies	Trent Bridge	1988	63
154	New Zealand	Edgbaston	1990	78
333	India	Lord's	1990	79
+123	India	Lord's	1990	79
116	India	Old Trafford	1990	80
+117	Australia	Adelaide	1990/91	84
+154*	West Indies	Headingley	1991	86
+174	Sri Lanka	Lord's	1991	91
+114	New Zealand	Auckland	1991/92	93
135	Pakistan	Headingley	1992	98
+133	Australia	Old Trafford	1993	102
+120	Australia	Trent Bridge	1993	104
210	New Zealand	Trent Bridge	1994	108

+ denotes 2nd innings
* denotes not out

Test Match Opening Partnerships

Partner	P/S	Runs Tog	Avge	100 P/S	Best Partnership		
J M Brearley	4	32	8.00	–	26[+]	New Zealand (Oval)	1978
G Boycott	49	1754	35.79	4	144[+]	West Indies (St John's)	1980/81
B C Rose	1	146	146.00	1	146	West Indies (Oval)	1980
C J Tavaré	2	237	118.50	1	155	India (Madras)	1981/82
G Cook	2	37	18.50	–	34	Sri Lanka (Colombo, PSS)	1981/82
R T Robinson	19	621	32.68	–	79[+]	Australia (Trent Bridge)	1985
W N Slack	6	161	26.83	1	127	West Indies (St John's)	1985/86
M R Benson	2	49	24.50	–	49[+]	India (Edgbaston)	1986
M D Moxon	6	95	15.83	–	27	New Zealand (Lord's)	1986
C W J Athey	1	38	38.00	–	38	New Zealand (Oval)	1986
B C Broad	14	506	36.14	1	125	West Indies (Trent Bridge)	1988
T S Curtis	7	182	26.00	–	56[+]	West Indies (Headingley)	1988
J P Stephenson	2	21	10.50	–	20[+]	Australia (Oval)	1989
W Larkins	4	214	53.50	1	112	West Indies (Port-of-Spain)	1989/90
M A Atherton	44	2501	56.84	7	225	India (Old Trafford)	1990
D I Gower	1	84	84.00	–	84[+]	Australia (Sydney)	1990/91
H Morris	6	271	45.16	1	112	West Indies (Oval)	1991
A J Stewart	15	528	35.20	1	123	Pakistan (Lord's)	1992

[+] denotes 2nd innings

Captaincy Record for England

Season	v	T	Toss	W	L	D
1988	WI	1	1	–	1	–
	SL	1	1	1	–	–
1989/90	WI	2	1	1	–	1
1990	NZ	3	–	1	–	2
	I	3	1	1	–	2
1990/91	A	4	2	–	2	2
1991	WI	5	2	2	2	1
	SL	1	1	1	–	–
1991/92	NZ	3	1	2	–	1
1992	P	5	3	1	2	2
1992/93	I	2	1	–	2	–
1993	A	4	2	–	3	1
TOTALS		34	16	10	12	12

Winning the toss and inviting the opposition to bat (3)

1989/90	WI	Port-of-Spain	Drawn
1992	P	Edgbaston	Drawn
1993	A	Old Trafford	Lost by 179 runs

Championship Hundreds

For Essex (72)

+114*	Leicestershire	Chelmsford	1974
100	Kent	Colchester	1975
+100*	Kent	Tunbridge Wells	1976
136	Worcestershire	Westcliff-on-Sea	1976
111	Lancashire	Old Trafford	1976
+105*	Warwickshire	Edgbaston	1977
108	Kent	Ilford	1978
129	Northamptonshire	Ilford	1978
109	Derbyshire	Chesterfield	1979
+108*	Glamorgan	Swansea	1980
+122	Kent	Ilford	1980
108	Surrey	Chelmsford	1980
134	Gloucestershire	Gloucester	1980
164	Leicestershire	Leicester	1981
146	Northamptonshire	Northampton	1981
+105	Leicestershire	Colchester	1981
+113	Glamorgan	Colchester	1981
+122	Somerset	Taunton	1981
+149	Kent	Canterbury	1982
+140	Surrey	Oval	1982
127	Kent	Chelmsford	1982
+110	Leicestershire	Chelmsford	1983
103	Worcestershire	Colchester	1983
111	Yorkshire	Chelmsford	1983
220	Hampshire	Southampton	1984
+108	Nottinghamshire	Chelmsford	1984
+113*	Leicestershire	Hinckley	1984
227	Derbyshire	Chesterfield	1984
131	Yorkshire	Headingley	1984
+105*	Middlesex	Lord's	1984
+160*	Surrey	Oval	1984
+202	Nottinghamshire	Trent Bridge	1985
+125	Kent	Dartford	1985
+173*	Somerset	Taunton	1985
132*	Surrey	Chelmsford	1985
+145	Middlesex	Lord's	1985
142	Yorkshire	Chelmsford	1985
151	Worcestershire	Southend	1986
171	Gloucestershire	Bristol	1987
159	Northamptonshire	Ilford	1987
275	Kent	Chelmsford	1988
139	Surrey	Chelmsford	1988
113	Sussex	Ilford	1988
123	Surrey	Oval	1988
+108	Northamptonshire	Chelmsford	1988
148	Derbyshire	Chelmsford	1989
124*	Leicestershire	Chelmsford	1989

158	Leicestershire	Leicester	1989
137	Middlesex	Lord's	1990
215	Leicestershire	Chelmsford	1990
121	Worcestershire	Worcester	1990
+120	Middlesex	Ilford	1990
+177	Lancashire	Colchester	1990
174	Northamptonshire	Northampton	1990
+126	Northamptonshire	Northampton	1990
+106	Middlesex	Lord's	1991
173	Northamptonshire	Colchester	1991
259	Middlesex	Chelmsford	1991
160	Leicestershire	Chelmsford	1992
113	Durham	Hartlepool	1992
102	Sussex	Southend	1992
+108*	Sussex	Southend	1992
+123*	Derbyshire	Derby	1992
+101	Gloucestershire	Bristol	1992
+159*	Worcestershire	Chelmsford	1993
109	Hampshire	Chelmsford	1993
+114	Hampshire	Chelmsford	1993
+123*	Hampshire	Southampton	1994
236	Kent	Chelmsford	1994
101	Worcestershire	Worcester	1994
+205	Worcestershire	Worcester	1994
140	Middlesex	Uxbridge	1994

+ denotes 2nd innings
* denotes not out

First-Class Opening Partnerships of over 150

Graham Gooch has had 39 different opening partners 1975–1994/95. He has had hundred partnerships with 23 of them, including 9 in Tests only. In all he has contributed 61 opening partnerships, the best of which are listed below. The most productive partnership has been with John Stephenson and in recent seasons they have compiled no fewer than 21 stands over 100. (See page 306 for the Test Match opening partnerships of 100.)

316	P J Prichard	Essex v Kent	Chelmsford	1994
293	L Seeff	Western Province v Eastern Province	Cape Town	1983/84
254	J P Stephenson	Essex v Derbyshire	Chelmsford	1989
238	J P Stephenson	Essex v Leicestershire	Chelmsford	1992
227	J P Stephenson	Essex v Northamptonshire	Northampton	1990
+220				
214	J P Stephenson	Essex v Worcestershire	Southend	1986
197	M H Denness	Essex v Gloucestershire	Gloucester	1980
189	J P Stephenson	Essex v Leicestershire	Leicester	1991
186*	G Boycott	England XI v South Zone	Hyderabad (I)	1981/82
179	J P Stephenson	Essex v Sussex	Southend	1992
173	G Boycott	England XI v Trinidad & Tobago	Port-of-Spain	1980/81
172	C Gladwin	Essex v Gloucestershire	Bristol	1987
170	M H Denness	Essex v Sussex	Southend	1979
+169	B R Hardie	Essex v Glamorgan	Colchester	1981
168	J P Stephenson	Essex v New Zealanders	Chelmsford	1990
168	N Shahid	Essex v Cambridge University	Cambridge	1991
+159	A W Lilley	Essex v Nottinghamshire	Trent Bridge	1978
+158	J P Stephenson	Essex v Lancashire	Colchester	1990
+152	J P Stephenson	Essex v Durham	Hartlepool	1992

+ denotes 2nd innings
* denotes unbroken partnership

Championship Five-Wicket Innings

7–14	Worcestershire	Ilford	1982
+5–46	Lancashire	Ilford	1985

+ denotes 2nd innings

Pairs

1.	1974	Essex v Gloucestershire	Bristol	
2.	1975	England v Australia	Edgbaston	Test debut
3.	1980	Essex v Kent	Folkestone	
4.	1983/84	Western Province v Northern Transvaal	Pretoria	
5.	1987	Essex v Warwickshire	Chelmsford	
6.	1987	Essex v Pakistanis	Chelmsford	

International Limited-Overs Matches Summary

Season		M	I	NO	HS	Runs	Avge
1976	WI	3	3	0	32	40	13.33
1978	NZ	2	2	0	94	94	47.00
1978/79	Aus	4	3	0	23	46	15.33
1979	W Cup	5	5	1	71	210	52.50
1979/80	WSC in Aus	9	9	0	69	181	20.11
1980	WI	2	2	0	12	14	7.00
1980	Aus	2	2	0	108	162	81.00
1980/81	WI	2	2	0	11	22	11.00
1981	Aus	3	3	0	53	101	33.66
1981/82	Ind	3	3	0	23	38	12.66
1981/82	SL	2	2	0	74	138	69.00
1985	AUS	3	3	1	117*	289	144.50
1985/86	WI	4	4	1	129*	181	60.33
1986	Ind	2	2	0	30	40	20.00
1986	NZ	2	2	0	91	109	54.50
1986/87	Sharjah	3	3	0	86	118	39.33
1987	Pak	1	1	0	9	9	9.00
1987/88	W Cup	8	8	0	115	471	58.87
1987/88	Pak	3	3	0	142	242	80.66
1988	WI	3	3	0	43	103	34.33
1988	SL	1	1	0	7	7	7.00
1989	Aus	3	3	0	136	198	66.00
1989/90	Nehru Cup	6	6	0	59	183	30.50
1989/90	WI	5	4	1	42	90	30.00
1990	NZ	2	2	1	112*	167	167.00
1990	Ind	2	2	0	45	52	26.00
1990/91	WSC in Aus	5	5	0	48	166	33.20
1990/91	NZ	3	3	0	47	105	35.00
1991	WI	3	3	0	54	65	21.66
1991/92	NZ	3	3	1	47	93	46.50
1991/92	W Cup	8	8	0	65	216	27.00
1992	Pak	4	4	0	45	121	30.25
1992/93	Ind	6	5	0	45	72	14.40
1993	Aus	3	3	0	42	63	21.00
1994	NZ	1	1	0	23	23	23.00
1994/95	WSC in Aus	4	4	0	38	61	15.25
	WI	32	31	2	129*	881	30.37
	NZ	16	16	2	112*	713	50.92
	Aus	32	31	1	136	1395	46.50
	P	16	16	0	142	517	32.31
	I	17	16	0	115	420	26.25
	SL	7	7	0	84	303	43.28
	Z	3	3	0	38	38	12.66
	SA	1	1	0	2	2	2.00
	Can	1	1	1	21*	21	–
Home		47	47	3	136	1867	42.43
Overseas		78	75	3	142	2423	33.65
Totals		125	122	6	142	4290	36.98

100	50	Ct	Balls	Runs	W	Avge	BB
–	–	–	–	–	–	–	–
–	1	1	60	29	2	14.50	2–29
–	–	–	8	2	0	–	–
–	2	–	48	36	0	–	–
–	1	4	185	181	4	45.25	2–32
–	–	–	42	30	2	15.00	2–30
1	1	1	60	45	2	22.50	1–16
–	–	1	48	20	2	10.00	2–12
–	1	3	126	109	0	–	–
–	–	3	132	92	4	23.00	2–25
–	2	2	90	68	0	–	–
2	1	1	90	70	2	35.00	1–10
1	–	1	48	41	1	41	1–0
–	–	1	–	–	–	–	–
–	1	–	66	68	0	–	–
–	1	1	36	34	0	–	–
–	–	1	18	12	0	–	–
1	3	2	90	79	1	79.00	1–42
1	1	2	–	–	–	–	–
–	–	–	30	15	1	15.00	1–12
–	–	–	66	35	2	17.50	2–35
1	1	2	–	–	–	–	–
–	2	2	241	151	5	30.20	3–19
–	–	2	90	63	1	63.00	1–26
1	1	–	24	23	2	11.50	2–23
–	–	–	–	–	–	–	–
–	–	1	60	39	1	39.00	1–39
–	–	1	180	104	1	104.00	1–40
–	1	2	108	77	3	25.66	1–9
–	–	1	–	–	–	–	–
–	3	1	–	–	–	–	–
–	–	2	–	–	–	–	–
–	–	5	12	13	0	–	–
–	–	1	–	–	–	–	–
–	–	–	–	–	–	–	–
–	–	1	108	80	0	–	–
1	4	7	461	372	11	33.81	2–12
1	4	4	348	232	5	46.40	2–23
4	9	14	692	542	9	60.22	2–32
1	1	6	96	44	3	14.66	3–19
1	1	9	193	158	4	39.50	2–25
–	4	4	228	138	4	34.50	2–26
–	–	1	48	30	0	–	–
–	–	–	–	–	–	–	–
–	–	–	–	–	–	–	–
5	10	15	738	549	16	34.31	2–23
3	13	30	1328	967	20	48.35	3–19
8	23	45	2066	1516	36	42.11	3–19

Domestic Limited-Overs Summary

	M	I	NO	HS	Runs
Sundays 1973–94	248	244	21	176	7906
Benson & Hedges 1973–94	100	100	11	198 *	4607
Gillette Cup/NatWest 1973–94	50	49	4	144	2383
Totals	398	393	36	198 *	14896

Hundreds in Limited-Overs Internationals

For England (8)   Match

				Match
108	Australia	Edgbaston	1980	27
115	Australia	Edgbaston	1985	39
117*	Australia	Lord's	1985	40
129*	West Indies	Port-of-Spain	1985/86	42
115	India	Bombay	1987/88	59
142	Pakistan	Karachi	1987/88	62
136	Australia	Lord's	1989	70
112*	New Zealand	Oval	1990	83

Fifties in Limited-Overs Internationals

(excluding hundreds – see above)   Match

				Match
94	New Zealand	Scarborough	1978	4
53	Australia	Lord's	1979	10
71	New Zealand	Old Trafford	1979	13
69	Australia	Sydney	1979/80	20
54	Australia	Oval	1980	26
53	Australia	Lord's	1981	30
64	Sri Lanka	Colombo, SSC	1981/82	36
74	Sri Lanka	Colombo, SSC	1981/82	37
57	Australia	Old Trafford	1985	38
91	New Zealand	Old Trafford	1986	48
86	Australia	Sharjah	1986/87	51
84	Sri Lanka	Peshawar	1987/88	55
92	West Indies	Jaipur	1987/88	57
61	Sri Lanka	Pune	1987/88	58
57	Pakistan	Peshawar	1987/88	63
52	Australia	Old Trafford	1989	68
56	Australia	Hyderabad (I)	1989/90	72
59	West Indies	Gwalior	1989/90	75
55	New Zealand	Headingley	1990	82
54	West Indies	Old Trafford	1991	95
51	India	Perth	1991/92	100
65	West Indies	Melbourne	1991/92	101
58	Australia	Sydney	1991/92	103

Avge	100	50	Ct	Ov	Runs	W	Avge	BB	4wI
35.45	12	52	90	912.2	4143	139	29.80	4–33	1
51.76	12	28	61	605.5	2118	69	30.69	3–24	–
52.95	6	15	24	273.1	847	28	30.25	3–31	–
41.72	30	95	175	1791.2	7108	236	30.11	4–33	1

Hundreds in Domestic Limited-Overs Matches

For Essex (30)

133	Oxford & Cambridge Universities	Chelmsford	1979	B&H
138	Warwickshire	Chelmsford	1979	B&H
120	Surrey	Lord's	1979	B&H
138	Somerset	Chelmsford	1981	B&H
101	Hertfordshire	Hitchin	1981	NW
100	Yorkshire	Chelmsford	1981	JPL
198*	Sussex	Hove	1982	B&H
122	Lancashire	Old Trafford	1982	JPL
116	Nottinghamshire	Trent Bridge	1983	JPL
176	Glamorgan	Southend	1983	JPL
122	Kent	Chelmsford	1983	NW
133	Scotland	Chelmsford	1984	NW
125*	Hampshire	Colchester	1984	JPSL
171	Nottinghamshire	Trent Bridge	1985	JPSL
100	Warwickshire	Chelmsford	1986	JPSL
120*	Kent	Canterbury	1988	B&H
117*	Warwickshire	Chelmsford	1988	B&H
100*	Hampshire	Chelmsford	1989	B&H
111*	Leicestershire	Chelmsford	1989	Ref
106*	Yorkshire	Southend	1989	Ref
102	Nottinghamshire	Chelmsford	1990	B&H
103*	Scotland	Chelmsford	1990	NW
144	Hampshire	Chelmsford	1990	NW
136	Nottinghamshire	Southend	1990	Ref
107	Somerset	Southend	1991	Ref
127	Scotland	Chelmsford	1992	B&H
119	Northamptonshire	Northampton	1992	B&H
105*	Gloucestershire	Cheltenham	1992	NW
130*	Leicestershire	Chelmsford	1994	B&H
101	Glamorgan	Southend	1994	AXA

Non-Test Match or County Championship Hundreds

For England XI (8)

115	Queensland	Brisbane	1979/80
117	Trinidad & Tobago	Port-of-Spain	1980/81
+122	Jamaica	Kingston	1980/81
119*	South Zone	Hyderabad (I)	1981/82
239	Jamaica	Kingston	1989/90
101RH	New Zealand Emerging Players	Hamilton	1991/92
102RH	Indian Under-25 XI	Cuttack	1992/93
+101	South Australia	Adelaide	1994/95

For Essex (7)

205	Cambridge University	Cambridge	1980
174	Cambridge University	Cambridge	1983
101	West Indians	Chelmsford	1984
102RH	New Zealanders	Chelmsford	1990
101RH	Cambridge University	Cambridge	1991
141	Pakistanis	Chelmsford	1992
105	Cambridge University	Cambridge	1993

For Western Province (4)

+104	Transvaal	Johannesburg	1982/83
126	Northern Transvaal	Cape Town	1982/83
163	Eastern Province	Cape Town	1983/84
+171	Eastern Province	Port Elizabeth	1983/84

For SAB English XI (1)

+109	South Africa	Johannesburg	1981/82

For MCC (1)

117	Rest of World XI	Lord's	1987

+ denotes 2nd innings
* denotes not out

Tours

Australia	1978/79, 1979/80, 1990/91, 1994/95
India	1979/80, 1981/82, 1992/93
West Indies	1980/81, 1985/86, 1989/90
Sri Lanka	1981/82
Pakistan	1987/88
New Zealand	1991/92

For limited-overs internationals only:

Sharjah	1986/87
World Cup	1987/88 (India & Pakistan)
	1991/92 (Australia & New Zealand)
Nehru Cup	1989/90 (India)
New Zealand	1990/91

INDEX